The College Learner

Reading, Studying, and Attaining Academic Success

SECOND EDITION

The College Learner

Reading, Studying, and Attaining Academic Success

Mary Renck Jalongo
Indiana University of Pennsylvania

Meghan Mahoney Twiest
Indiana University of Pennsylvania

Gail J. Gerlach
Indiana University of Pennsylvania

with Diane H. Skoner

Merrill,
an imprint of Prentice Hall
Upper Saddle River, New Jersey   Columbus, Ohio

Library of Congress Cataloging-in-Publication Data
Jalongo, Mary Renck.
    The college learner : reading, studying, and attaining academic
success / Mary Renck Jalongo, Meghan Mahoney Twiest, Gail J.
Gerlach, with Diane H. Skoner.—2nd ed.
        p. cm.
    Includes bibliographical references and index.
    ISBN 0-13-755570-9
    1. Reading (Higher education)—United States. 2. Study skills-
-United States. 3. College student orientation—United States.
4. Active learning—United States. I. Twiest, Meghan Mahoney.
II. Gerlach, Gail J. III. Title.
LB2395.3.J353   1999
428.4'071'1—dc21   97-50475
                                                        CIP

Cover photo: © FPG
Editor: Bradley J. Potthoff
Production Editor: Mary M. Irvin
Design Coordinator: Diane C. Lorenzo
Text Designer: John Edeen
Cover Designer: TOPEgrafix, Inc.
Production Manager: Pamela D. Bennett
Director of Marketing: Kevin Flanagan
Marketing Manager: Suzanne Stanton
Advertising/Marketing Coordinator: Krista Groshong

This book was set in Times Roman by Carlisle Communications and was printed and
bound by Courier/Kendallville. The cover was printed by Phoenix Color Corp.

 © 1999, 1996 by Prentice-Hall, Inc.
Simon & Schuster/A Viacom Company
Upper Saddle River, New Jersey 07458

Printed in the United States of America

10 9 8 7 6 5 4 3 2 1

ISBN: 0-13-755570-9

Prentice-Hall International (UK) Limited, *London*
Prentice-Hall of Australia Pty. Limited, *Sydney*
Prentice-Hall of Canada, Inc., *Toronto*
Prentice-Hall Hispanoamericana, S. A., *Mexico*
Prentice-Hall of India Private Limited, *New Delhi*
Prentice-Hall of Japan, Inc., *Tokyo*
Simon & Schuster Asia Pte. Ltd., *Singapore*
Editora Prentice-Hall do Brasil, Ltda., *Rio de Janeiro*

Preface

In 1996, we published *The College Learner,* a book that we hoped would be a significant departure from the skill and drill books that are commonly used in college reading and study skills courses. Before the year was through, we were already making plans with the publisher for the book's second edition. Evidently, there was a group of like-minded developmental educators who were seeking instructional materials that would support them in delivering a different kind of reading and study skills course, and all of us were approaching our work in similar ways.

Improvements With the Second Edition

We regard this second edition of *The College Learner* as an opportunity to make our book more learner centered, to offer more strategies that support learning, and to provide additional support for instructors who work with college freshmen to improve reading and study skills. New with this second edition are:

- a preface that deals with the issue of student motivation
- a stronger developmental reading emphasis
- a new chapter on critical thinking
- a synthesis of Chapter 1 (active learning) and Chapter 9 (lifelong learning)
- an emphasis on using technology and evaluating the authoritativeness of Internet sources
- an updated research/theoretical base and several new reading selections
- an expanded set of supplemental learning activities in the back of the book that instructors can use for small group work in class
- an exceptionally comprehensive instructor's manual, now available on computer disk, that not only contains a test item file, but also offers practical suggestions for presenting the content of each chapter

The Philosophy: Supporting Student Development

Developmental education is a massive, nationwide system of academic, social, and/or financial support that is designed to enable those who would not have been college bound in previous generations to begin college study, succeed in subsequent college courses, and pursue a career upon graduation. The underlying assumption of developmental programs is that students are lacking confidence and effective learning strategies rather than lacking ability (Brown, 1997; Maxwell, 1995; Miller, 1996). The National Association for Developmental Education (NADE) and the College Reading and Learning Association define developmental education as a field of research, teaching, and practice that is concerned with improving academic performance and that uses the principles of developmental theory to facilitate learning (Rubin, 1991).

In reviewing the literature on postsecondary education, critical thinking, and success for academically at-risk college students we find that our original concept for the book is consistent with what is being advocated by contemporary research (Reynolds & Werner, 1994). According to the U.S. Department of Labor and experts in the educational field, the "old basics" of reading and doing math at a high school level will no longer suffice to meet the demands of most entry-level jobs, much less the professional roles that most college students are studying to fulfill (Elias, et al., 1997; Murnane & Levy, 1997). Rather, these researchers call for education in the "new basics," the skills that are highly sought by twenty-first century employers. The second edition of *The College Learner* addresses the seven "new basics" for the new millennium that are listed below.

1. *Learning-to-learn skills that enable employees to reach their full potential, seeking growth and change.* Chapter 1, "Becoming an Active Learner," guides students in gaining insight into their learning processes. Likewise, Chapter 2 on critical thinking and Chapter 3 on time, study, and stress management support students in acquiring learning-to-learn skills.

2. *Acquiring competence in reading, writing . . . and technology.* Chapters 4 and 5 make up the section on reading and every chapter is replete with reading selections that are exceptionally varied as well as similar to the types of material that college students are expected to read and study. Unlike most college reading and study skills books, *The College Learner* includes a chapter on writing (Chapter 9). Even though college students have other courses in composition, we felt it was important to look at writing as a tool for completing other types of assignments. Additionally, each chapter includes a journal writing activity called "Writing and Reflecting".

One area that we wanted to strengthen with the second edition was the use of technology. Rather than devote a chapter to the topic, we made the decision to infuse the use of computers throughout all of the chapters so that students would be doing things such as learning how to evaluate the credibility of Internet sources or analyzing the ways in which technology is used on their campus generally and more specifically in their chosen fields.

3. *Thinking creatively and adapting to new situations, especially with regard to problem solving or in response to barriers/obstacles.* New with this edition of *The College Learner* is Chapter 2, "Developing Critical Thinking." This chapter directly addresses the reasoning and problem solving strategies of well-educated professionals.

4. *Listening and oral communication skills that foster dynamic interactions between and among workers.* Virtually no other college reading and study skills text includes information on effective listening and note taking (Chapter 6) as well as participating in class and making effective oral presentations (Chapter 7). We consider these abilities to be significant ways for students to demonstrate their mastery of course content, not only in learning support classes but throughout their college studies and professional careers.

5. *Goal setting/self-motivation that enables workers to pursue professional development goals and take pride in what they have accomplished.* Every chapter has several text features that promote goal setting and self-motivation. One of these features is "Assessing Prior Knowledge," an activity that helps students take stock of what they already know; another is the "Improvement in Action" boxes that get students involved in applying chapter material to their experiences.

6. *Working collaboratively with others through negotiation, teamwork, and other interpersonal skills.* The discussion of the new basic skill of collaborating in diverse groups is a strength of the first edition that we have preserved. Our book, much more than others, emphasizes group processes in a variety of ways. First, each chapter contains a "Cooperative Learning Activity" to promote cooperative learning. Second, the colored pages at the end of the book are replete with supplemental activities that instructors can use to guide small groups of students as they work together to master the course content. With the second edition, the supplemental activities are not only increased but also refocused to emphasize using technology.

7. *Making a contribution to the organization by developing leadership skills and enhancing the institution's effectiveness.* Our book does not approach learning support from a deficit model orientation. Rather, we encourage the instructor to offer the things that will enhance students' self-directedness and serve students well both now and in the future. One way of achieving this is to include material that builds skill in self- and peer evaluation. The "Self-Improvement Strategy" in each chapter, for example, invites students to keep track of their progress toward a goal that will reflect favorably on the institutions in which they are pursuing their degrees.

The Conceptual Framework: Enhancing Student Motivation

Because motivation is often a concern in required reading and study skills courses, *The College Learner* uses a variety of text features and materials in the instructor's manual to respond to the latest research on achievement motivation (Pressley, 1995).

- **Maintain an orderly, well-managed classroom with procedures that build student autonomy and encourage regular feedback.** Many instructors, for example, spend an inordinate amount of time returning papers. We offer suggestions in the instructor's manual for using a folder or portfolio system so that each student takes responsibility for turning in newly completed assignments as well as for reviewing previously submitted work that has been evaluated by peers/and or the instructor.

- **Let students know the learning objectives in advance.** Each chapter begins with prereading questions that help readers to understand the chapter's purpose. We also include the text feature "Assessing Prior Knowledge," which encourages students to access their schema before they begin to read.

- **Model interest in and enthusiasm for teaching and learning.** The instructor characteristic to which many students respond the most is enthusiasm. As authors and teachers, our collective experience would suggest that one of the best ways to maintain enthusiasm for teaching is to continue to develop as an instructor. Every chapter includes "Improvement in Action" boxes that instructors can use to experiment with more interactive teaching methods. Yet another alternative to lecture is found in over 50 learning activities in the supplemental activities section at the end of the book. The exceptionally detailed instructor's manual provides another rich resource for other in-class activities that offer alternatives to lecture.

- **Make the reasons for learning something clear.** We find that our students pay closer attention when we explain how, for example, a particular text-marking strategy will save them time or how they can analyze a test on which they performed poorly to do better the next time. Throughout the book, we do more than simply give the facts. We offer a practical rationale for the strategies that we are advocating.

- **Provide a task-oriented, low-anxiety environment in which students can attain success with reasonable effort.** Instructors sometimes feel that it is their responsibility to create college "boot camp" for students in the hope of toughening them for what lies ahead. In our experience, practices such as grading "on the curve" so that a predetermined number of people have to fail are demoralizing. Students should be helped to reach high expectations and have appropriate confidence that they can succeed with reasonable effort.

- **Make abstract material more personal, concrete, and familiar.** We use vignettes of college students' experiences at the beginning of each chapter to get students interested in the chapter content. Each chapter also includes "Voices of Students," helpful advice from college learners who were enrolled in learning support programs and successfully completed their undergraduate degrees.

- **Offer students choices about ways to learn content or topics to investigate and design learning outcomes that result in a high-quality product.** Rather than page after page of workbook-type exercises, *The College Learner* offers exceptional variety in learning activities and reading selections. We encourage students to become more actively involved through such things as conducting interviews, critiquing the written essay questions of anonymous students, or making a presentation about their major to peers. We endorse activities such as publishing a compilation of the class's best work. In other words, the opportunity to produce high-quality work is used as its own reward.

Purpose and Audience

As Fingeret (1991) contends:

> We must be clear that the construction of meaning is at the heart of literacy, and it is rooted in experience, culture and language. Respect for cultural and linguistic background is not simply a matter of motivating, recruiting, or retaining students. It has to do with dignity, power, strength, and authority. Cultural and linguistic diversity must be celebrated, respected and incorporated into the relationships among teachers and learners. We cannot separate literacy from experience, culture and traditions. (p. 10)

This textbook is intended for college freshmen who are enrolled in a developmental reading course, a study skills course, or some combination thereof. The book would also be useful as a text for high school seniors who are striving to improve reading and study skills prior to college entrance.

Overview of the Book

The second edition of *The College Learner* is divided into four parts: Learning in College, Advancing as a Reader, Participating Actively in Class, and Demonstrating Understanding.

Chapter 1, "Becoming an Active Learner," sets readers' expectations for the remainder of the book and encourages them to reassess their approaches and attitudes about various learning experiences. Chapter 2, "Developing Critical Thinking," is new with the second edition. It is designed to support students as they encounter the difficult material and complex ideas that are an inevitable part of their college experience. Chapter 3, "Managing Time, Study, and Stress," provides a basic overview of college study and survival strategies.

Part Two, Advancing as a Reader, includes Chapters 4 and 5. Chapter 4, "Building a Background for College Reading," emphasizes the role of prior knowledge in efficient, flexible reading. Chapter 5, "Applying Effective Reading and Study Strategies," includes reading strategies, such as identifying main ideas and reading between the lines, then moves to comprehension monitoring strategies, such as text marking and summarizing.

Because skill in oral language is fundamental to college success, Part Three (Participating Actively in Class) emphasizes listening and speaking abilities. Listening comprehension is a basic skill for college study and a foundation for reading, so we have devoted Chapter 6 to listening and note taking. Another language ability that exerts an influence on a student's success in college is the ability to make oral presentations based on reading and study. In Chapter 7, "Participating in Class Discussions and Making Presentations," we offer strategies that will enable students to develop oral presentation skills.

Part Four, Demonstrating Understanding, directly addresses the ways in which students demonstrate their knowledge and skills to their instructors. In Chapter 8, "Developing Test-Taking Strategies and Skill in Self-Evaluation," we take the traditional focus on test-taking strategies one step further by showing students how to monitor their own progress. Writing is a basic way of learning in college that relates not only to composition but also to study skills and to reading, so Chapter 9 concentrates on the writing process as it is used to complete assignments.

Matching the Book to Specific Course Goals

College reading and study skills courses are taught in different ways around the country. In some instances, they are separate courses; in others they are combined into a single "survival skills" course. The way that your particular course is structured will determine the best way to organize the chapters. The instructor's manual contains sample syllabi for courses that have three different emphases: a general reading/study skills course, a course in developmental reading, and a study skills course.

For a more general course that combines reading and study skills, you can use the existing organization of the book and emphasize the material that is most useful throughout.

For a course that focuses entirely on reading, we recommend that you begin with Chapter 1, "Becoming an Active Learner," and Chapter 2 on critical thinking, then emphasize the reading chapters (4 and 5) and use the remaining chapters as reading selections on which to practice the reading strategies. Our experience with college freshmen suggests that they generally are interested in reading "how to" self-improvement-type material; the remaining chapters of the book give you extensive resources in this area. For developmental reading instructors who want to focus on whole texts written by noted leading American authors, you may want to supplement this text with a book of readings. Still other instructors may want to use a popular periodical (such as *Newsweek* or *Time*) or a course packet of readings you have collected and for which you have obtained the copyright permission to use in class.

If you are teaching a course that focuses mainly on study skills, we suggest that you begin with Chapter 1 and emphasize Chapter 3, "Managing Time, Study, and Stress," as well as Chapter 8, "Developing Test-Taking Strategies and Skill in Self-Evaluation." The two chapters on reading (4 and 5) can be treated as a textbook study unit. Chapter 7, "Participating in Class Discussions and Making Presentations," can also be approached from a study perspective—how to communicate what students have learned from study to peers and the professor.

We have arranged the chapters in the order that makes the most sense to us, but that does not mean that they cannot be rearranged to meet the needs of your group. Although the chapters are related, each one can stand alone as appropriate reading material for college students and research-based recommendations for enhancing literacy processes. This is one reason we have compiled all of the group activities at the end of the book. Some fit better with the content of one chapter than another, but we leave it to the individual instructor to decide when to use an activity with a particular class.

We hope that this book supports you in your efforts to realize your teaching goals and create a new paradigm for teaching college reading and study skills courses.

Acknowledgments

We would like to thank the reviewers of our manuscript for their insights and comments: Lorraine Gregory, Duquesne University; Shuli Lamden, Santa Fe Community College; Thomas A. Marshall, Robert Morris College; Eleanor Myers, Kent State University-Trumbull Campus; Bill Ogletree, Western Carolina University; Elva I. Pena, Del Mar College; and Karen B. Quinn, University of Illinois at Chicago.

Mary Renck Jalongo
October, 1997
Indiana, Pennsylvania

References

Brown, O. G. (1997). *Helping African-American students prepare for college.* Bloomington, IN: Phi Delta Kappa.

Elias, M. J. et al. (1997). *Promoting social and emotional learning: Guidelines for educators.* Alexandria, VA: Association for Supervision and Curriculum Development.

Fingeret, A. (1991). Meaning, experience, and literacy. *Adult Basic Education, 1,* 4–11.

Maxwell, M. (Ed.). (1995). *From access to success: A book of readings on college developmental and education and learning assistance programs.* Clearwater, FL: H & H.

Miller, K .J. (1996). *Developmental education at the college level.* Bloomington, IN: Phi Delta Kappa.

Murnane, R. J., & Levy, F. (1997). *Teaching the new basic skills: Principles for educating children to thrive in a changing economy.* New York: The Free Press.

Pressley, M. (1995). *Advanced educational psychology for educators, researchers, and policymakers.* New York: HarperCollins College Publishers.

Reynolds, J. & Werner, S. C. (1994). An alternative paradigm for college and reading study skill courses. *Journal of Reading, 37*(4), 272–278.

Rubin, M. (1991). A glossary of developmental education terms compiled by the CRLA task force on professional language for college reading and learning. *Journal of College Reading and Learning, 23*(2), 1–14.

To the Student

If you are enrolled in a program that provides learning support to beginning college students, you are among the thousands of students nationwide enrolled in developmental education programs. Seventy-four percent of all higher education institutions in America offer at least one course designed to help postsecondary students succeed in college, and 30% of all college freshmen take at least one developmental education course during their careers (National Center for Education Statistics, 1991). If your college or university offers a course designed to prepare students for college-level study and/or reading, it is among the 93% of institutions that have one or more such courses (Boylan, Bonham, & Bliss, 1994).

The course you are about to take and this textbook that accompanies it represent a turning point in your educational career. Starting today, you have the opportunity to make daily decisions about how you will learn. These decisions will affect the story of your life. Will you decide that college is too hard, too stressful, too much work, and takes too long? Will you put socializing before your studies and find that you (and your friends) are soon out of the college scene? Or, will you—as we hope, as your professors hope, and others who really care for you hope—have the determination to make significant changes in your learning and master the strategies that will enable you to succeed in college? The answer to these questions lies, not merely in your words, but in your actions.

Only about one in three high schoolers even gives college a try (Lunenfeld & Lunenfeld, 1992). Nearly everyone in that one-third who begins college *intends* to be successful, yet not everyone *becomes* successful. Statistically speaking, even though virtually all college students hope they will succeed, about half of them fail and have to repeat courses or drop out entirely. We want you to be in the half that succeeds, but nobody can make you successful in college. It is something you must do for yourself, no matter how much encouragement or support you might get.

To a considerable extent, whether you will be numbered among the successful is based on making the right decisions. The first decision is that college is worth the effort. Without a college education, it is estimated that your income level will average about $8000 a year less than that of the typical college graduate. The second decision is the recognition that your first responsibility, your forty-hour-a-week job for the next four years, is to be a learner and a student. The third decision is that you must abandon those approaches to learning that have not served you well in the past and replace them with new, successful strategies even though it will take time and effort to master new methods of learning, thinking, studying, listening, reading, speaking, and writing. If you accept these three prime directives and decide that college is worth the effort, that being a student is your job, and that you must make changes in your habits, then your chances for success will increase dramatically.

Everything about the content and design of this book has been planned to make it a tool for supporting your decisions, your goals, and your learning. Before you begin reading, you need to understand the purposes of various aspects of the book and how they can help you to become a better college student. The features of the textbook are outlined here so that you can become familiar with them and their purposes before you encounter each feature in the chapters.

Prereading Questions

The purpose of prereading questions is to get you thinking about the topic of the chapter, to give you a head start by accessing what you already know about the material. Students often complain that their attention wanes while reading a chapter and that they quickly forget what they have read. But if you begin by really thinking about the topic, it will help you to get interested, get involved, and remember more of what you read. So don't skip over these questions to save time. Think of the time spent reflecting upon the prereading questions as an investment in better understanding and better recall of what you read.

Assessing Prior Knowledge

If you are like most students, you probably wish that you knew the secret of "speed studying," of finding a more rapid and efficient way of mastering material that you are required to read. Research on learning suggests that "taking stock" of what you already know about a subject before you begin studying it is the most efficient way of studying. That is why we have incorporated "Assessing Prior Knowledge." When we pose questions to you before you get into the body of the chapter, we are teaching you a strategy that makes the most of your study time. Naturally, you will be encountering many different types of reading material in college. If you learn this simple strategy of "taking stock" *before* you start reading, it will make all of your studying more effective and efficient. Then when you are faced with the big test and fear that your mind will draw a blank, there will be more in your memory bank to draw upon.

Vignettes

A vignette is a brief description of human behavior. The vignettes in this book are stories about college students we have known, their struggles in meeting the requirements of various courses, and the successes or failures that they experienced. Once again, you may be tempted to skip this part, thinking that it is not "essential" information. But research on narratives—on stories—suggests that the human brain "runs" on stories, that we remember information better and longer when it is presented in story form. So, give yourself the best chance for understanding and remembering the key ideas of the chapters and read about college students like you who have learned important lessons from their mistakes and from their successes. The vignettes are designed to put a face on what you are learning, to make it more personalized and interesting. Instead of just telling you what works in college, these vignettes show you what works—and what doesn't.

Chapter Content

Each of the nine chapters in this book is based on the latest research about success in college. You will find that there are many examples of students' work, charts and diagrams that enable you to see as well as read key concepts, and step-by-step instructions on how to complete college-level assignments in ways that lead to academic achievement. As you read through the chapters, search for the strategies that seem best suited to your individual needs. We have provided a range of options for people with different learning styles, learning problems, college courses, and professor expectations. As you read each chapter, keep asking yourself questions such as:

- How does this apply to my situation now?
- Is it something I might use later on in another college course?
- What changes do I apparently need to make in my behavior?
- What am I learning and how can I continue to make progress toward my goals?

Improvement in Action

As you scan through the chapters, you will see shaded boxes throughout that we call "Improvement in Action." Each one of these numbered boxes asks you to do something that will help to solidify your understanding of the material and really interact with what you are reading. You may want to jot down your ideas directly in your textbook or, if your instructor recommends it, you may want to begin a learning log and write your responses there.

Remember that the key to success in college study is not to simply "plow through" your assignments. Even if you have been using that approach with reasonable success in high school, you will find that it seldom leads to positive outcomes in college. Why? Because much of the college course material you will encounter is too complex, abstract, and difficult to master using the "once over lightly" approach.

The group of learners you are keeping company with in college is different from the ones you knew in high school where attendance was mandatory. Now that you are in college, the people who are there are the one-third who chose to be there (or at least had family members insist that they attend). As a result, expectations for your performance have risen. When you enrolled in college, you announced to the world that you wanted to pursue a professional career. Now you will need to act like a person who is serious about that career goal. One way of demonstrating your seriousness of purpose is to really work over your textbooks.

College-level learners who take the time and trouble to interact with textbook material are far more likely to make steady, continuous improvement. That is why we call this feature of your textbook "Improvement in Action"—it is only by becoming involved in what you read and really making it part of you that you can make significant gains in your academic achievement at the college level and meet your goals.

Voices of Successful Students

In our work with college students, we conduct interviews and survey students about those things that enabled them to be more successful. We include their advice and insights, stated in their own words, so that you can benefit from their experiences. Listen to their advice! It is worth thinking about because they were once in your same situation and made the best of their opportunity.

Cooperative Learning Activity

Even though most people think of study and learning as an individual activity, learning also has a social dimension. If interaction with other people made no contribution to the learning process, then everyone would simply stay home and take correspondence courses instead of going away to college. Lectures have their place, but you also need time to apply what you are learning and get feedback from others. That is why we have suggested a variety of activities that will give you the opportunity to work together with your peers under the guidance of an expert—your instructor for the course. Do not think of these cooperative learning activities as a time for casual conversation. They are designed to give you practical experience in working with others in a professional setting. They are "on-the-job training" for the kind of group work you will be expected to do later on in your chosen profession.

Self-Improvement Strategy

Improving your learning is strategic. In the "Self-Improvement Strategy" section of the chapter, we give you a helpful hint to try out and evaluate. Think of these strategies as the intellectual equivalent of going to basketball camp with a famous player. If you were in basketball camp, you would be hoping to learn some of the secrets to improving your game. Each self-improvement strategy is designed to do the same thing. We wanted to share some of the secrets to success in college with you.

Writing and Reflecting

College students can build and demonstrate their understanding of material better when they put it into their own words, strive to think more deeply about what they are learning, and relate it to themselves as individuals. As you go through your professional career, you will no doubt have professors who require you to keep a journal, a log, or observational notes. Often, this requirement is part of a writing course or part of an internship program, a time when you are required to put what you have learned into practice. Examples of internships include student teaching for an education major, working at a precinct for a criminology major, or working in industry for a business major. By keeping a journal or at least writing periodically about what you are learning, you will be using writing as a tool to improve your understanding. In fact, this view that writing can exert a positive influence on learning is so widely accepted among professors and other experts that it is sometimes called "writing to learn" or "writing across the curriculum (the program)."

Reading Selections

Reading in college will introduce you to a wide range of material. You might be reading the works of a great novelist at one moment, a science laboratory manual at another. You might be reading an ancient philosopher's words on Monday and an essay on a current controversy from *The New York Times* on Friday. You might be assigned to read 50 pages of a sociology textbook during the week, or to read and memorize 2 pages of conversation in Spanish. With this wide range of reading material, you will need to become a flexible and efficient reader. To aid you in this process, we have collected a variety of reading selections. Some are taken from actual college-level textbooks. Some are excerpts from books or articles about how to succeed in college. Others are from professional journals. Still others—most of the longer selections—were written by noted authors from various fields.

References

Each chapter also contains a complete list of the sources we consulted in writing the chapters. If you have a special interest in any of the sources and want to read more about a topic, be sure to consult your college library or visit your campus bookstore to examine these resources in greater detail.

Supplemental Learning Activities

Your instructor will decide how to use the supplemental learning activities that appear in the back of your book. Most of them are designed to be completed in small groups while you are in class.

We wish you success in the course that you are taking and hope that you find our book to be helpful to you in your college career.

Afterword

We have made every effort to fill this book with material that will be meaningful to you and useful in supporting your goal of completing a college education. We welcome your comments and suggestions about the book and will continue to do everything possible to make it a better learning tool for students. Write to us at the following address:

Drs. Jalongo, Twiest, and Gerlach
Professional Studies in Education
312 Davis Hall
Indiana University of Pennsylvania
Indiana, Pennsylvania 15705

References

Boylan, H. R., Bonham, B. S., & Bliss, L. B. (1994). Characteristic components of developmental education programs. *Research in Developmental Education, 11*(1).

Lunenfeld, M., & Lunenfeld, P. (1992). *College basics: How to start right and finish strong.* Buffalo, NY: Semester Press.

National Center for Education Statistics (1991). *College-level remedial education in the Fall of 1989.* Washington, DC: U.S. Department of Education/Office of Educational Research and Improvement.

Contents

Part Two   Advancing as a Reader   69

4   Building a Background for College Reading   71

5   Applying Effective Reading and Study Strategies   105

Part Three Participating Actively in Class   137

6 Listening and Note Taking in College Courses   139

7 Participating in Class Discussions and Making Presentations   165

Part Four Demonstrating Understanding

8 Developing Test-Taking Strategies and Skill in Self-Evaluation

Learning in College

Becoming an Active Learner

If you are about to start college, you are changing your environment. Few people will know you, and your daily routine will be brand new. So you have a chance to make yourself up any way you would like . . . you can decide to be a better student than you have ever been. Will that really make you a better student? It could. If you spend more time and energy on your schoolwork than you have ever spent before, you will learn more than you ever have, and your grades will improve accordingly.

The point is, you get to choose what sort of student you will be in college.*

—William Campbell

* From *The Power to Learn* (p. 4), by W. E. Campbell, 1993, Belmont, CA: Wadsworth. Copyright 1993. Reprinted with permission.

Prereading Questions

- How would you define learning and describe your learning process?

- How would you characterize your strengths as a learner?

- What strategies can learners use to compensate for their weaknesses?

- How do people become avid learners and continue to learn throughout life?

Assessing Prior Knowledge

Reflect for a few moments on your most and least successful learning experiences. They need not have taken place in school. Describe them. What made one experience satisfying and the other frustrating? Here is how LaMar, a college freshman, described his most successful learning experience:

> My most successful learning experience was learning how to swim. I learned how to swim at the age of 3 through a program at the city pool. You were supposed to be at least 5 years old to join the next program, but because I was so advanced, they let me stay. I ended up with three gold medals, two silver, and three ribbons. This was all at age 6. From that class I obtained all of my American Red Cross cards over a period of time. It took about 12 years to get my lifeguarding cards. It was a long and difficult process. In high school, I swam for the swim club. We traveled from state to state and I competed against top swimmers from all over the country. This year I ended up with a gold medal. From the first time I went to a swimming class, I learned; now I'm enhancing that experience. Almost every day I go to the university pool and practice.

Notice some of the essential features of LaMar's successful experience: He was motivated and interested, he had demonstrations of the proper technique by skilled individuals, he was in control of when to accept new challenges, and others gave him encouragement that built his confidence (Bent, 1990). Figure 1.1 contains additional examples of essays written by students.

Vignette: The First Class

The scene is a college classroom. Students move to empty seats, tentatively acknowledging one another. If you interviewed everyone here, each person would probably admit to some nervousness about what to expect from their first college course, yet the reasons for their anxiety are as different as their backgrounds. Consider, for example, the perspectives of four students who are beginning their college careers: Elisa, Jack, Charmaine, and Imani.

Sitting by herself near the window is Elisa, who resides in a small town about 40 miles from campus. After working as a cashier in a grocery store for a year when she graduated from high school, Elisa has decided to give college a try. In a way, she feels like a trailblazer because neither of her parents attended college, and her older sister got married while still in high school. Although her relatives are always insisting that she is the "brain" in the family, she doesn't feel that she deserves the honor. It was always difficult for her to get good grades in school. As Elisa scans her classmates' faces, she wonders just how much harder college will be.

Jack wishes he could have come to college sooner. After just two days, he has attended several parties and feels popular. He sits in the back of the room flanked on either side by friends from his old city high school. Together they have already explored the local scene and are looking forward to having a great time in college. Although Jack would never discuss it, he has many misgivings about his academic performance. Just sitting in a classroom causes all of his past school failures to resurface. Jack has learned to compensate for his reading difficulties by being charming, funny, and athletic. When the professor enters the room, his heart sinks. She doesn't look like she will be fooled by his routine.

Charmaine has given little thought to college because she is preoccupied with her home situation. She works during the day and takes community college classes at night, but she is always scrambling to find a good babysitter for her baby. She wonders whether she can keep juggling her home and school responsibilities, but she is convinced that college is her only way out of a minimum-wage job.

Imani leans sleepily on his desk and wonders how his mother is managing at home with his four younger brothers and sisters. The money he was making as a part-time waiter was their supplemental income, but now his mother has taken out a bank loan for his college education. He feels that he has an obligation to make the most of this experience, yet he worries that his limited proficiency with English will prove to be a major deterrent to success, especially in any course dealing primarily with reading and writing.

Each of these students has certain barriers to overcome, influences that will interfere with learning. Perhaps you can identify with one or more of the students or their circumstances.

Figure 1.1
Learning Experiences: Essays by College Students

One day I was going out with a couple of guy friends to a dance club. As I was getting ready to go, I decided to look real feminine that day—miniskirt, makeup, the works. I had my hair down, a dab of makeup here and there, wore a short, cute dress. When they came to pick me up, my friends were astounded. They kept on flattering me. When I got to the club and saw all my friends, they were very impressed. I met so many guys that night it was incredible. I couldn't believe how people were treating me so different. I never had so much attention before.

When I got home, I washed off all the makeup, put on my big, baggy t-shirt, and sat down to think. It was fun while it lasted, but I don't think I would do that again for a long time. It just wasn't me.

—Hee Chong Che

My worst learning experience happened last year. During my freshman year of college, being in the classroom and on the football team was a living hell. I was told by the coach that I could start on the varsity. Just my luck, the coach quit along with some of the assistant coaches.

As you could probably figure out, I didn't start. Heck, I didn't even play. It wouldn't have been so bad if I knew I wasn't going to play. Even worse, I went through all the training during the season. The practicing felt like boot camp in a desert. People who had been through football camp on the high school level were crying like little babies because it was so hard. You can imagine what I was going through. Then again, maybe not, because no words and no description in the English language could describe the pain and agony accurately. You just had to go through it to be able to relate.

After my freshman year, I was planning on giving up the sport I had grown to love and had become very good at. Thankfully, family members convinced me to keep striving. They told me that if you didn't lay down and hang up the cleats during the season, there is no reason to quit now. So I didn't. But I did transfer schools. That became my most successful learning experience.

—Raymond Miller

This book and the course that accompanies it are designed to help you become a better reader and college student. We begin with a discussion of active learning because it is the foundation for more effective college reading and study.

Redefining Learning

People often use the word *learning,* but do they fully comprehend its meaning? Many students mistakenly believe that learning in college is an outside-in operation; they think that it is their job to simply "soak up" information supplied by professors. This is a distorted and limited view of learning; real learning is a process that involves action, reflection, and restructuring (see Figure 1.2).

Action means that it is not enough for students to absent-mindedly take notes and memorize. Rather, they must actively engage with the material and think deeply about it. Psychologist William Glasser (1990) explains why memorization of information is not enough: "What happens outside of ourselves has a lot to do with what we choose to do, but the outside event does not cause our behavior. What we get—and all we ever get—from the outside is information. How we choose to act on this information is up to us" (p. 432).

The second key ingredient in learning is the process of reflection. *Reflection,* as it refers to learning, means that learning depends on thinking deeply about what you are learning. If we have truly learned something from a college course, it remains with us and continues even after the course is over. Real learning is a lifetime process, not merely semester-long. The process of learning to read and write is never officially finished. Rather, everyone is learning about language all of the time. Even people who are widely recognized as experts on language, such as English professors, editors, or novelists, encounter words or rules they did not know before and continue to learn about language.

The third and final feature of learning is *restructuring* or change. In fact, many psychologists define learning as a change in behavior. Consider, for instance, what we mean by learning to steer a car. If a driver goes on and off the road at first, we would not say that he had *learned* to steer until he makes a change in behavior and controls the car, keeping it in the correct lane.

Other, less directly observable changes occur as a result of college learning as well. If you read your institution's philosophy or mission statement, you will find that one major goal of a college education is to help people become more aware of the knowledge produced in many different fields or disciplines, to be more tolerant of varying perspectives,

Figure 1.2
Defining Learning

action—becoming involved with the information, working with it, and hands-on opportunities to practice

reflection—processing information, thinking deeply about ideas, and connecting them with personal experience

restructuring—making changes in thoughts and actions as a direct result of learning

---

BOX 1.3   *Improvement in Action* ▐▐▐▶

Now that you understand that learning is a process that involves the learner in action, reflection, and restructuring, reread the quotation from Campbell (1993) that begins this chapter on page 3. What kind of college student do you want to become? What changes will be necessary to achieve your goals?

to think more intelligently about information, and to deal with important issues. Therefore, restructuring thinking—expanding, enlarging, refining—is a highly desirable outcome of a college education.

Features of Authentic Learning Experiences

Authentic learning is first and foremost an active process of knowledge construction and sense-making by the student. Second, learning is social because we produce it, share it, and transform it as individuals and groups. And finally, learning is distributed among members of a group, and this distributed knowledge is greater than the knowledge possessed by any single learner (Shulman, 1986, p. 4). An overview of the features of authentic learning experiences is discussed in the next section. Keep them in mind as you continue to work on the project of improving your reading and study skills.

In order to have an authentic college learning experience, the following criteria need to be met (Knowles, 1975; Langer & Applebee, 1986):

Structure refers to the specific form that a learning experience takes. Ways of structuring learning experiences include such things as having a designated meeting time/place, following a course syllabus, and using a particular textbook. Real learning involves structures and routines but also offers enough flexibility for students in the class to explore possible alternatives, trying to be creative and innovative.

Ownership is the personal investment that learners make in the learning process. When learners take ownership, they accept responsibility for their own learning. Every person in the class shares responsibility for the success or failure of the course because everyone "owns" it.

Collaboration refers to the social nature of learning. Most of us learn better when we can interact, cooperate, and collaborate with other learners.

Internalization refers to the indelible marks that learning makes on the learner. Real learning is not easily forgotten because it is a part of you and continues throughout life.

Appropriateness refers to learning experiences that are at the right level of difficulty—neither too hard nor too easy. In order for the learning to be appropriate, the learner must be given the opportunity to exercise choices and see the personal value of what is being learned. Appropriateness also means that learners have some control over the pace of the learning experience and can decide when they are ready to move on to the next challenge.

Naturally, life is much easier for college students if every course they enroll in offers all the characteristics of an authentic learning experience. Yet, for a variety of reasons, this is not always the case. Active learners cope with these unfortunate circumstances by packing their own provisions—they *bring* and *build* the principles of authentic learning into every class. If, for instance, a faculty member does not provide opportunities for collaboration, active learners might create a study group; if the class is purely lecture with no discussion, students can internalize the material by talking about it outside the classroom; and if the material is inappropriate because it is too difficult, they can find a tutor. This problem-solving stance toward learning, even in very challenging situations, goes a long way toward building your college success. The next section gives more detailed advice on becoming an active learner.

How to Become an Active Learner

Clearly, learning is a complex process that is much more than "taking in" information. But how does a person become an active learner?

Active Learning Tip 1: Take Control of Your Own Learning

Many students mistakenly believe that their learning is completely controlled by others. If they fail an assignment because they did not follow instructions, they attribute their failure to the instructor's poor explanation rather than saying, "Why didn't I ask a question when the prof explained it?" If they write a paper with numerous spelling errors and their grade is low, it is because the instructor is too demanding, not because they did the assignment hastily rather than using the word processor at the campus computer lab and double-checking their spelling. If they are not permitted to register for courses in their major because their overall grade point average is too low, they attribute it to one particular course and instructor, not to the fact that they neglected their studies for the entire freshman year.

Active Learning Tip 2: Accept Responsibility for Success

When students perform exceptionally well in school, they often attribute it to luck or fate, the result of something or someone else's influence, saying, for example, "It must have been an easy exam" or "The professor must like me." As strange as it may seem, some students actually fear success (Brim, 1992). If they get an A on the first test and attribute it to luck, they worry that they cannot do that well again without good fortune on their side. At times, this fear of success is so overwhelming that students avoid investing time and energy in their work. That way, if they do poorly on a written assignment, they can shrug it off and say, "Oh, I didn't really work that hard on it." Be aware of this fear of success, for it is one of the damaging consequences of low self-esteem. See these reactions for what they are—counterproductive responses that will short-circuit your learning goals.

Active Learning Tip 3: Exploit Every Resource and Avenue for Learning

Increasingly, theorists and researchers are stressing the "multisource" nature of learning (Hartman & Hartman, 1993). This means that when we are engaged in active learning, we are using a wide array of materials, strategies, people, and contexts as resources. Take, as an example, Rhonda, who sings in a choir. In order to become an active member of the university's gospel choir, she did much more than memorize a few songs or read music, even more than following the choir director's instructions. Her learning is continuous and comes from a variety of sources—attending live performances, conversing with choir members, collecting recordings by famous choirs from different eras, reading books about choirs, watching television programs and specials, and browsing through sheet music at the local music store. In other words, Rhonda's learning is of a multisource nature (Iran-Nejad, 1990). Rather than relying on a single avenue for building her abilities, active learners like Rhonda seek out many different types of information and exploit all of those resources to build their understandings.

Figure 1.3 contains some suggested resources for expanding your learning beyond the classroom.

Now apply the multisource principle of learning to Charles, who is enrolled in Spanish 101. You might see him walking around with his headset and think he's listening to music, but more often than not, he is listening to Spanish tapes. When the Spanish Club meets, Charles takes the opportunity to interact with some native speakers of the language. He watches videotapes with English subtitles and close captioned television in Spanish. While he watches, he tries to get the gist of what is being said or to identify individual words, then looks at the bottom of the screen to see whether his predictions are correct. Because

Figure 1.3
Resources to Enhance Learning

To use the multisource nature of learning to its best advantage, consider using:

- **Technology**—CD Rom, web site on the Internet, word processing, spelling and grammar software, text scanners, self-improvement videos, audiotapes of lectures, using tapes as a memory aid, listening to books on tape, video and cassette tapes for studying languages, electronic dictionaries, electronic spellers and translators, public television

- **People**—peer tutors, study groups, student counseling services, academic advisors, graduate teaching assistants, instructors for courses, student organizations with an academic purpose, personnel at the library, writing center, computer center, learning assistance center, individuals who can be interviewed about a topic

Choose one resource from the list in Figure 1.3 to which you have access.

■ Resource:

Use that resource this week and jot down some notes about its usefulness here:

Then write about your experience with the learning resource in your journal.

Charles is planning to major in modern languages, he saved his birthday money and bought an electronic translator/dictionary that he carries with him and uses whenever he cannot think of a word in Spanish. As he rides in the car or runs around the track for exercise, he practices speaking and listening to Spanish. Last week, he met a student from Mexico, and they have agreed to help one another—Charles will speak to her in Spanish, and she will reply in English. That way, they will both get additional practice with the languages they are seeking to master.

Active Learning Tip 4: Use the 5 Rs of Learning: Relate, Recombine, Replace, Refine, Reevaluate

To become a more active learner and a highly successful college student, you must constantly monitor your own learning processes (Iran Nejad, 1990). To illustrate how this is accomplished, we will apply the 5 Rs (see Figure 1.4) of learning to a task familiar to most of us: learning to ride a bicycle. When children attempt to ride a two-wheeler for the first time, they *relate* their prior experience of riding a tricycle or other wheeled toys to the new challenge. But not all of the skills required for riding a two-wheeler are learned from riding a tricycle. So the child has to *recombine* the skills he or she already has, taking what is already known about pedaling and steering and combining it with what is known about balance from roller skating. At first, the child's attempts to ride the bicycle will be unsuccessful or shaky, but the child will continue to strive to eliminate or modify less successful behaviors and *replace* them with more successful ones. Now that the child can ride the bicycle in a straight line down the sidewalk, he or she needs to *refine* that skill until that skill is the best it can possibly be. New challenges are actively sought, such as steep hills or sharp curves. New levels of performance are pursued, such as a faster pace or a new bicycle stunt.

Figure 1.4
The Five Rs of Learning

Relate . . . prior knowledge to new challenge.
Recombine . . . old skills with new ones.
Replace . . . less successful behaviors with more successful ones.
Refine . . . new skills until they are flawless and automatic.
Reevaluate . . . progress continuously.

With each new challenge, the learner will *reevaluate* performance and decide whether his or her progress toward a goal is satisfactory.

All of the same principles of relating, recombining, replacing, refining, and reevaluating pertain to reading and college study. Until you become immersed in reading and study with the same enthusiasm and multisource approach that you use with your most successful learning projects, you cannot honestly say that you are an active learner, and your reading and study skills will not improve significantly. Common sense would dictate that if you want to learn to do anything successfully—singing, cooking, aerobics, hairstyling, playing basketball—you must find out all you can about these activities and participate in them frequently. The same holds true for college learning. People become better readers by reading, better writers by writing, and better students by studying.

Active Learning Tip 5: Overcome Obstacles and Develop Successful Coping Strategies

Every learner has barriers to overcome. In fact, if no obstacle existed, learning could not take place. Suppose, for example, that a person wants to learn a video game. If he or she completely masters the game and there are no more advanced levels to try, then the person would be likely to seek a different game to play. Without progressive challenge, most learners lose interest.

When learners are confronted with a difficult task, they sometimes respond by trying to defend themselves from failure rather than by trying to learn. Ironically, the strategy that they choose only exacerbates the problem by cutting them off from the learning that they need. Coping strategies such as disrupting the class, acting bored, or trying too hard to win the instructor's approval are generally unproductive; they are used to *avoid* learning rather than do the work required to replace ineffective strategies with effective ones.

Active Learning Tip 6: Strive to Attain the Satisfaction of Optimal Learning Experience

It is a common misconception that after elementary school, people are either "good" or "bad" readers and students. Actually, it would be more correct to say that there are learners and nonlearners, active and passive readers. Most college freshmen will strongly agree with the following statement: "If I really put my mind to something, I can do it." The critical question is, Have you ever really "put your mind to" school study in general, or reading in particular? Although it is commonplace to admire individuals who achieve peak physical performance, such as Olympic competitors, it is less common to think about ways to achieve optimal intellectual performance. Until we test the limits of our thinking abilities with the same determination that an athlete challenges the body, we cannot really say that we are active learners.

Psychologists have conducted extensive research on the concept of optimal experiences in learning and life (see Figure 1.5). The process of these peak experiences has been labeled "flow" (Csikszentmihalyi, 1990). Rhonda's experience as a singer, LaMar's experiences as a swimmer, and Charles's experience as a Spanish speaker are all good examples of achieving optimal experiences, or flow. Flow is characterized by:

1. intense and pleasurable involvement;
2. tasks that are matched to the person's skill level;
3. a lack of self-consciousness that enables the person to concentrate completely on the activity;
4. an activity that has clear goals and gives immediate feedback and a sense of accomplishment;

Figure 1.5
Optimal Experience: A Schematic for Flow

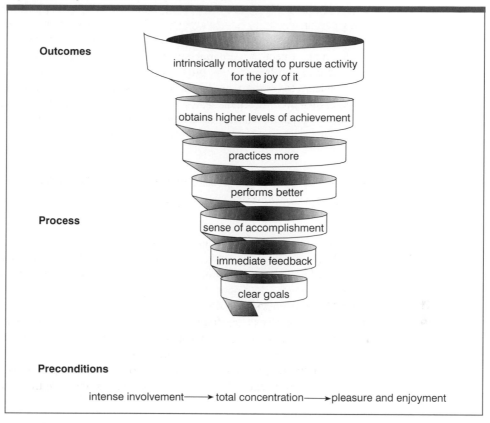

Outcomes
- intrinsically motivated to pursue activity for the joy of it
- obtains higher levels of achievement
- practices more

Process
- performs better
- sense of accomplishment
- immediate feedback
- clear goals

Preconditions

intense involvement ⟶ total concentration ⟶ pleasure and enjoyment

5. an upward spiral in which the person performs better, practices more, and there-fore achieves at an even higher level; and

6. such intense involvement that no extrinsic (external) rewards are necessary—the person pursues the activity for the joy of it.

In other words, you achieve optimal experience or flow when mind, body, and spirit soar to create a sense of satisfaction, wholeness, and ease. When LaMar feels like he is glid-ing ahead of his competitors in the pool, he experiences flow. When Rhonda feels uplifted by the beauty of the harmonious voices of the choir, she experiences flow. When Charles engages in a lively conversation with a native speaker of Spanish, he experiences flow. In fact, it is this feeling that keeps all three of them interested and motivated. Figure 1.6 dis-cusses research that has been done on why people attend college.

BOX 1.6   *Improvement in Action* ⅢⅢ➡

What about your optimal experiences? Have any of them been associated with learning, study, or reading? Was there a time in your school career when every-thing "clicked" and your learning progressed in a very satisfying way?

Figure 1.6
Why Attend College? What the Research Says

1. To increase earning power. People who attend college make more money and spend it more efficiently than non college-educated persons (Gardner & Jewler, 1992). From 1979 to 1987, the gap in pay between a male worker with a high school degree or less and a college-educated worker tripled (Whitehead, 1997). Generally speaking, a high school education by itself is no longer sufficient to equip a person to earn a middle-class income (Murnane & Levy, 1997). With more than one in five adults (23%) age 25 or older holding at least a bachelor's degree, those holding only a high school diploma operate at a serious disadvantage in the job market (Educational Testing Service, 1997). In fact, the Census Bureau (1995) estimates that, over a lifetime of work, the average high school graduate will earn $821,000 while the person with a bachelor's degree will earn $1,421,000—a lifetime earnings difference of $600,000.

2. To enhance self-esteem and social status. Education is the mechanism that leads you up or down the social ladder, regardless of the social class level of your family (Bee, 1992). Attaining a degree from a postsecondary institution is an accomplishment that contributes to self-esteem, thereby building confidence and persistence (Barton & Lapointe, 1995).

3. To lead a more satisfying life. College-educated adults report higher levels of psychological well-being (Barton & Lapointe, 1995). Overall they are healthier, more satisfied with their marriages, and happier with their lives (Bee, 1992). In a study of the first year after college, the researchers concluded that college plays an important role in providing a place to meet future spouses and that "Neither women nor men are willing to marry someone with poor income prospects. While such a preference is stronger for women, it is present for both genders" (Rindfuss, Kavee, & Cooksey, 1995, p. 433).

4. To stretch the intellect. Attending college has a positive impact on all areas of cognitive development including verbal and mathematical skills, oral and written communication, and intellectual flexibility (Pascarella & Terenzini, 1991).

5. To expand options. "America's higher education system is the envy of the world. It is noted for its accessibility, for its dazzling variety, and for the high quality of its many programs. . . . America's universities and community colleges have been unusually flexible and adaptive in meeting the rapidly changing needs of our agricultural, industrial, and technological societies" (Barton & Lapointe, 1995, p. 11). Those who attend college frequently discover that there are job opportunities they never knew existed that match their interests and talents. Perhaps most important, futurists predict that nearly 75% of workers will need retraining to keep their jobs in the future and that the average American worker will change careers—not jobs, careers—three times (Harris, 1990; Naisbitt & Aburdene, 1990). Thus, having a range of career options will become a "survival skill" in the twenty-first century.

6. To begin a professional network. One of the great resources of a college or university is the fact that it has a high percentage of talented, successful people who value education and are recognized as experts in their respective fields. College students can join professional organizations, identify role models, and establish mentorships with faculty. Someone with characteristics we admire can serve as a role model. It is not necessary to know a role model personally, only to have the opportunity to observe that person. A mentor, on the other hand, is someone you know whom you respect and admire and who is also in a position to help you achieve your goals. Mentors can introduce you to useful networks where you can meet other professionals and find jobs. Mentors and role models "provide shortcuts that allow us to avoid costly, time-consuming mistakes and focus our attention on proven techniques" (Cypert, 1993, p. 136).

7. To interact with a diverse population. One of the skills sought by employers today is the ability to collaborate in diverse groups (Murnane & Levy, 1997). Being exposed to a diverse population of people at the college level will enable you to learn more about human nature. You will meet individuals, for instance, with great talent who fail to use it, those with less talent who maximize it by working diligently, and those who are still trying to discover where their talents lie. "Because everyone must learn to live and work together, college provides a place and the opportunities for you to reach out to others in a spirit of friendship and community" (Kanar, 1995, p. 4).

8. To practice problem-solving. Most of the problems that people encounter in life are semi-structured, meaning that there are many approaches to the problem rather than one right answer. College life offers many opportunities to practice more complicated problem-solving skills, to exercise judgment, and to engage in moral reasoning (Barton & Lapointe, 1995). The problem-solving skills acquired during college "create, or reinforce habits that will affect later life experiences as well: a habit of reading and discussing

ideas; a tendency to be active socially and politically, analytic skills that assist in real-life problem solving" (Bee, 1992, p. 53).

9. To appreciate art, music, and cultural events. Every college campus has many curricular and extracurricular activities. Where else could a person listen to a jazz ensemble, gather for a poetry reading, watch an intramural basketball game, see a foreign film, watch an award-winning play, or listen to a famous speaker all in a month's time at little or no cost? Participating in these events enriches the lives of students in significant ways and creates an appreciation for cultural events that often lasts a lifetime (Barton & Lapointe, 1995).

10. To gain professional experience. College students get involved in a variety of "on-the-job" training programs or internships. Teachers, for example, typically spend a semester student teaching. Communications majors might work in television or radio. Nurses work in a hospital setting. All of these professional experiences enhance your credentials and provide employers with concrete evidence of your competence.

For many students reading is a chore. They stumble or plow through the material only because the teacher assigns it, because their grades depend on it, or because their future careers demand it. But if we think about Csikszentmihalyi's concept of optimal experience, it becomes clear that the most successful students find a way to experience flow *through* reading and study. Becoming an active learner requires much more than "going through the motions," even more than having an interesting and helpful teacher. To become a self-directed learner in college, you will need to have optimal experiences in connection with your studies. (The reading selection at the conclusion of this chapter will give you additional guidance on how to achieve flow.)

Active Learning Tip 7: Seek Role Models Who Are Avid, Successful Learners

Frank Smith (1992) contends that learning

> can be summarized in seven familiar words: we learn from the company we keep. We grow to be like the people we see ourselves as being like. Learning is therefore also a matter of identity, of how we see ourselves. . . . It is the *relationships* that exist within the classroom that matter: students' relationships with teachers and with each other and their relationships with what they are supposed to be learning—with reading and writing. (pp. 434, 440)

Identify the best company that the university has to offer. Often, they are the faculty who are the type of professional that you would like to become, called *role models* or *mentors*. Learn from peers. Examine closely what students who are academically successful, socially well adjusted, and respected by their instructors do to achieve that balance in their lives. You are likely to find that these students:

- make learning a top priority,
- use active learning strategies,
- plan both their work and recreation,
- use what they are learning inside and outside the classroom,
- give and receive help as necessary and appropriate, and
- work diligently *all* semester—even working ahead as necessary—to fulfill obligations and meet deadlines.

Remember that in college, you do not just study *subjects;* you also study and learn from *other people* and, in the process, gain insights *about yourself.*

Active Learning Tip 8: Set Reasonable Goals

Psychologist Gilbert Brim (1992) contends that most of us will pursue a goal with enthusiasm if we believe that we have a reasonable—more than 50%—chance of success. For complex goals, that often means breaking the challenge into more manageable parts. For instance, "I will attend every class possible, keep up with readings, and complete all assignments" is a more manageable goal than "I want to graduate in 4 years with straight As."

Active Learning Tip 9: Interact with Other Learners

A university is a place where students with diverse backgrounds at different levels of experience come together for the purpose of learning. One of the great mechanisms for learning is a dialogue between the more experienced and the less experienced. Because reading stimulates thinking, it makes that dialogue more interesting; it gives us something to talk about. Unless you develop reading relationships and use your readings as the basis for dealing with ideas and values, you will miss out on one of the greatest satisfactions that comes from college study. People learn to enjoy reading by sharing their reading experiences with others.

BOX 1.7   **Improvement in Action** ⅢⅢ➡

Why have you decided to pursue a college education? State your goal and write it here:

■ Goal:

Now break the goal down into its component parts:

1.

2.

3.

Making the Change to Active Learning

The first thing to remember about making a change in your learning habits is that no one else can do it for you. As Ferguson (1989) points out, "No one can persuade another to change. Each of us guards a gate of change that can only be opened from the inside. We cannot open the gate of another, either by argument or emotional appeal" (pp. 60-61). Making changes in your behavior as a learner is a type of risk taking because it requires you to abandon the ways of responding that are familiar and comfortable. Psychologists frequently conceptualize change as occurring at four different levels:

1. **Resisting the change** is the most common initial reaction. At first, we fall back on our earlier behaviors because that is less threatening than trying something new; we fear failure, and sometimes we fear that even if we succeed, we will set new levels of expectation that we cannot meet time after time. A college student who is at the resistance stage might say, for example, "Why do I have to take a college reading course, anyway? This class is going to be a waste of my time."

2. **Weighing the advantages and disadvantages of the change** is often the second step. We try to determine whether the proposed change is really worth all the effort. A college student at this stage might say, "This course might be difficult for me because I was never a good reader. But if I improved my reading and study habits now, it could help me in my major."

3. After we are convinced that the change is worth the additional effort, we usually **put our plans into action.** A college student at this stage might say, "OK, we have a lot of writing to do for this class, but if I get up one hour earlier on Monday, Wednesday, and Friday, I should be able to keep up. I'll start on that major paper early so that I have some flexibility in my schedule."

4. Finally, after the change is in place, we become involved in **maintaining the change** because we want the change to endure. An example of maintaining the change might be the student who says to herself, "This 'Intro to Theater' class is interesting, but the class notes are disorganized. I know how to cope with that; I'll *combine* my text and class notes and use these new notes to study."

One of the most important decisions you will make is whether to become a learner or a nonlearner. Learners change their behavior for the better. They keep striving for new strategies that will improve their power as learners. When something works, they expand and refine it. When something is unsuccessful, they take the lesson from it and leave the bad feelings behind. As the famous philosopher Jean-Paul Sartre once observed, "We *are* our choices." The choices you make about learning will exert a tremendous influence on your college achievement and your future career.

 Voices of Successful Students

We interviewed 20 college students who were enrolled in a college reading course as freshmen and are now on the dean's list with an overall grade point average of 3.5 or above on a 4.0 scale. Here is some advice from them on becoming more active learners:

QUESTION: *What strategies did you use to achieve your goal of a successful college career?*

"First, I had to focus on my schoolwork and put all other social things aside. Get your priorities straight—school first. Begin with a positive attitude and strive for success."

"Remember that you belong here as much as anyone else. Don't be afraid to ask for help when and if you need it. I tried to get to know my instructors. This helped when the time came for me to ask for help."

"Be open to other people, and don't be afraid to extend invitations to others in order to make friends and gain support. I formed study groups for courses that I found particularly difficult."

"I learned that if I kept abreast of my progress in a class, then I became more motivated to improve my grade. For example, if I knew that my overall grade was a mid-B, I became determined to make it an A."

"Never, ever be happy with just a passing grade. If you can honestly say that you've done your best and tried every resource imaginable—profs, tutors, computer resources, the library—only then should you be satisfied."

"Read more and more. The more you read, the better you comprehend. Write (take notes) *while* you read."

Extension Activities

Cooperative Learning Activity: I've Learned . . .

As you read through each "I've learned . . ." statement from *Live and Learn and Pass It On* (Brown, 1992), mark your favorites with a star.* Read back through them and circle your top five favorites. Then write several "I've learned . . ." statements of your own about college life, reading, learning, and success. Meet with your group and be prepared to share one of your statements with the other group members.

1. I've learned that if someone says something unkind about me, I must live so that no one will believe it.
2. I've learned that you can get by on charm for about 15 minutes. After that, you'd better know something.
3. I've learned that you shouldn't compare yourself to the best others can do but to the best you can do.

4. I've learned that trust is the single most important factor in both personal and professional relationships.
5. I've learned that nothing of value comes without effort.
6. I've learned that you can do something in an instant that will give you a heartache for life.
7. I've learned that people allow themselves to be only as successful as they think they deserve to be.
8. I've learned that if you pursue happiness, it will elude you. But if you focus on your family, the needs of others, your work, meeting new people, and doing the very best you can, happiness will find you.
9. I've learned that a good reputation is a person's greatest asset.
10. I've learned that it's easier to stay out of trouble than to get out of trouble.
11. I've learned that there's nothing you can't teach yourself by reading.
12. I've learned that you learn most from people who are learning themselves.
13. I've learned that encouragement from a good teacher can turn a student's life around.

*From *Live and Learn and Pass It On* by H. Jackson Brown, Jr., 1991, 1992. Copyright 1991, 1992 by Rutledge Hill Press, Nashville, TN. Reprinted by permission.

14. I've learned that if I don't try new things, I won't learn new things.
15. I've learned that when you judge others, you are revealing your own feelings and prejudices.
16. I've learned that when things go wrong, I don't have to go with them.
17. I've learned that I can't change the past, but I can let it go.
18. I've learned that if you keep doing what you've always done, you'll keep getting what you've always gotten.
19. I've learned that leisure is not enjoyed unless it has been earned.
20. I've learned that it's easier to *keep* up than to *catch* up.
21. I've learned that when bad things happen to me, I should keep the lesson but throw away the experience.
22. I've learned that choices made in adolescence have long-term consequences.
23. I've learned that it is impossible to teach without learning something yourself.
24. I've learned that if there were no problems, there would be no opportunities.
25. I've learned that success is more often the result of hard work than of talent.
26. I've learned that you always find time to do the things you really want to do.
27. I've learned that you should fill your life with experiences, not excuses.
28. I've learned that you can make a dime dishonestly but that it will cost you a dollar later on.
29. I've learned that worry is often a substitute for action.
30. I've learned that failures always blame someone else.
31. I've learned that enthusiasm and success just seem to go together.
32. I've learned that you shouldn't expect life's very best if you're not giving it your very best.
33. I've learned that it takes as much time and energy to wish as it does to plan.
34. I've learned that there's never a snow day on the day I have the big test.
35. I've learned that you don't miss fighting with your sister until she's left for college.
36. I've learned that I still have a lot to learn.

"I've Learned" Statements Written by College Students

1. I've learned that the more you sit back and relax, the more life passes through your fingertips.
2. I've learned that if you are not true to yourself, you are not true to anybody or anything.
3. I've learned that people who get taught don't always learn.
4. I've learned that you have to open your mind to let new experiences in.
5. I've learned that I can do a good job when I really apply myself.
6. I've learned that I had to adjust to living without constant adult supervision.
7. I've learned that I need to balance my social life with my academic obligations and adjust my study habits to my new environment.
8. I've learned to live on a budget. (Going to college was a major financial investment on my parents' part; therefore, I had to think of doing well as getting the most for the money.)
9. I've learned that you can't be a child forever and expect parents or others to do things for you all the time.
10. I've learned that if you concentrate on doing each step carefully, the pieces fall into place.
11. I've learned to deal with problems early before they get more difficult or get out of hand.
12. I've learned that going into things with a positive attitude and striving for success is important.
13. I've learned that it's better to just be yourself at college.
14. I've learned that I do my worst work when I am rushed.
15. I've learned to think of things that seem too hard as a challenge.
16. I've learned that you'll never know what's out there if you never try.
17. I've learned to be open to other people. I am no longer afraid to extend invitations to other people in order to make a friend I admire and respect.
18. I've learned to get as much out of every introductory class as I can and apply it to my "real" courses—courses in my major.
19. I've learned that I had to find myself, take control of my own life, and choose a career that was best suited to me.
20. I've learned that even if I don't ace a class, I need to be satisfied that I really learned something from it.
21. I've learned that college life is what you make it.

Writing and Reflecting: Becoming a More Active Learner

Use the Active Learning Tips on pages 10–16 for self-evaluation. Begin by rereading the list. Then think about how you can apply these principles to your current situation. Write a personal action plan that describes how you will go about becoming a more active learner in this college-level course.

Self-Improvement Strategy: Keeping a Reading Record

Keep track of how much time you devote to reading/studying and the types of material you read for 7 days. Also keep a record of other activities. How did you spend most of your time? Were there blocks of time that were wasted? What did you do to become more actively involved or think critically about material when your attention started to wane? This information will be used as the basis for discussion in class.

Reading Selections

Instructions: Begin by looking over the reading selections. Do not try to read them word by word; just skim them quickly as if you were looking for a number in the telephone book. Then go back and read each selection thoughtfully and answer the following five questions:

1. What was the author's purpose in writing this?
2. What was the main idea, the basic message of the selection?
3. What did you learn from reading it?
4. How does it relate to the ideas from this chapter?
5. How can you apply it to your situation?

Reading Selection 1

Many college students worry about their inability to concentrate during a class or while they are studying. In his book on studying, Jake Gibbs (1990) discusses basic principles that can help you focus better during class or study sessions. One basic principle is to have what the Zen masters refer to as "beginner's mind." This means that you approach each task with interest, enthusiasm, and a fresh perspective.

Applied to studying, beginner's mind means recognizing that each reading, writing, or problem-solving session is unique. In other words, each task must be approached as if it is being done for the first time, no matter how many times it has been done before. . . . If we do not give the task our complete attention, as a beginner would, we might miss that little or big something that is essential to doing the job right. For example, for the good baseball player there are no routine plays. Each play and each aspect of its execution require complete involvement. A minuscule lapse in concentration can mean a major error. . . . Beginner's mind is an open, flexible, empty mind. This is especially important for learning. If the mind is filled with preconceptions, judgments, and irrelevancies, including thoughts of self, it is difficult to learn. (pp. 28-29)

This is what Gibbs recommends on "being where you are" and exerting "right effort":

At this very moment, if you are reading this book, you cannot be anywhere else. There is only this place, this activity and this moment. You cannot actually be in the past or future, so you cannot be in another place doing something else, although you can think about it. You can only be in the present. You can only exist now.

To be fully engaged in the moment, you must give your full attention to what you are doing at the moment. If you are reading this book, read this book. If you are thinking about the great time you had last night, the gang of laundry you have to do tonight, or how you will outlaw English grammar when you are master of the universe, you are not fully engaged in the task at hand.

When you sit down to study or sit in a class, *be there*. You can't be anyplace else, anyway. Of course, you can get up and go do something else, but by the time you do this, it is a different moment. At the very moment you are studying or in class, it is futile to think that you can be somewhere else. It only causes problems and takes your mind away from what you should be doing.

When you sit down to study or sit in class, accept that you will have to be there for an hour or more, and concentrate on what you are doing. As long as you have to be there, *be there*. There is no place else you can be.

Living fully requires that you do only what you are doing while you are doing it. When you are studying, do not think of anything except that you are studying. Don't even think about how happy and proud you will be when you learn this lesson or many lessons. Concentrate totally on this lesson. Now! Don't just go through the motions. The time to learn is not in the future. The time to learn is now. (pp. 15-16)

Concentrating on what you are doing at the moment is simply a matter of letting go of what you are not doing at the moment. In other words, you have to accept being where you are and doing what you are doing. You have to let go of everything else.

You do not have to force other times and places, with attendant thoughts and feelings, from your mind. Just let them go. Allow your mind to concentrate its full power on what you are doing at the moment, for example, studying or writing. (pp. 18-19)

The Zen approach to unproductive thoughts and disquieting emotions is simply to recognize them for what they are and not let the mind abide in them. If you do not attach to them, they will pass naturally without great disturbance to your concentration or the task of the moment. Just relax, and let them go. Do not make them into more than they are. They are nothing special.

When your mind wanders from your studies, and thoughts of other times, places, and topics enter your mind, do not pursue them or suppress them. Just acknowledge them and return to work. If some thought is persistently intrusive or you have a wonderful insight while studying, write it down and return to it when you are finished studying.

Negative judgments and feelings will undoubtedly arise on your journey through school. At some time in our educational careers, we all feel bored, tired, angry, frustrated, confused, or depressed. The key to letting these feelings go and getting back to work is to treat them dispassionately. Do not associate them with yourself. Do not say, "I am bored. This is hopeless. I'll never learn this stuff." Simply say, "Boredom is here." Merely acknowledge that boredom has arrived on the scene. Do not try to get away from it. Do not get stuck in it. Let it go, and continue to do what you are doing at the moment. (pp. 20-21)

Gibbs follows with advice on confusion, uncertainty, and disappointment:

Do not be too quick to quit studying a subject or give up learning a new skill because you feel considerable confusion, doubt, or disappointment. It is not unusual to experience such feelings when doing just about anything in life that requires a sustained effort. These feelings can sometimes be the result of concentrating too much on goals or constantly comparing what is to what we thought would be. Goals and expectations are not what we are doing in the moment. They are not the reality of the here and now. They are at best abstractions of what will happen if everything goes according to plan. Since our plans and expectations are simplified versions of some future reality, the reality, when it arrives in all of its complexity and richness, seldom matches our simple, usually one-dimensional, expectations. If you are too strongly attached to future expectations and you are constantly comparing some desirable state that you think should have arrived to what is, you often will be disappointed and confused by the gap between your expectation and reality. . . .

Another common problem that spawns doubt and confusion among students is having vague goals. Some people do not have clear reasons for studying a subject or learning a new skill. They may have a vague notion that it is the right thing to do, and they may observe that everyone they know is doing it. But they may not have any clearly articulated educational or career goals.

If you are such a person, do not worry too much about it. Learning is a better thing to be doing than many other things you can do when you are trying to figure out what to do with yourself. If what you are learning brings you to college, for example, you are exposed to a wide variety of ideas and people, and you are encouraged to question and explore. Just take what comes in the moment, and do your best.

Keep in mind that your reasons for doing things, along with everything else in life, can change over time. You might go along taking a wide variety of courses for a while, and then one day it will dawn on you that you would like to write, for example, for a living. From this point on, writing will shape what is brought to you to be done in the moment, but it should not change your effort. Your effort should be right whether you have a definite goal in mind or some vague notion of how you want to spend some part of your life. (pp. 41-42)

On impatience:

[Impatience] occurs when you constantly worry about how long it is taking to complete a single task. For instance, you have three chapters to study for an exam, and while you are reading the first chapter you're watching the clock wondering if you will have time to finish all three before the test. You feel rushed and wish you were further along. After each page of chapter one, you turn to the end to see how many more pages you have to go.

You whiz through chapter one, consuming words but not digesting them. You finally finish. And . . . horrors! It's chapter two. How much more can you take? If chapter one was the introductory chapter, the one that always takes it easy on you, and it took you an hour to read it, chapter two will surely take you the rest of the night to read. It's hopeless. Give up. Why put yourself through this frustration?

The cause of this impatience is twofold: you did not allocate enough time for studying; and you're thinking about results, that is, finishing all the chapters instead of the process, that is, understanding what you are reading at the moment. A good general rule is to estimate realistically the amount of time it will take you to finish an assignment or study for an exam, then double it. This gives you enough time to deal with the unanticipated problems that always arise.

If you give yourself enough time, you will not feel pressed for time, and time and progress will not be on your mind so much. You will be much less likely to become frantic or feel hopeless. Finishing will not loom so large in your mind, and you will be better able to concentrate on what you're doing. You might even enjoy it.

Reading Selection 2

In *The Fifth Discipline*, MIT Professor Peter Senge (1990) talks about the discrepancy between the way things are (reality) and the way we would like them to be (vision).*

People often have great difficulty talking about their visions, even when the visions are clear. Why? Because we are acutely aware of the gaps between our visions and reality. "I would like to start my own company, but I don't have the capital." Or, "I would like to pursue the profession that I really love, but I've got to make a living." These gaps can make a vision seem unrealistic or fanciful. They can discourage us or make us feel hopeless. But the gap between vision and current reality is also a source of energy. If there was no gap, there would be no need for any action to move toward the vision. Indeed, the gap is *the* source of creative energy. We call this gap *creative tension*.

Imagine a rubber band, stretched between your vision and current reality. When stretched, the rubber band creates tension, representing the tension between vision and current reality. What does tension seek? Resolution or release. There are only two possible ways for the tension to resolve itself: Pull reality toward the vision or pull the vision toward reality. Which occurs will depend on whether we hold steady to the vision.

The principle of creative tension is the central principle of personal mastery. . . . Yet, it is widely misunderstood. For example, the very term "tension" suggests anxiety or stress. But creative tension doesn't feel any particular way. It is the force that comes into play at the moment when we acknowledge a vision that is at odds with current reality.

Still, creative tension often leads to feelings or emotions associated with anxiety, such as sadness, discouragement, hopelessness, or worry. This happens so often that people easily confuse these emotions with creative tension. People come to think that the creative process *is all about being in a state of anxiety.* But it is important to realize that these "negative" emotions that may arise when there is creative tension are not creative tension itself. These emotions are what we call *emotional tension.*

If we fail to distinguish emotional tension from creative tension, we predispose ourselves to lowering our vision. If we feel deeply discouraged about a vision that is not happening, we may have a strong urge to lighten the load of that discouragement. There is only one immediate remedy: lower the vision! "Well, it wasn't really important to shoot seventy-five. I'm having a great time shooting in the eighties."

Or, "I don't really care about being able to play in a recital. I'll have to make money as a music teacher in any case; I'll just concentrate there." The dynamics of relieving emotional tension are insidious because they can operate unnoticed. Emotional tension can always be relieved by adjusting the one pole of the creative tension that is completely under our control at all times—the vision. The feelings that we dislike go away because the creative tension that was their source is reduced. Our goals are now much closer to our current reality. Escaping emotional tension is easy—the only price we pay is abandoning what we truly want, our vision. . . .

But a one time reduction in the vision usually isn't the end of the story. Sooner or later new pressures pulling reality away from the (new, lowered) vision arise, leading to still more pressures to lower the vision. The classic "shifting the burden" dynamic ensues, a subtle reinforcing spiral of failure to meet goals, frustration, lowered vision, temporary relief, and pressure anew to lower the vision still further. . . .

The dynamics of emotional tension exist at all levels of human activity. They are the dynamics of compromise, the path of mediocrity. As Somerset Maugham said, "Only mediocre people are always at their best."

We allow our goals to erode when we are unwilling to live with emotional tension. On the other hand, when we understand creative tension and allow it to operate by not lowering our vision, vision becomes an active force. Robert Fritz says, "It's not what the vision is, it's what the vision does." Truly creative people use the gap between vision and current reality to generate energy for change. . . .

Mastery of creative tension transforms the way one views "failure." Failure is, simply, a shortfall, evidence of the gap between vision and current reality. Failure is an opportunity for learning—about inaccurate pictures of current reality, about strategies that didn't work as expected, about the clarity of the vision. Failures are not about our unworthiness or powerlessness. Ed Land, founder and president of Polaroid for decades and inventor of instant photography, had one plaque on his wall. It read: "A mistake is an event, the full benefit of which has not yet been turned to your advantage." (pp. 150-154)

Reading Selection 3

Selecting an Instructor: When Is the Tough Professor a Better Choice?

—Mary Renck Jalongo

My first semester of college, I stood in line for three hours to drop a Psychology 101 course. As a freshman, my schedule had been selected for me by computer and when other, more experienced students heard the name of my professor, they advised me to do whatever was necessary to change my schedule immediately. The prof was reputed to be a very demanding teacher, one who graded "on the curve" so that a predetermined number of students were destined to fail. I could not afford to take that risk, so I waited impatiently for a turn to plead my case at the drop/add table staffed by another faculty member. When that opportunity finally came, the faculty member said, "So, you want to drop Dr. X's section of Psych 101 and enroll in another section of the same course taught by a different instructor,

---

*From *The Fifth Discipline* by Peter N. Senge. Copyright 1990 by Peter M. Senge. Used by permission of Doubleday, a division of Bantam Doubleday Dell Publishing Group, Inc.

right? What's your reason—is he too tough for you?" I had just witnessed other students who were denied the drop, so I knew that being honest wouldn't work. The professor for the course happened to be blind and had a guide dog, so I blurted out, "I'm allergic to dogs" and my request for a schedule change was granted. Afterwards, my friends congratulated me on coming up with such an original and effective excuse. Yet now that I have been a student for many years and have become a college professor, my view of this incident has changed. I wonder if, by avoiding the more challenging class, I did myself a disservice. In late years, I deliberately went against the advice of other students and enrolled in classes taught by instructors who had a reputation for being tough. I have never regretted any of those decisions. Of course, there are different kinds of toughness. Dealing with difficult instructors is something that can be particularly troublesome for students, yet it is seldom addressed in any way other than the rumor mill. Here is my best advice on how to decide about enrolling in a class taught by an instructor who is reputed to be difficult.

1. *Consider the source of reputational information.* Students who are irresponsible will unavoidably have negative interactions with faculty. As a result, they are not a reliable source of information about an instructor's reputation. Speak with mature, successful students about their direct experiences with instructors rather than relying upon offhanded comments from a disgruntled student or two. Most colleges and universities have awards for excellence in teaching that are posted on a wall or listed in a publication at the library. Check the faculty newspaper and other public relations information published by the university to see which professors are very active professionally in writing, speaking, and conducting research. Why? Won't these instructors be too busy to have much concern for you? Over and over again, research on the effectiveness of college faculty supports the idea that the best instructors are frequently the best in other professional endeavors as well. They manage to do many things well. It's like the old saying, "If you want to get something done, ask a busy person." These instructors *are* busy, but less time with them may be more valuable because they have so much more to offer and are excited about what they are doing professionally. If a faculty member who is reputed to be demanding is also a superb teacher and/or a recognized expert in the field, it will probably be worth the effort to enroll in her or his section of the course—assuming that you have a choice.

2. *Determine if you have a choice.* As you move into your major area courses, there may be classes that are virtually always taught by one instructor who has specialized expertise in that area. So you may not have a choice of instructors for a particular course unless that faculty member retires, goes on extended sick leave, or takes an educational leave (called a sabbatical). If you have no choice, resolve to do your best instead of taking a defeatist or prejudicial attitude. Sometimes, students have already had a "run-in" with an instructor in a course and later find that they are required to take yet another course taught by this individual. Consider trying to re-establish your reputation with that professor. You might want to stop after class or during office hours and say something like what one of my students once said to me, "When you saw me in class, you probably wondered if I was going to be a lousy student again. I just wanted to let you know that I am a much better student now than I was a year ago and I hope that you'll give me a chance to prove it." I was very impressed by this forthright approach and responded, "As far as I'm concerned, each class is a new learning experience that begins with a clean slate. I'm looking forward to working with the new and improved you."

3. *Get specific about the instructor's reputation.* Anyone can acquire a reputation that is distorted or unfair. If another student cautions you to avoid a particular instructor, try to find out *why.* If it is because the professor is inept or hostile, that is a much different situation than if she or he simply has high expectations for students. Usually, instructors who were entertaining or easy graders are quickly forgotten. After you graduate and begin working, the instructors you once appreciated for making such minimal demands on your time and intellect are cast in a different light. You may even feel cheated by them when you realize that an area of your professional preparation is deficient. As one student put it, "We all loved Dr. T's class on Public Speaking—he could keep you alert, even during an 8:00 class with his wild antics and charming personality. But when I entered the world of business and had to make a speech, I realized that I had learned very little. I scoured the library and the bookstore searching for advice. In other words, I had to teach myself what I didn't learn in his class—the basics of public speaking."

Remember that real learning involves a change in behavior, and change is risky. The best learning experiences are a blend of challenge and support—a mixture that is usually found in classes taught by instructors who have a reputation for being tough.

4. *Accept responsibility for your own learning.* When I advise college students who are experiencing difficulty with a particular class, they usually say something like, "That class is so boring." As a start, try to keep in perspective that faculty are expected to be knowledgeable, not necessarily fascinating or entertaining. It would be preferable to have a terrific instructor for every class, but the reality is that you will not. You can't afford to get a poor grade every time an instructor isn't thrilling; that would ruin your record of academic achievement. In situations like these, view them as a challenge to your skill as an independent learner rather than a semester-long "sentence." Working to build interest in the subject by doing such things as relating course material to your personal experiences, discussing issues raised in the course outside of class, asking good questions in class, and doing more outside reading can all help you to succeed, even in a boring class. Even though you may have to suffer through uninspired instruction, that does not mean that you cannot learn or be successful in the class.

Conclusion

Ever since the first college was established, students have been "comparing notes" on their instructors. This informal sharing of impressions about a particular instructor can sometimes be useful in helping you to avert a disastrous class. At other times, the information you obtain can enable you to make a better impression—such as finding out a particular instructor's pet peeves. Every campus has its share of instructors that students prefer to avoid for one reason or another. Successful students have learned to weigh the evidence and to separate damaging rumors from legitimate concerns about an instructor's competence. As you make these important decisions, remember that it is the tough instructor—the one who urges you to stretch intellectually, the one who invites you to work at the edge of your competence, the one whose course causes a few butterflies in the stomach—who usually makes the most significant contribution to your learning, both now and in the future.

References

Barton, P. E., & Lapointe, A. (1995). *Learning by degrees: Indicators of performance in higher education.* Princeton, NJ: Educational Testing Service.

Bee, H. L. (1992). *The journey of adulthood* (2nd ed.). Upper Saddle River, NJ: Merrill/Prentice Hall.

Bent, E. (1990). Who should have control? In J. M. Newman (Ed.), *Finding our own way* (pp. 56-70). Portsmouth, NH: Heinemann.

Brim, G. (1992). *Ambition: How we manage success and failure throughout our lives.* New York: Basic Books.

Brown, H. J. (1992). *Live and learn and pass it on.* Nashville: Rutledge Hill.

Campbell, W. E. (1993). *The power to learn.* Belmont, CA: Wadsworth.

Census Bureau (1995, March). *Educational attainment in the United States.* Washington, DC: Author.

Copulsky, W. (1993). Do grades matter? *On Campus, 13*(3), p. 11.

Csikszentmihalyi, M. (1990). *Flow: The psychology of optimal experience.* New York: Harper & Row.

Cypert, S. A. (1993). *The success breakthrough: Get what you want from your career, your relationships, and your life.* New York: Avon.

Educational Testing Service (1997). *Plan smart series: What you need to know for college admission 1*(1), p. 5.

Ferguson, M. (1989). Quoted in Covey, S. (1989). *The seven habits of highly effective people: Restoring the character ethic.* New York: Fireside/Simon & Schuster.

Gardner, J. N., & Jewler, A. J. (1992). *Your college experience: Strategies for success.* Belmont, CA: Wadsworth.

Gibbs, J. J. (1990). *Dancing with your books: The Zen way of studying.* New York: Plume.

Glasser, W. H. (1990). The quality school. *Phi Delta Kappan, 71,* 425-435.

Harris, A. (1990). And the prepared will inherit the future. *Black Enterprise, 20*(2), 121-128.

Hartman, D. K., & Hartman, J. A. (1993). Reading across texts: Expanding the role of the reader. *The Reading Teacher, 47*(3), 201-211.

Iran-Nejad, A. (1990). Active and dynamic self-regulation of learning processes. *Review of Educational Research, 60*(4), 573-602.

Kanar, C. C. (1995). *The confident student* (2nd ed.). Boston: Houghton Mifflin.

Knowles, M. (1975). *Self-directed learning: A guide for learners and teachers.* New York: Cambridge.

Langer, J. A., & Applebee, A. (1986). Reading and writing instruction: Toward a theory of teaching and learning. *Review of Research in Education, 13,* 171-194.

Murnane, R. J., & Levy, F. (1997). *Teaching the new basic skills: Principles for educating children to thrive in a changing economy.* New York: The Free Press.

Naisbitt, J., & Aburdene, P. (1990). *Megatrends 2000: Ten new directions for the 1990's.* New York: Avon.

Pascarella, E. T., & Terenzini, P. T. (1991). *How college affects students.* San Francisco, CA: Jossey Bass.

Rindfuss, R. R., Kavee, A. L., Cooksey, E. C. (1995). The first year after college: Activities and their subsequent effects. *Journal of Higher Education, 66*(4), 415-446.

Senge, P. M. (1990). *The fifth discipline: The art and practice of the learning organization.* New York: Doubleday.

Shulman, L. (1986). Paradigms and research programs in the study of teaching: A contemporary perspective. In M. C. Wittrock (Ed.), *Handbook of research on teaching* (pp. 3-36). Upper Saddle River, NJ: Merrill/Prentice Hall.

Smith, F. (1992). Learning to read: The never-ending debate. *Phi Delta Kappan, 73*(6), 432-441.

Whitehead, R. (1997). High school and the new jobs. *The Atlantic Monthly, 280*(3), 112-115.

Developing Critical Thinking Skills

Real learning gets to the heart of what it means to be human. Through learning we re-create ourselves. Through learning we become able to do something we never were able to do. Through learning we extend our capacity to create, to be part of the generative process of life. There is within each of us a deep hunger for this type of learning. * *(p. 14)*

—Peter Senge

* From *The Fifth Discipline: The Art and Practice of the Learning Organization* (p. 14), by P. M. Senge, 1990, New York: Doubleday. Copyright © 1990 by Doubleday. Reprinted by permission of Doubleday, a division of Bantam Doubleday Dell Publishing Group, Inc.

Prereading Questions

- Of all the people you admire, whom do you admire the most as a thinker?
- How has your thinking changed over your school career?
- In what ways are you a good thinker?
- What challenges do you anticipate to your thinking skills in college?

Assessing Prior Knowledge

Some people say that they work well under pressure of a deadline, others do not. Some people need absolute quiet to study and concentrate, others are skilled at "tuning out" background noise. Part of becoming an effective learner in college is gaining insight into the particulars of your thinking processes. Evaluate your thinking skills using Box 2.1.

Vignette: Professors Who Challenge Students to Think

Imagine this scene: Two college seniors who are roommates are reminiscing about the college faculty member who exerted the most positive influence on their lives. Alaina says, "My first big culture shock was writing a paper in my Introduction to Philosophy class. Dr. Schutzinger had told us to select a subject that 'humankind has been trying to understand for centuries,' and I chose love. When I met with her to discuss my idea, she said, 'What type of love did you have in mind? The love of a mother for a child? Of friendship? Of brothers?' After I explained that I chose the topic because I was in love, she said, 'Ah, then it is personal love.' She lent me three books that were so hard to read and understand that I actually read them out loud at times, word by word. I reread some passages 4 or 5 times before I started to understand what these famous philosophers had to say about love. Dr. S. helped me to respect and appreciate great thinkers because she respected me as a thinker and expected me to understand the same things that she had studied." "Yes," her roommate Maria agrees, "The professor who influenced me the most was my advisor in my major, Dr. Cylkowski. He made Shakespeare come alive in his class and recommended me for a job as a tutor in the Writing Center. He also encouraged me to do an independent study in advanced composition. When I was trying to decide what I could do that would be worth 3 credits, he said, 'You have a double major in English and Spanish, correct? Why don't you think of a way to use your knowledge of both languages?' I ended up writing a paper on poetry that compared the sonnets written in English with those written in Spanish. For the first time in my life, I felt like a real scholar."

In both of these stories, it is clear that these admired instructors had several things in common: They challenged the assumptions of their students, encouraged them to think deeply about issues, and urged them to pursue the truth. Interestingly, the seniors' appreciation for these faculty was a delayed reaction. At the time, they admitted to some frustration when their professors refused just to give them the facts or tell them exactly what to do and how to proceed.

It takes time and maturity to realize that professors who have as many questions as they do answers are often the best role models. As a college student, you will no doubt have similar experiences. Have your previous school experiences really challenged your mind,

BOX 2.1 *Improvement in Action* ⦚▶

Use the plus/minus/interesting grid below to analyze your thinking skills. For example, you might list as a plus that you seem to be good at figuring out underlying motives for people's actions; you might list as a minus that you don't think well under pressure in a public situation; and it might be interesting to note whether you have a favorite place to go to think about important decisions.

Plus +	Minus −	Interesting !!

or were you usually functioning at the lowest levels, for example, being asked simply to memorize facts? How would you analyze and describe your ability to think? Many students find that their college instructors expect them to approach issues in ways that demand more from them as thinkers.

These college faculty members do not subscribe to the "suitcase packing" theory of teaching in which the teacher's job is to stuff in as much information as possible. Rather, they challenge students to think and to apply their thinking in a variety of situations.

The college environment is an appropriate place to develop and enhance thinking skills. You will be asked to think critically and make decisions that affect you personally. You will be asked to evaluate, make judgments, and formulate opinions more than ever before. These skills are necessary for learning, not only during college years, but throughout life.

In this chapter, we will examine the particular types of thinking required in a college career and beyond as you pursue your chosen profession. As you think about that profession, what is it that your prospective employers will be seeking? Of course, there are the basic skills of reading and doing mathematics at high school level. But the "new basic skills" that employers seek require much more. These expectations include problem solving, communicating orally and in writing, using technology, and collaborating in diverse groups (Murnane & Levy, 1997). From this it is clear that higher standards are being set for the thinking abilities of tomorrow's employees.

Redefining Thinking

As Collins and Mangieri (1992) point out:

> For most people, thinking represents a true contradiction. These individuals know how to think, but know little about what thinking is, how they learned to think and whether or not they are good at thinking. They would agree that it is a crucial ability, but yet these same persons are not concerned that they know so little about thinking. (p. xi)

At its best, human thinking may be defined as an active, purposeful, organized form of information processing that is used to improve our understanding of self, others, and the world (Chaffee, 1994; Pressley, 1995). The truth is that any conscious human being is thinking all of the time. Figure 2.1 identifies the general characteristics of good thinkers.

The ability to think at higher levels is so important, in fact, that it is referred to as critical thinking—critical not in the sense of finding fault, but critical in the sense of being absolutely crucial. When engaging in critical thinking, the learner has to go beyond the given, elaborate on the idea, and add complexity (Resnick, 1987). A good example is looking at a comic strip like "The Far Side," "Calvin and Hobbes," or a political cartoon. Usually, in order to "get" the joke, you need to "read between the lines" and elaborate, add complexity, or go beyond what is stated or pictured.

Traditionally, the "basic" thinking skills have been knowledge (memorizing information) and understanding (explaining information in your own words). Yet more often than not in a college class, students are expected to think at higher levels. They might be asked to do the following things:

■ Apply—use knowledge and understanding to complete a practical task. In a statistics course, for example: "Use what you know about probability and statistics to critique the following advertising claims that appeared recently in newspapers or magazines. Which claims are justified? Which are not? Why?"

Figure 2.1
Characteristics of Good Thinkers

Adapted from Pressley, M. (1995). *Advanced educational psychology for educators, researchers, and policymakers.* New York: HarperCollins College Publishers, and Borkowski, J.G., & Muthukrishna, N. (1992). Moving metacognition into the classroom: "Working models" and effective strategy teaching. In M. Pressley, K. R. Harris, & J. T. Guthrie (Eds.), *Promoting academic competence and literacy in schools* (pp. 477–501). San Diego, CA: Academic Press.

Good thinkers . . .

1. begin with a healthy, normally functioning brain.
2. regard growth of the mind as a gradual process.
3. know and use a large number of learning strategies.
4. match learning strategies to specific situations.
5. believe in the value of a carefully deployed effort.
6. understand their own learning needs and processes.
7. make efficient use of prior knowledge and short-term memory.
8. possess appropriate confidence in themselves.
9. keep failure in perspective and use it as a learning opportunity.
10. focus on completing tasks and gaining mastery rather than on immediate, tangible rewards.
11. approach learning situations with attitudes and emotions that support learning.
12. concentrate attention and inhibit inappropriate responses to situations.
13. contribute to their own education and development.
14. seek situations that provide stimulation and challenge.
15. imagine themselves in different roles in the near and distant future and envision new "hoped-for" selves becoming a reality.
16. turn to the right people for learning support.

- Analyze—break things down into their component parts. On an essay exam in English, for example: "Identify at least four examples of imagery used in the following sonnet, then analyze how the author uses imagery to create a mood."

- Synthesize—combine and integrate various sources of information. For example, on a final examination in ancient history class: "Synthesize your textbook readings, class notes, and outside reading to identify different viewpoints on the fall of the Roman Empire."

- Evaluate—assess the value, merit, or worth of something. For example, in an open-book exam (one during which you can refer to your notes) in a criminology course: "Describe the penal system in America from colonial days to the present. Using your class and text notes, evaluate the contributions and limitations of each era, and assess the influences of those previous trends on our modern concept of corrections." Figure 2.2 is a more detailed list of the critical thinking abilities emphasized and developed during college study.

Questions and learning experiences that require you to go beyond recalling facts, even beyond understanding them, are sometimes intimidating and confusing at first. Yet if you really focus on thinking during class, while studying, and as you read, you can approach such challenges with confidence.

Human Beings as Thinkers

Perhaps you have heard the human mind compared to a computer. Actually, the human brain is more powerful than any machine we know because it is capable of operating simultaneously on several different levels (Caine & Caine, 1997). "Numerous layers of organization within the brain act together . . . to handle not only memory, but also vision, learning, emotion, and consciousness " (Abbott, 1997, p. 12). You can, for example, be reading this book and trying to concentrate while all sorts of other thoughts creep in. These thoughts are like abbreviated bulletins about sensory impressions ("uncomfortable chair," "poor lighting"), your physiological needs ("lunchtime soon"), emotional messages ("need

Figure 2.2
Dimensions of Critical Thinking

Some of the critical thinking abilities expected of college students include the following (Chaffee, 1994; Kanar, 1995).

- thinking for yourself rather than going along with the crowd
- forming and applying new concepts
- setting goals and monitoring progress toward goals
- making responsible decisions
- analyzing the same issue from different perspectives
- reasoning about ideas in a logical, organized way
- supporting a point of view with reasons and evidence
- solving complex problems
- appreciating beliefs, values, and attitudes both different from and similar to your own
- thinking imaginatively and creatively

an A on test"), and distractors ("laundromat this weekend?"). The less effort you make to concentrate, the more likely these chaotic and often worrisome thoughts are likely to take over. When this multi-layered, simultaneous thought runs on without a clear focus, a person is apt to feel overwhelmed or confused. Thinking is the intellectual equivalent of keeping your eye on the ball in sports. You have to exercise conscious control over your own thinking processes, even when the material is not easy to grasp at first or outside your range of interest.

Even more impressive than the brain's ability to work on several different levels is its ability to seek patterns. You can read about political unrest somewhere in the world, for example, and think about the underlying motives of the groups in conflict, see connections between the causes of unrest in different parts of the world, analyze today's conflict from a historical perspective, or even make predictions for the course of future events. Most experts agree that few people have truly tested the limits of their brain power, and it is the rare individual who works at full intellectual capacity (Sylwester, 1995).

What deliberate efforts have you made to improve as a thinker? The typical young adult in America spends about 40% to 50% of his or her time in leisure activities, and few of those activities are used to build thinking abilities, particularly higher levels of thinking (Collins & Mangieri, 1992). This is one reason that the adjustment to college life can be so difficult; much more of successful college students' time must be focused on mental work, and often they are unprepared—or at least underprepared—for the change. Fortunately, there are many strategies emerging from research on the human brain and the field of cognitive psychology that can support you in your goal of becoming an effective thinker in college.

As a first step in improving thinking, consider the capabilities of the normally functioning human brain. Thinking processes of human beings are unique in a variety of important ways. As human beings, we possess numerous capabilities that distinguish us from other animals (Costa, 1996).

1. *Altering response patterns*. Human beings make conscious and deliberate changes in attitudes and behavior; animals are driven by instinct. Some good examples of altering response patterns would be making an effort to control your temper or training your body for competitive sports.

2. *Constructing meaning from experience*. Human beings are constantly striving to make sense out of what happens and to interpret the significance of events. If you see two paramedics walking down the corridor where your class meets, you will try to figure out what is going on. If you go out for football and end up sitting on the bench, you will try to make sense out of that experience too. Figure 2.3 highlights some of the thinking skills developed in college that enable students to make meaning out of their experiences.

3. *Handling abstractions*. Human beings can move beyond concrete experience to understand powerful and profound ideas. Animals operate in the world of direct, immediate experience. One of the hallmarks of human thinking is the ability to deal with the past and imagine the future. We are also capable of handling abstract ideas, such as explaining how it feels to be homesick or deciding what course of action would be consistent with ethical principles.

4. *Storing information outside the body*. Human beings retain, reorganize, and retrieve information. In fact, many of the institutions and much of technology that human beings have invented are designed to manage information, from the public library system to the Internet.

5. *Learning in reciprocity with others*. Human beings are fundamentally social and much of their learning takes place through dynamic interaction with other people. We can convey facts, ideas, and feelings to one another and effectively pool our resources to maximize learning. This is one reason why you are in college instead of studying alone at home. The assumption is that learning is more meaningful and enduring when it involves other people. You might be asked, for example, to join a discussion group on E-mail as part of a course requirement in order to learn in reciprocity with others.

6. *Finding problems*. Unlike animals who simply encounter problems, human beings actively seek out inconsistencies in situations and search for solutions. In fact, the essence of theory and research in any field you might study in college is this quest to identify problems and raise significant questions. Rather than rushing to an immediate answer or superficial solution, well-educated people realize that it takes time to find and formulate good questions.

7. *Thinking about thinking*. Human beings not only think, they think about thinking, a process called metacognition. An example might be a college student who was identified as learning disabled in elementary school. Perhaps that student feels that the label was inaccurate. Maybe that student agrees with the assessment and has learned to cope in a variety of ways. In both cases, the student is not merely thinking but thinking about his or her own thinking.

8. *Inventing new worlds*. Human beings are toolmakers, explorers, inventors. Whereas animals live in the here and now, human beings are capable of envisioning things

Figure 2.3
Thinking Skills Developed in College

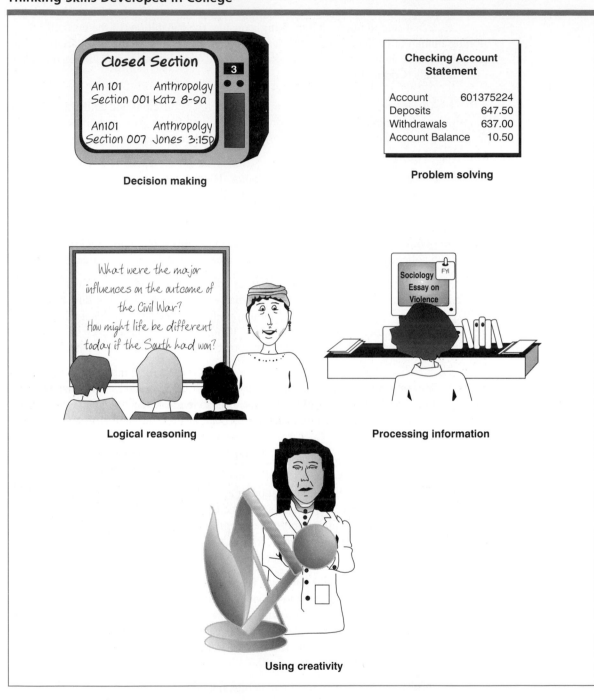

Closed Section

An 101   Anthropolgy
Section 001 Katz 8-9a

An101   Anthropolgy
Section 007 Jones 3:15p

Decision making

Checking Account
Statement

Account   601375224
Deposits   647.50
Withdrawals   637.00
Account Balance   10.50

Problem solving

What were the major
influences on the outcome of
the Civil War?
How might life be different
today if the South had won?

Logical reasoning

Sociology
Essay on
Violence

FYI

Processing information

Using creativity

they have never seen and creating imaginary worlds. The inventor who develops a new product and the science fiction writer are examples of this human ability to explore new worlds.

9. *Engaging in systems thinking.* Unlike animals, human beings can see the "big picture." We humans are capable, not only of perceiving patterns, but also of recognizing part-whole relationships. Suppose, for example, that your long-term career goal is to become a physical therapist. As a human being you are capable of recognizing all of the intermediate steps toward your goal such as attending class today or studying for a test tomorrow in order to reach your goal four years from now. You also are capable of seeing the many different influences on your professional aspirations—such things as health, finances, transportation, family support, and so forth.

Throughout your college career, you will be expected to develop these ways of thinking further.

Critical Thinking in College

In a synthesis of over 2,600 research studies on the effects of college, Pascarella and Terenzini (1991) found that attending college had a positive impact on all areas of cognitive development, including verbal and quantitative skills, oral and written communication, critical thinking, and intellectual flexibility. Additionally, they found moderate-to-strong evidence to support the contention that this positive impact goes well beyond the cognitive realm.

The positive changes that take place as a result of college continue to influence students throughout their lives and seem to "create, or reinforce habits that will affect later life experiences as well: A habit of reading and discussing ideas; a tendency to be active socially and politically, analytical skills that assist in real-life problem solving" (Bee, 1992, p. 53).

One important category of critical or higher level thinking is beliefs. Beliefs are strongly held views that affect motivation and behavior. Beliefs include such things as your religious creed, your political affiliations, and your scientific explanations for natural phenomena. You may engage in a heated debate with someone else who does not share your beliefs, particularly on a controversial issue, but have you ever really analyzed the characteristics of beliefs? Eleanor Duckworth (1996) has. Take a look at her thinking on paper and notice how she "sorts out" her thinking about beliefs. Her ideas are italicized, our examples follow.

- *You may have learned a belief by being told, or you may have concluded it yourself from evidence that you have been told about, or you may have developed the belief from your own personal evidence.* Belief in an afterlife, for instance, is often the result of religious training. There are people, however, who have had near-death experiences and therefore argue that they have evidence of and personal experience with life after death. Beliefs develop in a variety of ways.

- *An opposing belief is conceivable, and would give rise to different actions, in a situation where the belief is pertinent.* For example, some people view abortion as absolutely wrong under any circumstances while others view abortion as the absolute right of the woman to decide. Still others believe that abortion is acceptable in some cases, such as when a woman is raped. No matter how firmly you are committed to a particular point of view, other people exist who are equally convinced of an opposing view.

- *A belief can be confirmed or disconfirmed by further evidence (yet evidence that may be confirming or disconfirming to one person may be irrelevant to another).* Whereas one person who is convinced that AIDS can be transmitted by casual contact and reads several medical reports to the contrary might change that belief, another might disregard the information and fear any human contact with an AIDS patient. In other words, inaccurate beliefs can persist, even in the face of authoritative evidence to the contrary.

- *A verbal statement of the belief may not really mean that the belief is held. You may enunciate the belief because you think it is expected of you, even though you know you don't believe it, or you may think you believe it although you really don't—it conflicts with some other belief that really determines how you act.* Police officers are trained not to take the law into their own hands, yet if a member of their family or a fellow police officer is the victim of a violent crime, their true beliefs may surface. In other words, police officers' belief in "protecting their own" might override their stated beliefs about upholding the law.

Likewise, beliefs about college study are frequently based on high school experiences. When a typical college freshman first looks at the class schedule, it seems so open and easy in comparison to the all day/every day schedule of high school. But those "free" blocks of time are deceiving. Successful students are the ones who use a significant percentage of their out-of-class time—such as blocks of time during the day when the library is less crowded—to improve their thinking skills. They engage in activities such as preparing for class, studying for tests, and revising written assignments until their work is high quality.

Unsuccessful college students are not comfortable with thought and solitude. They feel that they always have to be in the company of groups of peers to prove that they are socially successful. Often, they spend their unscheduled time in activities that "switch their brains to off," like staring at television or talking about nothing in particular on the telephone. Unsuccessful students express concern about the 4 years it will take to finish college, yet experts estimate that the average person who lives to age 65 will spend the equivalent of 9 years watching television. In order to become a successful student, you will need to devote a substantial portion of your time to higher-level thinking. That is your full-time job as a student who is preparing for a future role as a professional.

Consequences of Neglecting Critical Thinking

Some students have the attitude that teachers who encourage them to think are trying to punish them or make them feel inadequate. Actually, nothing could be further from the truth. Responsible instructors know that achieving new and better ways of thinking is the key to success in college. The faculty member who expects less or "waters down" the curriculum might seem to be doing you a favor at the moment but is actually doing you a tremendous disservice. Raths and his associates (1986) have investigated what happens when students are not encouraged to think at the highest levels. Figure 2.4 is an overview of some of the consequences.

As you no doubt already know, self-confidence exerts a powerful influence on thinking. When people have difficulty thinking clearly, it is often more of a self-esteem problem than an intellectual one. One strategy for building confidence that is recommended by psychologists is the role of self-talk. Self-talk refers to the things that you say to yourself in your own mind. Studies show that as people's self-talk moves in a more positive direction, their confidence and competence builds (Manning, 1991). In your efforts to improve as a thinker and become a more active learner, try using the positive self-talk strategy. Figure 2.5 provides an example of self-talk related to college study and success.

Figure 2.4

What Happens When Students Are Not Encouraged to Think Critically?

Adapted from Raths, L.E., et al. (1986). *Teaching for thinking: Theory, strategies, and activities for the classroom.* New York: Teachers College Press.

Read the following list of behaviors and circle any that describe you:

1. **Low tolerance for ambiguity**—Students search for the answer and become frustrated when a single, obvious solution is not apparent.

2. **Overdependence**—Students doubt their own ability to think deeply about ideas and become overreliant on the teacher or some other authority for answers.

3. **Anti-intellectualism**—Students reject forms of intellectual activity (studying, using the library, discussing ideas) and regard them as a waste of time, as meaningless exercises done to please others. They may even ridicule classmates who take intellectual pursuits seriously.

4. **Impulsivity**—Students are impatient with reflective thinking processes and tend to jump to conclusions even though those conclusions are clearly faulty.

5. **Missing the meaning**—Students "go through the motions" of a learning activity but overlook the underlying purpose or goal.

6. **Dogmatism**—Students take an inflexible stand on an issue and refuse to reconsider, even though persuasive, authoritative evidence to contradict their perspective is presented.

7. **Learned helplessness**—Because students are treated as if their thinking processes are defective, many cope with this insult to their intelligence by "playing dumb." Eventually, they play the role so well that they cut off all forms of intellectual stimulation and become increasingly helpless as thinkers (Garber & Seligman, 1980).

Practically everyone exhibits the behaviors described here at one time or another. Are there any behaviors on the list that are particularly problematic for you? How can you counteract these influences and improve your thinking skills?

BOX 2.3   *Improvement in Action* ⫸

Use the list in Figure 2.4 on consequences of neglecting critical thinking to conduct a self-assessment. Which of these coping techniques have you used? Under what circumstances? How will you counteract your tendency to fall back on these unproductive ways of dealing with challenges to your thinking while you are in college?

The Well-Educated Person

When we say that a person is well educated, what does that mean? Why is it a desirable goal? As you read in Chapter 1, successfully completing a college degree offers many tangible and intangible rewards. Most of your instructors would agree that becoming a well-educated person is the most important outcome. One way to understand the concept of being well educated is to look at how such a person who has learned to think well approaches complex problems and difficult issues. Figure 2.6 identifies five fundamental questions that a well-educated individual raises about the world.

Figure 2.5
Positive Self-Talk

Adapted from Manning, B. H. (1991). *Cognitive self-instruction for classroom processes.* Albany, NY: State University of New York Press.

Level I   Negative Acceptance

Example of Level I self-talk: *I can't perform well in this class. If I could just pass this course, then maybe I could make it in college.*

Level II   Recognition of the Need to Change

Example of Level II self-talk: *I need to do well in this class. I should make a plan to study a little every day instead of waiting until test time. Cramming never works for me.*

Level III   Decision to Change

Example of Level III self-talk: *I never miss a study time. If I have to miss it on a particular day, I make it up another day. I no longer procrastinate and wait until a day or two before a big test to cram. I'll be less stressed-out if I take this one step at a time.*

Level IV   The Better You

Example of Level IV self-talk: *I am a successful student. I can see a direct relationship between the effort I put into studying and my grade point average. Now I know how to study and succeed. If I put my mind to it, I can do well in just about any class.*

Level V   Universal Affirmation

Example of Level V self-talk: *It is important for any college student to realize that studying is a major responsibility. Everyone needs to "hit the books" regularly in order to succeed. I say to anyone who complains about having to study or who asks my advice, "It's like exercise. Don't whine, just do it."*

BOX 2.4   **Improvement in Action** ⫸

Look at the examples of self-talk in Figure 2.5. Now think about a learning experience that you approached with some anxiety at first that turned out to be successful. Write examples of your self-talk at each stage as described in Figure 2.5.

Figure 2.6
Five Kinds of Questions the Well-Educated Person Raises About the World

Source: Meier, D. (1997). How our schools could be. In E. Clinchy (Ed.). *Transforming public education: A new course for America's future* (pp. 145–155). New York: Teachers College Press.

1. How do we know what we think we know? What's our evidence? How credible is it?
2. Whose viewpoint are we hearing, reading, seeing? What other viewpoints might there be if we changed our position?
3. How is one thing connected to another? Is there a pattern here?
4. How else might it have been? What if? Supposing that?
5. What difference does it make? Who cares? (Meier, 1997, p. 150).

BOX 2.5   *Improvement in Action* ⅢⅢ▶

Use the five questions in Figure 2.6 that a well-educated person asks about the world to think about a controversial topic that has been in the news lately. How did approaching the topic in this way enlarge your perspective?

Note that these questions are more "thought-full" than others that might be raised. They call upon the person to critically examine the situation rather than jump to conclusions or instantly reject opposing points of view. They get to the heart of the matter rather than stay at the surface level. All of these behaviors—raising thoughtful questions, using positive self-talk, examining beliefs, and thinking critically—are part of becoming a professional.

Interestingly, these behaviors also distinguish the thinking of novices or beginners in a field from the thinking of experts or those who are experienced. No matter what professional career you choose to pursue, the characteristics that distinguish experts from novices are relatively consistent. Studies of chess players, medical doctors, lawyers, teachers, and other professionals (Chi, Glaser, & Farr, 1988) suggest that experts think about their work lives in particularly effective and efficient ways. To preview the direction of the changes that your thinking about and within your career will be expected to take, look at Figure 2.7.

Figure 2.7
From Novice to Expert

Adapted from Pressley, M. (1995). *Advanced educational psychology for educators, researchers, and policymakers.* New York: HarperCollins College Publishers.

FROM	TO
general knowledge on a variety of topics	highly specialized expertise that enables them to excel mainly in one domain
FROM	**TO**
knowledge that is piecemeal and difficult to synthesize	a storehouse of cases, episodes, and accounts of experience that are stored in memory in narrative (story) format
FROM	**TO**
focusing on the surface and being overwhelmed or confused	seeing the big picture and recognizing large, meaningful patterns in their domain of expertise as well as representing problems on a deeper, more principled level
FROM	**TO**
being confounded by problems and making beginner's mistakes	spending proportionately more time analyzing problems qualitatively and then solving problems efficiently with few errors
FROM	**TO**
reliance on others to gain a sense of their progress and achievements	greater self-direction and strong self-monitoring skills

Conclusion

If you are a highly successful student in college, it will be because you discover a joy of learning in college, a joy that perhaps eluded you before. For learning to be significant, it must personally affect the learner; it must mean something to you. If your only reason for attending college is to please your family or teachers or to be with your friends, you are at a real disadvantage. Often learning for the sheer pleasure it brings to you is sparked by an enthusiastic teacher or an interesting experience. Although not all of your learning will be pleasurable, you may learn to enjoy thinking critically as you explore topics that interest you and expand your range of interests. Keep an open mind about the things you are learning. Having a positive attitude, one in which you seek to learn from all the situations you encounter, will enhance your chances of experiencing the joy of learning and becoming a better, clearer thinker in the process.

 ## Voices of Successful Students

Four college students who were interviewed about their thinking had this to say:

Bernard: "I guess I'm an all around team player. I think best with company. If it's up to me to study, I'll keep putting it off but when I know that I'll be meeting with my study group or my tutor, I don't want to let them down and come unprepared. These people are keeping me in good academic standing so that I can play sports and not lose my scholarship."

Maria: "If I expect to get anything out of a lecture, I have to take notes. If I want to organize my day, I have to write it down. If I have an important decision to make, I make a list of the advantages and disadvantages. I can't seem to think well without writing."

Janel: "When I found out that part of our grade in the World History class was based on talking about our projects, I was relieved. I'm not much of a writer, but talk? You'd best believe that I can do some serious talking. In the neighborhood where I grew up, you learned to think fast and talk even faster to stay out of trouble."

Ken: "I would be lost without my computer, the Internet, and access to the new technologies. It isn't just for academic stuff, it's also a way of connecting with other people. In my freshman class at this small Catholic college, anyone who is experiencing computer problems would probably say, 'Just ask Ken. He knows computers.' Helping people out is time-consuming, but I enjoy it."

Each of these students has learned to use different language tools to communicate and support their thinking processes. Whether it is Ken's facility with computer language, Janel's confidence with spoken language, Bernard's reliance on the social dynamics of language, or Maria's use of written language, all of these college learners have formed strong opinions about the conditions that enable them to think clearly and grapple with intellectually challenging material.

Cooperative Learning Activity: Profile of the Class as Thinkers

Use your evaluations of yourself as a thinker from boxes 2.1, 2.2 and 2.3 to create a one-page profile of yourself as a thinker. You may want to approach it like an advertisement and point out some of your best features. Compare your strengths as a thinker with those of the others in your group. How might you benefit from working together with someone who has different strengths to solve a problem or to complete a class project? What complementary strengths do you have?

Writing and Reflecting: Interview on Thinking

Use the following questions to conduct an interview with another student.

1. What, in your opinion, is distinctive about human beings' thinking processes? How does human thinking differ from that of other animals, for instance?
2. Of all the people who have lived throughout history, whom do you admire most as a thinker? Is there anyone living today you admire as a thinker? Who?
3. If you were asked to provide evidence to support your claim that these people are good thinkers,

what evidence would you provide? In other words, how do you go about determining who qualifies as a great thinker?
4. Do you consider yourself to be a good thinker? Why or why not? In what specific ways is your thinking strong?
5. How does a person go about improving thinking? What would the process be like?
6. What steps have you taken to improve your thinking? Describe what you did.

Self-Improvement Strategy: Self-Evaluation of Critical Thinking

Use Figure 2.2, Dimensions of Critical Thinking, on page 29 as a checklist for evaluating your use of critical thinking skills since you arrived on campus. For each item on the list, think of a specific example where you relied upon this thinking skill to make a decision or to solve a problem. In response to the first item, "thinking for yourself instead of going along with the crowd," you might offer as an example, "I decided to leave the group I was having lunch with early rather than risk being late for class." Continue in this fashion for the entire list. What have you noticed about your critical thinking processes?

Reading Selection 1

Evaluating Sources on the Internet: Let the Reader Beware

—*Reid Goldsborough**

The fact is, the Internet is chock full of rumors, gossip, hoaxes, exaggerations, falsehoods, ruses, and scams. Although the Net can reveal useful, factual information

that you'd be hard pressed to find elsewhere, it can also appear to be a gigantic electronic tabloid.

Can you ever trust the Internet? Sure you can. You just need to apply critical thinking in evaluating the information and advice you come across. Here's a six-step approach to doing this.

1. Don't judge a Web site by its appearance. Sure, if a Web site looks professional rather than slopped together, chances are greater that the information within it will be accurate and reliable.

But looks can and do deceive. A flashy site can merely be a marketing front for quack health remedies or an illegal pyramid scheme.

2. Try to find out who's behind the information. If you're looking at a Web site, check if the author or creator is identified. See if there are links to a page

---

* Reid Goldsborough is an award-winning journalist and the author of the book *Straight Talk About the Information Superhighway.* He can be reached at reidgold@voicenet.com or http://www.voicenet.com/~reidgold/.

listing professional credentials or affiliations. Be very skeptical if no authorship information is provided.

If you're looking at a message in a Usenet newsgroup or Internet mailing list, see if the author has included a signature—a short, often biographical, description that's automatically appended to the end of messages. Many people include their credentials in their signature or point to their home page, where they provide biographical information.

3. Try to determine the reason the information was posted. Among those who create Web sites are publishing companies, professional and trade organizations, government agencies, nonprofit organizations, for-profit companies, educational institutions, individual researchers, political and advocacy groups, and hobbyists.

Each has its own agenda—sometimes explicit, sometimes hidden. Unearth the agenda and keep it in mind when evaluating the information presented.

Similarly, look behind and between the words posted in Usenet and mailing list discussions. Is the author trying to promote his or her own ends, or be helpful? You can often do both, but not always.

4. Look for the date the information was created or modified. Unless you're doing historical research, current information is usually more valid and useful than older material.

If the Web site doesn't provide a "last updated" message or otherwise date its content, check out some of its links. If more than a couple are no longer working, the information at the site may no longer be up to date either.

5. Try to verify the same information elsewhere. This is particularly important if the information is at odds with your previous understanding or if you intend to use it for critical purposes such as an important health, family, or business decision.

Ideally, you should confirm the information with at least two other sources. Librarians and information scientists call this the "principle of triangulation of data." Spending a bit of time validating the material, through the Internet or at a local library, can be well worth the investment.

6. Try to find out how others feel about the reliability and professionalism of the Web site you're looking at. There are a number of review guides that offer evaluations of other sites. Here are three excellent, relatively new review guides that you may not have heard of:

Argus Clearinghouse
http://www.clearinghouse.net/chhome.html

Mining Company
http://miningco.com/

Reader's Digest's LookSmart
http://www.looksmart.com/

With any information you come across on the Net, the watchword is "Caveat lector"—Let the reader beware.

If you'd like to delve further into the issue of information credibility on the Internet, there are Web sites out there that let you do just that. Here are four good ones:

Evaluating Internet Information
http://www-medlib.med.utah.edu/navigator/discovery/eval.html

Evaluating Quality on the Net
http://www.tiac.net/users/hope/findqual.html

Thinking Critically about World Wide Web Resources
http://www.library.ucla.edu/libraries/college/instruct/critical.htm

Internet Source Validation Project
http://www.stemnet.nf.ca/Curriculum/Validate/validate.html

Reading Selection 2

Read the following poem about human potential. How does it relate to opportunities during college study?

stupid america

—Abelardo Delgado*

stupid america, see that chicano
with a big knife
in his steady hand
he doesn't want to knife you
he wants to sit on a bench
and carve christ figures
but you won't let him.
Stupid america, hear that chicano
shouting curses on the street
he is a poet without paper and pencil
and since he cannot write
he will explode
stupid america, remember that chicanito
flunking math and english
he is the picasso
of your western states
but he will die
with one thousand masterpieces
hanging only from his mind.

Reading Selection 3

As you read the following advice adapted from Brown and Holtzman 1987 by Meghan Twiest, consider the different ways in which career decisions call for the critical thinking skills of application, analysis, synthesis, and evaluation.

---

* Delgado, A. (1972). "stupid america" In *Chicano: 25 pieces of a Chicano mind.* Abelardo: Barrio Productions.

How To Choose a Career

1. Study yourself. Examine your strengths and weaknesses as well as your goals in life. Be realistic about your abilities, but remember that students often surprise themselves by doing well in difficult subjects once they see how they will be able to apply this information and are committed to learning it. If, for example you have always wanted to be a veterinarian but did not feel confident about your abilities, take an animal biology course. You may find that it is very interesting and that you are able to do well because the subject interests you.

2. Develop a time line. This will mean looking at what you need to accomplish each year much more carefully. Your adviser may have a "Planned Program of Study" that will enable you to see what criteria must be met during each year. For example, you know you want to do your student teaching in year 4. That means getting your pre-student teaching experience during your junior year. In order to do this you will have to take courses for teacher certification your sophomore year. Therefore, you have decided to try to get some of your elective courses this semester.

3. Make some predictions. Imagine yourself in a career. Envision problems you may encounter and what you would do to overcome them. You may know, for example, that as a hotel and restaurant management major you will probably be working in a large city sometime during your career. Because you will encounter people from all over the world, you decide to minor in a language to facilitate communication with the travelers with whom you will be working.

4. Learn about ways to get started in a career. Become familiar with the pathways for entering occupations that interest you. There are usually several ways to enter an occupation that interests you, and you will want to be familiar with all of them so that you can find the one that best suits you. Your advisers, mentors, and career placement service can help with these plans. As an early childhood educator, for example, you would like to operate your own day care center someday. You are considering the possibility of becoming a nanny in another state for the summer to get some experience. You have also made some appointments with directors of day care centers in your hometown to see whether there is volunteer work you can do.

5. Review your plans periodically with someone else. Talking over plans with your adviser or family helps you stay focused and monitor your progress. Often an adviser can foresee a problem with your plans that you have overlooked. Parents, because they are not as familiar with your academic life, can keep you in touch with your life outside of the college community. Questions such as, "How is this change in plans going to affect your graduation date?" must be seriously considered and are sometimes overlooked by students who may be quick to make decisions without thinking through the options clearly.

6. Start over if you have made a mistake. If you choose a career that does not suit you, you can start over. You may decide that another field is better suited to your talents and temperament. The time it takes for retraining is minimal compared to the length of time you will spend in that career.

Reading Selection 4

This reading selection gives you an idea about what to expect from your first job in your career field (Rigolosi, 1994).* Five suggestions are offered. Think about jobs that you have held and when you have done some of the things suggested in the article.

Your First Job: Reality Check

Your first job is going to be stimulating and challenging—right? Well, maybe not. Of course, you should look for a job that's going to let you use your skills and creativity. But 99 times of 100 you're going to start in an entry-level position—which means that you need to take the good with the bad. Here are some tips to help you negotiate your way through your first job.

1. Remember: You will make copies. You will also answer phones, take messages, run errands, and do the things no one else wants to do. Do everything cheerfully, and never take the attitude that this work is beneath you. Rather than complain, use your time constructively. If you're asked to staff the switchboard or make thousands of copies, bring a copy of Business Week (or some other industry magazine) to read while doing so.

Also keep in mind the reason that you're doing all these things. You are fresh out of school, the new kid on the block. Should your boss—who's much more experienced and highly paid—be spending his or her time at the copy machine? Be patient; in a few years you'll have someone to do clerical work for you.

2. Make yourself stand out. Today's job market is crowded with qualified people. That's why you need to show your employer why you are the best person for the job. Develop a skill that is in demand and demonstrable. In the global market of the 1990s, bilingualism can be a particularly strong competitive advantage for you.

Excellent communication skills can also make you stand out. Being able to communicate means being able to speak and write well. Speaking well means speaking clearly and at just the right speed. Writing well means knowing all the rules of spelling, punctuation, and grammar. It also means getting your point across clearly and concisely. Many reputations are made on the basis of high-quality presentations, memos, and reports.

3. Dress for the job you want, not the job you have. Today's companies are a lot less strict on dress codes than ever before. At most companies, the way you perform is more important than the way you dress. This does not mean, though, that your dress doesn't make an important psychological impression. Men who wear a suit and tie and carry a briefcase to work even

---

* From "Your First Job: Reality Check," by S. Rigolosi, 1994, *Keys to Success, 1*(2), 15, 21. Copyright © 1994 by College Marketing, Prentice Hall, Inc. Reprinted by permission.

when they're still on the lower rungs of the corporate ladder are sending a signal that they want to go places. The same holds true for women. If you tend to balk at having your individuality obstructed, remember that your job is not your life—you can dress however you want on your own time.

4. Make your supervisor look good. Many books have been written about employer-employee relations. The number one rule here is: Be a positive reflection on your boss. Most managers are rated (among other things) on the quality of the staff they hire and develop. When you perform above expectations, your boss's boss is impressed. The result? Your boss becomes more generous with raises, promotions, and added responsibilities.

Follow a few simple rules to keep your boss looking good. Always dress and act professionally at business meetings, particularly when people outside the company are present. Be extremely courteous (and not overly forward) when dealing with people from other departments within the company. Volunteer for projects that no one really wants to do and do a bang-up job on them.

5. Act professionally, but always keep a sense of humor. Though you will probably make many friends at your job, remember that work is not the place to socialize. Keep your life distinct from your job. The telephone is not there for you to talk to your friends or mother during lunch hours. (Did you know that most businesses pay telephone rates that are three times higher than those paid by residential customers?) Lunch hour is lunch hour, not 90 minutes.

All of this is not to suggest that you approach your job with Mr. Spock-like scorn for human relations. Smile and say hello to the people you meet in the hallways—including maintenance people and mail room personnel. Say thank you when someone does anything for you. If you see an article that might be of interest to someone, make a copy and send it to him or her. Meetings, which can sometimes get intense and frustrating, can be lightened up with a well-placed jocular comment. Take it on yourself to bring coffee and donuts once in a while. In general, develop the reputation for being a pleasant (and competent) person; success will follow. (p. 15)

References

Abbott, J. (1997). 21st century learning: Beyond schools. *Education Digest, 63*(2), 11–15.

Bee, H. L. (1992). *The journey of adulthood* (2nd ed.). Upper Saddle River, NJ: Merrill/Prentice Hall.

Brown, W. F., & Holtzman, W. H. (1987). *A guide to college survival*. Iowa City, IA: American College Testing Program.

Caine, R., & Caine, G. (1997). *Education on the edge of possibility*. Alexandria, VA: Association for Supervision and Curriculum Development.

Chaffee, J. (1994). *Thinking critically* (4th ed.). Boston: Houghton Mifflin.

Chi, M. T. H., Glaser, R., & Farr, M. J. (1988). *The nature of expertise*. Hillsdale, NJ: Erlbaum.

Collins, C., & Mangieri, J. N. (1992). *Teaching for thinking: An agenda for the twenty-first century*. Hillsdale, NJ: Erlbaum.

Costa, A. (1996) In Prologue to Hyerle, D. (1996). *Visual dimensions of critical thinking*. Alexandria, VA: Association for Supervision and Curriculum Development.

Duckworth, E. (1996). *The having of wonderful ideas and other essays on teaching and learning*. (2nd ed.). New York: Teachers College Press.

Garber, J., & Seligman, M. F. P. (1980). *Human helplessness*. New York: Academic Press.

Kanar, C. C. (1995). *The confident student* (2nd ed.). Boston: Houghton Mifflin.

Manning, B. (1991). *Cognitive self-instruction for classroom processes*. Albany, NY: SUNY.

Murnane, R. J., & Levy, F. (1997). *Teaching the new basic skills: Principles for educating children to thrive in a changing economy*. New York: The Free Press.

Pascarella, E. T., & Terenzini, P. T. (1991). *How college affects students*. San Francisco: Jossey Bass.

Pressley, M. (1995). *Advanced educational psychology for educators, researchers, and policymakers*. New York: HarperCollins.

Raths, L. E., et al. (1986). *Teaching for thinking: Theory, strategies, and activities for the classroom*. New York: Teachers College Press.

Resnick, L. B. (1987). *Education and learning to think*. Report. Washington, DC: National Academy Press.

Rigolosi, S. (1994). Your first job: Reality check. *Keys to Success, 1*(2), 15, 21.

Sylwester, R. (1995). *A celebration of neurons: An educator's guide to the human brain*. Alexandria, VA: Association for Supervision and Curriculum Development.

Managing Time, Study, and Stress

Perhaps the most valuable result of all education is the ability to make yourself do the things you have to do when it ought to be done, whether you like it or not; it is the first lesson that ought to be learned; and however early a man's training begins, it is probably the last lesson that he learns thoroughly. *

—Thomas Huxley

* Huxley, T., as cited in McWilliams, J. R., & McWilliams, P. (1992). *The portable life 101*. Los Angeles: Prelude.

Prereading Questions

- What are your personal organizational skills?
- Do you have long-term goals? Have you developed a plan for accomplishing those goals?
- What techniques enable successful students to use their time efficiently?
- What can you do to prepare yourself for stressful times during the semester?

Assessing Prior Knowledge

With all the people you are meeting as you embark on your college career, you have probably noticed some interesting differences. You probably know fellow students who are efficient. They seem to be able to locate information when needed, whether it be notes from chemistry class, an announcement about the health fair taking place on campus, or discount coupons for the pizza shop. They keep track of their possessions and are prepared for emergencies. In contrast, you probably also know people who are the opposite. These students seem to be the last to find out about early registration, are frequently running late, and have a hard time keeping track of their belongings. How do you compare with these two types of students? What would your friends say about you? Do you consider yourself to be an organized person? Evaluate your organizational skills using Box 3.1.

Vignette: Time to Run to Class

It is Monday, 7:50 a.m. The scene is a dark, quiet bedroom. The alarm rings, and Katrina jumps out of bed to push the button to end the persistent buzz of her clock. As she does, Katrina realizes that she has just 10 minutes to get to her first class. She throws on a pair of jeans and a sweatshirt that are crumpled up next to the bed from the day before and runs to the bathroom for a quick grooming. Upon returning, she hastily hunts for her chemistry notebook and textbook. After locating the textbook underneath her bed, she glances at a reminder she wrote last week: "LAB REPORT DUE MONDAY!" In order to turn her lab report in today, she will either have to write it during economics class or cut a class. Katrina can't find her notebook, so she rips a few sheets of paper from another notebook, grabs a pencil, and runs out the door. As she rushes to class, she thinks about the stress of college life: always running from one place to the next, barely completing one assignment

---

BOX 3.1   *Improvement in Action* ⅢⅢ➡

Identify one of your organizational strengths and one of your organizational weaknesses. For example, you may have all of your *Road and Track* magazines organized chronologically from 1989 but have difficulty remembering names. Or, you may be very careful about making lists but never seem to accomplish all the tasks on the list. Be prepared to discuss these characteristics with the class:

- Organizational strength:
- Organizational weakness:

before several others are due. Katrina wonders whether she can handle this for the next several years.

Every college student has had similar feelings and experiences. Reflect on Katrina's situation by completing Box 3.2. The keys to success in college are organizing yourself, managing your time, and, in the process, minimizing stress so you exercise greater control over your college career.

Adjusting to College Life

Students are often overwhelmed during their freshman year of college. There are so many new experiences, and each one requires adjustments in behavior. This extra effort of adaptation people make to function in their environments is called *stress*. Although most people think of stress as a negative state, psychologists argue that stress is simply the adjustment we make in response to a change in our environment. Thus, winning the lottery, falling in love, and owning a car for the first time are stressful even though they are generally regarded as positive events. Until people adjust to these experiences, they are stressful. At college, tasks that will later seem routine—such as finding unfamiliar buildings, getting to classes on time, and adjusting to commuting or to being away from home—all place new adaptive demands on you.

The high school experience differs considerably from the college experience. In high school, each day was structured for you and you merely moved from one class or activity to the next as scheduled. Other people (family members, friends, and school personnel) were there to assist in seeing you through your high school education. College is a much different situation. Now it is your obligation to structure your time throughout each day of the week. You have new opportunities and new decisions that are yours alone to make. Some of the more common decisions of college students can be stated as questions: "Should I go to class, or should I sleep in?" "Should I go to the dining hall for lunch, or should I eat a snack from the vending machine?" "Should I stay here this weekend and study, or should I go home and see my friends?" With all of the new opportunities and sense of freedom, it is easy to make the wrong choices.

BOX 3.2   *Improvement in Action* ▥▶

Now that you have read the opening vignette, answer the following questions:

1. How could Katrina organize her time and become more efficient?

2. Have you ever felt rushed, pressured, or embarrassed by your own disorganization? Write a short paragraph describing this incident.

For students who are returning to school many years after high school graduation, college can present a different set of challenges. Family members may have to contribute more to family duties, since much of your time will be focused on college. Additionally, older adults usually also have more financial responsibilities including home ownership, children who may also be in college, and caring for elderly parents. It may be difficult for loved ones to understand that you will need to be spending time at the library, meeting with other students after a class, or buying materials that are necessary for completing projects. In addition to these pressures, nontraditional students often express concern about being the only older person in a class or worry about being out of practice as students and writers.

Whether you are a recent high school graduate or an adult returning to college, you will soon find that time management is one of the most difficult tasks a freshman faces (Campbell, 1993). All of these new decisions force you to become more responsible, but this responsibility does not have to be overwhelming. If you learn to plan, organize, and identify goals, you can form successful habits that will last a lifetime.

Another change you may encounter is the distance between you and the support network you learned to depend on. Time constraints and distance may make it more difficult for you to communicate as regularly as you have in the past with family and friends. Furthermore, friends who are not in college may feel threatened by your decision to pursue a college career, and communicating with them may become increasingly difficult. You must be strong in your convictions and stick to your goals, even if it means alienating some members of your support network. If they really care about you, they will respect your decision to further your education and encourage you to succeed rather than attempt to hold you back.

College students are generally eager to make friends with whom they can share the new experiences of college life. Those students who live on campus must meet the challenge of living with a roommate. Because they get to know their roommates first, freshmen are often hopeful that they will become best friends, yet 4 years later very few of them will be friends, much less roommates. In the first few months, superficial relationships as well as lasting bonds are formed. Meeting new people, exchanging information, and discussing ideas lead to new friendships, and these peer relationships can enhance the college experience.

The new peers you meet, however, differ from your former network in one major way: They may not always have your best interest in mind. They might try to persuade you to join them in going to a party even though they know you have an exam the following day. They may have a personal problem that they need to talk with you about, even though it is getting late and you need to get some sleep so you can be alert the next day for your 8:00 a.m. class. They may want to borrow your notes, ask you to help them study for a class, or even ask you to do an assignment for them, when they obviously have not exerted the effort needed to understand the course material. Peers who really support you unconditionally and think about the long-term consequences of their actions on your college career may not be readily available. Therefore, it is up to you to determine what your priorities are.

Fortunately, universities are structured to provide you with a variety of support services (see Figure 3.1). Your institution probably has many people who are there to help,

Figure 3.1
Support People

Resident assistant	Approachable professor
Counseling Center staff	Tutors
Leaders of clubs or organizations	
Successful upperclass students	
Learning Center staff	Writing Center staff

such as those who work at the learning center, the library, a writing center, a counseling service, or a tutoring center. Your professors and academic adviser have an interest in your college career and are generally willing to help. There may be a resident assistant or a successful upperclassman you respect who could be a source of good advice. These support people can give you valuable insight when making decisions about classes to take, coping with a family crisis, or studying for tests. Take advantage of their experience. Make it a point to stop by regularly and talk with these people. Particularly if you are the first person in your family to attend college, these people can provide a type of support that you may not find from your family members or elsewhere. Use Box 3.3 to identify the people you can turn to.

Factors That Influence Success

Many other factors influence the success of college freshman (Jewler, 1989). Consider each of the statements in Box 3.4 and decide whether it is good or bad advice. This short evaluation will allow you to examine your priorities and enable you to make adjustments if necessary.

First-Semester Grades

The first semester of college is often a student's worst because he or she is adjusting to college life in general as well as specific academic demands. For some students, the freedom of being away from direct supervision is intoxicating and can override good judgment. As any college adviser can tell you, a college student may need years to make up for a bad first semester and to raise a grade point average.

Grade point average or quality point average (GPA or QPA) is an important indicator of your academic achievement. Instructions for calculating your GPA or QPA can be found in Figure 3.2. Knowing how to calculate your grade point average can enable you to monitor your progress. What are the consequences, for example, of a bad first semester? Consider the sample course record in Figure 3.3.

This student's academic achievement during the first semester was poor, partly because she had a difficult time adjusting to college life, but mostly because she had not developed good study habits and was spending many hours with her new friends. During the first semester, the student earned an overall GPA of 1.38. She made an effort to improve during her second semester, but because she was trying to earn some extra money with a part-time job, her semester GPA was only 2.25. Matters became complicated when she

---

BOX 3.3   **Improvement in Action** ||||➡

Identify people on campus with whom you feel you could talk and who would give you sound advice concerning the following situations:

■ Failing an important test
■ Using an unfamiliar word processing program to type a paper
■ Feeling very homesick
■ Having difficulty deciding a major

BOX 3.4 *Improvement in Action* ⫸

Self-Assessment: Keys to Success Your Freshman Year

True or False Indicate whether you think the following statements are true or false (circle your answer). Then check your answers to see whether you are aware of how you can increase your chances of success in college.

1. When students begin college, they must focus only on studying. Therefore, favorite pastimes, such as sports, reading for pleasure, and hobbies must be given up. **True / False**

2. Students who have parents who are wealthy are more likely to be successful students in college. **True / False**

3. Minority students have a more difficult time succeeding in a college environment. **True / False**

4. You can work your freshman year and still maintain good grades in your classes. **True / False**

5. Having difficulties maintaining a relationship back home has no bearing on your success in college. **True / False**

6. Freshmen who live on campus are more successful than those who live off campus during their freshman year. **True / False**

1. **False.** Nonacademic factors may have as much to do with staying in college as academic ones. College is an excellent place to develop personal interests or hobbies. Throwing a few pots on the pottery wheel or tossing the basketball around may be the ideal way to release some tension after not doing too well on a calculus test. It is important to pursue activities that make you happy.

Figure 3.2
Determining your GPA or QPA

It is easy to determine your GPA or QPA by numerically rating your grades and multiplying them by the number of credits earned. The most typical system is one in which every A is worth 4 points; every B, 3 points; every C, 2 points; every D, 1 point; and an F, 0 points. To calculate the quality points for a course, take the number associated with the grade (A = 4, B = 3, C = 2, D = 1) and multiply it by the number of credits the course is worth. For example, if you earn an A in a 3-credit course, this is worth 12 quality points (4 points for an A × 3 credits for the course = 12 quality points). If you earn a B in a 2-credit course, it will be worth 6 quality points (3 points for a B × 2 credits for the course = 6 quality points).

had to have a 2.5 to take courses within her major during her sophomore year. She had to postpone taking these courses and repeat others—something that may put her behind as much as an entire semester! Figure 3.4 illustrates the courses she took and the grades she earned during the third semester. Will she be able to take courses in her major now? Calculate her grade point average.

2. **False.** Success in college has less to do with wealth than with social support. If you are a single parent with no one to help you, you are obviously at a disadvantage in comparison to someone who can fully concentrate on academic responsibilities. But other things do matter, such as why you are coming in the first place. Do not expect to be successful if you are attending college just to please your parents or because your friends are all going. You must be attending college for yourself, and you should be able to identify why you are there.

3. **False.** Success in college has little to do with ethnic background. Even though a lower percentage of minorities attend college in the first place, cultural or ethnic background does not determine success. Success, once again, depends on your understanding that *only you* can determine whether you will succeed or fail.

4. **True.** Whether or not you work your freshman year does not matter, but how much you work does. The dropout rate for those who work more than 20 hours a week is five times higher. If you must work, keep your reasons for having a job in perspective. If, for example, you have a job so you can have a car, and you could ride the bus and eliminate the car expense, consider the alternative. Taking courses over because you did not do well the first time costs a considerable amount of money.

5. **False.** Personal problems can ruin your chances for success. When students withdraw from the university, it is usually due to emotional or physical health problems. Try to be mindful of your health and personal relationships.

6. **True.** Living on campus is a plus. Students who live off campus drop out nearly twice as much as those living on campus. Being close to your classroom buildings, having access to the library, and being able to talk with classmates are a definite advantage.

Figure 3.3
Sample Grade Report

Course	Hours Number	Hours Attempted	Earned	Quality Grade	Points
Fall, Freshman Semester					
Intro. to Art	AH 101	3.0	3.0	B	9.0
Geog. of U.S. & Canada	GE 102	3.0	0.0	F	0.0
Elements of Math	MA 151	3.0	0.0	F	0.0
Intro. to Religion	RS 100	3.0	3.0	C	6.0
Physics I	SC 101	2.5	2.5	C	5.0
			Semester GPA 1.38		
Spring, Freshman Semester					
Computer Literacy	CO 101	3.0	3.0	C	6.0
Personal Management	CS 101	3.0	3.0	B	9.0
Contemporary Lit.	EN 221	3.0	3.0	C	6.0
Fund. of Anthropology	AN 224	3.0	3.0	C	6.0
			Semester GPA 2.25		

Figure 3.4
Sample Sophomore Fall Semester Grades

Course	Grade	Credit Hours	
Intro. to Anthropology	B	3	3 × 3 = 9
Health and Wellness	A	2	4 × 2 = 8
Plant Biology	B	4	4 × 3 = 12
Bowling	A	1	4 × 1 = 4
Elements of Math	C	3	2 × 3 = 6
Criminology	B	3	3 × 3 = 9
Total Points			48

Total points (48) divided by the number of credits (16) = 3.0

This student has improved her average during the third semester to a 3.0 by earning a total of 48 points, which are then divided by the 16 credits she took this semester. But what about her overall or cumulative grade point average? In order to have a clear understanding of where the overall GPA is coming from, we need to examine her grade report from previous semesters. Return to Figure 3.2 to examine the grades she earned during the first two semesters. Her first semester, she earned a 1.38; the second, a 2.25; the third, a 3.0. Add those together for a total of 6.63. Divide that number by the number of semesters (three), and you find her GPA to be 2.21.

When averaged with her GPA from her most recent semester, you can observe that this student's grades were not good enough to take courses in her major. She is stalled at the sophomore level as most of her friends move on into the major she wants so desperately to pursue. It will take at least one more semester of excellent grades before she can take courses in her major. Of course, additional semesters will mean an additional commitment in terms of time and money. It could also mean graduating in the middle of the academic year, which may hinder her job search later on. As you can see, striving to make academic achievement the primary goal during your college career is well worth the effort. One way to improve academic achievement is to become more organized in how you manage your personal and academic responsibilities.

Organizing Time and Space

Are you an organized student? Order is not an end in itself and should not be looked upon as a drudgery. Some orderliness is necessary in college and throughout life because it enables you to accomplish the tasks that need to be done more efficiently, thus freeing more time to do the things you want to do.

The first step in organizing your time more efficiently is to identify long-term goals. By examining the "big picture," you will be able to formulate a plan that can help you meet those ends. Going from day to day without long-term goals will make it difficult to see what needs to be done. Then, before you know it, another year is gone and you will still feel that you have not accomplished much.

Identifying Long-Term Goals

Many adults—parents, advisers, and professors—assume that beginning freshmen have already decided what careers they want to work toward in college. Actually, the majority of college freshmen are uncertain about their majors and may even change their minds, some

Figure 3.5
Five Characteristics of a Useful Goal

From *Student Success—How to Succeed in College and Still Have Time for Your Friends* (p. 25), by T. Walter and A. Siebert, 1993, Orlando, FL: Harcourt Brace Jovanovich. Copyright 1993 by Harcourt Brace Jovanovich.

- Self-chosen
- Moderately challenging
- Motivating
- Slightly risky
- Within reach

BOX 3.5   *Improvement in Action* ⫸

Considering what you have read about goals, write a goal statement for this academic year. Put it in a place where you will have easy access to it so you can refer to it when you may ask yourself, "Why am I putting myself through all this?"

---

more than once. Still, it is part of your job to define, identify, reexamine, and refine your goals. In determining your goals, think about where you want to be next semester, in 1 year, or 5 years from today. Do you want to be a student in good academic standing? Do you want to be earning money? Do you want to develop a relationship? Think about the various aspects of your life when determining your long-term goals. Completing the Writing and Reflecting assignment later in this chapter will enable you to begin focusing on what your short- and long-term goals are.

Students who do have a career in mind are fortunate in that they already have an idea of what their primary professional goal is—becoming a teacher, a respiratory therapist, a biochemist, and so forth. To achieve this goal, the university has planned a sequence of courses and experiences called the *curriculum*. Students who complete their curriculum successfully are then eligible to get a job in a chosen field. If a student does not already know exactly what career path to take, he or she is not alone. In a survey conducted by the American College Testing program, two-thirds of the million students taking college entrance exams were unsure of what career path they would choose (Pelikan, 1983). Students are not the only individuals who have a difficult time recognizing what career will make them happy. In his book *Future Shock*, Alvin Toffler (1984) predicted that contemporary workers will change jobs an average of seven times during their lifetimes.

Selecting and setting a goal serves the purpose of providing a general direction in your life (Gibbs, 1990). Useful goals generally share five characteristics (Walter & Siebert, 1993):

1. The goal must be self-chosen. Your goals cannot be determined by someone else, although their opinions may be valuable to you.

2. The goal must be at least moderately challenging, if not very challenging.

3. You must be motivated to accomplish it. There must be some reward for putting forth the effort needed to achieve the goal.

4. The goal must be moderately risky. Being slightly nervous is natural when working toward something you really want.

5. You must feel that with good effort, you can reach the goal.

Figure 3.5 highlights these characteristics. Refer to Box 3.5 to identify your own goals.

Unfortunately, as McMahan (1996) describes, trying to accomplish a long-range goal can be difficult and unrewarding. Too much time can elapse with no reward with long-term goals. For example, graduating from college is certainly a long-term goal for those who are reading this text. However it will take at least 4 years to accomplish this goal; therefore, some short-term goals need to be set to keep track of your progress along the way. McMahan (1996) suggests that short-term goals are easier to deal with because they make it easier to know where to start, to monitor progress, to know when you're done and to feel rewarded.

To design short-term goals that support long-term goals, the size and complexity of the task is reduced to smaller tasks. Whether it be preparing for a long journey or graduating from college, each goal is reached one step at a time. It's a good idea to break your long-term goals into smaller time frames, such as by semester. For example, when taking a course it is necessary to begin studying the material on the first day, rather than waiting for the test or going into a panic the last week of classes. Organizing your time and the tasks you do are then directly correlated with your long-term goals.

Organization of Time

Smith (1991) identifies a business maxim known as Parkinson's Law that states, "Work expands to fill the time available for its completion." You may be able to identify with this. Did you ever have a whole weekend to finish an assignment and found that it did in fact take the whole weekend? What if you would have planned for it to take only one afternoon? Could you have done so? Time is limited, and everyone has the same number of hours in a day. The key to success is to use time wisely. Defining goals is the first step in becoming a successful student. With these goals in mind, you can develop a plan of action that will use your time most efficiently.

Most authorities on organizing time, as well as most efficient, successful people, have a system of time management that they use consistently. This can easily be accomplished by having two things available: a calendar and a small notebook. With these two tools, you can outline a logical plan of events. You should carry them at all times so that you can include important dates and times on your calendar and write down things to remember in your notebook as you think of them.

Many experts suggest monitoring your time, recording what you do every day for a week to get an accurate picture of how you spend your time right now (Brown & Holtzman, 1987; Ellis, 1984; Walter & Siebert, 1993). Record everything you do during a typical week using the chart in the Appendix at the end of this chapter. After completing the chart, calculate the total number of hours you spent doing activities such as eating, sleeping, grooming, watching TV, socializing, studying, attending class, working, exercising, or even day dreaming. What activities are occupying most of your time? Do you have more free time than you realized?

By monitoring your time for a week, you will probably see that you are not quite as busy as you thought and that you could make better use of your time. The idea of modifying your schedule is not to have your life so structured around studies that you have no time for recreation. Rather, the purpose is to plan, so that you do have time to do things you enjoy and keep yourself healthy as well as complete necessary tasks. Students who are able to manage their time get their work done with less "wear and tear on their emotions" (Armstrong & Lampe, 1990). After you have examined how you spend your time, use a fresh calendar to begin adjusting your schedule to make it work more efficiently.

Your calendar should be small enough so that you can have it with you most of the time but large enough so that you have enough space to write. A calendar is a vehicle for recording all appointments, due dates for assignments, tests, and deadlines. It is also a place where you can schedule time for personal activities as well as studying, reading tests, writing papers, and performing household duties. Organize time to study each day, rather than scheduling large study blocks once or twice a week. You will stay on task more using smaller blocks of time. If, for example, you have a test on Monday, you may want to block in some study time for test review on Saturday between 3:00 and 6:00 p.m. You might reserve time to go over notes on Sunday morning and block out Sunday evening after soccer practice for memorizing definitions that will be on the test and studying more in depth. Use the weekly organizer in the Appendix or your calendar to plan your week, using the previously mentioned suggestions.

Organization of Tasks

The other essential tool in keeping yourself organized and accomplishing long-range goals is a small notebook. (You may be able to use attached note sheets in your calendar for this, but pages may be too small or too few.) Some students use a sheet of paper with "things to do" at the top. This is convenient for carrying around in a pocket, but it is also easier to lose among other papers. A person can waste valuable time looking for specific papers. A small notebook is usually your best alternative.

Computers have personal "briefcases," and many small organizational gadgets are available. If you choose this option, remember you want to have it with you when you go to all your classes and it must include a calendar and a place to make notes.

Whether it be an electronic device or a notebook, record all the things you need to remember, such as telephone numbers, books you need to get from the library, or a list of things you need next time you go to the mall. Writing down information you will want later frees your mind from having to remember it.

The easiest way to get organized is to keep track of the things you need to do. You may keep just one ongoing list, or you may divide the list into more than one category such as "School" and "Personal." The personal list would include things such as "get hair cut," "get birthday present for Mom," "call Kenny about this weekend," or "get glasses adjusted." Items that would be appropriate under the "School" heading would be "go to the bookstore for art supplies," "get notes from Sondra," or "make appointment with Dr. Mahoney."

These items do not have to make sense to anyone but you. Whenever something needs to be done, put it on one of the lists. When the task has been completed, scratch the item from the list. You will be surprised at the satisfaction you get from crossing off each item from the list, especially the more tedious ones. It may take some time before you feel comfortable with this method of organization.

The list(s) you have written should then be used to compile a daily list of things you want to accomplish. It should include about 10 items and be as specific as possible. Check your calendar to see what is scheduled for that day or what might be coming up. Also include any tasks that have just arisen. Any items that have not been completed will be moved to the next day's list. Spend a few minutes the night before or in the morning compiling this list. Although it may seem difficult to sit down and think about this task when you are rushed or tired, it will be time well spent in the long run.

Many experts feel that prioritizing the items on your list is necessary (Lakein, 1973; Walter & Siebert, 1993; Winston, 1991). Otherwise, it's possible to get bogged down with completing easy, quick tasks (such as calling the bookstore) rather than ones requiring more effort and thought (such as studying for a final exam). Therefore, prioritizing activities on your daily list with a "1, 2, 3" or "A, B, C" method will give direction concerning how to arrange the day. Give urgent, stressful tasks or those that require creative thinking or time to plan a 1 or an A. These tasks are often things that remain on lists for long periods of time because they require more thought. Prioritizing assures that complex tasks that directly relate to your long-term goals are given daily attention too. Figure 3.6 illustrates the notebook of a student who is able to prioritize daily tasks on her "to-do" list.

Figure 3.6
Sample To-Do List

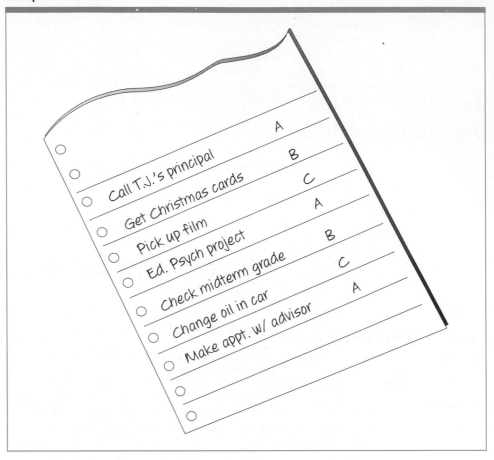

You can see from this list that this student has not included all the things she will actually do, such as going to class, but does include things that are easily forgotten or would not get done without a reminder. Seven items are on her list, because she has discovered that a list of more than 10 items rarely gets done. She knows that she can put items that were not accomplished on tomorrow's list.

Let us examine how this student, who happens to be a single parent, prioritized the tasks on her list. She gave calling her son's principal an A—top priority—because the principal gave a specific time when he could be reached. Working on the Educational Psychology project also rated an A because it is due in 3 weeks and she does not want to put it off until the last minute. Making an appointment with her adviser is also something she began putting off, but it needs to be done soon, with registration starting next week. Buying Christmas cards rates lower, a B priority, because she can purchase the cards Thursday if she forgets today. Picking up the roll of film she had developed can be done anytime, but she's anxious to see her vacation shots. She will find out her midterm grade Tuesday, but she wants to know how she did before then. Complete the task in Box 3.6 to practice prioritizing the things you need to do.

When planning the day, students also need to consider their energy flow. Are you a morning person or a night owl? Banks, McCarthy, and Rasool (1993) suggest using the circadian rhythm chart shown in Figure 3.7 to help you make optimal use of your body rhythms. Try to identify when you feel most alert during the day. Are you more likely to

Improvement in Action ⠀⠀▶

Complete a to-do list for tomorrow including at least two items in each of the categories.

A	B	C
Big projects, tasks you are not looking forward to, or things that must be done today	Tasks you would like to get done today but probably can wait until tomorrow if necessary	Tasks you would like to get done but do not really need to do today
1.	1.	1.
2.	2.	2.

Figure 3.7
Circadian Rhythm Chart

From *Reading and Learning across the Disciplines* (p. 57), by C. Banks, M. McCarthy, and J. Rasool, 1993, Belmont, CA: Wadsworth. Copyright 1993 by Wadsworth. Reprinted by permission.

Directions

1. Place a *P* for *peak* at the time of the day (morning, afternoon, evening, night) when you felt you had the most energy during the day.
2. Place a *V* for *valley* at the low point of your energy level each day.
3. Using a red pen, connect the *P*s to establish your high energy pattern.
4. Using a different-colored pen, connect the *V*s to establish your low-energy pattern.

	Monday	Tuesday	Wednesday	Thursday	Friday	Saturday	Sunday
Morning							
Afternoon							
Evening							
Night							

tackle tough calculus problems in the morning or after dinner? Try also to determine your low-energy time. Is this after meals, early afternoon, or midmorning? Save routine tasks that do not take a lot of mental concentration for this time.

We are learning more and more about our daily rhythms. This information will enable us to work with our natural energy flow rather than against it (Perry & Dawson, 1991). By identifying the times when you have the most energy, you will be able to incorporate the tasks from your to-do list that require the most energy.

In addition to examining your circadian rhythms, breaking down tasks into manageable chunks will also make accomplishing the task less of a strain. After writing down "Do sociology paper," decide how this should be accomplished and write down those components. In writing your sociology paper, you will need to accomplish several tasks, so write down things like "Do library research for paper," "Check writing center," "Revise again," and "Type final copy." Include these smaller tasks on your list and calendar. This approach gives you a sense of accomplishment as each segment is completed and prevents you from waiting until the day before a paper is due to start working on it.

By planning times when you do have to work on specific tasks, you can also see your unstructured or free time. Unstructured time is when you can get together with friends, read, watch TV, pursue personal hobbies, or do *nothing*. Unstructured time is important for your physical and mental well-being. How many times have you been watching a favorite TV program and felt guilty because you knew you should be studying? With the system just described, there is no guilt because you are allowing yourself time to work and time to relax. With practice, you will be able to organize your time so that you are able to manage your schedule and earn the grades you desire. An important component of this is knowing how to use your study time.

Using Study Time Efficiently

In *A Guide to College Survival,* Brown and Holtzman (1987) suggest several ways in which you can check whether you are using your study time wisely. Try to incorporate these modified suggestions into your weekly schedule.

Hints for Better Use of Study Time

1. **Plan for out-of-class time.** To estimate how much time you'll need to study for each class use the 2-to-1 rule; you can roughly figure 2 hours of outside work per week for every credit hour. If reading does not come easy to you, you may have to plan more time. Typically, the beginning of the semester does not seem to be quite as demanding, and the middle and end of the semester require more outside time. Often students who started out strong finish weak when the work demands increase later in the semester.

2. **Set realistic study requirements.** If you do not know how long it will take to translate two pages of French, do 10 calculus problems or read a chapter of sociology, estimate that French will take a little longer. If you finish early, it will be an added bonus.

3. **Study at regular times and places.** Knowing where and when you are going to study saves a lot of time in making decisions and locating necessary study materials. It is also helpful when your friends and family know your study schedule, so they will know you are at the library or will not disturb you at those times.

4. **Study as soon after class as possible.** Look over notes as soon after a lecture as possible, so that you can make additions to your notes if they do not seem as complete as they need to be.

5. **Use free time for studying.** Beginning college students often waste blocks of time during the day. Use the hour or two between classes to study, and you will have more free time later in the evening or on the weekends.

6. **Set a 2-hour limit on your studying.** Many students begin to tire after a couple hours, so take a short break. Switching to another subject is another way to give yourself a break.

Figure 3.8
Hints for Better Use of Study Time

Reprinted from *A Guide to College Survival* (pp. 35–36) published by The American College Testing Program, 1987. Reproduced with permission.

- Plan for out-of-class time.
- Set realistic study requirements.
- Study at regular times and places.
- Study as soon after class as possible.
- Use free time for studying.
- Set a two-hour limit on your studying.
- Study your hardest subject first.
- Study on weekends.

7. **Study your hardest subject first.** Your mind is fresh, and you will be able to concentrate fully. You may even want to reward yourself before going on to the next subject.

8. **Study on weekends.** Some time should always be scheduled on the weekends since this is a particularly good time to work on projects or use the library because it is usually less crowded.

Figure 3.8 summarizes these suggestions.

Organizing Your Work Area

Just as important as organizing your time is organizing your space. If you have gotten by so far in your life with haphazardly tossing things into corners and periodically losing things such as wallets, keys, and important papers, it may be time to make some modifications that will help you (and the people with whom you live) experience less clutter and frustration. Putting belongings in a particular place does have a definite advantage—it means that you will not have to waste time looking for them later.

Everyone needs a place where they can organize their schoolwork and keep class materials. The best place for this is a desk with a chair. If you do not have your own desk, delineate the space on the desk for you and the person you are sharing the desk with so that you have your own space. If you are living at home, you might find that an infrequently used space, like an attic or basement, is a better location for your work area. Alternatively, you may want to use a table or make a makeshift table with two stacks of bricks or blocks with a heavy board placed over the top. A desk does not have to be large or expensive, but it should be comfortable and well lit so that you can station yourself there and organize your study environment.

In a desk drawer, in a container, or on an area of your desk you should have a place for textbooks, notebooks, pens, pencils, stapler, paper clips, and highlighter pen. After the essentials, you may want to include other things that will motivate you to sit when you do not really want to, such as pictures of family and friends (those people who want you to succeed) and other memorabilia. A bulletin board is convenient for posting bills, receipts, and messages. Setting a small container somewhere in your room for small items that easily get misplaced is helpful. All students should have a folder for registration items—keeping a record of your progress from semester to semester—as well as a folder for school-related bills and checks. Also, keep copies of letters from and to your adviser, in case anything gets misplaced.

Winston (1991) has identified a system for "conquering the paper tiger." She suggests that when you are going through the mail, don't let important things get lost in the shuffle. Most mail can be sorted into three piles: toss, record, or take further action. If it is not information that is necessary to you, *toss* it into the wastebasket. You may receive a flyer about an upcoming event that you are interested in. Rather than keeping the notice, *record* the information on a calendar or datebook, then toss the notice into the wastebasket. If the piece of mail is something you want, then *take further action*. Maybe you want to check your test schedule and check with friends before deciding whether you want to attend a campus pottery sale. Maybe you have received a letter from home and want to respond before you file it with other letters. You need not spend more than 10 minutes per day on this task and will save hours of looking through stacks of paper when you need to find an important document.

You will probably spend much of your time studying in your dorm room, apartment, or house because it is convenient. However, it may not be the best place to study with all the activity that takes place when living with a large number of people. Try to analyze times that are best for studying. Usually living quarters are relatively quiet later in the evening and early in the morning. Study rooms are usually available in the dorms so that roommates will not be bothered. Another alternative is finding additional locations to study such as the library, where study carrels for individuals and study rooms for groups are available. If you decide to study at the library and do not have a private space, seat yourself in a seldom used area (like in the rare book collection) rather than on a major pathway where it is easy to be distracted by every passerby.

All of the techniques discussed in this chapter thus far will alleviate many sources of stress. By setting goals, managing your time, and organizing your space, you will feel more in control of your life as a college student. Despite your best efforts at organization, however, sometimes you will still feel stressed. By understanding what stress is and how to handle it in a positive way, you can reduce stress.

Coping With Stress

Stress is a term used to describe physical and psychological reactions that humans and animals exhibit in response to a stimulus or significant change in their environment (Levy, Dignan, & Shirreffs, as cited in Banks et al., 1993). As mentioned earlier, psychologists regard stress as neither good nor bad, although in everyday conversation it tends to have a negative connotation, as when we say, for example, "I'm stressed out."

Stress can be viewed as an inescapable part of everyday living. It can offer growth for the individual (such as getting a job promotion), or it can be damaging if the person does not have the ability to cope with the situation (such as dropping the football and losing the team championship). The intensity of stress seems largely dependent on three factors:

1. **The availability of external resources for support**—People who have resources such as friends or family to talk to can recover from stress more readily.

2. **The individual's stress tolerance**—This quality is associated with personalities. Someone who is excitable or nervous, for example, may have a lower stress threshold.

3. **The individual's perception of stressful events**—One person, for example may find it terrifying to give a speech in front of the classroom, while another may enjoy being in the limelight (Selye, 1974).

Consider Lijun, who is on her way to take an important test. She manifests all five of the physical responses to stress (adapted from Charlesworth & Nathan, 1984):*

---

* Adapted with the permission of Scribner, an imprint of Simon & Schuster, Inc., from *Stress Management: A Comprehensive Guide to Wellness* by Edward A. Charlesworth and Ronald G. Nathan. Copyright 1984 by Edward A. Charlesworth and Ronald G. Nathan.

- **Digestion slows so blood may be directed to the muscles and the brain.** As Lijun walks to the lecture hall, she has the sensation of "butterflies in the stomach."

- **Breathing becomes rapid to supply more oxygen for the needed muscles.** Lijun can feel her respiration rate increase as the test papers are distributed.

- **The heart speeds up and blood pressure soars, forcing blood to the parts of the body that need it.** When she reads the first question and cannot answer it immediately, Lijun is suddenly aware of the pounding in her chest.

- **Perspiration increases to cool the body and allows the body to burn more energy.** Lijun's palms become clammy as she searches for an easier question and begins to compose her answer.

- **Muscles tense for important action.** Lijun digs through her backpack after the test for an aspirin to relieve the terrible headache she has developed.

Evidence of stress in college freshmen can appear in response to a specific situation like Lijun's test, or the stress reaction can become more generalized. You may find yourself impatient, anxious, angry, lonely, or frustrated. You may even get sick more often because you are more susceptible to disease when you are feeling pressured or exhausted. All of these adverse effects are more generalized responses to more intense, long-term adaptive demands that a person finds difficult to meet.

What things do young adults consider to be most stressful? In a study conducted with 1,460 ninth- through twelfth-grade students, it was found that death of a family member was most stressful (Zitzow, 1992). Receiving a D or an F on a test ranked 6th out of 20 items, indicating that earning poor grades can be very stressful (see Figure 3.9). In fact, out of 20 items listed, 6 of them (items 4, 6, 8, 9, 12, and 15) were directly related to academic achievement and overall success in a college career.

Comparisons of schools in rural and urban environments yielded no differences in the intensity of stress experienced but significant differences in the *frequency* of experiencing the items listed in Figure 3.9. At one time or another, you may have experienced those stresses; perhaps you have experienced several of them simultaneously. Coping with some of the tragic situations on the list is not easy for anyone, yet working through these problems can make you a stronger and more caring individual.

Figure 3.9
Adolescents' 20 Most Stressful Situations

From "Assessing Student Stress," by D. Zitzow, 1992, *The School Counselor, 40*, p. 22. Copyright 1992 by the American Counseling Association. Reprinted with permission.

The following items are ranked from most to least stressful:

1. Death of a brother or sister
2. Death of a parent
3. Being responsible for an unwanted pregnancy
4. Being suspended from school or on probation
5. Having parents that separated or divorced
6. Receiving a "D" or an "F" on a test
7. Being physically hurt by others while in school
8. Giving a speech in school
9. Feeling that much of my life is worthless
10. Being teased or made fun of
11. Feeling guilty about things I've done in the past
12. Pressure to get an "A" or a "B" in a course
13. Pressure from friends to use drugs or alcohol
14. Fear of pregnancy
15. Failure to live up to family expectations
16. Feeling of anxiousness or general tension
17. Pressure to have sex
18. Feeling like I don't fit in
19. Fear of being physically hurt by other students
20. Past/present sexual contact with a family member

Use the following exercise to examine the stress in your life and determine how to make your level of stress more manageable.

1. List all the things that are causing you stress right now. Take at least 15 minutes to generate this list.

2. Put a check mark beside the items that you have control over. Circle the items that are out of your control.

3. Examine the items that you have circled. If you have no control over a problem or its outcome, it is time to reflect on what you learned, if anything, and spend your energy on the items with check marks next to them. For example, if you are stressed because you got an F on a test, there is nothing you can do about it. Examine why you did poorly, identify some ways to try to avoid this in the future, then stop worrying about it. Maybe you have spent a lot of energy worrying about your parents who are going through a divorce. This situation is very difficult to cope with, but it is also out of your control. Do not spend time wishing they would get back together; you are probably setting yourself up for disappointment. If you need to talk to someone about how the divorce is affecting you, do not be afraid to seek out a friend, college counselor, clerical member, or community organization to help you.

4. For those items that are checked, develop an action plan. What are you going to do about this? You may find the solution is quite clear—it is just a matter of taking action.

5. Prioritize the checked items, marking the problem causing you the most stress with a 1, and begin the plan of action now. Feeling in control is much better than feeling overwhelmed.

6. Identify a person who can help you resolve this situation. Next to each check mark, identify who could help you and contact that person. Maybe all you have to do is talk to your adviser. Maybe a trip to the writing center is in order. Maybe writing your best friend from home will help.

Although it is customary to think of stress as a debilitating force, many of the adaptive responses that result are actually beneficial. When you think about it, learning is almost by definition a stressful experience. Most psychologists define learning as a change in behavior, being able to do something you could not do before—and any change involves risk. But as with physical limitations, there are also limits to how far your mind can "stretch." The most probable time when students feel stretched to the breaking point is during midterms and finals. Organize yourself so that you are not pressed for time during these times. Remember that those stress-related physical responses will be making your mind sharp for that test and giving you that shot of adrenalin that will make you shine during that presentation. Look back at the goals you have written to remind yourself that there is a purpose for working as hard as you are. Use Box 3.7 to examine and evaluate the stress in your life.

Coping Mentally

Relaxation and clearing the mind are considered essential in both leading a healthy life as well as enabling you to concentrate when necessary (Gibbs, 1990; Hill & Stone, 1987; Ostrander & Schroeder, 1979). Make sure you allow time to be by yourself—take a walk, attend church service, or take advantage of a weekend when your roommate is away—to do some mental regrouping. Many books are available that explain different forms of mental relaxation techniques, including meditation. Check the library and local bookstores.

Experts in the field recommend trying some of the following techniques for mentally and physically coping with stress (Charlesworth & Nathan, 1984; Chickering & Schlossberg, 1995; Ellis, 1984). Read the suggestions and practice these techniques to help minimize stress.

1. **Take control of your feelings.** When you begin to feel tense, realize that you have control of your feelings and that you are not going to let the situation get the best of you. This realization momentarily breaks the pattern of panic, and you can refocus by using one of the following techniques.

2. **Mentally escape.** Think about a favorite location or vacation spot, where you feel you can really relax. Put yourself in that spot and visualize the sights, sounds, and smells that have made you feel relaxed and happy in the past.

3. **Contemplate the "worst-case scenario."** This approach invites you to explore just how awful the situation could be. It usually turns humorous, and you can see how unrealistic many of your fears are. Sometimes, simply ask yourself, "Fifty years from now, will this really matter?" Put your worries in perspective.

4. **Give yourself encouragement.** Telling yourself encouraging words gives you the confidence to make the best decision. Remind yourself of your success so far. Think positively.

5. **Picture yourself succeeding.** The key here is detail. Imagine it in complete detail: the sights, the sounds, and smells of the room and your triumphant feeling of knowing your presentation is going to be wonderful. Imagine each step. Include approaching the podium, making eye contact, using gestures appropriately, and finally seeing the approving nod of the instructor and hearing the applause of your peers.

Coping Physically

The physical aspects of stress can also be quite debilitating. Practice these techniques to alleviate the physical symptoms of stress:

1. **Breathe deeply.** Feel each breath as it enters and leaves your body. Concentrate on the life-giving capacity each breath of air holds. Feel your lungs expand and deflate, and feel yourself beginning to relax.

2. **Relax your muscles.** Beginning with your feet, relax all the muscles until they feel completely limp. Continue moving up the body—the ankles, calves, and so forth—until all the muscles are relaxed. Be sure to focus on the neck, back, shoulder, and facial muscles since these are often tense and can cause aches.

3. **Work your muscles.** Either exercise aerobically, or alternately tense and relax your muscles. By using your muscles, you can reduce body tension as well as improve your physical shape. If it is not an appropriate time to do physical exercise, such as before a test, exercise your muscles by tensing and relaxing specific muscle groups. This tires the muscles, allowing you to feel more relaxed.

4. **Express how you feel.** If you are feeling nauseous, have a headache, or feel like you are having difficulty breathing, focus on the physical sensation and describe it in great detail to yourself or someone else. Surprisingly, by fully experiencing the physical sensation, symptoms often disappear. People who are in chronic pain often use this technique to ease their suffering.

Managing your time, organizing your study schedule, and coping with the stresses of college life will be among the most important predictors of your success as a student. Your commitment to getting the most from your education will help you overcome the day-to-day situations that often prove to be challenging. As you encounter new situations, keep in mind that each new challenge is a learning experience, which is why you are in college. By incorporating the suggestions in this chapter into your daily routine, you will allow yourself the time to work at your fullest capacity. The suggestions in the chapters that follow will also help you attain success in your academic career.

 ### *Voices of Successful Students*

Here is what several students have to say about coping with stress:

"I think if you use positive thinking and have an open mind, a lot of stressful things may be eliminated."

"I have learned that there is always something that I will be able to do to deal with my stress."

"It really helped me to find out where my priorities are. I didn't enjoy thinking about all the stress in my life, but it was helpful when I identified the people who can help me."

"Now that I've sat down and thought about my problems, it doesn't seem that it will be that hard to handle anymore."

"I never wanted to examine it before, but now I realize what was stressing me out. Now I know what my problems are and I am going to do something to change them."

Extension Activities

Cooperative Learning Activity: Organizing Schedules

Get together with a partner to rehearse relaxation techniques described on page 61. One person will read the steps toward becoming relaxed as the other person practices the techniques. Do this several times a week so that after recognizing signs of becoming tense, you will begin the steps to relaxation automatically.

Writing and Reflecting: Writing a Letter to Yourself

Write a letter to yourself using one paragraph to address each of the areas listed. When considering your future, be descriptive as far as the activities with which you are involved. Don't limit yourself, but think about what you really want. Visualizing alone won't help

you reach your goals, but it will give you some direction concerning what you really want to do!

1. One goal you accomplished in the last year that you are really proud of
2. Where you see yourself next semester
3. Where you see yourself next year
4. Where you aspire to be in 5 years

Your professor may want to collect these letters and send them to you next semester to help you stay focused on your goals.

Self-Improvement Strategy: Getting Organized

Begin using a calendar and notebook to get organized, and develop weekly and daily plans to help achieve your long-range goals.

Reading Selections

Reading Selection 1

Read the following excerpts from an article about desk organizers by Betsy Bates (1994).* What is the writer's viewpoint? Can you identify any biases? Are the opinions of the writer supported with facts?

Organizers Replace Desks of Execs, Students

Organization and personal fulfillment await you—for as little as $19.99. At least that's what you might be led to believe by browsing the aisles of your favorite discount office supply store. While a free pocket calendar from the local dry cleaner used to suffice for the most harried business manager, America has now discovered the world of the personal organizer—a leather or vinyl bound binder that contains everything from today's schedule to your goals in life.

Devotees swear by them. . . . Stella Tan, 17, uses hers to keep track of course assignments, college application deadlines and activities at Van Nuys School. "I've had it for about a year. I like it a lot," says Tan. . . .

From a mere blip of stationery sales in 1980, personal organizers have bulged into a $500 million business that shows no sign of slowing down . . . .

Few people over the age of 12 have not at least considered moving their life's most important information into a combination date book/money manager/priority lists/goals reminder/little black book/calculator. . . .

"Organizers used to be something for business people who needed to keep track of their appointments and sales and expenses," said Karen Muller, public relations supervisor for Day Runner Inc., based in Fullerton. "Today, let's face it, everybody's a business person. Students are just as busy as adults. Everyone has an individual need to stay in control of their lives."

Author and organization guru, Stephanie Culp, says that organizers are, for most people, the key tool when they're learning to take control of their time. She cautions that "You have to be the power behind your planner. The tool doesn't get up and magically transform you. You really have to think about your goals and priorities for it to work." Culp said that people's goals can range from increasing their sales, to making the school track team, to meeting that special someone. Richard Putnam [director of investor relations that has a multi-million dollar time management business called Franklin Quest] states that, "In the 80's, people wanted riches [and] more toys . . . . The decade of the 90's is being billed as the decade of people who want richer lives. . . ."

"Either way, a personal system of organization can help," he said. "If you want to make a million dollars by the time you're 30, it will help you do that. If your goal is to enhance your family life, it will help you do that too.". . . Becoming organized is nothing less than a "life changing experience." (p. E2)

Reading Selection 2

Read the following passage from *The Journey of Adulthood* by Helen Bee (1992) on "Personality and Coping Strategies."* Then answer the following question as if it were an essay question on an exam: What coping behaviors are used to face stress?

Coping Behaviors in the Face of Stress

Suppose you have been trying for a particular promotion and find out that you didn't get it. Or suppose that your father has just died. How do you cope with these stresses? "Coping" is a very broad and fuzzy word to describe all the things you might think, feel, and do in response to such events in an effort to handle the stress. Lazarus and Folkman (1984) define it as "constantly changing cognitive and behavioral efforts to manage specific external and/or internal demands that are appraised as taxing or exceeding the resources of the person" (p. 141).

The number of different specific actions that might fall under this rubric is almost unlimited, so various theorists have attempted to categorize the possibilities. The most helpful category system, to my mind, is a combination of one proposed by Kobasa (Kobasa, 1982), who suggests two categories, *transformational* and *regressive* coping actions, and one offered by Moos and Billings (1992; Billings & Moos, 1981), who suggest a three-part division into *problem-focused* (what you *do*), *emotionally focused* (how you *feel*), and *appraisal-focused* (what you *think*) strategies.

In general, we ought to find that adults who use more transformational coping strategies deal with stress more effectively. They should be less likely to get sick, depressed, or anxious in the face of major life changes or chronic life strains. On the whole, that is what the research shows (Holohan & Moos, 1990, Lohr, Esses, & Klein, 1988), but there are some interesting exceptions.

For instance, Pearlin and Schooler, in their 1978 study of a representative sample of 2,300 Chicago-area adults, found that advice-seeking in the face of stress was associated with *higher* rather than lower rates of distress. Self-reliance, rather than help-seeking, seemed

*From "Organizers Replace Desks for Execs, Students," by Betsy Bates, January 2, 1994, *The Indiana Gazette*, p. E2. Copyright 1994 by the *Los Angeles Daily News*. Reprinted with permission.

*From Bee, Helen L., *The Journey of Adulthood*, 2nd ed., © 1994, pp. 250, 417–418. Reprinted by permission of Prentice Hall, Upper Saddle River, NJ.

to be a more effective coping strategy. They also found that selective ignoring (a regressive coping device) was actually effective if the stress was experienced in the area of finances but counterproductive if the stress was in marriage or family relationships. Among transformational strategies, too, particular coping devices worked better for some stresses than others. Negotiation appeared to be a particularly good strategy for a marital stress, while a reassessment of values or priorities worked when the problem was economic.

Thus, although it is roughly true that coping strategies from the transformational list are more likely to eliminate or alleviate the worst effects of stress, the best coping strategies will vary from one kind of stress situation to the next. Those adults who have a large repertoire of coping strategies are likely to be most successful in buffering themselves from the worst of potentially stressful life changes or daily hassles. (pp. 417–418)

Reading Selection 3

Before reading the next selection (*Health Secrets for Stressful Times*, 1993), construct a list of what you have learned about managing your stress. Then read the selection. Using a pen with a different ink color, add additional information you have gleaned from the reading. Compare how much you knew and what you have learned.

We all know that stress is dangerous. It contributes to cancer, stroke, heart, lung and liver disease, accidents, suicide, lowered immunity, and therefore, numerous other health problems.

Scary: Many people suffer from hidden stress—stress that has built up so slowly, they may not even realize it is there. Although most people try to get rid of stress by exercising or relaxing, these techniques do not address the root cause of stress—your thoughts.

The only way to really get rid of stress is to learn how to change your thinking. Benefits: Improved health, relationships, work, creativity . . . and joy in living.

What is stress? The definition of stress has changed—and along with it, our understanding of how to assess it and what to do about it. Assigned stress points to such events as moving, losing a job, divorce, the death of a loved one, etc., is no longer adequate.

More helpful: Understanding stress as a biochemical reaction to a perceived threat. It's not caused by things outside of you—traffic jams, your job, spouse, etc. It's an inner process caused by how you *think* about the people and events in your life.

If you think that you, your self-esteem or something else you value is being threatened, your body releases adrenalin and other chemicals into your bloodstream. This increases your blood pressure, heart rate and breathing. It decreases blood flow to your arms and legs, increases muscular tension and temporarily reduces your ability to reason.

This can trigger one or more of three emotions—anger, fear or depression. These emotions, while neither good nor bad in themselves, often lead people to take action that can set up a vicious cycle of negative stress.

How to master stress: The best way to master stress is to get rid of inaccurate—often subconscious—ways of thinking.

When you catch yourself feeling upset, stop to ask yourself, What am I thinking? Then take action to change those thoughts. Counterproductive thoughts to look for:

- **He/she/it makes me feel . . .** No one can make us feel anything. Our feelings are based on what we think is true.
  Watch for phrases such as "He makes me so angry . . . She drives me crazy . . . They hurt my feelings . . ." and so on. Let the words be a cue for you to pause and take responsibility for your own feelings.
  Example: My co-worker got a compliment from our boss and I feel jealous . . . because I am thinking that a compliment given to my coworker is a put-down to me. That thought, not the compliment scares me. I know my work is good.

- **It's not fair . . .** Many people become upset and stressed because they think that they aren't being treated fairly. Their outrage prevents them from making constructive changes.
  Problem: We learn from childhood games to expect that people should be fair. But as adults, we need to accept that life is often an unrealistic expectation. It's more likely that others will treat us in ways that they believe are in their own best interest. And once we understand this, we can leave resentment and blame behind, and work to effect positive change.
  Example: Vicki was able to show her husband how it would serve his best interest if he took on more of the housework.

- **What people say matters most . . .** When we write, it can take several drafts for people to express what we really mean. Yet we unreasonably expect others to say precisely what they mean when they say things . . . and then we hold them to what they say. When you believe you are upset by something someone says, stop to make sure you understand what he/she means.

- **Other types of counterproductive thoughts.** Many habits of thought produce stress. Examples: I can't . . . if only . . . I just know . . . I should/shouldn't . . . poor me . . . I always/never . . .

Watch for these thought patterns, and look for ways to eliminate them from your life.

Check yourself: Making progress on even a few of these thought patterns can help you build your self-esteem and eliminate even your hidden stress. (pp. 1–3)

Reading Selection 4

The following reading selection summarizes a research study that was conducted to examine factors that influence drug use (Collins & Kuczaj, 1991). At the college level, you will read about many such research studies. To gain a better understanding of what a published research article looks like, read the following selection, then go to the library and find an actual research study on the topic of drugs. Journals with the word *research* in their titles will be your best bet for finding this type of article. The article should address the following points:

1. A statement of the problem
2. The hypothesis
3. A review of the literature
4. The design of the study
5. The data analysis
6. The summary and/or conclusions

Make a copy of this article and read it. Determine what you think the study is about and be prepared to discuss it in class.

Adolescent Drug Use: A Long View

Understanding the nature and causes of adolescent drug use presents a number of difficult problems for researchers. One is that it is difficult to follow over a period of time to get information about whether drug use was a short-term experiment or the beginning of a long-term pattern of behavior. Another is that it is necessary not only to monitor drug use itself, but also to continue to gather information about the factors that seem to go along with drug use and abuse and to learn about what fosters initial drug use and what maintains drug use across time.

Psychologists Judith Stein, Michael Newcomb, and P. M. Bentler (1987) have recently completed an extensive longitudinal study of drug use in which they followed 653 adolescents from junior high school until they were several years beyond high school graduation age. As a group, the participants in the study were representative of young adults nationwide, as determined by the National Survey on Drug Abuse (Miller et al., 1983). Stein, Newcomb, and Bentler wanted to examine the relative importance of the individuals' peer and adult models, perceived community standards for drug use, and problems associated with family disruption in predicting (1) changes in drug use over the course of the study and (2) whether or not the participants were experiencing problematic drug use during adulthood.

Their findings supported many of the conclusions drawn from other studies:

- Individuals who reported using drugs in junior high school were likely to be using drugs as young adults. However, there was a greater stability of drug use from late adolescence (age 18 or 19) to young adulthood than from early adolescence to late adolescence. The specific drugs used by a young person may change, of course, but the tendency to use or not use drugs was remarkably consistent across the years. Drug use in adolescence did not necessarily presage *problem* drug use in young adulthood, however.
- Perceptions of drug use by parents and peers influenced drug use in adolescence and young adulthood alike to a greater extent than did perceptions of community behavior and standards. Adult and peer influence varied somewhat by the type of drug used. Perceptions of adult use particularly influenced alcohol use by young people, whereas perceptions of peer drug use influenced use of marijuana and hard drugs.
- Parental drug use and family disruption seemed to be intertwined in their influence on drug use during adolescence and young adulthood. For example, early exposure to alcohol uses by adults was correlated with drug-related problems many years later. This may have been due to early modeling of drinking and drug use. Another possibility is that early exposure to drug use was associated with family disruption, and drug use may be one way in which adolescents have learned to cope with the stress of family problems.

Personality characteristics associated with rebelliousness and low social conformity were linked to problem drug use in adolescence and in young adulthood. Lack of social conformity itself was strongly correlated with family disruption, implying that family disruption may be linked to drug-related problems via its effects on personality characteristics. As researchers frequently note, social factors (for example, peer and parent drug use) may influence whether or not a person uses alcohol and drugs, but personality characteristics and individual stressors determine whether or not that use attains problem dimensions. (p. 610)

Reading Selection 5

Don't Ever Say . . .: Interacting More Successfully With Professors

Every instructor and adviser has a mental list of comments from college students that she or he finds especially aggravating. We share them with you here so that you can avoid making these remarks and be perceived more positively by your college instructors and advisers.

Never say, "I missed class last week. Did we do anything important?

Most professors are insistent on class attendance. This is not a matter of big egos; it is simply the case that students who miss class generally do not perform as well in the class. So the minute you start talking about being absent, you are dealing with some resistance from your instructor. Naturally, the reason for that absence is important. If you have a legitimate reason, by all means, share it.

Asking whether "anything important" happened adds insult to injury. Just think about why. First, it suggests that the class is generally boring and uneventful. Second, it implies that the faculty member should drop whatever he or she is doing and give you a private tutoring session on what you missed. Finding out what you missed in class is clearly your responsibility as a student. If you can anticipate that you will have to miss a class, such as when you are a member of a band, in a sports competition, or have a doctor's appointment, the best thing to do is plan ahead for it.

Never say, "I stopped by your office, but you're never there."

In a study of higher education sponsored by the Carnegie Foundation, Jaroslav Pelikan (1983) defined a university as "a place where professors are paid to study." A busy office with telephones ringing, classes full of students walking by, and constant interruptions is simply not conducive to the kind of study that faculty need to do in order to remain current and contribute to their fields.

The first thing to understand is that a college faculty member is obligated to be a scholar. Professors who are musicians need to study and perform music, those who are philosophers need to study philosophy and philosophize, those who teach art need to be artists themselves. None of these activities can be easily pursued in a busy departmental office. Even everyday activities, such as evaluating students' work, are better accomplished in a quiet place—usually the faculty member's office at home.

Beginning college students expect their professor to be there whenever they drop by or feel like talking to him or her. Yet many faculty are on a completely different schedule from their advisees. They may be "on the night shift" and teach undergraduate or graduate classes in the evening. They may have off-campus classes to teach or may be traveling to various workplaces to supervise interns during practicum experiences. (An *internship* or *practicum* is an apprenticeship in a real-world job situation, like student teaching for education majors or working for a newspaper for journalism majors.)

Sometimes, students will see a note on the door indicating that the faculty member is out of town at a conference. Even though the location of the conference may sound inviting, this should not be interpreted as "going on a vacation." Faculty must be involved in their professional organizations to keep up-to-date and network with other experts in their fields.

Even if the faculty member is sitting in his or her office when you walk by, do not automatically assume that it is for the purpose of holding office hours. They may be gathering materials and on their way to one of the many committees on which the faculty member typically serves. It is best to ask "Is this a good time for you to talk?" and, if not, "Can I make an appointment to see you?" As a courtesy, let them know whether you have just a quick question or will need more time.

The most reasonable expectation for meeting with faculty is to expect what you would expect from a medical doctor: to go to the office during scheduled office hours and/or make an appointment.

Never say, "Could I take the test some other time?"

One grouchy professor we know used to say, "There is only one reason for missing a test, a death in the family—YOURS!" Students will often find that, unlike high school, many instructors' class policies prohibit rescheduling a test. Think about why. If a professor allows you to take the test late, it is not fair to all those who had to be prepared earlier. If a professor teaches several sections of the same course, he or she may have already made up two or three versions of the test in the interest of test security. If you take a test at any time other than the scheduled one, the faculty member now has to make up another test just for you.

Desperate students sometimes feign an illness or claim a tragedy when they are unprepared for an exam. Then when the instructor tells them that they will be given an all-essay test or be questioned in person in place of the written examination, these same students frequently have a miraculous recovery and agree to take the written test they were too ill or too stressed to consider previously. One faculty member told the story of three students who went to Florida over spring break. They called his office to report that they had a flat tire and would not be able to make it back to campus to take the test. The faculty member had his doubts, but because they had been responsible students throughout the semester, he agreed to allow them to take the test as soon as they arrived back on campus. When they came to the office, he put them in three separate rooms to take the test. The first question, for 15 points, read, "Which tire was flat?" As it turned out, they had lied about the tire, they had just wanted to spend an extra day in the Florida sunshine. As this story illustrates, instructors can be rather creative and devious when checking up on an alibi.

So do not assume that a test can be made up later. It is not unusual to get an F on a test if you fail to show up at the scheduled time.

Never say, "I had my assignment done but . . . the computer broke, . . . my typist didn't get it finished," and so forth.

A student burst into an instructor's office waving a sheaf of papers in his hand while saying, "I really do have my assignment done—it just isn't typed. I could get it to you tomorrow." The faculty member replied, "The most important thing to me is that you did complete your work. I'll overlook your technical difficulties and read your handwritten copy so that I can give you full credit for the assignment." "Oh, no," the student protested, "you couldn't possibly read this." "I'm certain that I can," said the faculty member, taking the papers from his hand. You can probably guess what happened here. The student had in no way completed the assignment. The papers were simply some notes and a couple of paragraphs of ideas jotted down. As a result, he not only failed the assignment, he also lost credibility with his instructor.

Never say, "What grade am I getting? I have no idea what grade I'm getting in this course."

When students speak of "giving" or "getting" grades, the implication is that grades are assigned arbitrarily by the instructor or that they are like the lottery—the result of good or bad fortune. It is not an inconsequential matter of semantics when a professor replies, "The grade you have *earned* is. . . ." Most college instructors are very offended by challenges to their fairness. Usually they go to some trouble to ensure that the students who perform the best in the course are the ones who receive the best grades. So you do *earn* your grades.

Some college students mistakenly assume that it is exclusively the professor's job to keep track of how they are doing. Yet, as a student, you have a responsibility to keep a record of all the feedback that you receive. Grades on tests, written papers, class presentations, group projects—all of these things should be recorded and kept in a place where you can refer to them easily. When work is returned to you, keep it in a folder labeled with the course title and number. A student who is completely unaware of how he or she is doing in the class is a student who has not learned the importance of monitoring his or her achievement. As with any other endeavor, humans perform better when they have a clear idea of where they are at the moment, know where they are headed and set reasonable goals. If you see that you had a C on the first test and a B on the second test, and one major written assignment remaining, you can begin to coach yourself with self-talk like, "OK, I am improving. If I can get As and Bs on the other two tests and really work on my written assignment, which is a third of my grade, I might even be able to get an A." Monitoring your own progress is essential for motivation.

Never say, "But I did all the work. I spent hours on it."

When students earn grades that are lower than expected, they frequently argue that they "did the work." But evaluation isn't based solely on completing work; it is based on the *quality* of that work in comparison with other students at various times who have taken the course. Arguing that the work is completed is analogous to an automobile mechanic who spends hours rebuilding your car engine yet does not succeed in getting the car to run. Although the mechanic may be a nice person who smiles and says, "But I did all this work and spent so much time on it," that will not make you any more willing to pay the bill. Students sometimes feel betrayed when a professor who is pleasant and encourages them to try hard ultimately judges the quality of their work to be inferior. There is no question that time and effort are important but the bottom line, just as with the car engine, is an evaluation of the quality of the results.

Learning to interact more successfully with faculty is one small yet important key to your college success. Avoiding these common gaffes in your conversations with instructors and advisers will enable you to put your best foot forward as a college student (Jalongo, 1995).

References

Armstrong, W., & Lampe, M. (1990). *Pocket guide to study tips.* New York: Barron's Educational Series.

Banks, C., McCarthy, M., & Rasool, J. (1993). *Reading and learning across the disciplines.* Belmont, CA: Wadsworth.

Bates, B. (1994, January 2). Organizers replace desks for execs, students. *The Indiana [PA] Gazette,* p. E2.

Bee, H. (1992). *The journey of adulthood.* New York: Macmillan.

Brown, W., & Holtzman, W. (1987). *A guide to college survival.* Iowa City: American College Testing Program.

Campbell, W. E. (1993). *The probe to learn.* Belmont, CA: Wadsworth.

Charlesworth, E., & Nathan, R. (1984). *Stress management—A comprehensive guide to wellness.* New York: Ballantine.

Chickering, A. W., & Schlossberg, N. K. (1995). *How to get the most out of college.* Boston: Allyn & Bacon.

Collins, W. A., & Kuczaj, S. A. (1991). *Developmental psychology: Childhood and adolescence.* Upper Saddle River, NJ: Merrill/Prentice Hall.

Ellis, D. (1984). *Becoming a master student.* Rapid City, SD: College Survival.

Gibbs, J. (1990). *Dancing with your books—the Zen way of studying.* New York: Plume.

Health secrets for stressful times. (1993). N.p.: Boardroom Reports.

Hill, N., & Stone, W. (1987). *Success through a positive mental attitude.* New York: Pocket.

Huxley, T., as cited in McWilliams, J., & McWilliams, P. (1992). *The portable life 101.* Los Angeles: Prelude.

Jalongo, M. R. (1995). Don't ever say . . . interacting more successfully with professors. *College On-Line.*

Jewler, J. (1989). Making the transition. In J. Gardner & A. Jewler. (Eds.), *College is only the beginning.* Belmont, CA: Wadsworth.

Lakein, A. (1973). *How to get control of your time and your life.* New York: Penguin.

McMahan, I. (1996). *Get it done.* New York: Avon.

Ostrander, S., & Schroeder, L., with Ostrander, N. (1979). *Super learning.* New York: Dell.

Pelikan, J. (1983). *Scholarship and its survival.* Princeton, NJ: Carnegie Foundation for the Advancement of Teaching.

Perry, S., & Dawson, J. (1991). What's your best time of day? In H. Weiner & C. Bazerman (Eds.), *Reading skills handbook* (pp. 387–388). Boston: Houghton Mifflin.

Selye, H. (1974). *The stress of life.* New York: McGraw-Hill.

Smith, B. D. (1991). *Breaking through college reading.* New York: HarperCollins.

Toffler, A. (1984). *Future Shock.* New York: Bantam Books.

Walter, T. & Siebert, A. (1993). *Student Success—How to succeed in college and still have time for your friends.* Orlando, FL: Harcourt Brace Jovanovich.

Winston, S. (1991). *Getting organized.* New York: Warner Books.

Zitzow, D. (1992). Assessing student stress. *The School Counselor, 40,* 20–23.

Weekly
Time Chart

Complete the chart with activities such as watching tv, eating, and studying for each hour of each day. At the end of the week, total the number of hours for each activity.

	Mon.	Tues.	Wed.	Thurs.	Fri.	Sat.	Sun.
6:00–7:00 a.m.							
7:00–8:00 a.m.							
8:00–9:00 a.m.							
9:00–10:00 a.m.							
10:00–11:00 a.m.							
11:00 a.m–12:00 noon							
12:00–1:00 p.m.							
1:00–2:00 p.m.							
2:00–3:00 p.m.							
3:00–4:00 p.m.							
4:00–5:00 p.m.							
5:00–6:00 p.m.							
6:00–7:00 p.m.							
7:00–8:00 p.m.							
8:00–9:00 p.m.							
9:00–10:00 p.m.							
10:00–11:00 p.m.							
11:00 p.m.–12:00 mid.							

Advancing as a Reader

Building a Background for College Reading

[R]eaders construct their own meaning. That meaning probably resembles the meaning the author had in mind in setting pen to paper, but no reader will develop the same model as the author; nor will any two readers develop exactly the same model. Each of us prints a unique personal stamp on every act of reading we undertake.*

—P. D. Pearson, L. R. Roehler, J. A. Dole, and G. G. Duffy

*From "Developing Expertise in Reading Comprehension," by P. D. Pearson, L. R. Roehler, J. A. Dole, and G. G. Duffy, 1992, in S. J. Samuels and A. E. Farstrup (Eds.), *What Research Has to Say about Reading Instruction* (2nd ed., p. 149), Newark, DE: International Reading Association.

Prereading Questions

- Define reading and explain the reading process.

- Why is it important to access information that you already know about a topic when reading?

- What strategies can you use to enhance your reading comprehension and vocabulary?

- How do expert readers behave? What behavioral changes will you need to make to become an expert reader?

Assessing Prior Knowledge

If you were asked to define reading, how would you do so? Think of all the different types of reading you do in the course of a day. You begin the day by reading the time on your clock radio; you read a bus schedule; you read the student newspaper; you read your textbook assignments; you read the menu at the dining hall. You read many different types of text. So, what is reading? Generate some ideas by responding to the question in Box 4.1.

Vignette: Effective and Ineffective Reading Strategies

Tony and Melinda both have a 15-page reading assignment for a history class. The format for the chapter is comparable to many other college textbooks: The chapter opens with objectives; the content is organized in sections; and tables, charts, drawings, and photographs with captions are used to break up the text. The chapter concludes with questions for self-evaluation and class discussion. Both students arrange their study time so they could legitimately say, "I've read the chapter twice"; yet this is where similarities in their approaches end.

BOX 4.1   *Improvement in Action* ⫸

What words or phrases come to mind when you think about the word *reading?* Write your responses at the end of the "spokes" radiating from the word *Reading.* As you read this chapter, you can continually modify your responses as you learn more about reading.

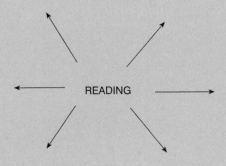

READING

As you read the following description of how Tony and Melinda approach their study of the chapter, think about their techniques and predict who would perform better on an unannounced quiz that the professor might give on the chapter content at the beginning of the class period.

Melinda opens her book to the appropriate chapter, begins reading, and highlights important information. In an effort to save time, she skips over the graphic illustrations including a timeline, a chart of major historic trends, and the captions under the illustrations. While Melinda rereads portions of the text, her mind wanders to a party she is planning to attend. She finishes the chapter and promises herself that she will reread it, this time paying close attention to the information that she has highlighted. The next day she does that prior to class.

Before Tony opens his book, he reflects for a moment on what was presented in the previous class. Next, he recalls the purpose for the reading assignment that he is about to begin. When these issues have been addressed, Tony opens his book to the appropriate chapter and spends *5 minutes* previewing the chapter. He uses previewing strategies recommended by leading experts in reading (Grant, 1993). That is, he

- reads the chapter objectives or questions,
- scans the section headings,
- notes boldfaced and italicized type,
- looks over graphic illustrations (charts, tables, and graphs),
- thinks about the chapter summary, and
- reflects on what he already knows about the topic.

When 5 minutes have elapsed, Tony is finished previewing and he begins reading the chapter. While reading, he continues to relate what he already knows to the content. Unlike Melinda, Tony monitors his comprehension for understanding. That is, when he does not comprehend what the author has written, he rereads to make corrections for what he does not understand. When he finishes reading the chapter, Tony takes a second look at the questions or objectives to assess his understanding, because those are the ideas that the author considers to be important. As Tony rereads the chapter, he will put a check mark beside important ideas and make notes in the margins of the book. Throughout his interaction with the text as described here, Tony's focus will continue to be on the objectives.

The next day the professor gives an unannounced quiz on the chapter. Melinda gets a C on the quiz, while Tony receives an A. Although both students have spent the same amount of time studying the chapter, one has gotten more from the reading. Both students may have "read the chapter twice," but Tony's reading was more interactive, intensive, sharply focused, and therefore more efficient. The expression "study smarter, not harder" describes the difference between Melinda's and Tony's approaches to reading. Tony has learned how to make the most of his study time; he has "studied smarter."

College students who develop greater proficiency in reading have the potential to get a better job and earn more money upon graduation. In a recent study, researchers found that, in general, people with better developed reading skills acquired the best jobs and earned the highest salaries ("The Education Illusion," 1997). You, as a reader, need to understand how to acquire those skills that will enable you to ultimately succeed in your field of study.

The Reading Process

Imagine that a person from an alien culture where the practice of reading was unheard of asked you to explain the reading process. How would you define reading for someone who has no concept of reading? What would you list as the essential features? How would you differentiate between real reading and going through the motions of reading, for example? Now think about your own reading process—does it operate more like that of the C student or the A student described in the opening vignette? One of the most common concerns expressed by our college reading students is difficulty in maintaining attention during reading. Yet it is easy to see how a few simple strategies, applicable to many different types of reading assignments, can help focus attention.

Over the years, the prevailing views of reading have changed, enlarged, and become more sophisticated. It was once thought that reading comprehension was a fairly straightforward process in which readers would first determine accurate meanings of words and eventually use those words fluently (Devine, 1986). We now know that reading involves more than "sounding out" words, because pronouncing a word does not guarantee a full understanding of its meaning. You can decode or pronounce the word *jib,* for instance, but if you don't know what it means, you are not truly reading that word. (A jib, by the way, is a small sail on a boat.)

Currently, reading is thought to be a much more active and complex process. Readers actively build meaning from the printed text by drawing upon their background knowledge and relating this knowledge to what they read (Pike, Compain, & Mumper, 1997). The interactive reader

- previews the material,
- relates background knowledge to the content,
- monitors his or her comprehension,
- fills in the gaps in understanding, and
- uses the chapter questions as a focus for reading and as a check of comprehension when reading a textbook.

Being an interactive reader may sound complicated, but the effort pays off. The interactive reader may be compared to a skilled baseball pitcher. Refer to the approach of the interactive reader in Figure 4.1. The interactive reader previews material to be read and relates background knowledge; the skilled baseball pitcher "previews" the hitter and relates background knowledge about the hitter before determining which pitch to use. The inter-

Figure 4.1
The Interactive Reader

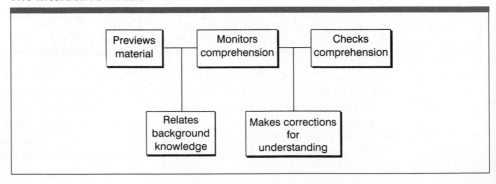

active reader monitors comprehension, checks for understanding, and makes corrections as needed; the skilled baseball pitcher continually monitors accuracy and makes adjustments to pitches. Keep in mind the characteristics of an interactive reader as you read the material for your college courses.

Research on the Reading Process

As you might guess, reading is so essential to learning that it has been the focus of extensive research (Anderson, Hiebert, Scott, & Wilkinson, 1985). As a college student striving to improve your reading, you will find the following five major conclusions from research helpful in understanding the reading process.

1. **Reading depends on background knowledge.** The reader's background knowledge, commonly referred to as *schema,* will influence the interpretation of what is read. A reader with broader knowledge of a topic will find it easier to comprehend a topic than someone who is reading about a topic for the first time. For example, a computer science major will find it easier to understand the instructions that accompany a piece of computer software than someone who has never used a computer even though their general reading abilities are similar.

2. **Reading requires motivation.** This means that readers must have (or develop) positive attitudes about reading. The student quoted in Box 4.2 realized the importance of reading and became motivated to read. At first, she had a negative attitude toward reading and dismissed reading as boring. Now that she is in college, she sees reading as essential to life. Attitudes are powerful; they influence behavior (Ellis, 1984). For example, maybe you are reading something that is difficult, like philosophy. Because you are determined to comprehend it, you discuss the reading with a classmate, relate the information you read to your lecture notes, and reread the material. A positive attitude about reading motivates you to comprehend what you read.

You need to analyze your negative feelings about reading and work to overcome them in order to improve as a reader. Complete Box 4.3 to assess your attitude about reading. Think about incentives to improve your reading skills. These could be to do well in college or achieve in your major. According to Silha (1992):

> The age of electronic communication may be here, but it doesn't mean we don't have to read. If anything, today's citizens are asked to read more; from computer screens, to fax messages, to specialized magazines. Then there's the fine print in those Internal Revenue Service forms, insurance policies and job applications. Information abounds.

BOX 4.2   ***Improvement in Reading*** ‖‖➡

As one student shared, "I got off to a bad start in reading, but I am working hard to better my skills. At first, I thought reading was boring, but I have found out that it is an essential part of my life. Advice to others is to give reading a chance."
    What might have changed this student's negative attitude about reading?

■ _____

■ _____

■ _____

What's more, reading is a basic building block underlying the survival skills of to-day's information-based economy: absorbing information, analyzing, organizing, inter-preting, communicating, understanding, learning. (p. 1)

Sawyer and Rodriguez (1992/93) present additional reasons some adults want to im-prove their reading and writing skills in Figure 4.2.

3. Reading is a continuously developing skill. Reading skill is developed through-out life, beginning with the first time that a child is exposed to text. It is a common miscon-ception among college students that a person is either a "good" or "bad" reader and that read-ing abilities are fully formed by junior high or high school. Yet college faculty with Ph.D.s who are considered experts on a subject continue to read materials that they find very diffi-cult to understand—material that places ever-increasing demands on them as readers.

Reading for pleasure is one way to continuously develop skill in reading. In his pop-ular book *The Success Breakthrough,* Cypert (1993) suggests that self-improvement should be a part of everyone's daily routine. During this time, your full attention should be given to reading and thinking. Your "daily ritual should include setting aside time—preferably the same time every day—to read the newspaper, a trade magazine, or a good book. Seek vari-ety in your reading. Whatever you read will help expand your mind. Make notes, save clip-pings, and train yourself to retain information that is of value to you" (Cypert, 1993, p. 17).

If you have not done a lot of reading for pleasure in the past, you may not know how to begin looking for a book that interests you. Check some of your favorite magazines. Of-ten they have book reviews that summarize and critique recent releases. Libraries, book-stores, and newspapers all carry lists of best-sellers that will also help you make a selection many other individuals have enjoyed. Check the bookstore to discover what books (other than textbooks) students across the United States are reading on campuses. What types of books are most popular? Fiction? Self-help? Completing the activity in Box 4.4 will give

Figure 4.2
Adults' Reasons for Wanting to Improve Reading and Writing Skills
Adapted from Sawyer and Rodriguez (1992/93).

Family—to make my family proud of me, to be a good parent someday

Economic—to have a career and a higher income

Community—to contribute to the solution of social problems

Personal—to have greater self esteem and confidence

Knowledge—to be better informed

Instrumental—to deal more effectively with college-level study and job-related demands

Entertainment—to get pleasure and enjoyment from reading and writing

Culture—to learn more about my cultural heritage

BOX 4.4   *Improvement in Action* ▐▐▐▶

To find out what students are reading in their leisure time, look in a newspaper called *The Chronicle of Higher Education*. Every 2 weeks it publishes a column called "What They're Reading on College Campuses." Make a copy of this list and use it to conduct a survey. Ask five students the following questions:

- Please look at the list of top 10 books on college campuses. Which ones have you read? Which ones would you like to read?

- Are you currently reading a novel or book that is not required reading? If so, what is the title? Who is the author? Have you read any other books this author has written?

- If you are not currently reading a book for pleasure, have you read any book or novel in the past year? What is the title of the book you enjoyed most? Who is the author? Have you read any other books this author has written?

Bring this list to class so that a class list of popular books can be compiled from your survey.

---

you an idea of what students are reading on your campus. Whatever you choose to read, you will be expanding and training your mind to retain information.

4. **Reading must be strategic.** Each reader must have a plan for reading. Think back to Tony's approach to his reading assignment. He had a plan for reading the assignment. He followed his plan and was successful on the unannounced quiz. Research on college readers documents that they can benefit from learning to use specific reading strategies (Rinehart & Platt, 1984). Before you assume that you are a "bad" reader, try being a *planned* reader—someone who experiments until she or he finds the strategies that work best.

5. **Reading must be fluent.** Unless readers can interpret meaning and pronounce words quickly, they find it difficult to concentrate on understanding the text. What if you know before you begin that you will be encountering many new words that will make you less fluent? Efficient readers get prepared to read. For example, a psychology major may

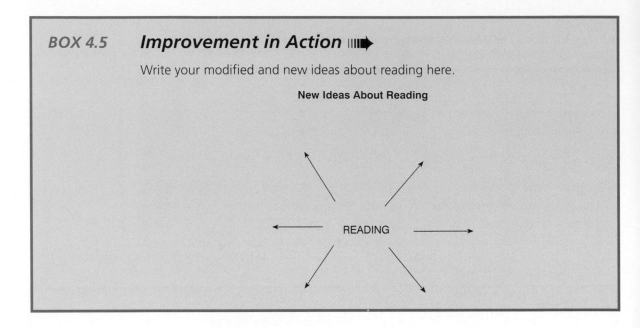
attempt to understand italicized vocabulary words introduced in a chapter by checking the glossary of the textbook prior to reading the chapter.

Now return to Box 4.1 and review your list of ideas about reading. How would you modify your ideas on the basis of what you have read so far in this chapter? Record your ideas in Box 4.5.

This book is based on the premise that every reader must continuously strive to further develop reading skills. Beginning college students are sometimes overwhelmed by the variety of challenging reading materials they encounter. Each discipline—whether science or sociology, mathematics or marketing—has a different perspective, style, and professional vocabulary. That is why it is particularly important for you to be cognizant of the reading process and develop strategies that enhance comprehension in the many different types of reading material. When you consider that during a single semester you might be expected to read and understand the words of great philosophers, the text of a Shakespearean play, a description of psychological theory, and the symbols for complicated mathematical formulas, then you begin to appreciate the importance of developing a wide array of effective reading strategies. A presentation of schema theory will help you understand how to activate and enhance your knowledge base.

Understanding Schema Theory

According to schema theory, knowledge is compartmentalized into parcels or packets of information (Rumelhart, 1984). These parcels are everything that we know or think we know about a particular topic. They may contain both accurate information and misconceptions that will be corrected later on as we know more. For example, before you came to college, you had an idea of what a college class would be like, based on one source or a combination of sources. One source may have been your knowledge of a high school class, which you assumed would be very similar to a college class. An additional source may have been information that a college friend shared with you about classes on campus. Still another source that could set your expectations may have been several college catalogs you had read

Figure 4.3
How a Schema Is Built

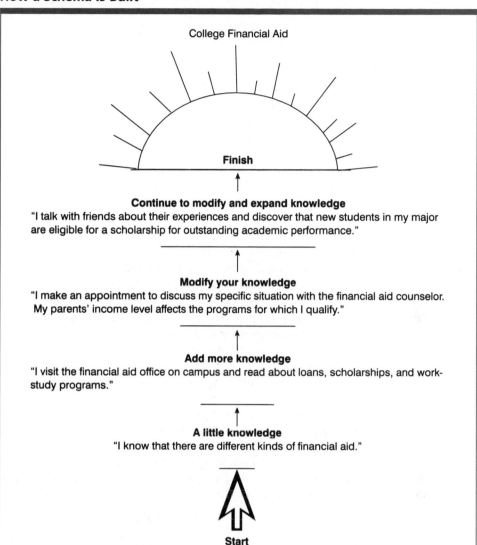

College Financial Aid

Finish

↑

Continue to modify and expand knowledge
"I talk with friends about their experiences and discover that new students in my major are eligible for a scholarship for outstanding academic performance."

↑

Modify your knowledge
"I make an appointment to discuss my specific situation with the financial aid counselor. My parents' income level affects the programs for which I qualify."

↑

Add more knowledge
"I visit the financial aid office on campus and read about loans, scholarships, and work-study programs."

↑

A little knowledge
"I know that there are different kinds of financial aid."

⇧

Start

as you were preparing to apply for admission to colleges. Another source may have been the college class that you observed when you came to campus for orientation.

You could also have some misconceptions about a college class based on your schema. Perhaps you think that you will need a hall pass to leave the classroom, but you find out this is not done in college. You might think that when test papers are returned, you are expected to tell others how you did, good or bad. But in college, your grades are considered to be private and yelling out, "Hey! I got an A!" is considered to be immature and inappropriate.

Obviously, the more information you have about a topic, the better you will understand or conceptualize it. Drawing upon your knowledge of college to understand a college class would give you some idea of what the college class is like. But if you added information from a variety of sources, you would have a more thorough understanding of a college class. Figure 4.3 shows how a schema is built for understanding college financial aid.

Attending your first semester of college classes would help you continue to modify your concept of a college class. As this example illustrates, schemas can be modified or enhanced (Rumelhart, 1984). Modification or enhancement of a schema occurs automatically. New information is added to the schema; incorrect or obsolete information is discarded. For example, one student expected college to be like it is depicted in movies and found that the Hollywood version is very inaccurate. He expected classes to be in a large lecture hall in tiered rows taught by an older male professor with graying hair and wearing a rumpled corduroy suit. His schema for college was modified when he went to college. Classes varied in size—some classes had only 25 students; lecture and cooperative group work were common; and professors, both males and females, varied in ages. If you were the student, you would be unaware that your schema for college is changing. However, when you recall your schema for a college classroom at a future date, the schema will reflect the changes that have occurred. In other words, your background knowledge is constantly updated and reorganized even when you are unaware of it.

You also may develop a schema for a topic totally unfamiliar to you. Suppose you are at freshman orientation and a dean is discussing your general education requirements. The dean mentions you will have course options called *electives,* which she also refers to as free electives. You relate the word to the concept of making a choice, based on your knowledge of the base word, *elect;* still, you have no idea how to make decisions about electives in your program. Since the dean focuses on freshman general education courses, there is no information that would help you build a schema for electives. You check the college catalog to find that electives are offered as part of the general education program, as well as within your major. When you meet with your adviser, you are guided in making choices that match your interests and develop your skills. Now, you have added to your schema of an elective course.

During your junior year, you enroll in an elective course in your major. Now you fully conceptualize an elective course, based on the course that you are taking. Your schema of an elective, however, can still be modified. For example, you could discuss with classmates the elective courses they are taking. Friends from home who are studying at another university might tell you that they can take their electives pass or fail rather than for a specific grade. Once again, your schema for an elective course continues to be enriched and enlarged.

No two people have exactly the same schema for a concept (Harris & Sipay, 1990). The schema may be similar, but it will not be exactly the same. You can discuss the elective course with your friend; however, your schema for the course will differ depending on your background of experiences.

According to Bransford (1979), many college students have difficulty transferring information gleaned from one source to another, yet critical reading depends on relating prior knowledge to what is being read (VanderStoep & Seifert, 1994). To be a skilled reader, you need to make a concerted effort to access your schema or background knowledge prior to reading and build on that schema during and after reading.

As you are preparing to read, it is important that you think about what you already know about the topic. In other words, you relate your background information or schemas to the text. Ask yourself three basic questions: "What experiences have I had that are like this?" "What do I already know about this topic?" and "What would I like to know about this topic?" (May, 1990, p. 165).

For example, in response to the self-questioning about past experience, prior knowledge, and future interests in the topic, a reader's thoughts when reading a chapter titled "The Return of Family Cohesiveness" might sound something like this: "Cohesiveness in my family was always evident. My parents were supportive of me and my brothers. We were close. What I already know about this topic is that not all families are close. In fact, I know some families who live in the same house, but that appears to be all that they share. What I would like to know about this topic is the meaning of the title of the chapter. In what ways is family cohesiveness returning? What impact will this have on society?"

Improvement in Action ⟫

Chapter Titles

- "Using Mail Merge for Letters" (in a computing course)
- "Effective Community Action to Deter Crime" (in a criminology course)
- "Classroom Management Skills" (in an educational psychology course)
- "Assertiveness Training for Professional Women" (in a business course)

Questions to Ask About Each Title

- What experiences have I had that are like this?
- What do I already know about the topic?
- What would I like to know about this topic?

Read the titles of the chapters in Box 4.6. For each, answer the questions to assess your background knowledge.

Strategies for Building Prior Knowledge or Schema

There are numerous ways to compensate for insufficient background knowledge or schema. One way is to begin a graphic organizer in which you jot down everything, however sparse, that you know about the topic, then build on this map as you become more knowledgeable. Another technique to build prior knowledge that can be used to enhance the map is prior reading, including complementary articles and books about the topic. A third way to enhance schema is to use a multimedia approach—videos, computer software, CD-ROM and the Internet—to build background knowledge.

Accessing Schema through Graphic Organizers

In elementary school, you probably were taught how to outline text as you were reading. An outline is an organizer set up to show the hierarchy of ideas. The Roman numerals represent major ideas, the capital letters represent minor ideas clarifying the major ideas, and lowercase letters identify points that further explain the minor ideas. The arrangement of the ideas with indentations presents the ideas in abbreviated form showing a hierarchy. One drawback of outlining is that the material has to be extremely well organized and hierarchial in order for it to be outlined with ease. As a result, outlining is not quite as flexible as some other methods of organizing ideas. Other graphic organizers that represent that relationship of concepts give more of a visual representation than an outline.

One of these is a map that shows the relationships of ideas. Figure 4.4 illustrates a map of the concepts related to an elective course described earlier. Note the hierarchy of ideas that is presented in a more informal way than with an outline. An advantage of the map is that it is easy to visualize and expand as more information becomes apparent. A map is an excellent vehicle for first plotting your schema related to a topic before you begin to read. Then, as you read, you can expand or modify the map. For example, suppose that in a sociology of sport class you were going to read about the effect of television on

Figure 4.4
Elective Courses

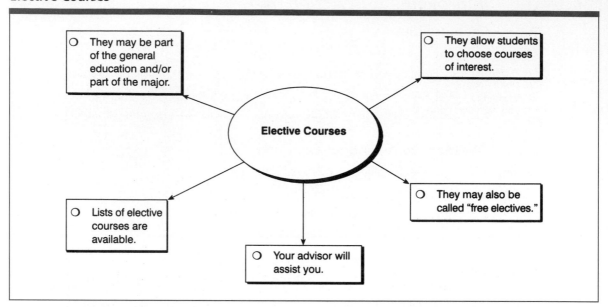

Figure 4.5
Effects of TV on Professional Sports

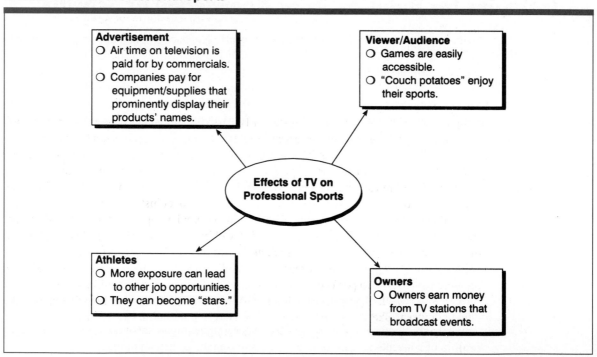

professional sports. You begin by assessing your schema related to this topic and draw a map (see Figure 4.5). Once you have completed prereading strategies, you begin reading the text. You discover that "Television has affected the economy, the ownership and location of franchises, as well as the scheduling, staging, management, dynamics, and even the aesthetics of sporting events" (Leonard, 1993, p. 435). You can modify your concept map accordingly as you confirm or reject your ideas or add new ones to your schema.

Figure 4.6
Mapping

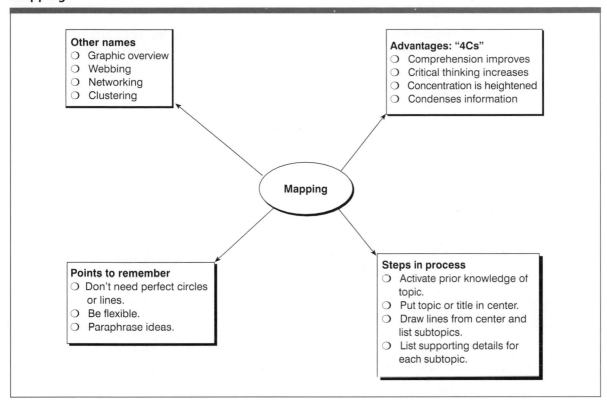

How to Map

Mapping is easy to do. According to Richardson and Morgan (1994), you should map parts of a chapter or article that will help you understand the "superordinate and subordinate relationships" (p. 159). Begin anywhere on the page and write the topic, main idea, or question. Next, draw lines and write and connect secondary ideas to the topic, main idea, or question. Then, find supporting details and write and connect them to the category that they support. Figure 4.6 presents features of maps and additional instructions.

Try mapping for yourself. Once again you are previewing a chapter assigned in your sociology of sport class. This time the topic is the effects of imposing the professional model of sports on youth sport programs, such as Little League. Think of the issues involved in children's early participation in organized competitive sports. Some concerns might be the pressure on children to perform, costs associated with participation (uniforms, equipment, travel), and the lack of good role models in coaches. Think of other problematic issues. Take a few minutes to sketch a map showing these effects as you understand them.

Note that other students may produce a very different map of the same topic because of their schemas. Compare and contrast your map of the effects of imposing the professional model of sports on youth sport programs with a map on the same topic in Figure 4.7.

When you have finished the map on the effect on youth sports programs, you begin reading the chapter and discover the following:

> Not all juvenile sport programs stress winning, but when the professional model is imposed on youth programs, numerous undesirable consequences may result. Cutting, or eliminating children from sports programs, can be a serious problem, and those cut may experience *aversive sport socialization* experiences, which later condition their future

Figure 4.7
Professional Model Imposed on Youth Sports Programs

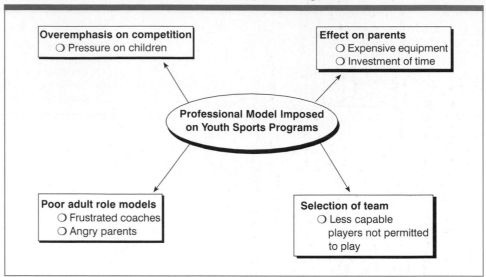

sport interests, perspectives, and behaviors. . . . Expecting too much from a youngster at an early age can and has produced various forms of psychological damage, as is evidenced by *Little League syndrome*. (Leonard, 1993, p. 134)

After reading the text, you can add information to your map.

Accessing Prior Knowledge Through Other Reading

By previewing the text chapter or an article to be read, you can determine the topics included in the piece. You may want to read other related material to access prior information or build background knowledge before you do the actual reading of the text or article. Suppose you are taking an introduction to computers course and have been assigned a chapter on selecting and purchasing your own computer. You construct a map on the process based on your schema of buying a computer. As you preview, you notice that notes in the margin indicate some pertinent issues to consider when buying a computer: your computing needs, your budget, and the software you are interested in using (Ingalsbe, 1992). Before reading the chapter, you refer to a computing magazine in the library to assess the author's ideas related to this purchase. Once again, you modify your map. Your next task is to read your text. As you read, you continue to embellish your map and build your knowledge base.

A student who reads alternative sources of information, whether before or after reading the text, is going to build a much stronger knowledge base of the topic than someone who does not. You may prefer to read supplementary sources of information after you have completed reading your assignment. Either way, you build a broader base of information.

Multimedia Approaches to Building Prior Knowledge

College libraries have extensive collections of video cassettes and CD-ROM (compact disks) on a range of topics. Your syllabus indicates the particular topics to be studied for the semester. You can check ahead of time to determine whether any videos or CD-ROM are available on these topics. Prior to reading your assignment, view the video or access the CD-ROM to enhance your knowledge base. For example, in your nutrition and wellness class, you know that the relationship of food and exercise will be studied. Check your library to determine whether any video or CD-ROM exists on this topic. View the video or access the CD-ROM topic and then do your assigned reading.

Another source to build background or schema is the Internet. The Internet provides immediate access to virtually unlimited sources of information (Ryder & Graves, 1996/1997) in the form of databases, library services, electronic journals, essays, graphs and maps, photographs, as well as movie and sound clips (Mike, 1996). The computer labs on your campus will enable you to "surf the Net" for information that will support and expand topics you are studying. This can be done relatively quickly if you are experienced with search engines and the World Wide Web. If you are unfamiliar with the Internet, check technology support on your campus for assistance or enroll in a course that provides instruction in using the Internet.

All of these strategies for accessing schema, graphic organizers, supplementary reading, and multimedia used separately or in combination will help you build not only schemas but a better understanding of the topic. The extra time that these strategies take pays off as you are held accountable for the content of a discipline by your professor. Ultimately, your grades will show your efforts.

The concepts that you learn in one course may build the foundation for topics studied in subsequent courses. This process necessitates your active involvement. For example, the schemas that are the knowledge base of your major are built from the introductory course in your major and in all other courses until you have met all of the graduation requirements. In fact, schema enhancement is a lifelong process. It also involves metacognitive processes, or thinking about your individual ways of processing information.

Reading as a Metacognitive Process

Using metacognitive strategies during reading puts the reader in a position of power, of control. Metacognition is "thinking about thinking" (Jacobs & Paris, 1987). For example, if you are asked to multiply 12×12, you might retrieve the solution or quickly solve the problem. You can say to yourself, "How do I know that answer?" and think that you memorized this fact years ago in elementary school. Or you might say, "I can visualize the answer: 10 groups of $12 = 120$ plus 2 groups of $12 = 24$ for a total of 144." In both situations, you are thinking about your thinking—not simply rushing to an answer but trying to figure out *how* and *why* you know the answer.

Metacognition involves two basic processes: (a) knowing which processes are needed to complete a task effectively and (b) monitoring task performance and making corrections if the task is not proceeding correctly (Baker & Brown, 1984). Skilled readers know how to approach the reading task to get the most from reading. They also know how to determine whether the reading is not going well and what to do about it. Many inefficient college readers tend to flit through reading assignments without much focus. They turn their attention to whatever catches their eye, rather than focusing attention on what is really important. Others tend to plow through reading material long after they have lost comprehension. Then they say that they "just didn't understand it" or blame it on poor memory. Neither "flitting" nor "plowing" through reading works well. Monitoring your understanding and making corrections when you are not understanding avoids both of these mistakes. This comprehension monitoring is one type of metacognitive strategy.

Other metacognitive strategies can be used to increase the comprehension of text, regardless of the type of reading assignment. It is important that each strategy becomes automatic. Have you ever heard of accounts of people who get the gist of an entire book in a

Figure 4.8
Guidelines for Previewing a Chapter

Follow these steps while thinking about what you already know about the topic.

- Think about the purpose of the assignment.
- Read the chapter objectives.
- Read the title and subtitles.
- Read the first and last paragraphs.
- Read the boldfaced and italicized words.
- Read the graphic illustrations.
- Read the summary.
- Read the end-of-chapter questions.

few minutes? Chances are, they used a strategy called previewing. When you begin a book, chapter, or section, there is no need to ask, "What do I do first?" because you automatically preview the chapter. There is no need to wonder, "What do I preview?" because you know all the components to be previewed. There is no need to think, "How much time should I spend previewing?" because you already know that previewing should take about 5 minutes. In fact, your sense of this time period becomes so natural that there is no need to look at a clock.

How does previewing work? First, you open a book to read a chapter. You automatically read the objectives, first and last paragraphs, title and subtitles, boldfaced and italicized words, graphic illustrations, summary, and questions. Throughout this process, active readers reflect on why the professor gave the assignment. They continually think about what you already know about the topic. For example, as you read the title and subtitles, you say to yourself, "What do I already know about this topic? What do I think will be included in this section?" As you look at an illustration, you ask yourself, "What does this picture describe? How will it be related to what I am going to read and to what I already know?" Refer to Figure 4.8 for a list of these guidelines.

Occasionally, you come across text that does not have special features, such as subtitles or graphic illustrations, to preview. In that situation, read the title, read the first and last paragraphs, and quickly skim the selection to get the general idea of its content.

Having previewed the chapter, you are ready to interact more fully with the text. Initially, it would be a good idea to use five key phrases to remind you how to improve your comprehension (May, 1990). Think about these key phrases for effective reading as a marathon: The purpose for reading is to get to the finish line; the reading rate is comparable to the running time; relating background information is like the preparation that you have made for the marathon; attending to organizational patterns is analogous to attending to the rules for the marathon; and monitoring your understanding for greater clarity can be compared to the adjustments in pace and strategy that the runner makes. Refer to Figure 4.9 to review the analogy of the key phrases for reading and the marathon. Each phrase will be elaborated upon in the next section.

Effective Reading Key 1: Set a Purpose for Reading

You, the reader, determine the reasons for reading a selection. Usually, our primary purposes for reading fall somewhere along a continuum with two broad categories at either end (Rosenblatt, 1978). At one end is reading purely for information, such as reading instructions on how to assemble a bookshelf, and at the other extreme is reading entirely for aes-

Figure 4.9
Keys to Effective Reading: A Marathon Analogy

1. **Set a purpose: Get to the finish line.**
(Set a purpose for reading.)

5. **Adjust pace and strategy.**
(Make corrections for greater clarity.)

2. **Select a running rate.**
(Select a reading rate.)

3. **Preparation for the race.**
(Relate background information.)

4. **Follow marathon rules.**
(Attend to organizational patterns.)

BOX 4.7   *Improvement in Action* ▐▐▐➡

What would be your purpose for reading each of these texts?

■ The university's financial aid bulletin
■ A love letter
■ An interview with a college sports star
■ Your favorite magazine
■ A movie review

What might cause your purpose to change?

---

thetic purposes, such as enjoying the beauty of a poem. Of course, most of the reading we do is not purely for information or aesthetic purposes. More often, it is some combination of the two. But every piece of reading has a purpose. It may be to interpret the meaning of a piece of literature or to understand scientific terms. In reading your assignment, your purpose may be to understand a controversial idea or to figure out which five items from a chapter are important enough to be on the daily quiz. As you read, ask yourself, "Am I reading the text with the purpose in mind? What is this purpose?" To gain valuable experience in applying purposes for reading text, complete Box 4.7.

When your study schedule requires preparation for class by reading assignments, studying for a test, or writing on an assigned topic, you will approach the tasks differently. Each of these topics will be considered more in depth in other chapters; reading is the focus of this chapter. In each case, it is important to read the syllabus carefully to be sure you understand the required assignment.

Reading as Preparation for Class. Begin your preparation by considering the use of the reading assignment that you are to do. Will the information be incorporated into the lecture? Will the instructor depend on students to respond to issues that were in the reading assignment? Will there be an unannounced quiz? Will there be cooperative learning groups that complete an in-class learning activity based on the reading assignment? Will the content of reading be ignored until it is time for a test? Prepare for the reading with a focus on the anticipated use of the content of the reading assignment. For example, if you anticipate the purpose to be to discuss controversial issues in the assignment, you would key in on issues that might be debated as you read. If you anticipate that the class will be mostly lecture with an incorporation of content from the reading, you might consider only the main ideas or most important points. If you know that the period will begin with a quiz on terms and their definitions, your study would focus on new vocabulary and definitions for terms.

Regardless of the purpose for which you prepare, the professor will ultimately hold you accountable for understanding the content of the course. This may be in the form of a test.

Reading as Preparation for Tests. When you prepare for tests, your purpose for rereading/studying the material or your notes must give special attention to those issues that were read and/or emphasized in lectures. For example, you might be told that you were going to be asked to compare and contrast various types of telecommunications channels. If the instructor did not inform you specifically of this question, you might assume it is based on the reading and emphasis in class. The text might have presented three types of channels: wire cable, microwave signals, and fiber optics (Ingalsbe, 1992). You should think about knowing in detail what each of these communication channels is, what the current state of their implementation is, the future applications of each, and how they are similar and different. Focus on these issues prior to studying to maximize the use and quality of your study time, as well as your preparedness for the test.

Reading as Preparation for Writing. The majority of your college writing assignments will require you to prepare by extensive reading. After the assignment has been made, you will need to go to the library to gather resources. Reading to prepare for writing involves skimming sources of information to identify pertinent information on which you will take notes. Initially, you will do skimming or previewing of information and find detailed information to enhance your schema or background knowledge. The more extensively you read, the better you will be prepared to write your paper. Writing will be easier because you understand the information.

Effective Reading Key 2: Determine a Reading Rate

College students sometimes say that they would like to learn speed reading so that they can finish their assignments sooner. Actually, you already know some secrets to speed reading—the preview of the chapter that takes just 5 minutes is called *skimming* and, in effect, is speed reading. Our best advice is to be flexible and use the reading rate that matches your purpose. Should you scan or read rapidly to locate specific information? Should you skim or preview the material to get a general idea of its content? Should you read the material carefully or slowly with considerable concentration? Varying the reading rate depends on your purpose. If you are looking for the meaning of a word in the dictionary or checking a number in the telephone book, you scan. That is, you quickly look only for that specific piece of information. In these situations, most readers move their eyes rapidly along the page. They do not stop to read other things they come across, nor do they read carefully—until they find the one piece of information for which they are searching.

Reading carefully is the slowest mode of reading. You read carefully when you read instructions about how to complete a class assignment or when you follow the steps in assembling an object. Even reading carefully has variations, such as reading more quickly if you are familiar with the topic of the text. Reading technical material or reading about a topic that is new to you requires slow, careful reading. If a reading task is particularly difficult or frustrating, you might even catch yourself reading it aloud. Have you ever tried to follow difficult instructions from a computer manual? During a task such as this, readers often resort to reading the steps one at a time, slowly, deliberately, and out loud.

On the other hand, if you are reading for enjoyment—a novel or the sports page—you would use a medium rate of reading, somewhere between slow, careful reading and skimming. Force yourself to pick up a little reading speed. Do not be concerned if you come across an unfamiliar word, unless the word interests you. Many readers read carefully when

BOX 4.8   *Improvement in Action* ||||➡

For each type of reading material, determine whether the reader should read carefully, read at a medium rate, preview/skim, or scan for a specific piece of information.

1. Your insurance policy after an accident
2. A consumers' digest article of mild interest
3. An article from the sports page to review the game
4. A mystery for relaxation
5. A potential error on your credit card bill
6. A chapter on the American Revolution for class
7. A table of contents to get an idea of the contents
8. A glossary to locate the meaning of a word
9. An article for your term paper

List the numbers of the types of reading material here.

Rates of Reading

Carefully (slow)	Medium Rate	Preview/Skim	Scan (fast)

they could read more efficiently by using a medium rate of reading. They think that they are trying harder if they slow down to a tedious word-by-word reading even though that rate and style of reading are unsuited to their purposes at the time. Students who have become accustomed to reading carefully most of the time may find it difficult at first to use a little faster rate of reading, but the time that it saves makes it worth the initial effort.

The reading rate called skimming (also called *previewing*) was introduced in the section on previewing. Skimming is reading quickly to get a basic idea of the content. That is exactly what a reader does when previewing a chapter or selection, catching the highlights to prepare for more careful reading. As Spargo (1994) advises, "[L]et your eyes run down the page, snatching ideas on the run. Do not stop to read; do not pause to reflect. Try to let the words trigger your mind as you race by" (p. 126). Skimming is like looking for shells on the beach. You quickly search an area while you walk.

Assess appropriate reading rates by answering the questions in Box 4.8.

Effective Reading Key 3: Relate Background Information

Relate information you know, as described in the section on the role of schema. Ask yourself, "Have I had any experiences with this topic? What do I know about it?" For example, in your psychology text you are beginning to read about motivation. Think about what you already know. Ask yourself, "How do I motivate myself? Do I know anyone who is good at motivating other people? I know that I am highly motivated to dance. How do psychologists assess motivation, and what do they recommend when people lack motivation? What techniques motivate me in this class?"

Sometimes as you begin to read, you may be able to relate only minimal information to the topic. For example, if you are taking a health and wellness course, you may come across several examples of physician-assisted suicide for terminally ill patients. Perhaps you recall watching news about Dr. Jack Kevorkian who has been arrested for helping terminally ill patients end their own lives. You begin to build background knowledge about this issue and the controversy that surrounds it. That is, you start to understand the concept of euthanasia, which is the practice of ending the life of someone who is terminally ill or suffering from an incurable illness.

Relating prior knowledge to the topic does not occur only as you preview the text. It is a continuous process as you read. Use what you know to remember and understand what you are reading.

Effective Reading Key 4: Attend to Organizational Patterns of Text

When readers are aware of the sequence of events or the logic of the text, they are attending to organizational patterns. Although not all paragraphs can fit neatly into a specific organizational pattern, there are four general ways of structuring text: chronological, listing of ideas, comparison-contrast, and cause and effect.

If the text is one in which sequence is important, ask, "What is the chronological order or time order of events?" The following text, describing how to ride a chair lift when skiing, gives an example of *chronological order.*

> The skiers stand side by side on a wooden ramp or platform. They look over their shoulders to see the lift man guiding the chair towards them. As the edge of the seat knocks them behind the knees, they sit down. . . . As soon as they are airborne they pull down a metal "gate" behind their heads. This acts as a safety bar. . . . The last pylon before the top of the lift usually carries a warning sign which tells you to raise the safety "gate" and push it back over your head. (Evans, Jackman, & Ottaway, 1979, p. 124)

If the text is a listing of ideas, ask, "What point is the author trying to make?" In a listing of ideas, the order of presentation of points is not important. Remembering this statement will help you differentiate between listing of ideas and chronological order. The following example about the NASA SpaceLink presents text with the *listing of ideas* pattern.*

> The Marshall Space Flight Center . . . operates the NASA SpaceLink, a space-related informational database. Information on aeronautics, NASA news, NASA educational services, and the International Space Year . . . can be examined. (Kehoe, 1993, p. 49)

If the text is comparing and contrasting ideas or issues, ask, "What are the comparisons? Comparisons are similarities or differences. What are the contrasts or differences?"

The following text gives an example of a *comparison* of an e-mail address with a Postal Service address showing how they are similar:

> When an e-mail address is incorrect in some way (the system's name is wrong, the domain doesn't exist, whatever), the mail system will *bounce* the message back to the sender, much the same way that the Postal Service does when you send a letter to a bad street address. (Kehoe, 1993, p. 9)

---

* From *Zen and the Art of the Internet: A Beginner's Guide,* by B. P. Kehoe, 1993, Upper Saddle River, NJ: Prentice Hall. Copyright 1993 by Prentice Hall. Reprinted by permission.

Figure 4.10

Common Organizational Patterns of Text and Words That Indicate These Patterns

Chronological Order	■ Past ← Present → Future
	■ 1st step, 2nd step, 3rd step, etc.
	■ *first, second, before, after, last, next, later, initially, finally*
Listing of Ideas	■ point 1, point 2, point 3
	■ Look for a series of commas.
	■ *a few, some, another, in addition, too, as well, furthermore, moreover*
Comparison-Contrast	■ similarities, differences
	■ *similarly, in the same way, alike, further, in contrast, conversely, but, not, yet, though, although, even though, despite the fact that, on the other hand, also*
Cause and Effect	■ Causes → Effects
	■ *as a result, since, because, consequently, hence, therefore, due to*

Here is an example that *contrasts* different on-line services, showing how they differ:

> Inter-connectivity has been and always will be one of the biggest goals in computer networking. . . . Note that some services are not (nor do they plan to be) accessible from the "outside" (like Prodigy); others, like GEnie and America Online, are actively investigating the possibility of creating a gateway into their system. (Kehoe, 1993, p. 83)

If the text is specifying cause and effect, ask, "What is the cause; what is the effect?" The following excerpt about a computer virus gives an example of the *cause-and-effect* pattern:

> On November 2, 1988, Robert T. Morris . . . wrote a self-replicating, self-propagating program called a *worm* and injected it into the Internet. Morris soon discovered that the program was replicating and reinfecting machines at a much faster rate than he had anticipated—there was a bug. . . . Ultimately, many machines at locations around the country either crashed or became "catatonic." (Kehoe, 1993, p. 63)

Figure 4.10 visually depicts these organizational patterns and lists words that give clues to them.

Are you able to identify some organizational patterns in this text? Try the application exercise in Box 4.9.

Effective Reading Key 5: Make Corrections for Greater Clarity

Realizing that you do not understand is an indication that you are monitoring your comprehension. Efficient and flexible readers clarify what they do not understand, or seem to misunderstand, by rereading a section of the text. This strategy is called *fix up*. This assumes that the reader needs to stop periodically to think about what has just been read. A reader can fix up or repair understanding at any time during reading when what is read is not clear. Ask yourself, "Did I understand the paragraph? Did I get the important details?" Generally speaking, easy-to-read text will require few repairs; more technical text will require frequent repairs. However, the need for repairing or fix up depends on the reader's background.

BOX 4.9   **Improvement in Action** IIII➡

Identify the organizational pattern of each of the following paragraphs from this text.

Page	Paragraph	Organizational Pattern
52	6 "By monitoring . . ."	
119	Box 5.7 "Like newspapers . . ."	
86	3 "Having previewed . . ."	
117	1 "Bazerman (1992) . . ."	
7	2 "Action means . . ."	
109	2 "In general . . ."	
52	4 "Most authorities . . ."	
44	2 "It is . . ."	

Here are some of the sources you can use for fix up:

■ Read a previous paragraph.

■ Read beyond the spot where you are confused.

■ Check a glossary or dictionary for a word meaning.

■ Refer to an alternate source of information, such as a library book on the topic or an encyclopedia.

■ Check with other people—a well-informed friend, study group members, a tutor from the learning center, a graduate assistant, or the professor for the class.

Try repairing your comprehension while reading the following paragraph, which may have content that is unfamiliar.*

> Almost eighty years after the first intelligence tests were developed, a Harvard psychologist named Howard Gardner challenged this commonly held belief. Saying that our culture had defined intelligence too narrowly, he proposed in the book *Frames of Mind* (Gardner 1983) the existence of at least seven basic intelligences. In his theory of multiple intelligences (MI theory), Gardner sought to broaden the scope of human potential beyond the confines of the IQ score. He seriously questioned the validity of determining an individual's intelligence through the practice of taking a person out of his natural learning environment and asking him to do isolated tasks he'd never done before—and probably would never choose to do again. Instead, Gardner suggested that intelligence has more to do with the capacity for (1) solving problems and (2) fashioning products in a content-rich and naturalistic setting. (Armstrong, 1994, p. 1)

Here is a "walk-through" of how a reader might have repaired comprehension while reading Armstrong's paragraph:

> *Almost eighty years after the first intelligence tests were developed, a Harvard psychologist named Howard Gardner challenged this commonly held belief* ("What is this commonly held belief? I better go back and read the previous paragraph.") *Saying that*

---

* From *Multiple Intelligence in the Classroom* (p. 1), by T. Armstrong, 1994, Alexandria, VA: Association for Supervision and Curriculum Development. Copyright 1994 by ASCD. Used with permission.

our culture had defined intelligence too narrowly, he proposed in the book Frames of Mind *(Gardner, 1983) the existence of at least seven basic intelligences.* ("How has culture defined intelligence? Does this mean IQ?") *In his theory of multiple intelligences (MI theory), Gardner sought to broaden the scope of human potential beyond the confines of the IQ score. He seriously questioned the validity of determining an individual's intelligence through the practice of taking a person out of his natural learning environment and asking him to do isolated tasks he'd never done before—and probably would never choose to do again.* ("Gardner must mean multiple-choice IQ tests with that reference to 'isolated tasks.'") *Instead, Gardner suggested that intelligence has more to do with the capacity for (1) solving problems and (2) fashioning products in a content-rich and naturalistic setting.* ("If we quit using IQ tests, what would we use to assess intelligence? I need to read further to determine what [2] means.")

This section on metacognitive processes has introduced five important strategies for monitoring your reading. Try to visualize the marathon runner in Figure 4.9 and the five keys to reading. Can you list the five keys to active reading? They are as follows:

1. setting a purpose for reading,
2. determining a reading rate,
3. relating background information,
4. determining organizational patterns, and
5. fixing up or repairing for greater clarity.

You will have additional practice with these metacognitive strategies with longer selections at the end of this chapter.

Understanding Unfamiliar Vocabulary

How do you determine the meaning of an unknown word in text? Think of the previous metacognitive strategies. If you are constantly monitoring your understanding of what you read, you will be aware of unfamiliar words (Duffy & Roehler, 1989). Next, you need to make a decision about how to learn the meaning of that word. For example, three students in a marriage and family relations course encounter the word *polygamous*. One uses the glossary, another uses the context in the sentences in the paragraph, and the other uses the dictionary. Another student may try to analyze the word and use the context, noting the prefix *poly* means many. Since *monogamous* means married to one person, *polygamous* must mean married to more than one person.

You have options in your approach to determining the meaning of an unfamiliar word (Blachowicz & Zabroske, 1990; May, 1990). By asking the following questions, you can quickly resolve the issue:

1. Can the meaning of the word be determined by looking in the sentence in which the word appears or the sentences that surround it? For example, in the sentence in this chapter "Using metacognitive strategies during reading puts the reader in a position of power, of control," you may not have known the meaning of the word *metacognitive*. If you read the next sentence, it is defined for you. ("Metacognition is thinking about thinking.") In some paragraphs, you may need to read beyond the next sentence to determine the meaning of the word.

Many authors define a discipline-related vocabulary word immediately after the word. For example, in the sentence "The freshman matriculated (enrolled) at the university closest to his home," *matriculated* is further explained by the parenthetical information (*enrolled*).

2. Can I relate this word to another word that I know? For example, the word *fix up* was used in this text. Even though fix up has a specific meaning related to comprehension monitoring, you know the general meaning of *fix up* and can relate it to the specific meaning needed.

3. Can I infer a possible meaning for this word? In the sentence in this text "If you are looking for the meaning of a word in the dictionary or checking a number in the telephone book, you scan," you can infer that *scan* means to look quickly, because you can visualize the type of reading that you use to locate information quickly.

4. Do I need to ask someone or check the meaning in the dictionary or the glossary of the textbook? If you cannot determine the meaning of the word using the first three approaches, you may need to check one of the following sources: ask someone who knows the word, look in the dictionary, or look in the glossary.

Of course, as soon as the meaning of the word is determined, the search for the meaning can be discontinued, so all steps may not be needed. Figure 4.11 presents an algorithm using key terms related to these steps that you can remember.

Perhaps you have been told that you should always stop reading and look up words in the dictionary. The difficulty with this as the only approach to determining the meaning of unfamiliar words is that it can disrupt the reading repeatedly, break your concentration, and discourage you from completing the assignment. Once again, consider your purpose when deciding how to approach an unfamiliar word. Sometimes the easiest and best way to determine the meaning of an unfamiliar word is to ask someone. If a precise definition of the word is essential, using context clues (those clues in the sentence or sentences surrounding the word) may not be sufficient to determine the meaning of the word. In this instance, a glossary might be best. Sometimes students know a word but do not realize it because they are pronouncing it incorrectly. A dictionary can help with that. Dictionaries are also useful for determining word origins, common foreign language phrases, and abbreviations.

When you enroll in college as a freshman, you may be advised to purchase a college dictionary and thesaurus. A thesaurus is a reference used for identifying synonyms (words with the same meaning) and antonyms (words with opposite meanings) of words, something that is especially useful for writing assignments. Words that are not highly specialized or technical vocabulary are often better understood by using a thesaurus. Suppose you saw the word *poignant* in the sentence "She had poignant memories of her childhood." You could check the thesaurus to determine that some synonyms for *poignant* as it is used in the sentence are *moving, intense,* or *impressive.* Some students prefer to buy an electronic dictionary/thesaurus since these are more compact, approximately the size of a checkbook. Some of the newer electronic dictionaries will pronounce the words not only in English, but also in other languages. You may also rely on the spell checker and thesaurus in your word processing software.

Figure 4.11
Algorithm for Determining the Meaning of an Unfamiliar Word
Adapted from Blachowicz & Zabroske, 1990; May, 1990.

1. *CHECK the context* of the word in the sentence it appears and in other sentences in the paragraph.
2. *RELATE the word* to other words that you know.
3. *INFER a possible meaning* of the word.
4. *INVESTIGATE resources,* such as the dictionary or glossary, or ask someone what the word means.

As a reader, you will find that knowledge of words falls along a continuum (Dale, 1965). You may 1) know one or several meanings of the word, 2) recognize the word in the context of the sentences and know it has something to do with something else you know, 3) you may have heard the word but don't know what it means, or 4) you may have never seen the word. Of course, a word you fully understand needs no further attention. The meanings of words in a meaningful context in sentences can be determined, as described earlier. Generally speaking, the words that are most problematic are those you've heard but don't understand or those you have never seen before.

When you come across unfamiliar words, you need to make a decision as to the importance of the word for your study. Words may be general or technical. Knowledge of a general word may be necessary to comprehend the text. For example, you may come across the word *attribute* in a history course. Using the context, you may be able to determine that an attribute is a characteristic. An education major may read about pedagogy as it relates to teaching. This is a technical word that is an important part of an educator's professional vocabulary and may need further exploration. In checking the definition, the student would determine that pedagogy refers to the art of teaching and all methods and practices that are used to help children learn. Understanding the word needs to go beyond the dictionary definition. Parks and Black (1992) have identified ways to think about a topic. Figure 4.12 is an adaptation of their model for thinking about a word. This model could be used with any word. The example will focus on the word *Internet*.

After you have identified those words on which you need to focus and understand their meanings, it is important to provide a vehicle for future rehearsal of the words. Two rehearsal strategies are suggested by Kanar (1995). They are recording words on note cards or in a notebook and reviewing the words until they are known.

Both strategies are easy to use. The note card system simply involves recording the word on one side of the notecard and the definition on the second side. Kanar (1995) suggests that on the second side you include any memory cues that help you recall the word, the word in a sentence that shows meaning, and possibly the part of speech. If you are going to need to spell the word, highlight any problem letters. Carry the cards with you so when you have a little extra time, such as standing in line, you can review the words and definitions.

The second strategy for learning new words involves using a notebook. Kanar (1995) suggests drawing a line to make a three inch column on the left side of the page. The word

Figure 4.12
Do I Really Know It?

Example: The Internet	
What kind of word is it?	a noun that describes a communication network
What are some examples?	World Wide Web Yahoo (Search Engine) e-mail
What are some similar, yet distinctive ideas?	other efforts to create communications systems: postal system, telephone system
What are its important characteristics?	speedy transmission of information accessed by computer or television hook up enormous storage capacity continuously updated
What is a definition?	The Internet is a large collection of networks that can be used to access information by anyone with a computer and modem.

is written in that column with the definition and any other notes across from the word. To rehearse the words, cover one of the columns, either the word column or the definition column, and recite the definition (or word, if the other column is covered). Slide the paper down the column to uncover the next word. Continue to review all words with which you are somewhat familiar or are unknown until you learn them.

All of the issues raised in this chapter are helping you understand the reading thought processes and become an expert reader. According to Smith (1985):

> The phrase "learning to read" can be misleading, if it leads to an assumption that there is a magical day in every literate person's life, some kind of a threshold, on which we become a reader but before which we are merely learning to read. We begin learning to read the first time we make sense of print, and we learn something about reading every time we read. (p. 116)

The Expert Reader

By now, your sense of what reading is has expanded. You realize that "Reading occurs when people assimilate information through their eyes and act upon it" (Hobson & Shuman, 1990, p. 350). What do expert readers do differently than novice readers? Research has determined that expert readers have acquired the following habits:

- Search for connections between what they know and the new information they encounter in the texts they read.
- Monitor the adequacy of their models of text meaning.
- Take steps to repair faulty comprehension once they realize they have failed to understand something.
- Learn early on to distinguish important from less important ideas in texts they read (addressed in the next chapter).
- Are adept at synthesizing information within and across texts and reading experiences.
- Draw inferences during and after reading to achieve a full, integrated understanding of what they read.
- . . . [A]sk questions of themselves, the authors they encounter, and the texts they read. (Pearson et al., 1992, p. 153)

Searching for connections, monitoring reading, and repairing faulty comprehension have been discussed in this chapter. Additional strategies for interacting with text will be discussed in the next chapter.

 Voices of Successful Students

"Always go to class prepared so that you can relate better to the subject being discussed."

"Read more books, go over things, and if you still don't understand, get help."

"Always read required texts and books."

"How do you get better at reading? By reading, reading, and more reading."

"When I don't understand a passage, I reread it. If I come to a term I do not know in a textbook, I look it up in the glossary or ask someone."

Cooperative Learning Activity: Mapping

Choose a topic that is likely to be discussed in a college course, such as reading approaches to use when completing your class assignment. These approaches could include information about schema, metacognition, and other topics in this chapter. Independent of other members of your group, build a map based on your personal schema of the topic. Remember, a map begins with the topic in the center, in this case "Reading to Prepare for Class," and lines radiating out from this central topic with the major ideas. When individual maps have been completed, combine the maps into one comprehensive map. Discuss the use and value of this map as a prereading strategy, as well as during and following reading.

Writing and Reflecting: Becoming an Active Reader

Think about the amount of reading you typically do during the day. Do you read, or at least skim, the newspaper on a daily basis? Do you subscribe to magazines? Do you read in your sparc time, such as before you fall asleep at night? How much time are you spending reading textbooks each day? Reflect on the amount of reading that you do, and determine what kind of reader you would like to be in the future. Are you reading enough to be the kind of reader you would like to be? What adjustments can you make to become a more active reader? Write your response in your journal so you can refer to it when necessary.

Self-Improvement Strategy: Complementary Reading

For one of your courses, do some background reading on one of the topics that seems particularly difficult or unfamiliar before you actually read the chapter. To determine what to read, look at the course syllabus and the table of contents of your text to key in on the issues related to the topic. For example, if the topic is the genetic influence on diseases, you might go to some contemporary sources to read about recent discoveries. This reading may be from another book, an article, or a newspaper. After reading this complementary text, read the assigned chapter. Then, evaluate your understanding of the topic as it was presented in the textbook. Did the prior reading enhance your schema of the topic? If so, in what ways?

Reading Selections

The following selections will help you further apply the reading thought processes described in this chapter. Read each one as if you had been assigned the reading for one of your classes and you were going to be held accountable for understanding the issues raised in the selection.

Follow these specific directions:

1. Set a purpose for reading.
2. Briefly preview the selection. Since most of the selections have few special features, preview by reading the title, subtitle, and first and last paragraphs.
3. Determine a reading rate before beginning.
4. Attend to the overall organizational pattern.
5. Fix up or repair for greater clarity if your mind wanders or you are unfamiliar with the topic.
6. Map the major points of each selection after you have completed the reading.

Reading Selection 1

The following selection is from a college English handbook (Skwire & Wiener, 1993).* As you read the selection, think about sexist language that you commonly hear and see in print.

---

* From *Student's Book of College English* (p. 515), by D. Skwire and H. S. Wiener, 1993, Boston: Allyn & Bacon. Copyright 1993 by Allyn & Bacon. Reprinted with permission.

Sexist Language

Sexist language is language that displays prejudice and stereotyped thinking about the roles, character, and worth of both sexes, though women have most frequently been its victims. Avoiding sexist language is a moral issue, of course—the sexist bigot is not more appealing than the racial, religious, or ethnic bigot. It is also a stylistic issue because language reflects social realities, and habits of language may continue long after the social realities have changed. Sexist language is sometimes more the product of habit than of intention.

To prevent or eliminate sexist language, pay particular attention to the following suggestions.

- *Avoid stereotypes in occupations.* The notion of distinctive man's work and woman's work has by and large become outdated.
  Sexist Language
  A nuclear physicist needs to take his environmental responsibilities seriously.
  Adele is hoping to become a policeman.
  Carla Rodriguez is an outstanding lady doctor.
  Our file clerk quit yesterday, and we need a new woman for the job.
  Improved
  Nuclear physicists need to take their environmental responsibilities seriously.
  Adele is hoping to become a police officer.
  Carla Rodriguez is an outstanding doctor.
  Our file clerk quit yesterday and we need to find someone new for the job.
- *Avoid stereotypes in character and social behavior.* Not all women giggle, gossip, and want to have babies any more than all men swear, drink beer, and overdose on football.
  Sexist Language
  A good cook always seems to have a secret recipe for her Thanksgiving stuffing.
  The wise shopper can save real money by remembering to use her coupons.
  Her woman's heart melted when she saw her new grandson.
  Improved
  A good cook always seems to have a secret recipe for Thanksgiving stuffing.
  A wise shopper can save real money by remembering to use coupons.
  Her heart melted when she saw her new grandson.
- *Avoid insulting and condescending language.* Some sexist words are obvious insults and easy enough to recognize: *babes, dames, dolls, broads,* and the like. Other words and phrases masquerade as affectionate tributes or compliments but can, in fact, be extremely patronizing: *the fair sex, the gentle sex, my better half, girl* (when used to describe a grown woman), and so on. Avoid both types.
  Sexist Language
  When Jenny left the company, it was hard to find another girl to replace her.

My aunt was thoughtful, helpful, and compassionate—a truly gracious lady.
President Bush said that his wife Barbara had been a main source of strength.
Improved
When Jenny left the company, it was hard to find anyone to replace her.
My aunt was thoughtful, helpful, and compassionate—a truly outstanding person.
President Bush said that Mrs. Bush had been his main source of strength.

- *Avoid using* man, men, *and* mankind *as synonyms for humanity, people, and the human race.*
  Sexist Language
  Man's future is uncertain.
  Men must first learn to love themselves before they can love anything else.
  Are you telling me that mankind is on the brink of doom? What else is new?
  Improved
  Humanity's future is uncertain.
  People must first learn to love themselves before they can love anything else.
  Are you telling me that the human race is on the brink of doom? What else is new?
- *Avoid using the pronoun* he *when sex is unknown or irrelevant.*
  Sexist Language
  We need a person who can offer a few hours of his time each week.
  Everyone wants to feel that he is esteemed.
  A liar needs to make sure that he has a good memory.
  Improved
  We need a person who can offer a few hours of time each week.
  All people want to feel that they are esteemed.
  Liars need to make sure that they have good memories. (p. 515)

Answer these questions in the space provided:

1. What was your purpose for reading?

2. How did you preview the selection?

3. What reading rate did you use? Why?

4. What is the overall organizational pattern?

5. Where did you fix up, and what strategies did you use?

6. Draw your map here.

2. How did you preview the selection?

3. What reading rate did you use? Why?

4. What is the overall organizational pattern?

5. Where did you fix up, and what strategies did you use?

Reading Selection 2

The following is an excerpt from a textbook on multicultural education (Au, 1993).* As you read the selection, relate the ideas to your culture.

Culture may be defined as a system of values, beliefs, and standards which guides people's thoughts, feelings, and behavior (Hernandez, 1990). While this system forms an integrated whole, it is by no means static. Culture involves a dynamic process which people use to make sense of their lives and the behavior of other people (Spindler & Spindler, 1990).

The complex and dynamic nature of culture is highlighted in the following characteristics (Gollnick & Chinn, 1990). First, culture is learned. People are not born knowing their culture but are initiated into it through the actions of family members and others. People actively seek to construct an understanding of the different cultures in which they participate. Even so, no individual ever learns everything there is to know about a particular culture, and each individual's understanding of a culture is somewhat different from that of every other individual (Wolcott, 1991). Second, culture is shared. Members of a cultural group have a common understanding of the system, of ways of thinking and behaving. Third, culture is adaptation. A culture may adapt to its natural environment or to particular political and economic conditions. Fourth, culture is continually changing. Changes may be as minor as a new hairstyle or as dramatic as a long-term trend such as the replacement of industrial workers by robots. (p. 4)

Answer these questions in the space provided:

1. What was your purpose for reading?

6. Draw your map here.

Reading Selection 3

The following is an excerpt from a chemistry textbook (Petrucci & Harwood, 1993).* As you read the selection, compare and contrast the interests of the various types of chemists.

Many chemists work in more traditional fields of chemistry. Biochemists are interested in chemical processes that occur in living organisms. Physical chemists work with fundamental principles of physics and chemistry in an attempt to answer the basic questions that apply to all of chemistry: Why do some substances react with one another while others do not? How fast will a particular chemical reaction occur? How much useful energy can be extracted from a chemical reaction? Analytical chemists are investigators; they study ways to separate and identify chemical substances. Many of the techniques developed by analytical chemists are used extensively by environmental scientists. Organic chemists focus their attention on substances that contain carbon and hydrogen in combination with a few other elements. The vast majority of substances are organic

* From *Literacy Instruction in Multicultural Settings* (p. 4), by K. H. Au, 1993, Fort Worth, TX: Harcourt Brace Jovanovich. Copyright 1993 by Harcourt Brace Jovanovich. Reprinted by permission.

* From *General Chemistry: Principles and Modern Applications* (6th ed., p. 2), by R. H. Petrucci and W. S. Harwood, 1993, Upper Saddle River, NJ: Merrill/Prentice Hall.

chemicals. Inorganic chemists focus on most of the elements other than carbon, though the fields of organic and inorganic chemistry overlap in some ways. (p. 2)

Answer these questions in the space provided:

1. What was your purpose for reading?

2. How did you preview the selection?

3. What reading rate did you use? Why?

4. What is the overall organizational pattern?

5. Where did you fix up, and what strategies did you use?

6. Draw your map here.

Reading Selection 4

The following is an excerpt from a chemistry textbook (Petrucci & Harwood, 1993).* As you read the selection, note Rutherford's contributions to scientific understanding of the composition of the atom.

In 1909, Rutherford with his assistant, Hans Geiger, began a line of research using alpha particles as probes to study the inner structure of atoms. Based on Thomson's "plum pudding" model . . ., Rutherford expected that a beam of alpha particles would pass through thin sections of matter largely undeflected. However, he believed that some alpha particles would be slightly scattered or deflected as they encountered electrons. By studying these scattering patterns, he hoped to deduce something about the distribution of electrons in atoms.

. . . Alpha particles were detected by the flashes of light they produced when they struck a zinc sulfide

screen mounted on the end of a telescope. When Geiger and Ernest Marsden, a student, bombarded very thin foils of gold with alpha particles, here is what they observed.

- The majority of α particles penetrated the foil undeflected.
- Some α particles experienced slight deflections.
- A few (about one in every 20,000) suffered rather serious deflections as they penetrated the foil.
- A similar number did not pass through the foil at all but "bounced back" in the direction from which they had come. The large-angle scattering greatly puzzled Rutherford. As he commented some years later, this observation was "about as credible as if you had fired a 15-inch shell at a piece of tissue paper and it came back and hit you."

By 1911, though, Rutherford had an explanation. . . . The model of the atom he proposed is known as the *nuclear* atom and has these features.

- Most of the mass and all of the positive charge of an atom are centered in a very small region called the *nucleus*. The atom is mostly empty space.
- The magnitude of the positive charge is different for different atoms and is approximately one half the atomic weight of the element.
- There exist as many electrons outside the nucleus as there are units of positive charge on the nucleus. The atom as a whole is electrically neutral.

Protons and Neutrons

Rutherford's nuclear atom suggested the existence of positively charged fundamental particles of matter in the nuclei of atoms. Rutherford himself discovered these particles, called *protons,* in 1919, in studies involving the scattering of alpha particles by nitrogen atoms in air. The protons were freed as a result of collisions between alpha particles and the nuclei of nitrogen atoms. At about this same time, Rutherford predicted the existence of the nucleus of electrically neutral fundamental particles. In 1932, James Chadwick showed that a newly discovered penetrating radiation consisted of beams of *neutral* particles. These particles, called *neutrons,* originated from the nuclei of atoms. Thus, it has been only for about the past 60 years that we have had the atomic model. (p. 40)

Answer these questions in the space provided:

1. What was your purpose for reading?

2. How did you preview the selection?

3. What reading rate did you use? Why?

4. What is the overall organizational pattern?

---

* From *General Chemistry: Principles and Modern Applications* (6th ed., p. 40), by R. H. Petrucci and W. S. Harwood, 1993, Upper Saddle River, NJ: Merrill/Prentice Hall.

5. Where did you fix up, and what strategies did you use?

6. Draw your map here.

4. What is the overall organizational pattern?

5. Where did you fix up, and what strategies did you use?

6. Draw your map here.

Reading Selection 5

The following is an excerpt from a philosophy textbook (Stewart & Blocker, 1992).* As you read the selection, compare and contrast the goals and concerns of epistemology and psychology.

Perhaps the goals and concerns of epistemology will be clearer if we contrast them with the goals and concerns of psychology. Both epistemology and psychology are concerned with human consciousness, and it might at first appear that epistemology is only trying to do what psychology is in a position to do better. But there is a fundamental difference between the two approaches. Psychology is an attempt to *describe* the way the human mind actually operates, epistemology seeks to establish normative criteria for how we *ought* to think. In its more experimental mode, psychology centers its attention on the physiological aspects of the knowing process—on the brain, stimulus-response mechanisms, the nervous system, and so forth. As a descriptive enterprise, it is not the purpose of psychology to delve into the intricacies of separating opinion from knowledge and belief from opinion. Whereas the epistemologist is concerned with standards of acceptability in terms of which to judge beliefs, the psychologist is mainly interested in understanding the *how* of human thinking. (p. 185)

Answer these questions in the space provided:

1. What was your purpose for reading?

2. How did you preview the selection?

3. What reading rate did you use? Why?

Reading Selection 6

The following is an excerpt from a foods textbook (McWilliams, 1997).* As you read the selection, think about the different types of food poisoning—maybe you have had one of them.

Salmonellae cause salmonellosis when they are consumed in large numbers. The symptoms, which develop between 6 and 72 hours after eating the offending food (most commonly at about 12 hours), include nausea, abdominal cramps, fever, and diarrhea. Streptococcal infections are most commonly transmitted through poultry, but are also found in raw milk. A sore throat is characteristic of this problem. Staphylococcal poisoning is characterized by the symptoms of vomiting, diarrhea, and abdominal cramps which begin between 3 and 8 hours after ingestion and last for a day or two. Perfringens poisoning, which results from consumption of contaminated and improperly chilled cooked meats, causes acute inflammation of the stomach and intestines and diarrhea about 8 hours after ingestion and lasts a day. One of the most dangerous of the foodborne illnesses is botulism, which usually causes death unless the appropriate antitoxin is administered promptly. Onset is usually 12 to 36 hours after eating food containing the toxin produced by viable spores of *C. botulinum,* the usual source of which is inadequately heat-processed canned, low-acid foods such as vegetables and meats. (p. 531)

Answer these questions in the space provided:

1. What was your purpose for reading?

2. How did you preview the selection?

3. What reading rate did you use? Why?

4. What is the overall organizational pattern?

5. Where did you fix up, and what strategies did you use?

6. Draw your map here.

References

Anderson, R. C., Hiebert, E. H., Scott, J. A., & Wilkinson, I. A. G. (1985). *Becoming a nation of readers: The report of the Commission on Reading.* Washington, DC: National Institute of Education.

Armstrong, T. (1994). *Multiple intelligences in the classroom.* Alexandria, VA: Association for Supervision and Curriculum Development.

Au, K. H. (1993). *Literacy instruction in multicultural settings.* Fort Worth, TX: Harcourt Brace Jovanovich.

Baker, L., & Brown, A. L. (1984). Cognitive monitoring in reading. In J. Flood (Ed.), *Understanding reading comprehension: Cognition, language, and the structure of prose* (pp. 21–44). Newark, DE: International Reading Association.

Blachowicz, C. L. Z., & Zabroske, B. (1990). Context instruction: A metacognitive approach for at-risk readers. *Journal of Reading, 33*(7), 504–508.

Bransford, J. D. (1979). *Human cognition: Learning, understanding and remembering.* Belmont, CA: Wadsworth.

Cypert, S. A. (1993). *The success breakthrough—Get what you want from your career, your relationships, and your life.* New York: Avon.

Dale, E. (1965). Vocabulary measurement: Techniques and major findings. *Elementary English, 42,* 895–901.

Devine, T. (1986). *Teaching reading comprehension.* Boston: Allyn & Bacon.

Duffy, G. G., & Roehler, L. R. (1989). *Improving classroom reading instruction: A decision-making approach* (2nd ed). New York: Random House.

Ellis, D. B. (1984). *Becoming a master student.* Rapid City, SD: College Survival.

Evans, H., Jackman, B., & Ottaway, M. (1979). *We learned to ski.* New York: St. Martins.

Grant, R. (1993). Strategic training for using text headings to improve students' processing of content. *Journal of Reading, 36*(6), 482–488.

Harris, A. J., & Sipay, E. R. (1990). *How to increase reading ability: A guide to developmental & remedial methods* (9th ed.). New York: Longman.

Hobson, E., & Shuman, R. B. (1990). *Reading and writing in high schools: A whole-language approach.* Washington, DC: National Education Association.

Ingalsbe, L. (1992). *Using computers and application software* (2nd ed.). Upper Saddle River, NJ: Merrill/Prentice Hall.

Jacobs, J. E., & Paris, S. C. (1987). Children's metacognition about reading: Issues in definition, measurement and instruction. *Educational Psychologist, 22,* 255–258.

Kanar, C. C. (1995). *The confident student* (2nd ed.). Boston: Houghton Mifflin.

Kehoe, B. P. (1993). *Zen and the art of the Internet: A beginner's guide.* Upper Saddle River, NJ: PTR Prentice Hall.

Leonard, W. M., II. (1993). *A sociological perspective of sport* (4th ed.). Upper Saddle River, NJ: Merrill/Prentice Hall.

May, F. B. (1990). *Reading as communication: An interactive approach* (3rd ed.). Upper Saddle River, NJ: Merrill/Prentice Hall.

McWilliams, M. (1997). *Foods: Experimental perspectives* (3rd ed.). Upper Saddle River, NJ: Merrill/Prentice Hall.

Mike, D. G. (1996). Internet in the schools: A literacy perspective. *Journal of Adolescent & Adult Literacy 40*(1), 4–13.

Parks, S., & Black, H. (1992). *Book I Organizing thinking graphic organizers*. Pacific Grove, CA: Critical Thinking Press & Software.

Pearson, P. D., Roehler, L. R., Dole, J. A., & Duffy, G. G. (1992). Developing expertise in reading comprehension. In S. J. Samuels & A. E. Farstrup (Eds.), *What research has to say about reading instruction* (2nd ed., pp. 145–199). Newark, DE: International Reading Association.

Pike, K., Compain, R., & Mumper, J. (1997). *New connections: An integrated approach to literacy* (2nd ed.). New York: Longman.

Petrucci, R. H., & Harwood, W. S. (1993). *General chemistry: Principles and modern applications* (6th ed.). Upper Saddle River, NJ: Merrill/Prentice Hall.

Richardson, J. S., & Morgan, R. F. (1994). *Reading to learn in the content areas* (2nd ed.). Belmont, CA: Wadsworth.

Rinehart, S. D., & Platt, J. M. (1984). Metacognitive awareness and monitoring in adult and college readers. *Forum for Reading, 15*(2), 54–62.

Rosenblatt, L. (1978). *The reader, the text, and the poem: The transactional theory of the literacy work*. Carbondale: Southern Illinois University.

Rumelhart, D. E. (1984). Understanding understanding. In J. Flood (Ed.), *Understanding reading comprehension:* *Cognition, language, and the structure of prose* (pp. 1–20). Newark, DE: International Reading Association.

Ryder, R. J., & Graves, M. F. (1996/1997). Using the Internet to enhance students' reading, writing, and information-gathering skills. *Journal of Adolescent & Adult Literacy 40*(4), 244–254.

Sawyer, D., & Rodriguez, C. (1992/93). How Native Canadians view literacy: A summary of findings. *Journal of Reading, 36*(4), 284–293.

Silha, S. (1992). Reading: Connecting with the real world. *Progressions, 4*(4), 1–3.

Skwire, D., & Wiener, H. S. (1993). *Student's book of college English* (6th ed.). Upper Saddle River, NJ: Merrill/Prentice Hall.

Smith, F. (1985). *Reading without nonsense* (2nd ed.). New York: Teachers College.

Spargo, E. (1994). *The college student* (4th ed.). Providence, RI: Jamestown.

Stewart, D., & Blocker, H. G. (1992). *Fundamentals of philosophy* (3rd ed.). Upper Saddle River, NJ: Merrill/Prentice Hall.

The Education Illusion. (1997, October 15). *Investor's Business Daily*, p. B1.

VanderStoep, S. W., & Seifert, C. M. (1994). Problem solving, transfer & thinking. In P. R. Pintrich, D. R. Brown, & C. M. Weinstein (Eds), *Student motivation, cognition, and learning: Essays in honor of Wilbert J. McKeachie* (pp. 27–50). Hillsdale, NJ: Lawrence Erlbaum.

Applying Effective Reading and Study Strategies

With any piece of writing we usually do not read to memorize the text. Rather we transform it for our own understanding and purposes. Even an actress who must memorize the script of her part must then interpret that part through her delivery of the lines, gestures, and actions. Just as the actress must create life on stage out of the dead words on the page, we must do the same with our reading: convert someone else's words into our own meanings, thoughts, and actions.* (p. 5)

—C. Bazerman

---

* From *The Informed Reader: Contemporary Issues in the Disciplines* (p. 5), by C. Bazerman, 1989, Boston: Houghton Mifflin.

Prereading Questions

- How do you interact with the textbooks that you are assigned to read? Do you, for example, highlight? Underline? Write notes in the margins?

- How important are graphic aids?

- Identify strategies you use to improve your memory of the material you have read.

- Have you ever studied in a group? What factors would need to be considered when organizing and working in a study group?

Assessing Prior Knowledge

Suppose that a professor makes an assignment to read two chapters. Just think of the range of responses to this course requirement. Some students will scarcely look at the book; others will spend hours going over it. Some students will leave their books untouched; others will underline certain passages. Some students will hurry through the reading; others will take the time to interact or become involved with the text.

When you are completing the assignment, how much time do you spend? Do you read the chapter once or twice? Do you "interact" with the content? That is, do you underline, annotate, summarize, or map information? Do you use text features, such as the table of contents, objectives, questions, and the summary, to preview and review? According to Jensen (1979), studying efficiently involves more than reading and rereading. Effective study includes reading, writing, thinking, and recalling.

Some students complete the reading of a text and do no further reflecting on what they have read (Paris, Wasik, & Turner, 1991). They think that they have a reading problem or, worse yet, lack the brain power to succeed when what they really need are new approaches that get them involved with what they read. The mistake of thinking that reading is a "once over lightly" activity appears to have been Sondra's problem in the following vignette.

Vignette: Going Beyond Reading the Chapter Once

Sondra had a 3.5 cumulative grade point average in high school. She read chapters and articles that were assigned but never felt the need to go beyond reading the assignment once because the teachers usually repeated the same material during class. Sondra thus could understand the chapter's content with minimal effort.

Sondra has just completed her first semester in college, and her grade report, which arrived last week, was a shock. Enclosed with the grade report was a letter informing Sondra that she is on academic probation. After Sondra discovered that she had earned a 1.9 grade point average for the semester, she met with her academic counselor. One conclusion that the counselor reached was that the reading strategies Sondra had used successfully in high school simply did not work with the more challenging material she encountered in college. Sondra needs to modify her reading strategies and learn how to study.

No matter how intelligent you are, your college career will demand that you enhance your reading comprehension and improve your ability to remember what you are reading. Strategies used to accomplish this goal of wider knowledge and deeper understanding are called "thinking about text" strategies. These techniques can help you study more effectively and efficiently in any college-level course.

Thinking About Text

A high school ice hockey player saves money to enroll in a camp taught by a National Hockey League player. Why? Because the student believes that the player is an expert, and he assumes that the player has more knowledge about hockey than most other people. You are attending college for a similar reason. College study puts you in the company of experts and ultimately enables you to develop your own expertise in an area of study. Even before you begin to specialize in college while you are still taking general courses, professors expect you to actively build a knowledge base in each course in which you enroll. Later, when you make a career choice and select a major, your knowledge will need to be more specialized and comprehensive.

In this chapter you will learn how to read and study using a number of basic strategies.

Identifying Topics

If you are like many students, the moment you hear the words *topic* and *main idea,* you groan, "Not that again!" Instead of tuning it out, think about why identifying these points is taught. An efficient reader has to be able to discriminate between information of primary and secondary importance. To accomplish this, the reader needs to determine the topic of text and the main idea in passages of text.

A topic is the subject of what has been written. For example, the topic of this chapter is *applying effective reading and study strategies.* The subtopic in this section is *identifying topics and main ideas.* In most textbooks or articles, topics of chapters or sections can easily be identified by the headings and subheadings. Topics of paragraphs are not as readily identifiable because paragraphs do not generally have titles. However, topics succinctly describe what the paragraph is about and are usually stated as a phrase. They are comparable to the front labels on canned goods—they tell what is inside but not in great detail. If you look at a can of spaghetti sauce, for instance, you know that there are many specific ingredients—tomatoes, salt, seasonings, and so forth—but just two words, *spaghetti sauce,* adequately describe the contents.

The following paragraph, written using the listing of ideas pattern, addresses a topic or subject. Read the paragraph and identify the topic.

> European immigrants, who constituted by far the largest numbers of minorities in America, also encountered much hostility in the United States. In general, however—although there certainly were exceptions—they received better treatment than Asians, Mexicans, blacks, and Indians. As the Europeans assimilated into American society and adopted American cultural mores as their own, they became indistinguishable from other whites. But until the assimilating process had eradicated their foreign ways, they did not enjoy the privileges of equal status. (Dinnerstein, Nichols, & Reimers, 1990, p. 240)

As you were able to determine, the topic of this paragraph is "Attitudes toward Europeans" or "European Immigrants' Treatment in America." You can assess the accuracy of the topic by asking, "Would this phrase serve as an appropriate title of the paragraph?" For this paragraph, that topic would serve as a fine title because it describes the general, overall content of the paragraph.

Now try to determine the topic of another paragraph written using the comparison/contrast organizational pattern:

> There are two basic methods of conducting a physical inventory count. One alternative is to take inventory at a regular interval. Many businesses take inventory at the end of

the year. . . . This periodic physical count generates the most accurate measurement of inventory. The other method of taking inventory involves counting a number of items on a continuous basis. . . . Such a system allows for continuous correction of mistakes in inventory control systems and detects inventory problems sooner.* (Scarborough & Zimmerer, 1993, p. 689)

The topic of this paragraph is "Methods of Inventory Control," which is an appropriate title.

Stating the Main Ideas

Once the topic has been identified, the reader probes more deeply to uncover the **main idea.**

The main idea is more than a general label. The author's apparent purpose for writing something gets added to the topic in order to get at the main idea. The main idea expands the topic and stands for the most important ideas that are being said or written about the topic. Whereas the topic is expressed as a phrase, the main idea is usually written in a complete sentence. The complete sentence ensures a clearly stated main idea. For example, the overall main idea of this chapter is "Background knowledge is built by applying many reading strategies." The main idea of the sections on topics and main ideas is "Topics and main ideas can be identified by determining what the section is about and the important ideas that are written about the topic."

Sometimes main ideas are actually stated, included as sentences or phrases that are within the paragraph. If a main idea is stated, the most likely location for the main idea sentence would be the first sentence in the paragraph. In the first selection on the treatment of Europeans, the first sentence is the statement of the main idea: "European immigrants, who constituted by far the largest numbers of minorities in America, also encountered much hostility in the United States." In the second selection from the business text, the first sentence is also the statement of the main idea: "There are two basic methods of conducting a physical inventory count."

The next most frequent location of the main idea is the last sentence of a paragraph. In the following paragraph from an economics book, the last sentence is the statement of the main idea.

> Do you like anchovies on your pizza? How about sauerkraut on your hot dog? Is music to your ears more likely to be new wave, heavy metal, rap, reggae, or country and western? Choices in food, clothing, movies, music, reading—indeed, all consumption choices—are influenced by consumer tastes. *Tastes* are nothing more than your likes and dislikes as a consumer. What determines tastes? Who knows? . . . Economists do recognize, however, that tastes are very important in shaping demand, and that a change in tastes can change demand. (McEachern, 1994, p. 56)

You can see that most of the sentences in the paragraph are details that lead to the main idea stated in the last sentence and the author's **purpose** for writing this: to show how changes in tastes affect demand for products.

Sometimes, the main idea in a paragraph is implied, not stated in any sentence. The following paragraph from the preface of a book has no stated main idea. The main idea is implied and must be inferred by the reader.

> Judith Greissman helped to bring this book to fruition, and several friends and colleagues—Milton Mankoff, Jon Peterson, and Mary Ryan—read various chapters and

---

* From *Effective Small Business Management* (4th ed., p. 689), by N. M. Scarborough and T. W. Zimmerer, Upper Saddle River, NJ: Merrill/Prentice Hall. Copyright 1993 by Prentice Hall, Inc. Reprinted by permission of Prentice Hall, Upper Saddle River, NJ.

gave me valuable criticism. I owe special thanks to my editors at Atheneum—to Tom Stewart for his unflagging support and to Ilene Smith for editing the manuscript with extraordinary skill and perseverance. (Steinberg, 1989, Acknowledgments)

This paragraph acknowledges the assistants who supported the author during the writing of the text. No introductory or final sentence states the main idea. The main idea, "The author is grateful to many individuals who assisted him in the writing of this book," is clear when we consider *why* the author of this passage is writing this—he wants to thank his assistants.

In general, if you turn your main idea sentence into a question and the selection as a whole answers the question, you have probably identified the main idea correctly. For example, the implied main idea previously stated, "Many individuals assisted the author in the writing of this book," as a question would ask, "Who assisted the author in writing the book?" You can refer to the paragraph and answer that question, so the main idea is accurate.

Identifying topics and stating main ideas are ways that you can "study smarter." It will allow you to focus on what is really important in 100 pages of assigned reading instead of being overwhelmed. Refer to Box 5.1 for more practice in identifying topics and stating main ideas.

Using Graphic Aids in the Text

Graphic aids can enhance understanding of main ideas. Graphic aids, such as charts, maps, figures, and graphs, are included in printed materials to condense and clarify information and to convince the reader (Smith, 1989). Figure 5.1 shows four types of graphic aids—from left to right, top to bottom—a bar graph, line graph, circle or pie graph, and map. These visual representations can provide simple, meaningful explanations when used in combination with text. Believe it or not, many novice readers tend to skip the graphic aids. In doing so, they miss an important enhancement to text.

Graphic aids should be used several times in the course of interacting with a reading selection: when previewing, when reading and studying, and when reviewing the text. During previewing, the graphic aids will give an indication of the content of the text. During reading and study, the graphic aids can clarify meaning by serving as summaries of text. These visual summaries are again invaluable as you review the text.

Reading graphic aids is easy and can be done quickly. The time invested is worthwhile. Figure 5.2 presents directions for reading graphic material.

BOX 5.1　　*Improvement in Action* ▐▐▶

Identify the topic and main idea of this paragraph:

In 1840 Charles Darwin began to keep a diary on the activities of his first-born son, William. Darwin noted William's early reflexes, contrasting them with subsequently learned behaviors. He examined the child's sensory systems, noting for example that William gazed at a candle on his 9th day, attended to a brightly colored tassel on his 49th day, and attempted to seize objects on his 132d day. (Gardner, 1991, p. 23)

Topic: Main idea:
Discuss your answers with other students in your class.

Figure 5.1
Four Types of Graphic Aids

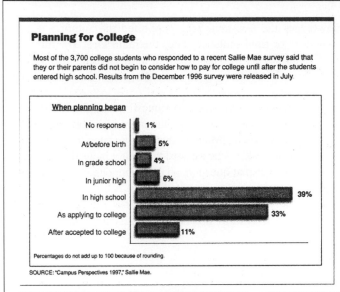

Planning for College

Most of the 3,700 college students who responded to a recent Sallie Mae survey said that they or their parents did not begin to consider how to pay for college until after the students entered high school. Results from the December 1996 survey were released in July.

When planning began

No response	1%
At/before birth	5%
In grade school	4%
In junior high	6%
In high school	39%
As applying to college	33%
After accepted to college	11%

Percentages do not add up to 100 because of rounding.

SOURCE: "Campus Perspectives 1997," Sallie Mae.

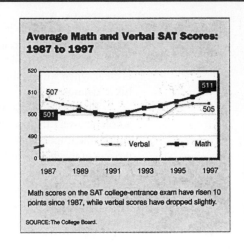

Average Math and Verbal SAT Scores: 1987 to 1997

507 ... 511
501 ... 505

1987   1989   1991   1993   1995   1997

— Verbal   — Math

Math scores on the SAT college-entrance exam have risen 10 points since 1987, while verbal scores have dropped slightly.

SOURCE: The College Board.

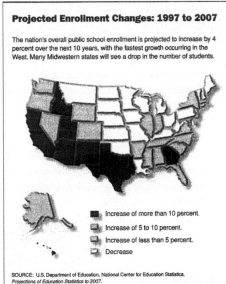

Projected Enrollment Changes: 1997 to 2007

The nation's overall public school enrollment is projected to increase by 4 percent over the next 10 years, with the fastest growth occurring in the West. Many Midwestern states will see a drop in the number of students.

■ Increase of more than 10 percent.
▨ Increase of 5 to 10 percent.
▧ Increase of less than 5 percent.
▢ Decrease

SOURCE: U.S. Department of Education, National Center for Education Statistics, *Projections of Education Statistics to 2007*.

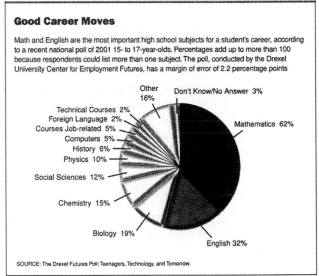

Good Career Moves

Math and English are the most important high school subjects for a student's career, according to a recent national poll of 2001 15- to 17-year-olds. Percentages add up to more than 100 because respondents could list more than one subject. The poll, conducted by the Drexel University Center for Employment Futures, has a margin of error of 2.2 percentage points

Other 16%
Technical Courses 2%
Foreign Language 2%
Courses Job-related 5%
Computers 5%
History 6%
Physics 10%
Social Sciences 12%
Chemistry 15%
Biology 19%
Don't Know/No Answer 3%
Mathematics 62%
English 32%

SOURCE: The Drexel Futures Poll: Teenagers, Technology, and Tomorrow.

Reprinted with permission from *Education Week*. Vol. 17, *1*, Sept. 3, 1997. Vol. 17, *2* Sept. 10, 1997.

Figure 5.2
How to Read Graphic Material
Adapted from Kanar (1995) and Smith (1989).

Read the title. The title describes or summarizes the presentation.

Read all narrative text, including footnotes and italicized material.

Note the source and date of the data. Is the graph based on current information?

Read the labels and legend. How are the numerical values presented? In thousands? In millions? In percentages?

Note the trends. Find the extremes, averages, and increases and decreases.

Draw conclusions. What does it mean? How does it relate to the text you read?

Complete Box 5.2 for practice in interpreting graphic aids.

The graphic aids in Figure 5.1 were presented without text. In print material, these aids are usually presented with detailed text material. Your approach when reading and studying should be to refer to graphic aids for clarification.

Refer to some of the graphic aids in this or previous chapters in this book. Read the text that accompanies the graphic aid and note how it condenses and clarifies information. Does the graphic aid convince you of the position presented?

Using graphic aids enables you to go beyond the text. Next you will learn to read between the lines.

Reading Between the Lines

Suppose that your steady date says, "I think we should start seeing other people." If you read "between the lines" of this statement, you may infer that the person is really saying, "I want to break off this relationship without hurting you too much." As the person who hears this statement, you simultaneously evaluate it. Reading between the lines and critically evaluating words are just as essential in college reading as they are in personal relationships.

Evaluating the texts you read and making inferences about implied meanings are important skills for college study. Thistlethwaite (1990) suggests that you should think about the following things as you read:

1. **The credentials or authority of the writer**—What is the author's background? Is this background sufficient to write this text? For example, has the author written other books on the same or related topics? Does the author have a degree in the field that is the basis for the book? Not every source of opinion is equally valid. For example, a rock star who becomes a political spokesperson is unlikely to be as well informed about legal issues as a district attorney.

2. **The biases or objectivity of the writer**—Does the author present one side or both sides of the issue? Are certain points omitted that should have been presented to the reader? Some writers are one-sided to stimulate controversy or promote a single viewpoint. For example, you would expect antiabortionists to present one perspective and to believe that they are right. You would not expect their leaflets to present the viewpoint of the pro-abortionists.

3. **The purpose for writing the article, poem, editorial, or story**—Is the author attempting to make readers aware of a problem, inform them about an issue, appeal to their emotions, persuade them to a certain viewpoint, entertain them, critique something, or convince the reader to take action? For example, an editorial in a newspaper usually has the purpose of persuading the reader or "winning over" the reader to the author's point of view, while the purpose of a movie review is to critique the film.

4. **The recency of the information**—What indication is there that the text is based on recent information? If the material is not current (check the copyright date), is there a need for more recent information to be included? For example, a position on nuclear armament that is supported by voter data collected in 1985 would be less convincing than data collected during the current year.

5. **Support for issues**—Which issues raised by the author are factual? Which are the author's opinion? Does the author use connotative words to persuade the reader? Connotations are words that the reader associates with positive or negative emotions. For example, consider the difference in shades of meaning in these word clusters: *gaunt* and *slender; obese* and *husky. Gaunt* and *obese* have negative connotations; *slender* and *husky* are more positive ways to describe someone's appearance. If a writer says that the voter turnout was low, it has a very different connotation from saying it was "disappointing" or "pitiful."

6. **The writer's conclusions**—What are the author's conclusions? Do these conclusions make sense in view of the text that has been presented? For example, if one research report states that "44% of the respondents . . ." and another says that "nearly half of all . . . ," the second sounds stronger, even though the data are the same.

7. **The biases or objectivity of the reader**—What background do you have that will enable you to read the text critically? What are your biases regarding the topic? Note that number 2 in this list of issues to consider when reading between the lines refers to the writer's objectivity. A reader who is actively lobbying for gay rights, for example, might respond differently than another person to an article demanding that information about HIV-positive patients be divulged to all employees.

Refer to Box 5.3 to evaluate some sources of information.

Next is a selection on day care and the notes of a reader who has thought critically about the selection. Read the selection, then note the thought processes of the critical reader who has applied the items noted previously. Refer to Figure 5.3 to review these strategies. Keep in mind that the selection is a small portion of a chapter.

> The greatest controversy around maternal employment is associated with the fact that a majority of women with babies under one year of age are now working outside of the home, often leaving their infants in day care. In 1986, the noted psychologist Jay Belsky expressed some reservations about placing children in day care for more than twenty hours a week during their first year of life, suggesting that this posed a "risk factor" for "insecure attachment" to mothers. A recent study in Dallas, Texas, found that the children of mothers who returned to work during their child's first year scored more poorly than did other children in social and academic functioning. But other studies do not replicate the Texas finding, even for mothers who return to work very shortly after birth. And Belsky himself has strongly objected to conservative attempts to turn his tentative cautions into a full-scale indictment of early day care. In Sweden, Belsky notes, where women have more well-resourced child-care centers to choose

**Figure 5.3
Reading Between the Lines**

Consider:

Reader's

- background
- objectivity

Author's

- credentials
- objectivity
- conclusions

Text's

- purpose
- recency
- supporting information

from after their six months of paid parental leave are up, studies find no such negative effects of maternal return to employment before the child's first birthday.* (Coontz, 1992, p. 217)

Reader's critique: The author's credentials, presented in the preface, are sound. Coontz has written a previous book on families and had the content of the book from which this paragraph came reviewed by individuals who are knowledgeable in the field. She seems to be objective, quoting research that supports the issue. The only date quoted is 1986. A reader might wonder how recent the research is. Would current research show the same results? The author draws no conclusions in this selection.

Naturally, the reader's critique is tentative because it is based on one small part of a whole section on day care in a book chapter. But it is enough to give you an example of how to critique using Figure 5.3 as a guide.

Now try to critique the following piece of writing, keeping in mind factors to consider when reading between the lines. The author of the article in which this excerpt appears is an associate professor of strategic management and public policy. He served as a research consultant for a tobacco company.

Implicitly or explicitly, teenage smokers are treated as passive victims of social forces compelling them to smoke, forces that are utterly beyond their control. In sharp contrast, careful statistical analysis of actual smoking behavior indicates that teenagers' decisions are, in an economic sense, rational: teens assess the expected benefits and costs of smoking and make their decisions accordingly. (Beales, 1994, p. 22)

Discuss your critique of this selection with someone who has read the selection. Do the two of you agree on your critique?

Throughout this chapter so far, you have been actively involved in thinking about text. Next, you will use writing as a way to interact with text.

---

* Selected excerpt from *The Way We Never Were* by Stephanie Coontz. Copyright 1992 by BasicBooks, A Division of HarperCollins Publishers Inc. Reprinted by permission of BasicBooks, a division of HarperCollins Publishers Inc.

Interacting with Text by Using Your Pencil and Other Study Tools

When you think about studying, what comes to mind? Respond to the questions in Box 5.4 to focus on studying.

Anderson and Armbruster (1984) write, "Studying is a special form of reading" (p. 657). Studying is engaging in tasks that can be identified, such as outlining, summarizing, or mapping. Studying involves the rehearsal of the text, which enables information to be put into long-term memory. Study is imperative to mastering content.

Several reading and study strategies involve writing directly inside your textbook, as this book encourages you to do. Some students avoid writing in textbooks that they purchase to "save" the text for resale at the end of the semester. Textbooks are expensive; however, the resale value is a very small portion of the original price of the book. We strongly encourage students to make maximum use of their books by "working them over"—that is, inserting post-it notes with key phrases on selected pages, making notations in the book by underlining or highlighting, and annotating in the margins to enhance the comprehension of material and to use for future study.

Campbell (1993) recommends using a pencil while reading:

> Always read with a pencil in your hand and use it. . . . Just as taking notes in class helps you attend to the lecture, using your pencil while you read helps you attend to what you are reading. . . . [T]he primary reason for using your pencil is to help you concentrate. (p. 116)

Campbell (1993) further notes that some students indicate that concentration is best accomplished by reading through quickly first and then revisiting the text to mark it. We concur with this procedure, for reasons that will become clear in the next section.

Underlining or Highlighting

Experts on studying agree: Underlining or highlighting is one of the most popular aids used to study text (Anderson & Armbruster, 1984; Harris & Sipay, 1990). This study strategy should be used after the initial reading of text. According to Harris and Sipay (1990), waiting to underline is important because summary statements may occur later in the paragraph,

---

BOX 5.4   *Improvement in Action* ⅢⅢ➡

Compare and contrast your study habits with those used by successful students.

	Me	Successful Students
Definition of studying		
Behavior while studying		
Frequency of study		
Results of study		

section, or end of the chapter. Sometimes you can waste 5 minutes searching for five points in the text only to discover that they are in the box on the next page or listed at the end of the chapter. These statements might be the key information that needs to be underlined. So, once again, previewing can help save you time and enable you to study smarter.

In highlighting or underlining, some notational system should be used to differentiate more important from less important information (Harris & Sipay, 1990). This could be as simple as a double or wavy underline for main ideas and a single underline for supporting details. Some students prefer to a use a highlighter to mark main ideas and a highlighted underline for details that support, enhance, or expand on the main ideas. One of the most common errors students make is highlighting too much (Harris & Sipay, 1990). It is important to differentiate between primary and secondary information. We know of students who underline virtually everything and thus do not discriminate between main ideas and supporting details. This approach makes the highlighted information useless for study at a later time because too much text must be reread. Remember that underlining and highlighting are designed to help you concentrate and save time.

Study the following paragraph, noting the information that has been underlined. Think about the topic, main idea, and supporting details. Envision an outline of this information. Identify the salient points and note that they have been underlined. Main ideas have a double underline; supporting details have a single underline. *EX* is an abbreviation used in the paragraph to identify an example.

> Robert Nisbet (1988) writes eloquently on the connection between war and change. Change is created through diffusion as war breaks down insulating barriers between societies. The crossbreeding and intermingling of cultures during and following a war leave all societies involved different than they were before the conflict. Wars also promote invention and discovery. *EX* During the first World War (1914–1918), the U.S. government was able, because of the pressure of war, to promote and finance the development of such technologies as the airplane, automobile, and radio, each of which contributed to the social and cultural revolution that followed the war. And America's culture, both during and after World War I, was exported to societies all over the world. (Shepard, 1993, p. 580)

Notice the features of the underlined components of the paragraph. The main idea sentence, if it is stated, is usually the only fully underlined sentence; key words in sentences with supporting details are also underlined. Examples should be marked *EX* or *e.g.* (Latin for *exempli gratia*) and not underlined. As you read, associate the example with the points being made in the paragraph—in this case, the effect of World War I on cultural change.

Now read the paragraph in Box 5.5 that has no underlining or highlighting. Then, revisit or review the paragraph, this time underlining ideas using a double underline for the main idea and a single underline for supporting details. Finally, check your underlining with the model-marked paragraph in Box 5.6. Remember to be selective in underlining.

Your marking may not exactly match the model marking; however, compare the markings in general. Did you differentiate between main ideas and supporting details? Were you selective in your underlining?

Another rereading strategy allows the reader more interaction with text than underlining or highlighting. This strategy is annotating and involves writing in the text margins.

Marginal Annotating

Putting ideas and responses into your own words (paraphrasing) really helps make the information stay with you. Associating something familiar with some new information helps you remember the new information. For example, an incident or experience in your biology lab in high school could help you remember information related to the topic when you

BOX 5.5   *Improvement in Action* IIII➡

The echo sounder works by transmitting sound waves toward the ocean bottom. A delicate receiver intercepts the echo reflected from the bottom, and a clock precisely measures the time interval to fractions of a second. By knowing the velocity of the sound waves in water (about 1,500 meters per second) and the time required for the energy pulse to reach the ocean floor, the depth can be established.* (Tarbuck & Lutgens, 1990, p. 482)

Also, identify the topic and main idea.

Topic:

Main idea:

---

* From *The Earth: An Introduction to Physical Geology* (3rd ed., p. 482), by E. J. Tarbuck and F. K. Lutgens, 1990, Upper Saddle River, NJ: Merrill/Prentice Hall. Copyright 1990 by Prentice Hall, Inc. Reprinted by permission of Prentice Hall, Upper Saddle River, NJ.

BOX 5.6   *Improvement in Action* IIII➡

The echo sounder works by transmitting sound waves toward the ocean bottom. A delicate receiver intercepts the echo reflected from the bottom, and a clock precisely measures the time interval to fractions of a second. By knowing the velocity of the sound waves in water (about 1,500 meters per second) and the time required for the energy pulse to reach the ocean floor, the depth can be established. (Tarbuck & Lutgens, 1990, p. 482)

Topic: Echo sounder

Main idea: The echo sounder measures the depth of the scan.

come across it again. A note of this incident in the margin of your textbook will aid remembering information.

According to Bazerman (1992), interacting with the text by underlining important ideas, marking supporting arguments, and determining the meanings of unfamiliar words deal with the "surface meaning of the text." One way to get below the surface meaning is to make marginal annotations that will help you clarify or evaluate the text. For example, note the annotations on the following text:

In Chapter 6.2 we discuss some of the hazards in the workplace for *both* male and female workers. For women, however, a unique danger exists on the job, *sexual harassment*. Although workplace dangers such as unsafe working conditions are of an impersonal nature, sexual harassment is different, entailing violence perpetrated in a personal manner. Moreover, sexual harassment exists in settings other than the workplace and is committed by others than one's employer. For these reasons we discuss sexual harassment as interpersonal violence, rather than corporate crime. (Beirne & Messerschmidt, 1991, p. 89)

Bazerman (1992) makes some suggestions for annotating text. He stresses that you should freely write your reactions. These may include approval/disapproval, disagreements, exceptions, examples, implications, associations, and underlying assumptions of the text. Once you get a sense of annotating, you can forget thinking specifically about these categories and just react. Try annotating the text that follows and compare your annotations with those of a classmate. Remember, your annotations may differ from another's annotated text due to the readers' different perspectives. You may need to check your dictionary for any unfamiliar words; those definitions can become marginal notes.

We need a national commitment to eliminate ghettos. It is remarkable how we, as a nation, have become inured to the odious moral connotations of this term. We talk about "ghettos" with the same neutrality that we talk about "suburbs." Ghettos are nothing less than the shameful residue of slavery. It took one century after this nation declared its own freedom from colonial domination to abolish slavery. It took another century, and a protracted bloody civil rights struggle, to end official segregation. It is time for a third stage that will eliminate racial ghettos, and destroy the less visible and tangible barriers that manifest themselves in a host of inequities ranging from lower incomes to higher mortality.* (Steinberg, 1989, p. 293)

Interacting with text does not always occur on the pages of the text. The same notetaking strategies that you use during a class—mapping, summarizing, and taking notes—can be used with a textbook.

Mapping

Mapping, a form of summarizing introduced in Chapter 4, is a graphic presentation of content similar to what would be included in a traditional outline. Mapping takes a little more time than underlining or annotating. Like those strategies, it is valuable for students who are visual learners; that is, they learn best by seeing information on paper (Campbell, 1993). Mapping, which causes students to look for relationships in text, is a very efficient strategy to use when learning from text (Ruddell & Boyle, 1989). McTighe and Lyman (1988) believe that mapping helps the reader organize the information, which leads to improved critical thinking. Maps aid comprehension because they help relate prior knowledge and ideas (Richardson & Morgan, 1994).

As noted in Chapter 4, mapping begins in prereading and is completed during postreading. The finished map can be used to review (Harris & Sipay, 1990). Remember the directions for mapping from Chapter 4: Begin anywhere on the page and write the topic, main idea, or question. Next, draw lines and write and connect secondary ideas to the topic, main idea, or question. Then, find supporting details and write and connect them to the category that they support. Remember to use the author's organization as reflected in the headings and subheadings of the chapter or the chapter outline to guide you.

---

* Reprinted with the permission of Scribner, an imprint of Simon & Schuster, Inc., from *The Ethnic Myth: Race, Ethnicity, and Class in America* by Stephen Steinberg. Copyright 1989 by Stephen Steinberg. Reprinted by permission.

Prepare a map on the topic of summarizing, which will be discussed next. Begin by thinking about any previous instruction that you have received on summarizing. Put the word SUMMARIZING in the middle of a sheet of paper and record thoughts that come to mind about summarizing text. Next, preview the section on text summarizing, then read it. Use the information from that section to complete your map.

Summarizing

When you read the sports page the morning after the game, you are reading a summary. When you turn to the wedding announcements, you are reading a summary. In both cases, the summary or synopsis enables readers to recap an event in which they participated or, if they did not participate, gives them the essence of what they missed.

Text summary is an important strategy in college material to use when reading to monitor comprehension and when revisiting or reviewing the text. Summarizing text positively affects comprehension and recall of text (Pearson & Fielding, 1991). Harris and Sipay (1990) define a summary as "a brief statement that represents a condensation of information and that reflects the gist of the text" (p. 616).

Casazza (1993) uses a set of guidelines for evaluating summaries. These guidelines, also useful for writing summaries, can be grouped into categories. The first category deals with recognizing the author's purpose and emphasis, and the topic and main idea. The second category includes combining related key ideas while omitting minor details such as examples or the author's personal opinions. The final category emphasizes that summarization should be so selective that the summary length should not exceed one-third of the original text. The "one-third rule" is a general guideline and certainly would not be appropriate for summarizing lengthy text, such as a book. In this case, the summary would be much shorter. For example, read the following selection from a book on classroom discipline and management and the summary that follows (Edwards, 1997).

> To determine what discipline approach to use, you must first determine your personal philosophy and values. This determination will provide guidance as you decide which of the available discipline models is most attractive. An extensive analysis of existing theories is essential in this process. If you find that you consider the available models of discipline inadequate, you may decide to create one of your own. Then, armed with a discipline approach that has been carefully analyzed and mastered, you will be better prepared to meet the challenges of the classroom.
>
> A good discipline program should be comprehensive. Components designed to prevent as well as correct discipline problems are essential. In addition, a comprehensive discipline program should include schoolwide applications. This unit is designed to help you make these decisions. (p. 265)

The author's purpose in this textbook excerpt is to introduce the concept of selecting an approach to discipline. To summarize the excerpt, a sound approach is first to identify the topic and main idea. The topic is a brief label or title in the form of a phrase. In the previous excerpt, the **topic** is "Selecting a Discipline Approach." The **main idea** expands on the topic and should be stated in a complete sentence. It gives the essential message and reflects the author's purpose for writing or orientation to the topic. For example, the main idea of the previous excerpt could be "Careful selection of a discipline approach will enable the teacher to be prepared for teaching." The sample summary could be "Careful selection of a discipline approach will help the teacher to be prepared for teaching. First look carefully at theories of discipline. You may want to create your own. The discipline program should be comprehensive and useful beyond your classroom, and it should include prevention and correction of discipline problems."

Note the components of the summary and the conciseness of the wording. The summary is 50 words long, a bit more than one-third the length of the original text, which was

131 words. Some of the author's words are incorporated in the summary; however, the context for those words has been provided by the writer. The author's words have been paraphrased. Refer to Figure 5.4 to review key issues in summarizing text.

Read the paragraph in Box 5.7 on the events leading to the development of the popular novel, identify the main idea and supporting details, map it, and summarize the paragraph using Casazza's (1993) guidelines in Figure 5.4. Then, compare your summary to that of a classmate.

Summarizing is one writing strategy for revisiting text. Another strategy is note taking from text. Using this strategy, the reader focuses on aspects of content that differ from the focus for summarizing.

BOX 5.7   *Improvement in Action* ⅢⅢ➡

Identify the topic or main idea; map and summarize this paragraph.

Like newspapers, novels became enormously popular between 1830 and 1860. Of course, novels had been read long before 1830, and authors, among them the Scot Sir Walter Scott, had gained a wide following. But the cost of novels before 1830 had restricted their sales. Each of Scott's novels, for example, was issued in a three-volume set that retailed for as much as thirty dollars. During the 1830s and 1840s, the impact of the transportation revolution and technical advances in printing brought down the price of novels. As canals and railroads opened crossroads stores to the latest fiction, publishers in New York and Philadelphia vied to deliver inexpensive novels to the shelves. By the 1840s cheap paperbacks that sold for as little as seven cents began to flood the market. (Boyer et al., 1993, p. 363)

Does your summary adhere to Casazza's (1993) guidelines?

Figure 5.4
Guidelines for Writing Summaries

Adapted from Casazza (1993).

- Recognize author's purpose.
- Identify topic and main idea.
- Paraphrase accurately.
- Delete minor details.
- Combine/chunk similar ideas.
- Reflect author's emphasis.
- Recognize author's organization.
- Adhere to appropriate length (one-third original text).
- Exclude personal opinions.

Other Guidelines

- Work from your notes.
- Condense evenly. Be sure that your summary has information that is representative of the whole text.
- Give credit to the source in the form of a reference.

Note Taking

Nist and Simpson (1987) promote the idea of writing as a means of monitoring reading. They believe that reflecting on reading in this way gives the reader a sense of control. These authors suggest one strategy, called the *double-entry journal*, which requires reflecting on difficult-to-understand theories, concepts, and words. These are the guidelines suggested by Nist and Simpson (1987):

1. Write for a minimum of 1/2 hour.
2. Divide paper in half lengthwise. Mark the lefthand column "Copy" and the righthand column "Response."
3. In the lefthand column, copy directly from the book quotes, theories, etc., that are difficult to understand, interesting, of key importance, or need clarification.
4. In the righthand column, record whatever thoughts, questions, or comments come to mind as you attempt to make sense of what was copied. (p. 622)

Try this double-entry journal approach with the selection that follows. Using these guidelines, copy selected text on the left side of the paper; use the right side to record your thoughts, questions, and comments. Record your entries in Box 5.8.

Of all the misconceptions about love the most powerful and pervasive is the belief that "falling in love" is love or at least one of the manifestations of love. It is a potent misconception, because falling in love is subjectively experienced in a very powerful fashion as an experience of love. When a person falls in love what he or she certainly feels is "I love him" or "I love her." But two problems are immediately apparent. The first is that the experience of falling in love is specifically a sex-linked erotic experience. We do not fall in love with our children even though we may love them very deeply. We do not fall in love with our friends of the same sex—unless we are homosexually oriented—even though we may care for them greatly. We fall in love only when we are consciously or unconsciously sexually motivated. The second problem is that the experience of falling in love is invariably temporary. No matter whom we fall in love with,

---

BOX 5.8   ***Improvement in Action*** ▮▮▮▶

Compare your entries with that of a classmate. Remember that both copy and response entries of two individuals will probably differ.

Copy	Response
Example: "The first is that the experience of falling in love is specifically a sex-linked erotic experience."	*Example:* Sex-linked erotic response??? There is more to it than that!

we sooner or later fall out of love if the relationship continues long enough. This is not to say that we invariably cease loving the person with whom we fell in love. But it is to say that the feeling of ecstatic lovingness that characterizes the experience of falling in love always passes. The honeymoon always ends. The bloom of romance always fades. (Peck, 1978, p. 84)

Recall that the double-entry journal is especially suited for difficult-to-understand or technical material. It would not be reasonable to expect college students to use it with everything they read. Think of the double-entry journal as the "heavy artillery" you will use when other methods of study fail.

Read the following selection from a science text (Miller, 1993). Record your copy of hard-to-understand text and responses in Box 5.9. Again, compare your responses with those of a classmate.

A favorite debating and advertising trick is to claim that something "has not been scientifically proved." But scientists don't establish absolute proof or truth.

Science is the acceptance of what works and the rejection of what does not. That's why scientific theories may be modified, or even discarded, because of new data or more useful explanations of the data. It's also why advances in scientific knowledge are often based on vigorous disagreement, speculation, and controversy.

Scientific laws and theories are based on statistical probabilities, not certainties. Scientists trying to find out how oak trees grow cannot study any more than a minute fraction of Earth's oak trees. The growth of oak trees is affected by numerous variables—factors that vary from site to site. Scientists can study only a small number of the thousands, perhaps millions, of possible interactions of these and other variables. (p. 37)

Answers to your questions in the double-entry journal might be found in the text or answered by your professor, a classmate, a tutor, or your study group. It would be worthwhile to return to modify your notes based on follow-up discussions or further clarification. Other notes, such as those taken in class lectures, should be integrated with text reading.

Integrating Class Notes With Textbook Readings

Professors vary in their lecture styles. Some professors lecture spontaneously, relating interesting anecdotes that maintain students' attention the full class period. Other professors read their notes from behind a lectern and do not make much eye contact with the class. Still others vary the class period with some lecture, discussion, and group work. The content of lectures varies, too. Some lectures focus on the content of the reading assignment or textbook; some refer occasionally to the assignment, while other lectures seem to be unrelated to the reading assignment. Regardless of lecture style or content, it is important that you relate your lecture notes to the reading assignments that you complete. One way to do this is

BOX 5.9	*Improvement in Action* ⅢⅢ➡	
	Copy	Response

write lecture notes on alternate lines of your notebook leaving an empty space between each line of notes, or use a split-page approach similar to the double-entry journal. That is, you can put notes from the lecture on the left side of the page and related notes from the text on the right side. After the lecture, review your notes and revisit the reading that you have done for the assignment. Within your notes, make brief notations showing the relationship between the content of the lecture and reading. These notations could consist of key words or references to page numbers in the book where ideas were discussed.

Lecture notes are one way to interact with the text. Using a student study guide, if one is available, is another way of improving your study skills.

Using a Student Study Guide

Some textbook publishing companies produce a student study guide to accompany the text. The purpose of the student study guide is to elaborate on the information in the text and provide students with additional practice with textbook material. These guides usually include summaries of the chapters, suggestions for additional reading, related issues, exercises with answers, and self-test quizzes. Figure 5.5 shows a sample selection from a student study guide.

The study guide must be purchased separately from the textbook and may not seem worth the additional price, given a college student's limited budget. Look carefully at the study guide before making a decision whether to purchase it. Some study guides are quite valuable in extending interaction with the text and are worth the purchase price if you will

Figure 5.5
Sample from a Student Study Guide in Educational Psychology
From *Educational Psychology: Student Study Guide* (p. 234), by M. M. Bierly, D. C. Berliner, and N. L. Gage, 1979, Chicago: Rand McNally.

Application of Key Concepts

The terms listed below refer to important concepts that were discussed in this chapter. Carefully read each descriptive statement, and identify the concept or concepts each statement implies. Place the corresponding letter of the concept(s) you select in the space provided.

Concepts A. genuineness
B. empathy
C. facilitator of learning
D. positive regard for others
. . .

Descriptive Statements

_____ 1. I think that your idea of starting a school newspaper is a good one, and since I don't have enough background to help you, why don't you arrange for an interview with the editor of the newspaper here in town. . . .

_____ 2. Look, this hasn't been one of my better days, so if you could all please relax for a minute, I'll try to explain this problem to you.

_____ 3. I think I know how you feel about not being chosen to be on the team.

_____ 4. Sam, you're certainly entitled to your opinion about this—it's as valid as anybody else's.

. . .

Answers: 1C, 2A, 3B, 4D

take time to use them. If your instructor ordered the student study guide to the text, some of the course assignments may be from the student study guide. If you are still unsure of the study guide's importance, wait until the first class meeting and ask the instructor about it.

If you spend the money for the student study guide, you will certainly want to use it. Before reading the assigned chapter, you could use the guide to preview chapter content and get a sense of the important concepts in the chapter. After you read and revisit the chapter, select sections of the student study guide to complete. Vocabulary review and exercises to enhance understanding and recall are important. Try the quizzes and check your answers. These will enhance your memory along with other memory aids and contribute to your confidence with the material. By the way, this book has the study guide built into it, mainly through the "Improvement in Action" boxes and the activities at the end of the chapters.

Use Box 5.10 to revisit the strategies for interacting with text presented in this chapter.

Memory Aids to Reading

Many college students express the concern that they read but do not seem to retain what they have read. This problem affects all readers at times, even the most proficient ones. Usually, the influences that seem to erase information from memory include a host of things that interfere with active reading:

1. **Preoccupation with other matters**—your thoughts keep wandering to all you have to do rather than remaining focused on the reading.
2. **Repeated interruptions**—your train of thought keeps being derailed by visitors, telephone calls, and so forth.
3. **Work with unfamiliar material**—you are encountering reading material for which prior knowledge is absent or insufficient.

The strategies you have learned thus far in this chapter are all designed to enhance your ability to remember what you have read—if you make a commitment to use them. In his book *The Seven Habits of Highly Effective People,* Covey (1989) suggests that the upward spiral in any undertaking begins with **learn, do,** and **commit** and follows through with these three elements on increasingly higher levels. Figure 5.6 explains how to apply learn, do, and commit to the reading strategies in the chapter. You will be more likely to remember what you have read because you have actively interacted with the text.

Understanding the memory process helps you realize that the strategies learned in this chapter are valuable for remembering information. The process of remembering begins when you first attend to information by listening or reading. To begin, you selectively attend to information that enters the brain through your senses. You may totally disregard the information if it does not concern you, or, if it does, the information may be entered into short-term memory. Short-term memory is working memory. An individual who reads a chapter of a book by just reading over the words and not interacting with the text in some way commits the information, at best, to short-term memory. It is quite possible that the information might be discarded even before it gets into short-term memory. What does all of this mean for you as you study? It means that readers who fail to interact with the text will not remember much. A student might say, "But I read the chapter," yet that student has not read the material in the sense of comprehending its meaning. Smith (1985) contends that real reading stops when meaning is lost. So, in many cases, it would be more accurate to say that students "look at" their books rather than actually read or study them, and so they do not recall what they have read.

Improvement in Action ‖‖➡

From the list, choose the three strategies that you consider to be of greatest value to you for study. Indicate the value of each.

Strategy	**Value for Me**
Underlining or highlighting	
Marginal annotating	
Mapping	
Summarizing	
Note taking from text	
Integrating class notes with textbook readings	
Using a study guide (if available)	

**Figure 5.6
Learn, Do, and Commit
Applied to Reading
Strategies**

- **Learn**—first master reading strategies.
- **Do**—practice them regularly.
- **Commit**—make a conscious decision to apply them to increasingly challenging tasks.

To put the information into long-term memory, the reader has to get actively involved by rehearsing information. For example, if you memorize and frequently use that phone number you looked up, you will remember it. If a period of time elapses without your using the number, you will forget it. That is the way it is with studying. You need to engage in strategies to put information into long-term memory and keep it there until you no longer need it. We do not expect to pull money out of our wallets if we have not put any money into them (Pauk, 1984). The same holds true for recall of what we have read—you get out of it what you put into it.

You can use four techniques to enhance your memory (Ellis, 1984):

1. **Relate what you learn to your goals.** When you want to remember, you usually can. Suppose that there is a musical performance by your favorite artist on television. Your goal is to see it, and you will do what it takes to make sure you do not forget to watch, including such things as marking the TV listings, posting a note by your favorite chair, setting the VCR, or adding the program to your list of things to do. If your purpose is to score well on an exam, you must invest even more energy in studying than you would in making sure you see that program.

2. **Make associations between your prior experiences and your reading.** Suppose you are reading an article about high blood pressure, a health problem that your mother has. As you read, you will relate information in the article to her behavior. The article says, for instance, that consistency in taking medication is a must, so you ask yourself, "Does Mom take her medication regularly?" Visualize the new information in relation to what you have read already in the text. For example, if you were reading about a theory of human cognitive development in psychology, think about this theory in relation to another theory that has been presented in the book.

3. **Rehearse information.** Suppose you had the lead in a play. You would rehearse your lines by yourself and with the play cast until you had committed the lines to memory. Reciting aloud provides triple-strength learning (D. Skoner, personal communication, December 5, 1994), which means you are three times more likely to remember the information. Recite and repeat aloud something you want to remember. For example, if you need to memorize a definition for a word, recite it aloud again and again—overlearn it.

4. **Distribute your learning.** If you are practicing to run a marathon, you are more likely to increase your endurance by running 10 miles three times a week than running 30 miles once a week. Generally speaking, your memory works more efficiently if you study for two 2-hour periods rather than for one 4-hour session. For example, when you are studying for a history exam, distribute your study over several days rather than cramming one evening.

All of the techniques used to study from text—underlining, annotating, mapping, summarizing, and taking notes—will enhance your memory of the text content. However, other memory aids can support the learning of text material, too, including creating mnemonics, chunking information, and using text features to review.

Creating Mnemonics

Knowing information helps you feel more confident (Richardson & Morgan, 1994). Mnemonics is simply making associations with familiar information to help remember new information. This technique is especially valuable when information is difficult to remember because the components are mostly unrelated. For example, *ROY G. BIV* is commonly used to help remember the name of each color in the spectrum of light: *R*ed, *O*range, *Y*ellow, *G*reen, *B*lue, *I*ndigo, and *V*iolet. This acronym is easy to remember because it contains the first letters of each of the words and can be associated with those colors.

Other forms of mnemonics are also frequently used. For example, a mnemonic could be in the form of a sentence, such as "Every good boy does fine," for the notes of the lines of the treble clef (E, G, B, D, F). A mnemonic could be stated as a rhyme, like "Thirty days has September, /April, June, and November." Another type of mnemonic that can be used for remembering is to visualize and relate the items. Using this technique, you associate and connect images. For example, suppose you were learning Ellis's (1984) techniques to enhance your memory discussed previously: (a) relate, (b) associate, (c) rehearse, and (d) distribute. You could visualize brain activity: "memory—mind; relate—in the brain information is related; associate—new information is associated to information already in the brain; and so on. Visualizing this information supports your efforts to remember.

Suppose that you wanted to create your own mnemonic for summarizing the steps in Casazza's (1993) guidelines for evaluating summaries suggested previously. You could use *RCOL*: *R*ecognize the author's purpose, topic, and main idea; *c*ombine key ideas while *o*mitting minor details; *l*ength should be less than one-third of the original text. As this example illustrates, mnemonics can be personal creations that enable readers to remember.

Now try to create a mnemonic for Nist and Simpson's (1987) double-entry journal system for note taking introduced earlier in this chapter. Remember, a mnemonic is your creation. One we might develop would differ from yours; that does not matter. What counts is that the mnemonic does what it is supposed to do—aid your memory. An appropriate place to record your mnemonics would be in the margin of the text. When reviewing using your annotations, you would soon know whether the mnemonics are working for you. Do they help you recall information?

Refer to Box 5.11 and try to determine when a mnemonic might enhance your memory.

Larger amounts of information than those appropriate for mnemonics can be grouped for easier remembering by using a technique called *chunking* (Richardson & Morgan, 1994).

Chunking Information

Saturday is often errand day for college students. How could you remember this list of errands (without a note pad) by organizing them geographically? That is, think about the route you will travel to complete them. The list of errands:

- Do laundry.
- Shop for food.
- Pick up a birthday card.
- Get a haircut.
- Buy a pen refill.
- Buy a university-imprinted sweatshirt.

The "route" could be go to the laundry (it is on the next floor and less crowded early on a Saturday morning); then go to the bookstore and get a birthday card, pen refill, and sweatshirt; walk downtown and get a haircut; then go food shopping. These could be regrouped for different rationales; however, the map provides the plan. You probably would not need to look at your to-do list once you thought about the route. You have just "chunked" information.

Chunking is done by categorizing related information. For example, read the following list of assumptions about educational leadership by Frymier (1991).* As you read, think about ways to categorize the assumptions.

1. Each person is unique.
2. Every person has worth.
3. All people can learn.
4. Schools exist to help students learn.
5. Curriculum is the major means by which the schools help people learn.
6. Curriculum includes what is taught and how it is taught.
7. Curriculum can and must be improved.
8. Those most directly concerned with curriculum (students, teachers, parents, and administrators) should be involved in curriculum improvement efforts.
9. Those who willingly work on curriculum improvement will be influenced by the developmental efforts.
10. The basic responsibility of those in educational leadership roles is to improve curriculum. (p. 163)

---

* From "Reflections on Principles of Educational Leadership" (p. 163), by J. Frymier, in D. L. Burleson (Ed.), *Reflections: Personal Essays by 33 Distinguished Scholars*, 1991, Bloomington, IN: Phi Delta Kappa. Copyright 1991 by Phi Delta Kappa. Reprinted by permission.

One way to relate the information would be to group items 1 and 2 about the individual; items 3, 4, and 5 about people learning; items 6 and 7 about what is curriculum (what is studied in school); and items 8, 9, and 10 about curriculum improvement. Note that the last item in each set leads into the next category. You may have "chunked" differently; that is fine. The issue here is that you thought about this list in terms of categories that helped you remember the items and related them. Look at Figure 5.7 for hints in chunking various types of information.

Chunking enhances memory because of the necessity for relating information and visualizing it, which enables you to recall more information. Another technique used to refresh your memory is referring to text features.

Using Text Features to Review

Features of the text such as the table of contents, chapter objectives, questions, and summaries can be used to refresh your memory. Many tables of contents in books provide a detailed chapter summary in list format. Reviewing these major topics in the chapter would indicate to you how much you can recall from the information presented. Figure 5.8 presents a sample table of contents to accompany a chapter on how to get started in writing for publication.

Other valuable chapter components for review are chapter objectives found at the beginning of the chapter, or prereading questions like those found at the beginning of each chapter in this book and chapter questions found at the end of the chapter. The chapter summary, also, serves as an abbreviated review of the chapter. Remember that sometimes it helps to read the end of the chapter or the summary section first.

Strategies for study generally are used independently. However, your knowledge base, understanding, and thinking can be extended through a study group.

Figure 5.7
Hints for Chunking Information

*From "Reflections on Principles of Educational Leadership" (p. 163), by J. Frymier, in D. L. Burleson (Ed.), *Reflections: Personal Essays by 33 Distinguished Scholars,* 1991, Bloomington, IN: Phi Delta Kappa. Copyright 1991 by Phi Delta Kappa. Reprinted by permission.

After determining that the information needs to be remembered:

1. look for items that could be grouped for ease in remembering—that is, some relationship exists among them;
2. group the items; and
3. memorize them, using a mnemonic, if desired.

Figure 5.8
Sample Table of Contents

From *Writing for Successful Publication* (p. viii), by K. T. Henson, 1991, Bloomington, IN: National Education Service.

Chapter Three: Getting Started 29

1. The Right Title 29
2. Selecting Titles for Nonfiction Journal Articles 31
3. Writing the First Sentence 34
4. Paragraphing 37
5. Go Ahead and Write 38

Study Groups

One popular study arrangement on college campuses is a study group. This strategy is valuable in courses with complicated and technical material or when varying viewpoints add insight into the information being studied. Study groups may form as the need arises or involve a group of students in a course who get together at regular intervals to study.

Ellis (1984) feels that a study group provides support by encouraging you to study. It also offers the opportunity to develop relationships with other students. Ellis notes that some days you just do not feel like studying; however, your commitment to a study group makes it more likely that you will study on those days.

Organizing a Study Group

Ellis (1994) gives numerous suggestions for organizing a study group. First, you will want to study in a group that has similar goals to yours, with students who are serious about their academic progress. This is one time when friendship and popularity are not the best criteria for selection. Choose classmates who are good students, participate actively in class, and experience success in college. Your best approach is to make personal contacts and invite classmates to form a study group. If these contacts do not work, advertise on the chalkboard in your class, in the student newspaper, or in other places on campus where notices can be posted. Do try to be selective in forming a study group. Ellis (1994) suggests that the study group be limited to five or six members to be effective.

Locating a Place and Time to Meet

Establishing a location for the study group to meet may be more problematic than recruiting students for the study group. On your campus, the library or residence halls may have small group study rooms available. These may need to be reserved well in advance of your planned study session. Often classroom buildings are open for student use. A classroom might be available, especially in the evening. A student apartment might be a good site; however, probably the more formal the setting, such as a library study room, the less distracted your group will be by other activities.

Determining a time when everyone in the group can meet may be more problematic than finding a location. Students have busy schedules juggling classes, library research, and often work and family responsibilities. Decide on a time that meets everyone's schedule and stay with it, so that study group members can easily remember it and consistently attend.

Conducting the Session

Ellis (1984) suggests how to manage the study group sessions. First, set the dates to meet and the length of the time period, and establish the responsibilities for each group member. At the beginning of each session, review the agenda for the session. Activities can include discussing and debating issues for greater understanding, comparing class notes, and testing each other by asking questions for general review purposes or for preparation for exams. At the end of the study, establish the agenda for the next session before the group disbands. Make sure that each group member prepares for the meeting, so that everyone contributes to the session (Pauk, 1984).

Tackling Difficult Assignments

Recall that the double-entry journal is especially well suited for challenging reading material. A difficult assignment is a perfect example of what the study group might discuss and clarify. Each member would come prepared with an interpretation, including clarification through additional reading or discussion with the instructor or a tutor. The contribution of each member would enhance understanding.

Solving Problems

Problems may occur in your study group. Some problems might be lack of regular attendance by members, conflicts with each other, lack of preparation by all members, or the inability to stay on task, which results in a lack of productivity in the session. Establishing some ground rules when the group initially organizes might help in these instances. For example, define the consequences if an individual does not attend the study group regularly or does not prepare for the sessions. Determine how the group will monitor its off-task behavior. Predetermined guidelines will help monitor situations like these and keep the group working cohesively.

Make every effort to get your study group to work. An added advantage of studying together is "While schools emphasize competition, study groups foster cooperation and getting and giving help so that all may achieve academic success" (Gall, Gall, Jacobsen, & Bullock, 1990, p. 83).

Study Group Alternative

Students on some campuses form study groups that "meet" electronically. Through electronic mail (e-mail) individuals in a study group can send messages to each other, pose questions for study, and respond to those questions. A discussion group can be formed using a LISTSERV (Parson, 1997; Ryder & Graves, 1996/1997). All members on the list automatically receive the messages anyone sends. The discussion is ongoing but students check and respond to this type of e-mail at their convenience. The topics discussed could be the same as those discussed when the study group meets: reactions to interesting issues, viewpoints of supplementary reading, requests for clarification on class notes or text material, or review of potential test questions. If your group wants to interact with each other simultaneously like a real study session, you can set up a CHAT ROOM for your group. For instructions on using the Internet for interacting with each other, check the technology service on your campus.

 ### *Voices of Successful Students*

"I have been exposed to a mountain of reading. This amount has forced me to learn to read things more than one time if I don't understand, then highlight the main ideas to remember."

"I found out that the more I read, the better I comprehend. It wasn't until I started writing while I was reading that my comprehension really started to improve. I had never done this before in high school, and I suddenly realized that the most successful students had been doing this all along."

"Try to find a quiet place to read. Set reading intervals to maybe a half an hour, then take a break."

"I've improved reading by the amount of reading that I do each day—most of my classes in my major require a lot of reading. I comprehend it well because I am interested in it."

Cooperative Learning: A Study Group

Practice organizing a study group. Work with four or five students in your class. Follow the guidelines suggested by Ellis (1994) and establish the framework for a study group. Then, with your study group, use "reading between the lines" as a study topic. Review the strategy and then, independently, write the answers to the short quiz here. Compare the answers of group members. At the end of the session, evaluate the session and make suggestions for improvement.

Quiz

1. Why must the biases of both the writer and reader be considered when interpreting text?
2. How do you know whether the author is qualified to write on the topic?
3. How would you respond to a classmate who remarks, "I don't have time to read between the lines"?

Self-Improvement Strategy: Text Revisitation

Choose one of the text revisitation strategies mentioned in this chapter, other than underlining or highlighting, then revisit an assigned reading from another class using this strategy. Prepare to report on the application of the strategy, evaluating its values and limitations. Report your reaction to the class.

Writing and Reflecting: Self-Prescription for Study Improvement

Using what you have learned in this chapter, write a "self-prescription" for study improvement; that is, in your piece identify the strategies that you are committed to implement to improve your interaction with text. For each strategy, indicate the value that you see in the strategy and how it will enhance your learning.

Reading Selections

Follow the directions specified for each reading selection. You may need to review the text revisitation strategies before implementing them.

Reading Selection 1

What do you propose as a way to solve the crime problem? As you read the following selection, think about the differences in the three ideological approaches (Conklin, 1995).*

Identify the main idea for each approach. Use this main idea as a basis for highlighting or underlining the salient points of the selection.

---

* From *Criminology* (5th ed., pp. 526–528), J. E. Conkoin, 1995, Boston: Allyn & Bacon. Copyright 1995 by Allyn & Bacon. Reprinted by permission.

Ideological Approaches to Solving the Crime Problem

Three general ideological orientations toward the crime problem can be delineated: a conservative approach, a liberal approach, and a radical approach. Each position includes a set of general beliefs and assumptions about the causes of crime and the appropriate ways to reduce it. The assumptions of each position underlie the policies proposed by its adherents, even though those assumptions may not always be made explicit (Miller, 1973; Fairchild & Webb, 1985; McGarrell & Flanagan, 1987).

The Conservative Approach

The **conservative approach** seeks to preserve the status quo of criminals, who are seen as challengers to the existing social order. Conservatives focus on the high costs of crime and the criminal justice system. They emphasize conventional crimes such as the FBI's index offenses; white-collar crime and government corruption are ignored, denied, or even justified.

Conventional crime is attributed to the lower and working classes, who are thought to be improperly socialized or irresponsible. Crime is said to be caused by the defective family structure of the poor and by the failure of those families to inculcate in children the values appropriate to a law-abiding life. Conservatives' concern with the permissiveness and immorality of groups that have high rates of conventional crime has a long history, going back to at least as far as nineteenth-century Paris, where crime was attributed to the "dangerous classes," a term synonymous with the lower and working classes (Chevalier, 1973).

The conservative solution to the crime problem is to encourage "adherence to the legitimate directives of constituted authority" (Miller, 1973: 144). The means to do this include the improvement of family life, better discipline, more self-control, and harsher and more certain penalties. Because conservatives are ideologically opposed to the intrusion of the government into homes, even into homes that produce criminals, they rarely give much attention to programs to strengthen the family or to teach parents better ways to instill law-abiding values in their children. Instead, conservatives emphasize deterrence, incapacitation, and just deserts, and rely on the criminal justice system to mete out certain, severe, prompt, and just penalties. Conservatives call for a larger, more efficient, and less restrained police force; a higher conviction rate in court; less probation and parole; longer prison sentences; and more capital punishment. Conservatives are often willing to sacrifice or abridge the procedural rights of defendants, and indeed the rights of the entire population, in order to increase the chances of arrest, conviction, and punishment.

The Liberal Approach

The **liberal approach** holds that crime can be reduced by policies that attack its underlying causes. Liberals claim that people are the products of the social and economic system in which they live. Inequality of income and power and the lack of opportunities for certain groups increase the probability that more members of disadvantaged groups will engage in behavior defined as criminal by those who hold power.

Liberals believe society can be reformed in ways that will reduce the crime rate, but they reject the idea that a full-scale revolution is required. They tend to focus on conventional crimes, which they see as a lower-class and working-class phenomenon that results from poverty, discrimination, and oppression. As a consequence, they propose that educational and vocational training, welfare assistance, job opportunities, antidiscrimination laws, and community organization and change can reduce the crime rate. Liberals traditionally have argued that the primary function of criminal penalties should be the rehabilitation of convicted offenders, but with growing evidence that many treatment programs do not work, some liberals have shifted to a theory of punishment that stresses just deserts to a better degree (Bayer, 1981).

The Radical Approach

A third perspective on the crime problem is the **radical approach.** This viewpoint focuses on crime by both the underprivileged and the privileged, and attributes crime by both groups to the conditions of a capitalist society. Radicals point to evidence—such as some self-report studies—that indicates that crime is more evenly distributed among the classes than is suggested by official crime statistics. Differences in crime rates among various groups are then attributed to the differential handling of groups by the criminal justice system rather than to actual differences in their criminal behavior. The crime problem is regarded as a socially defined product of selective crime reporting and recording, media attention, and differential treatment by the criminal justice system.

The radical approach places greater emphasis on white-collar crime and political corruption than do the conservative and liberal approaches. Conventional criminals are seen as victims of a capitalist system, rather than as offenders against society. Radicals shift attention from the criminal offender to the social and economic system that defines certain behavior as criminal and pushes people into crime by failing to meet their needs. The radical perspective emphasizes justice rather than crime, and looks at the negative implications of values such as competition and material success.

The radical perspective offers few specific solutions to the crime problem, other than calling for the construction of a new and basically different social system, one that is vaguely described as communist or socialist. Whether such a society now exists anywhere or can be created in the future is open to question; radicals rarely describe in detail the alternative society that might keep crime to a minimum. (p. 525)

Reading Selection 2

Suppose that you invented a new piece of computer software—something that took you over 2 years of work. Any pieces of your software that are illegally copied will rob you of your income. Now read this selection to discover the rights of the software buyer and seller (Ingalsbe, 1992).*

Read between the lines and note your reactions in the margins. Make a map of this selection, also.

Ethics of Copying Software, and Software Licenses

Unauthorized copying and distribution of software is illegal, period. It is also an unethical use of the software to which you have access.

When an author creates a new book, such as the one you are reading, the author can obtain a copyright, which provides legal protection against unauthorized copying or use of the author's work. Similarly, computer software can be protected legally by a copyright, which

---

* From *Using Computers and Applications Software* (2nd ed., p. C-32), by L. Ingalsbe, 1992, Upper Saddle River, NJ: Merrill/Prentice Hall. Copyright 1992 by Prentice Hall, Inc. Reprinted by permission of Prentice Hall, Upper Saddle River, NJ.

establishes a limitation on how a person may legally use the program. . . . Other legal protections, such as trademark registration and coverage by patent law, are also granted.

Generally, you do not really buy the software when you acquire an application software package; you actually are buying the right to use the package according to instructions contained within a software license. The software license is often printed on the box or envelope containing the software, with a warning that opening the wrapping containing the software constitutes your acceptance of the developer's conditions of use.

In most cases, you are given the right to use the software on one computer and to make a single **archival copy** of the software as a backup to guard against accidental loss. Sometimes a software company will grant the buyer the right to use the software on more than one computer; a **site license,** for example, grants the right to use the software on all computers installed at a single location or within a company.

Although you may "get away" with making a copy for a friend, you really are breaking the law, unless the software you are using is public domain software or shareware that gives you the right to copy it. Actually, you do not gain by "pirating" a copy of software. If you do not have a legally obtained copy of the software, you will not be able to get assistance from the developer, and you will not be notified of special offers for updated versions. Very importantly, you probably will not have access to the program's operating instructions which are usually contained in the manual shipped with the legal copies. (p. C-32)

Reading Selection 3

Believe it or not, there is not just one theory of human development. Read the following selection to discover three ways in which our development can be explained (Steinberg & Belsky, 1991).*

Summarize the selection, and use a mnemonic to remember the major theories of human development. Also, prepare double-entry journal entries for the three theories.

The major theories of human development fall into three categories: psychoanalytic, behavioral/learning, and cognitive. Each type of theory tends to focus on a different aspect of development. Psychoanalytic thinkers, who study human **emotions,** are particularly interested in the psychological conflicts that arise at different stages of development. Learning theorists, or behaviorists, in contrast, focus on **behavior** rather than feelings. Outside stimuli in the environment, not internal feelings, they contend, model and shape behavior. Finally, cognitive theorists are concerned with processes of **thought:** with how people perceive, understand,

and think about their world. This school argues that we can best understand development by looking closely at how individuals reason. No one theory is complete, but together these different theoretical perspectives provide insights that help us understand the path of development from infancy through adolescence. (p. 7)

Reading Selection 4

Are you going steady, engaged, or married? If so, how did you find your partner? Compare and contrast your search for a partner with Bee's (1992) explanation of selecting a partner.*

Take notes on any concepts that are new to you in this selection. Then write a summary paragraph of the selection.

Finding a Partner

The process of mate selection preoccupies most of us in our teens and twenties; for many adults it becomes a preoccupation again after a divorce. We are searching for a partner with whom we hope to spend the rest of our lives. Just what attracts one person to another? How does a couple move past passion or intimacy to commitment? Why do some early combinations break up, while others become stable? Social scientists have tried very hard to answer these questions, but despite the efforts, understanding still largely eludes us.

The most widely accepted theories describe mate selection as a series of "filters" or steps (Perlman & Fehr, 1987). One example: Bernard Murstein (1970, 1976, 1986) suggests that when you meet a prospective partner, you first check for the degree of match on basic "external" characteristics, such as appearance, or manners, or apparent social class. If this first hurdle is passed, you then check for a match on attitudes and beliefs, such as politics, sex, or religion. Finally, if you are still interested in one another, the degree of "role fit" becomes an issue: Do your prospective partner's expectations fit with your needs or inclinations? Is there sexual compatibility, or agreement on sex roles?

There is some support for filter theories of courtship, but the filtering process probably occurs very early in the courtship process rather than over a period of months or years as Murstein originally suggested and may not follow a strict sequence. The one thing that is clear is that we choose our partners more on the basis of similarity than on any other single basis—a process sociologists refer to as *assortive mating* or *homogamy.* We are far more likely to choose someone who is similar in age, social class background, race or ethnic group, religious preference or involvement, interests, attitudes, and temperament than someone who differs from us in these respects. Furthermore, long-term partnerships based on such similarity are more likely to endure than

* From *Infancy, Childhood, and Adolescence: Development in Context* (p. 7), by L. Steinberg and J. Belsky, 1991, New York: McGraw-Hill. Copyright 1991 by McGraw-Hill, Inc. Reprinted by permission.

* From *The Journey of Adulthood* (2nd ed., p. 250), by Helen L. Bee, 1992, Upper Saddle River, NJ: Prentice Hall. Copyright 1992 by Prentice Hall, Inc. Reprinted by permission of Prentice Hall, Upper Saddle River, NJ.

are those in which there are wide differences between the partners (Murstein, 1986).

Several studies of couples who eventually marry also show that there are distinct changes in facets of the relationship as a couple moves from casual dating to greater commitment to marriage (Huston, et al. 1981). Feelings of belongingness and attachment (what Sternberg would call intimacy) increase over time as do "maintenance behaviors," such as disclosing feelings, trying to solve problems, and being willing to change in order to please the partner. Both ambivalence and conflict also increase early in relationships, with the peak just before a commitment to marriage is made, after which they decline. Ted Huston and his colleagues also found a sex difference in these patterns: Women appear to be more cautious about forming an attachment or making a commitment, but once it was made, they took on more of the task of relationship maintenance—a standard female sex role task in this culture. (p. 250)

Reading Selection 5

Using a credit card seems so easy. Have it imprinted and approved and you are on your way. Read this selection to discover how the credit card user pays for this convenience (Scarborough & Zimmerer, 1993).*

Before reading, map your knowledge of the use of credit cards, considering the advantages and disadvantages of their use. As you read, make marginal notes on the salient issues in this selection. When you finish reading the selection, add to your map on credit card use.

Credit Cards

To avoid the expense and the hassle of maintaining their own accounts receivable, many small businesses rely on credit cards as a source of consumer credit. This "plastic money" is extremely popular among consumers; the total number of credit cards in the United States now tops *one billion.* Customers use cards to pay for $28 out of every $100 spent on consumable goods and services. . . . In addition, the average credit card purchase is $50, twice the average cash purchase. . . . One recent study found that use of credit cards increases the probability, speed, and magnitude of customer spending. In addition, credit programs enhance a store's image. Surveys show that customers rate businesses offering

credit-installment credit, charge accounts, or credit cards higher on key performance measures. . . .

Almost every financial institution issues credit cards: Visa, Mastercard, Diner's Club, American Express, or Discover. These cards allow small companies to offer credit without putting a burden on their cash flows because they receive almost immediate credit for credit card purchases. Credit card companies usually bear the risk of bad debts (except on invalid or unauthorized cards).

Surveys show that retailers lose sales if they fail to display signs showing which credit cards they accept. Customers are too embarrassed to ask if a business accepts a particular card; instead, they leave the store without buying anything at all. According to one retailer, credit cards are "the basis of business today." . . . Such dependence on credit cards holds potential disadvantages for small companies, however.

The convenience of credit cards is not free to business owners. Companies must pay a fee—typically 1 to 6 percent of total credit card charges to use the system. Given customer expectations, small businesses cannot drop major cards, even when the big card companies raise the fees merchants pay. Fees operate on a multistep process. On a $100 Visa or MasterCard purchase, a processing bank buys the credit card slip from the retailer for $97.44. Then, that bank sells the slip to the bank that issued the card for about $98.80. The remaining $1.20 discount is called the interchange fee, which is what the processing bank passes along to the issuing bank. . . .

Some small businesses issue their own credit cards for customer convenience and to build customer loyalty. These private label cards typically are good only at the sponsoring company, thus encouraging customer loyalty and enhancing the businesses' image. "A private label credit card offers small businesses the clout to compete with major department stores, which have their own credit card programs," says one credit service manager. . . .

Private label cards also give small businesses fast access to the cash from credit sales without the hassle of keeping accounts receivable records. Plus, any losses due to customer defaults typically fall on the credit service that actually issues the card, not the small business sponsoring it. The credit service handles all billing and collection activities. "Normal fees for these services run about 2 percent," says one credit service manager. "But with higher volumes, lower fees can be negotiated." . . .

Offering private label cards can attract more business with minimal effort. "The whole process is easy to implement," says the owner of a small furniture store offering customers its own credit card. "Our private label card program definitely contributes to higher sales volume and add-on business." . . . Most companies place a credit limit on each customer's account and compute interest charges on the customer's average daily balance during the billing cycle. State usury laws set the maximum interest rate the company can charge on credit cards. (p. 399)

* From *Effective Small Business Management* (4th ed., p. 399), by N. M. Scarborough and T. W. Zimmerer, 1993, Upper Saddle River, NJ: Merrill/Prentice Hall. Copyright 1993 by Prentice Hall, Inc. Reprinted by permission of Prentice Hall, Upper Saddle River, NJ.

References

Anderson, T. H., & Armbruster, B. B. (1984). Studying. In P. D. Pearson (Ed.), *Handbook of reading research* (pp. 657–679). New York: Longman.

Bazerman, C. (1989). *The informed reader: Contemporary issues in the disciplines.* Boston: Houghton Mifflin.

Bazerman, C. (1992). *The informed writer: Using sources in the disciplines* (4th ed.). Boston: Houghton Mifflin.

Beales, J. H. (1994). Teenage smoking: Fact and fiction. *The American Enterprise, 5*(2), 20–25.

Bee, H. L. (1992). *The journey of adulthood* (2nd ed.). New York: Macmillan.

Beirne, P., & Messerschmidt, J. (1991). *Criminology.* San Diego, CA: Harcourt Brace Jovanovich.

Bierly, M. M., Berliner, D. C., & Gage, N. L. (1979). *Educational psychology: Student study guide* (2nd ed.). Chicago: Rand McNally.

Boyer, P. S., Clark, C., Kett, J., Salisbury, N., Sitkoff, H., & Woloch, N. (1993). *The enduring vision: A history of the American people* (2nd ed.). Lexington, MA: Heath.

Campbell, W. E. (1993). *The power to learn.* Belmont, CA: Wadsworth.

Casazza, M. E. (1993). Using a model of direct instruction to teach summary writing in a college reading class. *Journal of Reading, 37*(3), 202–208.

Conklin, J. E. (1995). *Criminology* (5th ed.). Boston: Allyn & Bacon.

Coontz, S. (1992). *The way we never were: American families and the nostalgia trap.* New York: Basic Books.

Covey, S. R. (1989). *The seven habits of highly effective people.* New York: Simon & Schuster.

Dinnerstein, L., Nichols, R. L., & Reimers, D. M. (1990). *Natives and strangers: Blacks, Indians, and immigrants in America* (2nd ed.). New York: Oxford.

Edwards, C. H. (1997). *Classroom discipline and management* (2nd ed.). Upper Saddle River, NJ: Merrill/Prentice Hall.

Ellis, D. B. (1984). *Becoming a master student* (4th ed.). Rapid City, SD: College Survival.

Ellis, D. B. (1994). *Becoming a master student* (7th ed.). Boston: Houghton Mifflin.

Frymier, J. (1991). Reflections on principles of educational leadership. In D. L. Burleson (Ed.), *Reflections: Personal essays by 33 distinguished educators* (pp. 162–172). Bloomington, IN: Phi Delta Kappa.

Gall, M. D., Gall, J. P., Jacobsen, D. R., & Bullock, T. L. (1990). *Tools for learning: A guide to teaching study skills.* Alexandria, VA: Association for Supervision and Curriculum Development.

Gardner, H. (1991). *The unschooled mind: How children think and how schools should teach.* New York: Basic Books.

Harris, A. J., & Sipay, E. R. (1990). *How to increase reading ability: A guide to developmental and remedial methods* (9th ed.). New York: Longman.

Henson, K. T. (1991). *Writing for successful publication.* Bloomington, IN: National Educational Service.

Ingalsbe, L. (1992). *Using computers and application software* (2nd ed.). Upper Saddle River, NJ: Merrill/Prentice Hall.

Jensen, E. (1979). *You can succeed: The ultimate study guide for students.* New York: Barron's.

Kanar, C. C. (1995). *The confident student* (2nd ed.). Boston: Houghton Mifflin.

McEachern, W. A. (1994). Economics: *A contemporary introduction* (3rd ed.). Cincinnati, OH: South-Western.

McTighe, J., & Lyman, F., Jr. (1988). Cueing thinking in the classroom: The promise of theory-embedded tools. *Educational Leadership, 45*(7), 18–24.

Miller, T., Jr. (1993). *Environmental science: Sustaining the earth* (4th ed.). Belmont, CA: Wadsworth.

Nist, S. L., & Simpson, M. L. (1987). Facilitating transfer in college reading programs. *Journal of Reading, 31,* 178–181.

Paris, S. G., Wasik, B. A., & Turner, J. C. (1991). The development of strategic readers. In R. Barr, M. L. Kamil, P. Mosenthal, & P. D. Pearson, (Eds.), *Handbook of reading research* (Vol. 2, pp. 609–640). New York: Longman.

Parson, P. T. (1997). Electronic mail: Creating a community of learners. *Journal of Adolescent and Adult Literacy, 40*(7), 560–562.

Pauk, W. (1984). *How to study in college* (3rd ed.). Boston: Houghton Mifflin.

Pearson, P. D., & Fielding, L. (1991). Comprehension instruction. In R. Barr, M. L. Kamil, P. Mosenthal, & P. D. Pearson, (Eds.), *Handbook of reading research* (Vol. 2, pp. 815–860). New York: Longman.

Peck, M. S. (1978). *The road less traveled.* New York: Simon & Schuster.

Richardson, J. D., & Morgan, R. F. (1994). *Reading to learn in the content areas* (2nd ed.). Belmont, CA: Wadsworth.

Ruddell, R. B., & Boyle, O. F. (1989). A study of cognitive mapping as a means to improve summarization and comprehension of expository text. *Reading Research and Instruction, 29*(1), 12–22.

Ryder, R. J., & Graves, M. F. (1996/1997). Using the Internet to enhance students' reading, writing, and information-gathering skills. *Journal of Adolescent & Adult Literacy, 40*(4), 244–254.

Scarborough, N. M., & Zimmerer, T. W. (1993). *Effective small business management* (4th ed.). Upper Saddle River, NJ: Merrill/Prentice Hall.

Shepard, J. M. (1993). *Sociology* (5th ed.). St. Paul, MN: West.

Smith, F. (1985). *Reading without nonsense* (2nd ed.). New York: Teachers College Press.

Smith, B. (1989). *Bridging the gap: College reading* (3rd ed.). Glenview, IL: Scott, Foresman.

Steinberg, L., & Belsky, J. (1991). *Infancy, childhood, and adolescence: Development in context*. New York: Mc-Graw-Hill.

Steinberg, S. (1989). *The ethnic myth: Race, ethnicity, and class in America*. Boston: Beacon.

Tarbuck, E. J., & Lutgens, F. K. (1990). *The earth: An introduction to physical geology* (3rd ed.). Upper Saddle River, NJ: Merrill/Prentice Hall.

Thistlethwaite, L. L. (1990). Critical reading for at-risk students. *Journal of Reading, 33*(8), 586–593.

Participating Actively in Class

Listening and Note Taking in College Courses

Too often people think of the listening experience as a passive activity in which what they remember is largely a matter of chance. In reality, good listening is hard work that requires concentration and willingness to mull over and, at times, verbalize what is said. Good listening requires using mental energy. If you really listen to an entire 50-minute lecture, when the lecture is over you will feel tired because you have put as much energy into listening as the lecturer put into talking.* (pp. 133–134)

—James F. Shepherd

---

* From *Reading Skills for College Study* (3rd ed., pp. 133–134), by J. H. Shepherd, 1988, Boston: Houghton Mifflin.

Prereading Questions

- How would you define listening?

- What influences make it easier or harder to listen?

- Why are listening skills so important during college study and in later professional life?

Assessing Prior Knowledge

Becoming an active listener is a key ingredient of a successful college career. In this chapter, you will learn how to apply active listening skills in the college classroom. Before you begin reading, identify misconceptions about listening and note taking you may have by taking the listening quiz in Figure 6.1.

Vignette: Three Students Listen in Class

A professor in Philosophy 101 is explaining the requirements for a major course assignment. The assignment will include writing a paper on a contemporary ethical issue, then analyzing it from a famous philosopher's point of view. Dionne tries to pay attention, but the explanation is rather lengthy and his attention begins to drift. "Oh, well," Dionne thinks, "I'll check with Tonya about it later. She's writing down everything, as usual."

Kay, on the other hand, is giving the professor's explanation her undivided attention. She knows that she is not a good test taker, and she sees this paper, which is a third of her total grade, as a way of improving her grade for the course. She listens to every word, yet when the explanation is over, she is still unclear on several important points and has many questions about how to proceed.

Tony listens, takes a few notes on key points, and, when the professor asks whether there are any questions, he asks, "What is usually the best way to get a sense of a particular philosopher's viewpoint?" The professor responds, "Begin with your readings and class notes. I have a variety of books on reserve at the library that will help. If you still have questions, come to see me during my office hours." Later on during the discussion, Tony says, "I seem to learn best by example. Do you happen to have any examples of excellent student papers that we could look at in class?" The professor agrees to share an example of an outstanding student paper on the overhead projector during the next class meeting.

Each of these students recognized the importance of listening, yet only one—Tony—was an active listener. Dionne, who planned to get another student's notes, never got around to asking her until the week the assignment was due. By that time, he could not make any sense out of them. Although Dionne knows how to look like he is listening to avoid insulting the teacher, he fails to get involved with the course material. Kay was confused by her own notes because she had tried too hard to listen intently to every word the professor spoke instead of remembering her purpose—listening for instructions. Tony was an active listener because he did more than receive the spoken message. Not only did he listen for the requirements—he also acted on that information. Tony's focus was on fulfilling his responsibilities in completing the assignment. In fact, through his questions, Tony indirectly helped nearly every one of his classmates do a better job with the philosophy assignment. As a college student and listener, Tony is aware of how his listening and note-taking strategies influence the success of his college career.

Figure 6.1
Listening and Note Taking: A Quiz

How much do you know about listening, and how much of what you believe is inaccurate? Respond to each true/false item below.

1. Adults devote about half of their total verbal communication time (this includes reading, writing, speaking, and listening) to listening.

2. Most college students feel that their note-taking skills are adequate.

3. Listening and note taking are passive activities; students can simply write down whatever the professor says without thinking about it much and take good notes.

4. Good listeners have to ignore much of what they hear.

5. If a student gets permission and has a classmate make an audiotape of a lecture, listening to the tape will take the place of being in class.

6. If a student can repeat the exact words that a professor just said, the student has been practicing active listening skills.

7. Expectations for listening skills are identical in different societies around the world.

8. Learning to listen is automatic.

Now compare your answers with the following quiz answers:

1. True. Estimates of the total communication time devoted to listening are about 55% (Werner, 1975). The average businessperson spends about 40% of the time listening; it is estimated the business *executive* devotes even more—as high as 80%.

2. False. In a survey of college students in a southwestern college, 75% reported that their note-taking skills were inadequate and that their notes were virtually useless in preparing for a test (O'Hair, Wooden, & O'Hair, 1987).

3. False. Listening is actually the process of constructing meaning from the message heard. College students who daydream through a lecture and write notes often find that their notes are meaningless when they try to study (O'Hair, et al., 1987).

4. True. Good listeners must learn to tune out as well as to tune in. Unless they can ignore at least some of the many sounds and messages vying for their attention, they will not be able to focus on what is important. College students take meaningful notes in class, for example, as a result of carefully planned listening for structure and fighting distractions, not absentmindedly writing down whatever the professor says (O'Hair, et al., 1987).

5. False. Communications experts estimate "only 10% of our communication is represented by the words we say. Another 30% is represented by our sounds, and 60% by our body language" (Covey, 1989, p. 241).

6. False. Being able to repeat a message word for word is not the best way to assess listening comprehension—paraphrasing is. If you can translate the speaker's message into your own words, it is a better indicator of understanding.

7. False. Ways of listening are particularistic and culture-bound. Our patience with long or ambiguous messages, how frequently we give nonverbal or verbal signs of listening (a nod of the head, "Hmmm . . . ," "Exactly!"), how focused we are on the speaker, whether and when we consider interrupting—all of these things are a function of our socialization into the role of listener and speaker, something that is greatly affected by cultural background.

8. False. Just as we learn to read or write or talk, we *learn* to listen—it is not something that we can take for granted, nor is it a character trait that is an unchangeable part of our personalities. Rather, active listening is a learned response that is greatly influenced by sensory acuity, motivation, and behavior.

In order to become active, effective listeners, college students must get involved, ask questions, seek clarification, and pursue solutions when difficulties arise.

A Definition of Listening

When we hear the word *listening*, most of us think of simply receiving a message. Yet everyone who hears something does not always listen. In fact, we can give all of the outward appearances of listening carefully when we are only listening marginally or not at all. Hearing is a physiological capacity and natural ability; listening is a practiced skill and art. To illustrate this point, think about something you have listened to with great intensity recently. Chances are, you were involved *both* intellectually and emotionally with the message.

Listening is categorized as a receptive language art (like reading) because the major purpose is to receive a message, but even so, it is both *interactive* and *constructive*. Listening is interactive because good listeners get involved with the message; it is constructive because listeners build meaning from what they hear. Actually, listening is more than hearing—it is the process of converting spoken language into meaning in the mind (Lundsteen, 1979).

Improvement in Action ▓▶

Think about a time when you listened exceptionally well, a time when you were totally absorbed in what you were hearing. Maybe it was your favorite musical artist's new CD. Maybe it was words of love. Maybe it was advice about getting financial aid. Perhaps it was when someone was evaluating the quality of your work. Now describe your good listening experience. What enabled you to concentrate completely on the message you heard?

In most cases of careful listening, your emotions as well as your thoughts are involved. That is why it is important to *develop* an interest in a class, even if the subject seems boring. The simplest way to achieve this is to invest time and energy in the course; after you have made that investment, you will be more emotionally involved in what you hear.

The Value of Listening—Before, During, and After College

Why is there such an emphasis on listening throughout life? From the earliest days of school, teachers insist that students "pay attention" because it helps students learn, enjoy, appreciate, get information, act and react, recognize danger, make decisions, develop attitudes, clarify values, and develop thinking skills (Jalongo, 1991).

At the other end of the spectrum, developing active listening strategies remains important long after your college career is completed. Being a good listener is a highly prized ability in every professional field and in society at large. In a study of organizational environments, for example, interactive listening behavior was frequently regarded as the single most important skill in employees (Tuttle, 1988). Many corporations, convinced of the importance of effective listening, have begun to offer formal training programs to develop higher-level listening abilities in their employees. On the job, the failure to listen can result in costly errors that waste time or the material resources of the organization. Mistakes can also be costly in the sense of creating misunderstandings between coworkers.

In addition to being valued before and after a college career, active listening is essential during college. Of all the language skills college students use, listening is the one they use the most because listening is essential to the learning process. If we logged the hours that a typical college student devotes to the other communication activities of speaking, reading, and writing, it would take all of them combined to equal the time devoted to one activity—listening (Verderber & Elder, 1976).

What Is Active Listening?

Without a doubt, college students have ample opportunity to listen. But listening *more* is not the solution; listening *better* is (De Haven, 1983). In his best-selling book *The Seven Habits of Highly Effective People*, Covey (1989) emphasizes the importance of active listening for interpersonal relationships:

> When another person speaks, we're usually "listening" at one of four levels. We may be **ignoring** another person, not really listening at all. We may practice **pretending.** "Yeah. Uh-huh. Right." We may practice **selective listening,** hearing only certain parts of the conversation. . . . Or we may even practice **attentive listening,** paying attention and

focusing energy on the words that are being said. But very few of us ever practice the fifth level, the highest form of listening, **empathic listening** . . . seeking *first* to understand, to really understand. . . . Most people do not listen with the intent to understand; they listen with the intent to reply. . . .

"Oh, I know exactly how you feel!"

"I went through the very same thing. Let me tell you about my experience.". . .

In empathic listening, you listen with your ears, but you also, and more importantly, listen with your eyes and your heart. You listen for feeling, for meaning. You listen for behavior. (pp. 239-241)

Higher-level listening skills essential for college study include:

Interpretation—visualizing what is heard, listening "between the lines," and making meaning out of messages

Evaluation—weighing the evidence, comparing/contrasting, or making professional judgments as we listen

Response—connecting and interacting with the message, applying it to our situation

Empathy—connecting both intellectually and emotionally with the speaker and the message

Are You an Active Listener?

Research suggests that even individuals without any hearing impairments listen with only 25% efficiency, which means that they are distracted and do not understand or remember three-quarters of what they hear (Hunsaker, 1990). Do you consider yourself to be a good listener? The following indicators, stated here as questions, will help you decide:

Do I come prepared to listen? Good listeners begin with a positive attitude and expect themselves to attend to the speaker's message.

Do I strive to resist distractions and focus on the task? Good listeners keep their purpose in mind and focus on the message. In the process, they overcome distractions and develop greater powers of concentration. When a speaker pauses, for example, do you use that time to reflect on what the speaker has said, or does your attention wane? Maintaining eye contact with the speaker, sitting up front, and taking notes are all ways to improve your ability to stay focused.

Do I consciously practice and try to improve my listening skills? Successful college students practice their listening skills with a wide variety of materials and in many different contexts—not only during class lectures but also while talking with a troubled friend, listening to a poetry reading, or evaluating a political speaker. In this way, they become more flexible listeners. When you are listening in a college class, try predicting what the speaker will say next and visualizing what the speaker is saying, for instance.

Do I wait to hear people out? Good listeners allow others to express their thoughts without interruption, except for clarification. They are patient with the speaker, even if it takes a rather long time to get to the point. Listen to the speaker first; evaluate the quality of the message later.

Do I listen "between the lines"? Good listeners do more than listen to the words; they strive to understand the underlying meaning. They interpret both verbal and nonverbal messages—not only the speaker's words but also the nonverbal signals that accompany those words, including facial expressions (such as looking quizzical), body posture (such as sitting with slumped shoulders and looking defeated), and gestures (such as hand movements). They also listen for verbal cues to the underlying structure of messages—"three causes . . . ," "a historic overview . . . ," "major controversies . . . ," "steps in the process . . . ," and so forth.

Do I avoid jumping to conclusions? Good listeners avoid getting wrapped up in their own point of view. Even when the topic is controversial and elicits strong emotional responses, they strive to focus on the speaker's message.

Becoming an Active Listener

Even if you are not an active listener, you can take certain steps to improve.

Make the Commitment to Listen

Often, beginning college students will say that if a class is boring, they just can't seem to pay attention. But as they gain experience, they begin to recognize that even a faculty member who has much to offer them professionally may not be a dynamic speaker. Conversely, after students go out into the workplace, they sometimes conclude that a faculty member who was witty and entertaining actually cheated them by failing to educate them. This is one reason that it is important to "hear out" every faculty member and make a sincere effort to listen—even when the message does not seem particularly exciting. *Liking* a class is not necessarily *learning* from a class.

Even if you are entirely justified in disliking a particular class, do not allow your feelings to control and defeat you. Some freshmen will stop attending a class they do not like. Then they usually fail the course, have to repeat it (sometimes with the same professor!), and may end up on academic probation. After all these negative things occur, it matters little whether you were right about the class being boring. You have allowed a bad course to make things bad for you, and now it will take much more time, effort, and money to correct it than sticking with the course in the first place ever could. It may even jeopardize your college career. You do have the mental ability to make yourself concentrate for a few unpleasant hours each week and the determination to get through a difficult or tedious course. It might be worth the effort now to save so much effort later.

BOX 6.4   ***Improvement in Action*** ⫸

Review the list of active listening behaviors below and rate yourself:

5 = excellent, 4 = good, 3 = average, 2 = fair, 1 = poor				
1. Resisting distractions	5	4	3	2	1
2. Striving to improve listening skills	5	4	3	2	1
3. Waiting to hear people out	5	4	3	2	1
4. Listening between the lines	5	4	3	2	1
5. Avoiding jumping to conclusions	5	4	3	2	1

What will you need to do to engage more fully in listening?

Override Your Biases

Both speakers and listeners are affected by perceptions, expectations, stereotypes, social status, and the social context. Many times, listeners make the mistake of thinking that a speaker must be "just like me" in order to have anything significant to say. A listener who is very informal in his style of speech, for instance, may be put off by a speaker who uses very formal speech, or a college student may immediately stereotype an elderly professor as being less up-to-date than a professor who is new to the field. Beware of allowing your biases to affect your perceptions and expectations.

Activate Prior Knowledge

One of the best ways to build prior knowledge is to do the assigned reading before coming to class. Students often say that they are worried that they will ask a stupid question and look foolish in front of their peers. But if you have done the background reading, you will be well informed and feel confident that your questions are good ones. Feeling free to ask questions will help maintain your interest and attention as well as build your understanding of the course content.

If the background reading contributes little to your understanding because it is difficult or confusing, try consulting other sources on the same topic, such as a film documentary, an encyclopedia article, or even a photo essay on the subject. Such strategies for building prior knowledge are particularly important when students have reading difficulties, inadequate high school preparation, or limited proficiency with English.

Build Personal Interest

Try to discover how the information would benefit you personally (O'Hair & Wooden, 1988). If a psychology professor is talking about self-esteem, for example, you might think "Do I have self-esteem?" or "She is listing some of the consequences of low self-esteem—is there anyone I know who seems to fit either of these profiles?"

Predict-Then-Confirm

Applying this to the same lecture on self-esteem, you might think, "It seems like she's going to talk about causes now. I predict that one cause of low self-esteem is overly critical parents. Let's see if I'm right."

Recognize Barriers to Listening

Based on our informal interviews with highly successful college students who were enrolled in a college reading course as freshmen, the number one deterrent to listening in class was a physical condition—not getting sufficient sleep. Obviously, if you cannot keep your eyes open, you can hardly be expected to give a message your full attention. So one of the simplest steps that you can take to improve your listening habits is to make certain that you get adequate rest.

Set a Specific Purpose for Listening

Remember the three students in the opening vignette? Tony knew how to listen because he had a purpose and interacted with the message. He did not commit either of the two most common mistakes: being indifferent to the message or attempting to listen to and remember every word. He listened *for* the relevant information and *worked with* the information until he achieved a thorough understanding.

Instead of listening to everything, listen *for* something (Funk & Funk, 1989). This is a very useful distinction. Some students listen for funny remarks or an interesting example rather than listening for what will probably be on the test. Then, when they are confronted with the information on the examination, it seems unfamiliar and intimidating. It is fine to enjoy an illustration that a professor uses to make a point, but do not lose sight of your purpose in taking notes or allow it to distract you from your primary purpose for listening—to understand the course material.

One quick and easy way to set a purpose for listening is to take the topic of the lecture and turn it into a question or questions you would like to have answered. If the topic is self-esteem, for example, you might ask, "What causes people to have high or low self-esteem? Is my self-esteem average, low, or high?"

Know When to Listen Rather Than Talk

Did you ever notice that when the professor suggests what to study for a test, the room grows very quiet? Clearly, this is a time when it is important to give your full attention to the message. But there are other times that students sometimes overlook. One is the beginning of class. Many faculty begin the class period by taking roll, making announcements, and responding to any questions. If you are habitually late for class or miss class entirely, you may not hear that a quiz date had to be changed or that an essay question will be on the exam—things that affect how and when you study. Some students also make the mistake of sitting beside a talkative friend during class and conversing or passing notes throughout the class period. Class time is a time when you should be listening or, if talking, discussing course content at appropriate times.

Adapt to the Particular Features of the Listening Environment

Generally speaking, a listening environment should be relatively free from distractions or interruptions and have clear operating procedures for both the speaker's and listener's participation. Yet the particular features of a listening situation call for different kinds of behavior on the listener's part. Consider three situations in which listening to a conversation is important. The first is at a lively party with loud music; the second is in a coffee shop seated at a table face-to-face with another person; the third is listening to a young child who is just learning to talk. In each circumstance, the listener would have to behave differently. The same holds true for college students' in-class listening. Your listening intensity must change to suit your purposes, depending on whether you are listening primarily for enjoyment, understanding, or evaluation (Shepherd, 1988).

One of the most important types of variations you can make is adjusting to the pace of the lecture. Too often, students allow themselves to become frustrated when the pace is too fast or uninterested if the pace is too slow (O'Hair & Wooden, 1988). Once again, you can exert some control over the pace of a class by becoming involved. If the professor is hurrying through information, you could slow things down with questions like, "Would you mind going over those last two points again? I'm not clear on the distinction between the two" or "Could you leave that transparency up for a minute?" If the presentation is too slow, you could liven up the lecture by making a comment, asking for an example, or raising a question. In both instances, you are adapting to the message and its pace.

Figure 6.2 is an overview of eight specific counterproductive listening habits and ways to counteract them.

Assess Your Strengths and Weaknesses as a Listener

Listeners are affected by their auditory functioning, motivation/disposition, cultural background, conceptual level, and previous experience (Bromley, 1988). Specific listening strategies, such as connecting new information with prior information or actively participating, also influence listening. Many people who are awaiting the opportunity to enter into a discussion, for example, become so focused on what they are going to say that they stop listening. A better idea would be to jot down a few key words of the point you want to make in the margins of your

Figure 6.2
Counterproductive Listening Habits

Adapted from the Indiana University Career Development Center, Bloomington (1990).

Counterproductive Habit 1: Dismissing a Subject as Dull

Ineffective listeners . . .
decide a lecture is going to be boring and "turn off" the speaker.

Effective listeners . . .
listen closely for information that can be important or useful.

Counterproductive Habit 2: Prejudging or Overreacting to a Speaker

Ineffective listeners . . .
find fault with a speaker, criticizing voice, looks, clothes. They anticipate that the speaker will say nothing of importance and become so emotionally involved in disagreeing with the speaker that they miss most of the message.

Effective listeners . . .
look for the ideas presented, not superficial characteristics of the speaker. They try to be more objective and listen with their minds. If there is a point of disagreement, they make a note of it to raise as a question later, then go on listening.

Counterproductive Habit 3: Listening Only for the Facts

Ineffective listeners . . .
want only the facts they will be tested on and disregard examples or supporting details that help clarify content.

Effective listeners . . .
listen for examples and details that support and elaborate on the facts.

Counterproductive Habit 4: Forcing a Lecture to Fit a Formal Outline

Ineffective listeners . . .
miss important content and become frustrated because they are so preoccupied with making a lecture fit into a rigid mold.

Effective listeners . . .
adjust their note taking to the speaker's topic, style, and patterns of organization.

Counterproductive Habit 5: Faking Attention

Ineffective listeners . . .
look at the speaker but do not really listen; they expect to get the material from the textbook later.

---

notebook but continue to listen to the conversation. If you stop listening altogether, you run the risk of repeating what someone else has already said or missing an important shift in the discussion. If the discussion is going in another direction by the time that you have a chance to ask your question, do not be discouraged. You can bring everyone back to an important issue by saying something like, "I would like to return to a point that was made earlier."

Interact With Other Listeners and the Sender to Clarify Messages

College faculty are responsible for much of the talk that students are expected to hear and understand. Senders of messages exert a positive influence on the listening process by speaking audibly and clearly, using nonverbal communication effectively, clarifying when necessary, and avoiding distracting habits. Most instructors recognize when their students are confused and quickly adjust by making corrections, offering clarifications, or even starting all

Effective listeners . . .
realize that all the information in the lecture may not be in the textbook. They also understand what the professor chooses to discuss in class is often what he or she considers to be most important.

Counterproductive Habit 6: Allowing Distractions

Ineffective listeners . . .
use little distractions—someone dropping a notebook, a truck passing by outside, a whispered comment—as an excuse to stop listening.

Effective listeners . . .
filter out distractions and concentrate on the speaker's message.

Counterproductive Habit 7: Ceasing to Listen When the Topic Becomes Technical or Difficult

Ineffective listeners . . .
seek entertainment, not learning. They cease listening when complex ideas or arguments are presented.

Effective listeners . . .
are not put off by tough, technical, or complex ideas. They will work hard to learn something new and try to understand. If the speaker is moving too quickly, they try to slow him or her down with a question or comment. If the speaker is moving too slowly, they take that time to think about what he or she is saying.

Counterproductive Habit 8: Allowing Attention to Wane When the Speaker Is Moving Too Quickly or Slowly

Ineffective listeners . . .
daydream and move along lazily if the speaker is moving slowly or grow frustrated and "tune out" if the material is being covered too quickly to suit them.

Effective listeners . . .
understand that thought moves more rapidly than speech (the speed of talk is about 150 words per minute, while the speed of thought is about 400 words per minute) and use this speed differential to their advantage. They use any extra time or pauses in the presentation to reflect on what the speaker is saying, summarize the main points, or make predictions about the remainder of the lecture. If the speaker is moving too quickly, they ask a question or make a comment ("Could you leave that on the chalkboard for one more minute, please?") to try to slow the speaker down.

over again. If a faculty member fails to do these things automatically, active listeners should raise specific questions ("You have discussed forces that contribute to political unrest. Would it be safe to assume that the reverse of each influence on that list contributes to political stability?"), ask for an example ("You've defined the term *displacement,* and I'm familiar with it from physics. But can you give an example of its meaning in psychological terms?"), or attempt to paraphrase what you think the person said ("Let's see if I'm interpreting this correctly. You're saying that . . ."). Notice how much more focused and specific these questions are than the typical "I'm so confused" or "I don't understand any of this."

Generally speaking, messages that are long, vague, abstract, distorted in some way, or that contain complex vocabulary are poorly understood by listeners. Conversely, messages that are clear and concise, introduce new vocabulary in context, and use concrete objects to illustrate or emphasize key points tend to be well understood. By listening and participating more fully in the class, you can make the material more understandable.

Plan for a Meaningful Follow-Up

As a college student, you can assume that you will be asked to use what you have heard during class and written in notes on future tests or written assignments. If you actually *use* what you have heard—before your grade is on the line—you will become a better listener. Allow what you have heard in class to follow you outside class. In order to use what you are listening and learning about in everyday situations, you could do such things as

- apply your knowledge of world history to a controversy on the national news;
- ask your roommate the question that was raised in class, then explain the ideas and describe the discussion that took place;
- critically analyze information in the newspaper based on a class lecture; or
- use a particularly thought-provoking message for dinner table conversation, or relate what you heard in one course to the discussion in another.

The more you use the messages you have heard, the more motivated you will become to be a better listener.

By instituting all of the active listening practices outlined here, you can quickly improve your listening habits and significantly improve them over time. Remember, "If you listen actively in class, you will put as much energy into listening as your teachers put into lecturing" (Shepherd, 1988, p. 130).

Recognize the Influence of Listening for Overall Success

Because college students are expected to spend so much time listening, it would stand to reason that improving listening and note taking would improve their chances for success in college. Some research supports this view. In a study conducted by the director of a learning center, students were enrolled in a listening enhancement program. Later, when they were taking their other college-level courses, these students were compared with another group that did not work on improving its listening skills. The overall grade point average of 85% of the students who used active listening strategies improved by at least 0.6. This means that if they had a 2.0 overall grade point average (C) and their major requires a 2.5, a course in listening made the difference between being in academic trouble and being in academic good standing. Furthermore, 37% of the students who took the listening improvement course improved their overall grade point average by 1.00—one full grade on a 4-point scale (O'Hair et al., 1987). If findings like these are any indication, applying active listening strategies could make the difference between success and failure in your college career.

Listening and Note-Taking Strategies

Listeners must use note-taking strategies that match the speaker's style and their best style of learning (Hamp-Lyons, 1982). As a first step, try to analyze your instructor's style—what college students refer to as "psyching out" the instructor. Try to categorize your instructors along a continuum from those who are rigidly structured, extremely methodical, and linear in the way they present material, all the way to the other extreme—faculty who are disorganized "free spirits" and talk about whatever is on their minds at the moment. Note taking has to be different for professors of various types. It will only frustrate you to try to outline the free spirit's notes, for example. With such lecturers, you will want to select a less structured approach to note taking. Is the instructor exceptionally well organized in how she or he presents course material? If so, you might be able to use an outline for your notes. Naturally, you will also want to consider your best style of learning. If you prefer a high level of organization in material, you may need to take relatively unstructured notes during class and organize them later with the material from the required readings for the course.

Always try to find out early in the semester what the instructor will emphasize on the exams. Some faculty tend to explain what is already in the book and use a collection of test items actually written by the textbook author, for example. Others use the textbook as background reading and place much greater emphasis on class notes. On the first day of class, when the instructor introduces the course requirements, set a purpose for your note taking by asking, "What do you emphasize most on the exams, the textbook or the notes?" This will help you concentrate your listening, note-taking, and study efforts. Figure 6.3 presents a helpful note-taking checklist.

Figure 6.3
Note-Taking Checklist
Adapted from Reynolds (1992); Banks, McCarthy, and Rasool (1993).

1. I assess my prior knowledge of the topic to be addressed before I begin to read or study.
2. I read assigned material before class and mark places that I don't understand with a question mark (?) in the margins.
3. I generate a list of questions that I still have about the topic.
4. I know that I am listening attentively because at any given point in the lecture, I could paraphrase the instructor's words.
5. I listen for cues that help to focus notetaking, such as "It is *crucial for . . . ,*" "*the* four types of *. . . : ,*" "*effects on employers,*" or "*the results* of this research."
6. I watch for cues—gestures, voice, writing something on the chalkboard—to signal that the instructor thinks something is important.
7. When taking notes, I do not attempt to write down everything the instructor says. I also use abbreviations to save time (*ex.* for example, *def.* for definition, etc.).
8. During notetaking, I have a system for indicating key points or ideas (e.g., a wavy line under definitions, a star in the margin for possible exam questions, numbering important details, etc.).
9. When I am unclear about something presented in class, I specify the kind of help and clarification that I need (e.g., "Could you explain that definition in another way?" "Could you give an example of _____?") rather than saying "I'm so confused" or "I just don't understand."
10. During the lecture, I listen to make certain that the questions I had during my reading are answered. If they are not, I ask a question during the discussion.
11. During a class discussion, I listen not only to the lecturer but also to the other students.
12. When the instructor asks a question, I attempt to answer it, even if I do not answer it verbally.
13. I volunteer to share ideas and experiences that are relevant to the lecture/discussion.
14. As soon as possible after class, I review my notes to fill in any gaps and make certain that my questions have been answered.
15. I review my notes from the previous class shortly before the next class meeting.
16. I recognize that my notes are more than transcribing information—they are my interpretation of the course material written in a way that I can understand.
17. I use a system of symbols to indicate my individual responses to the information on which I take notes, such as a question mark (?) for confusion, an asterisk (*) for important points, or an exclamation point (!) for a surprising piece of information.
18. I realize that borrowing someone else's notes or relying on a tape recording is generally less effective than being an active listener and taking my own notes.

BOX 6.5 ***Improvement in Action***

As you read the questions in Figure 6.3, keep score on your note-taking habits. Rate yourself using the following scale:

18–14	Superlative note-taking practices
13–10	Good note-taking practices
9–6	Average note-taking habits
5 or below	Real deficiencies in note taking—improvement is essential.

The sections that follow take you from the least to most structured methods of note taking.

The Shopping List

The shopping list is just what it sounds like—a simple listing of items with categories or headings supplied where they are obvious, but without a highly structured format (Hamp-Lyons, 1982). It is called the shopping list because if you were preparing to go to the grocery store, you would probably begin with a disorganized list of the items you need and later categorize them by the areas of the grocery store—produce, dairy, meats, and so forth—to make your shopping trip more efficient. The same clustering strategy can be used in note taking when the material is not clearly organized and the speaker tends to go off on tangents and digress frequently from the original topic. Applied to taking lecture notes on child development, it might look something like the depiction in Figure 6.4.

Figure 6.4
Shopping List Note Taking

Developmental Influences on Child

Intellectual/cognitive	○ mental capacity ○ thinking skills ○ experiences and opportunities
Social	○ parents/family ○ peers ○ community ○ culture/ethnicity
Emotional	○ self-esteem ○ self-knowledge ○ coping strategies
Physical	○ physiological characteristics ○ health/nutrition ○ psychomotor skills

Figure 6.5
T-Formation Notes

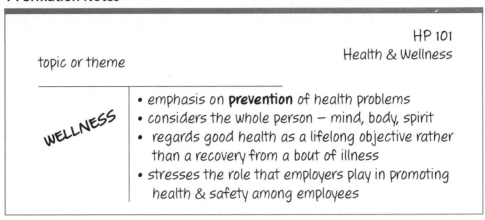

If you learn best when things follow a clear sequence, you will probably find that the shopping list does not meet your study needs. Try using it initially, then revising the notes into a more structured style later.

The T-Formation

If the speaker has a somewhat more organized style and provides an overall topic on the course syllabus and a thesis statement for the presentation or lecture, try the T-formation. It separates the basic concept or main topic from the supporting details by placing the main idea on the left-hand side of the paper and supporting details or examples on the right-hand side (see Figure 6.5).

Graphic Organizers

As you know from the previous chapters, graphic organizers look like diagrams, charts, or maps. Graphic organizers are a very flexible note-taking strategy because they can be used with both highly and loosely structured lectures. If you tend to be a visual learner, this technique will be especially useful. When selecting a graphic organizer, try to consider the organizational structure of the message. Basically, there are five structural patterns in messages and accompanying note-taking structures (Smith & Tompkins, 1988).

The **definition or description** graphic organizer is designed to tell all about something. This is often used with vocabulary that is new to people who are not experts in the field. Consider the education major who is enrolled in a human development course. The professor begins the class period by saying that she will be giving an overview of preschoolers' intellectual, physical, social, and emotional development. The student sketches a small stick person and draws four lines radiating from the figure. As the lecture/discussion continues, the student writes only the key points under each of the four categories of development.

The **chronological or procedural** graphic organizer is arranged by time; it chronicles the history of something or explains how to do something step by step. The chronological organizer is often used in a survey course like history and philosophy of education, while the procedural approach is often used in a presentation designed to teach a practical skill, such as how to use the videotape editing machine in a communications course.

The **categorical** graphic organizer classifies things into types, based on purpose or function. In a discussion of literary elements in an English course, for example, students would be introduced to the basic literary elements—plot, theme, setting, characters, and style. During the discussion, each category and its function in a work of literature would be discussed, and students would be asked to suggest examples of each literary element from novels they had read.

The **comparative** graphic organizer uses likenesses or differences as a way of organizing. For example, in an introductory religion class, the instructor might discuss creation stories from major religions, what they have in common, and how they are unique.

The **causative** graphic organizer answers how and why by presenting causes and effects or problems and solutions, or problems, solutions, and results. In a world history course, for example, the topic for the day is revolution. The students could identify several different instances of the concept—the American Revolution, the French Revolution, anti-apartheid in South Africa—and look at causes and effects. Similarly, in a sociology course, the topic might be poverty, solutions that have been attempted, and the results of efforts to eradicate poverty in the United States.

Figure 6.6 shows a note-taking structure for each type of material.

Figure 6.6
Graphic Organizers for Note Taking

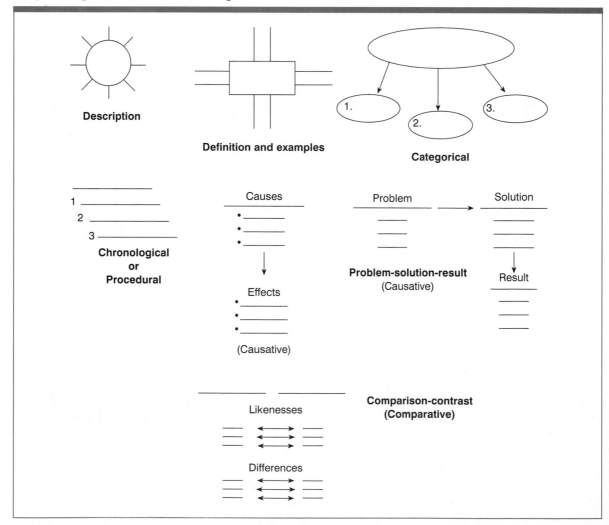

Illustrated Notes

You may also use pictures in your note taking. We know that good listeners use mental imagery to create pictures in their minds that clarify ideas, so you can put this ability to good use. Try illustrating your notes like the example in Figure 6.7.

Formal Outline

Students are often told to outline their notes, but the speakers must be very precise, organized, and structured in their style for this note-taking strategy to work well. If you are taking notes from a textbook, the formal outline may be more appropriate because books tend to be more structured than a lecture or a discussion. An example of outlined notes is in Figure 6.8.

Figure 6.7
Illustrated Note Taking on Howard Gardner's Theory of Multiple Intelligences

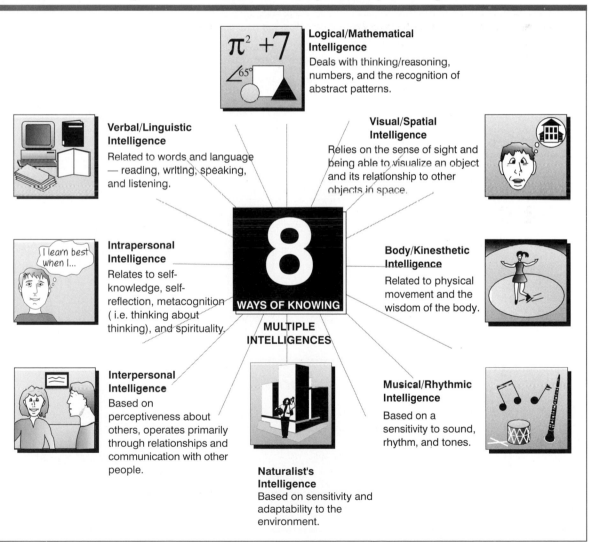

Figure 6.8
Outlined Notes

Adapted from: Gregorc, A. (1982). *An adult's guide to style*. Maynard, MA: Gabriel Systems.
Messick, S. (1976). *Individuality in learning.* San Francisco: Jossey-Bass.
Reiff, J. (1992). *What research says to the teacher: Learning styles.* Washington, DC: National Education Association.
Resnick, L. B. (1987). *Education and learning to think.* Washington, DC: National Academy Press.
Adapted from Reiff (1992).

Topic: Learning Modalities, Types, Rates, and Styles

I. Sensory Modality

    A. Which type of sensory input do you favor in learning?

        1. Visual—you learn best from what you see (real objects, pictures, words)

        2. Auditory—you prefer to "listen and learn."

        3. Tactile—you learn best by a "hands-on" approach, actually manipulating materials.

        4. Kinesthetic—you learn best when you can involve your whole body in learning and physically perform a learning task.

II. Cognitive Style

    A. What is your rate of dealing with ideas?

        1. Reflective—you tend to be patient, size up a situation thoroughly before beginning, work at a somewhat slower pace, and be very concerned about making mistakes.

        2. Impulsive—you tend to be impatient, dive into a task, work quickly, and be relatively relaxed about committing errors, assuming that you will correct them later.

    B. What is your general approach to processing information?

        1. Global—you tend to focus on the "big picture," to want to see the forest before examining individual trees.

        2. Analytic—you tend to focus on details, to want to look at individual trees and put them together as components in the forest.

How to Use Your Notes

After you have listened actively, selected an appropriate note-taking strategy, and taken good notes, now what? The real value in note-taking is that it enables you to review in the truest sense of that word: to see (*view*) again (*re-*). Reviewing good notes again and again is the best way to internalize the course material, to make it a part of you so that it is not subject to forgetting. Box 6.6 gives an example of using your notes to study for a test.

BOX 6.6   ***Improvement in Action*** ⫸

Do you have a driver's license? Think about the way you behaved when you were studying for the written portion of the driver's license test. You probably read the questions aloud, asked others to quiz you, talked with people about any laws that you did not understand, and maybe even made flash cards to study with. Right before the test, you were probably quickly reviewing what you had studied. Make a list of all the strategies you used with this very important test. How can you apply those same strategies to ace your next college course?

What is the best way to review using class notes from a lecture or presentation? Here are some suggestions:

1. Strive for understanding. Have you ever thought you understood something and then felt inadequate when you tried to explain it to someone else? Suppose that you just studied photosynthesis for a multiple-choice test and did well on the exam. Yet the following week, when you try to explain the process of photosynthesis to someone else, you have forgotten much of what you thought you learned. Situations like these illustrate one of the most common reasons that we forget information: because we did not fully understand it in the first place. If you really work to understand the material that was presented in class, you will be less likely to forget it. One excellent test of your understanding is the ability to put the material into your own words, to paraphrase. If you can interpret information and paraphrase it without introducing any inaccuracies, then you will be certain that you understand it well and feel confident that you can remember it later on.

2. Review your notes. Have you ever returned to notes taken a week earlier and wondered what they were about? Unless you go back and look over your notes after class, this can easily happen. If you do not review notes soon, they can become completely unfamiliar by the midterm or final exam. Then the task of studying for the test is totally overwhelming and you are likely to give up. But if you devote just 5 or 10 minutes to reviewing as soon as possible after each class, you will find that your notes are familiar, that you feel comfortable with the material, and that you feel more confident about speaking up in class. Spargo (1994) gives an excellent reason for reviewing notes when he says, "Consider for a moment what good sense this makes: you may have spent an hour studying and learning something; 5 minutes devoted to reviewing is insurance that you won't forget and that the hour's study won't have been wasted" (p. 142).

3. Talk about the course material. Another way of using notes and preventing yourself from forgetting material is to discuss it with others. One of the reasons that you are in an academic environment instead of taking a correspondence course is because learning is a social process, and having the opportunity to interact with others about ideas is important. Staring at a page of notes in confusion will not accomplish much. A better use of your time is to pick up your notebook and walk down the hall of the dormitory to discuss it with another serious student from the class or to phone a helpful, knowledgeable classmate to clear up your misunderstanding. This is particularly true if you have to miss a class and borrow someone else's notes, because another student's system of note taking may be difficult to interpret, and, if you were not there for the class, the notes might not make much sense. The opportunity to discuss course material with others is another way in which a study group can help. If you have regular opportunities to wrestle with new and sometimes difficult ideas in the company of supportive peers, you will gain competence and confidence.

4. Look for the big ideas. Every student has had the feeling of despair that comes from leafing through page after page of class notes and the textbook and saying, "How can I ever remember all of this?" Too often, students think of study and review as working with hopelessly large quantities of information that can never be mastered. Instead, try to figure out what the instructor thinks is important. Some clues to watch for are when the instructor devotes more class time to a topic, writes more notes on the board about the topic, or gives some hints about what to concentrate on for the test. After you have made an attempt to figure out what an instructor will stress on the test, go back through your notes and identify some major, general ideas or themes—five to seven key points—that are essential. Learn them well enough that you can state them without looking back at your notes. In this chapter, for example, you have encountered many ideas about listening and note taking. Instead of trying to memorize them, you could make a plus/minus chart of things that improve listening, memory, and note taking and the things that interfere with them.

5. Make learning efficient. Two ways of making learning more efficient are to connect it with prior knowledge and to use it. We remember better if we connect new learning with previous learning, so be sure to exploit this way of enhancing memory. For example, has it occurred to you that many of the things that you learned in Chapter 1 about active learning apply directly to this chapter? Active listening is one type of active learning—the two are clearly connected. You can use connections like these to increase your understanding.

By making learning more meaningful, becoming an active listener in all of your college courses, and selecting the note-taking style best suited to the particular situation, you can become a master student.

 Voices of Successful Students

Here are successful students' comments on strategies to improve listening skills:

"Get enough rest so that you can stay alert in class."

"Participate as much as possible."

"Read the chapter to be discussed prior to class—it helps a lot."

"Try to relate lectures to personal situations or ideas."

Extension Activities

Cooperative Learning Activity: Comparing Notes

Compare and contrast the note-taking style you use with each of the Reading Selections at the end of this chapter with the notes taken by other members of the group. Were some approaches better than others? Why? What did you learn about your own note-taking skills?

Self-Improvement Strategy: Note-Taking Self-Evaluation

Review your evaluation of your note-taking strategies from Box 6.4. What have you learned from this chapter that will correct your weaknesses? Write a "prescription" for what you can do to improve your note taking.

Writing and Reflecting: Taking Notes on Professional Readings

The purpose of this reading activity is to expand your knowledge of your major field and develop your skills in summarizing.

First, locate a professional journal article related to your major. A journal differs from a magazine or newspaper in that it is written for an audience of professionals with specialized training rather than for a general audience. Check the list of periodicals at the library for titles of major journals in your field.

Second, read and annotate the article. Make certain that you can:

- state the author's main idea,
- identify the major points in the article using a list or graphic organizer, and
- briefly describe supporting evidence/details.

Third, write a one-page paper with three parts:

1. Explain why you selected this particular article.
2. Summarize the article (main idea, major points, brief examples of supporting evidence).
3. Evaluate the article. Do not simply say, "I liked it" or "I didn't like it." Critique the article in terms of its content, clarity, organization, persuasiveness, writing style, and so forth. For example, what did you learn from reading it? Did the author answer all of the questions you expected to have answered, based on the title?

Reading Selections

Reading Selection 1

Do not read the following passage on television viewing yet. **Ask someone to read it to you aloud.** While you listen, take notes on the key points. Then go back and read the passage yourself and highlight the main ideas. Look over the notes you took as the passage was read aloud. Did you do a good job of listening and note taking? How did hearing the passage read aloud enable you to improve your understanding?

Television and the Real World of College Study

Even though—if you are anything like the average young adult—you are accustomed to averaging about 16 hours of television per week, this habit will hinder your success in college. Why? Because college is focused on developing higher-level thinking skills, and most television viewing operates at the lowest levels of thinking. Mostly, people just look at television. To elaborate further on the contention that the great majority of television watching is basic visual image processing, consider these points from leading communications expert Neil Postman (1982):

- **Little preparation is required.** From toddlerhood on, you already know most of what you need to watch most television programs. There is no such thing as a television-watching course or remedial television watching because virtually anyone who can see and hear can join the ranks of the television audience.
- **Little skill is involved.** Even after 65 years of practice watching television, your ability will remain pretty much at the same level. That is because minimal skill is involved in the first place. Watching television does not move hierarchically from beginner to advanced, for example, and little practice is required to become perfect at staring at the tube.
- **Sight is more important than sound.** The ability to recognize electronic images instantly is the main ac-

tivity while watching television; sound is secondary. You can, for example, turn the sound off on your set and still get the gist of what is happening on most television programs.

For all of these reasons, television does little to contribute to the life of the mind or to present new intellectual challenges. It is accessible to anyone who can see, it is understandable almost immediately, and it relies more on sensory input than on thought.

But what about those talk shows—aren't they intellectually stimulating? Actually, most popular talk shows are designed to be emotionally charged rather than informative. Furthermore, few of the guests on these programs are experts on the subjects that they talk about. Instead of interviewing a researcher about child abuse, for example, it is more common to invite an abused person to talk about his or her experiences or to confront the abusive person on stage. Because these programs often involve more theatrics and showmanship than well-reasoned arguments, few real experts will consent to appear on them. Over the years, there have been numerous instances of the guests on talk shows being impostors. For all of these reasons, the authoritativeness of talk show information is suspect. Talk shows frequently select material on the basis of how shocking, sensationalistic, or titillating it is. As a result, much of the information on talk shows is unreliable, distorted, pure opinion, or simply untrue.

But what about public television and all those educational programs? Be honest. What percentage of your television watching time is actually devoted to documentaries or other educational programs? When people watch television, it is mostly for the purpose of switching their brains to off—one reason that Marie Winn titled her best-selling book about television *The Plug-In Drug*. Few people look to television as a means of intellectual stimulation. In fact, with the advent of the remote control, few people watch any one program long enough to know what it is about. Mainly, they just flip from channel to channel or "channel surf" to see what else is on. As Lunenfeld and Lunenfeld (1992) observe:

In college, television is about as unimportant as it will ever be. Many college professors do not even own a set, and, even if they do, they are unlikely to be watching the situation comedies, soap operas, talk shows, or late-night programs that are most popular in the ratings. The emphasis in college is on seeking accurate, authoritative information from expert sources, deepening your understanding of ideas and issues, making a commitment to a career, and learning the values of your professional field. Television has little to do with any of this. Instructors seldom appreciate any references to television, and, unlike high school, the main topic of discussion the next day will not be what was on television the night before, unless war was declared or your college sports team made it to the national playoffs. (p, 15)

But what if you really like watching television? What if you are a self-confessed addict? What should you do? Here are four suggestions for weaning yourself away from the screen:

- **Analyze the time you devote to watching television.** Take a cold, hard look at your television-viewing patterns by keeping a log for 1 week of the number of minutes you devote to watching. Consider limiting your viewing to just one or two programs per week. Even the most avid watcher has to admit that there usually is not much on anyway, and whatever *is* on, if it is good, will usually be repeated . . . and repeated . . . and repeated. If someone offered to make your productive, waking day 2 hours longer without asking you to sacrifice any sleep, you would probably jump at the chance to have that extra time. Yet TV watchers often overlook the fact that they spend at least that much time watching television every day. All it takes is one movie or a couple of programs. Many of the students who claim to have no time in their schedules to study or get involved in extracurricular activities would free up their schedules and improve their grades significantly by switching off the set.

  If you are from a home where the television set is on constantly, you do not have to keep up this family "tradition." Be rebellious! Make your own life now that you are out on your own. Break those habits that interfere with your concentration and success in college. Instead of joining the "nation of spectators" Americans have become from watching television during their leisure time, break free from its domination and do something more meaningful and productive with your life and talents.
- **Think objectively about how much television controls you.** A student who was in danger of being dismissed from college due to his low grade point average helps illustrate how television can control you. His academic adviser was bending over backward to find a time in her busy schedule when they could meet, but he refused two different possible appointment times because they conflicted with his favorite television programs! Finally, she said, "It sounds to me like you are going to have to make a decision. Do you want to stay in college or stay home and watch TV?" Evidently, the student made his decision. He now has plenty of time to keep up with television because he dropped out of college. He had the choice,

and he made it. But will he be happy with that decision 10 or 15 years from now? If he is, fine. But what if he regrets abandoning his college career and finds his current job unfulfilling? What if his disappointment affects his self-esteem and relationships? Most of the programs that this student regarded as so important were probably rerun in the summer. Was television worth abandoning a college education over? Probably not.

Instead of being tied to the set, take control. Give someone some blank videotapes and ask them to record your favorite show. Then, next time you are sick in bed, home on break, or snowbound, you can look forward to catching up. The idea is for *you* to schedule television rather than allowing it to schedule you. Exert some personal control over television.
- **Choose real activities over televised ones.** On most college campuses, there are usually several real, live events you can participate in every week—a film, a sporting event, a lecture by a famous speaker, a debate on a controversial issue, a professional conference in your chosen field. Do not waste your time sitting alone in your room staring at a television set. Get out and meet interesting people, think about big ideas, and talk about important issues. This is the best preparation for your chosen profession, where you will be expected to know how to do all of these things as a well-educated person. In many ways, participating in the special events on your campus form a "hidden curriculum" of college. By becoming actively involved outside class in intellectual pursuits, you can learn just as much as you do while in your classes, and that learning often makes the difference between an ordinary student and an outstanding one.
- **Put your studies first.** Think about how television affects your academic decisions. Did you ever schedule classes around a soap opera? Did you ever turn down an invitation to an intellectual event on campus just because it interfered with your favorite program? Now think how your grades might look if a significant portion of the time you devoted to watching television had been devoted to study instead. It is estimated that only about 23% of students spend more than 16 hours per week studying (Lunenfeld & Lunenfeld, 1992, p. 14). When that 16 hours is added to a common semester course load of 15 hours, that still is only 31 hours. But if you had a real job, your standard time commitment would be 40 hours. Actually, in order for college life to be anything like the real world of work, you would need to study for *25 hours per week.* Remember that "40 quality hours strikes experts as enough for any student to study, week after week. The beauty is that you can stretch your 40 hours over 7 days and not have to cram it in during an exhausting, 5-day, 9–5 routine. . . . Distribute the study hours sensibly. Do your homework 4 1/2 hours a day, Monday through Friday. Get them in when it's convenient, but get them in. Be as consistent as if you were punching a time clock. Take Friday night and Saturday for whatever you want, picking up the slack on Sunday with 7

hours of study" (Lunenfeld & Lunenfeld, 1992, p. 14). If you follow a real-world work plan and shut off the TV, it is amazing how much you can accomplish.

You have no doubt heard people say that college is what you make it. This means that a college education is not simply a matter of the prestige of your school or how difficult your major is considered to be. It depends on your personal investment of time and energy at your campus in your field of study. A thousand students with the same major at the same institution can come away with very different levels of education. You can be sure that the students who got the most benefit from their educational experience were the ones who knew how to pull the plug on the television set. (Jalongo, 1996)

Reading Selection 2: Short Passages

In the following quotations, authors talk about theme, plot, and point of view in literature (Safire & Safir, 1994).* As you read each selection, imagine that you are hearing the words spoken (or ask someone to read them to you). Go back and read each passage as if you were studying your class notes. Then do the following:

1. Decide which note-taking strategy on pages 152–156 would best capture the highlights of each passage.
2. After choosing an appropriate strategy, use it with the passage.
3. Write a sentence or two explaining why you selected that note-taking strategy.
4. Evaluate how well it worked.

On Theme

Isabelle Ziegler (1994) makes some important observations about literary themes. Imagine that you are hearing these words spoken, and take notes on the main ideas. Be sure to select a note-taking style that matches the content.

Leading all themes is the fight to survive. People want to read about this whether it concerns the survival of a man, a mouse, or a worm. The second most demanded theme is man's ability, in William Faulkner's words, not only to survive but to prevail. Another successful theme is how to prevail and be happy at the same time. How to be and how to do are almost certain guarantees of a successful book or article: how to be beautiful, happy,

---

* From *Good Advice on Writing* by William Safire and Leonard Safir. Copyright 1992 by Cobbett Corporation. Reprinted by permission of the author.

popular, healthy, strong, successful (socially, sexually, professionally, spiritually) and how to do anything from subdividing a tiny planeria to visiting another planet. Still another popular theme is the veil of mystery, going behind the scenes and observing how other people live, prevail, and die. (pp. 154–155)

On Plot

Rita Mae Brown (1994) has this to say about plots:

I believe there are four main plots. They are as follows:

- The Self vs. The Self   Internal Conflict
- The Self vs. Another   Internal Conflict (Personal)
- The Self vs. The State   External Conflict (Impersonal)
- The Self vs. Time/Nature   Perspective Conflict

For 99 percent of all novels, conflict is the core of the plot. Without it there is no tension and there's no reason to turn the page. Essays are the place for gentle reflection. Novels are not. (pp. 177-178)

On Confusion Between Plot and Theme

Phyllis Reynolds Naylor (1994) makes the following suggestions for distinguishing between plot and theme:

If you sometimes confuse plot with theme, keep the two elements separate by thinking of theme as what the story is about, and plot as the situation that brings it into focus. You might think of theme as the message of the story—the lesson to be learned, the question that is asked, or what the author is trying to tell us about life and the human condition. Plot is the action by which this truth will be demonstrated. (p. 251)

On Point of View

Cleanth Brooks and Robert Penn Warren (1994) explain four basic points of view in writing:

This [point of view] involves the question of who tells the story. We may make four basic distinctions: (1) a character may tell his own story in the first person; (2) a character may tell, in the first person, a story which he has observed; (3) the author may tell what happens in a purely objective sense—deeds, words, gestures—without going into the minds of the characters and without giving his own comment; (4) the author may tell what happens with full liberty to go into the minds of characters and give his own comment. These four types of narration may be called (1) first-person, (2) first-person observer, (3) author-observer, (4) omniscient author. Combinations of these methods are, of course, possible. (p. 193)

Reading Selection 3: Building Interest

Here is some expert advice on maintaining concentration:

Try to maintain an interest in what you are studying.

(a) *If you do not already have an interest in the course you are taking, try to develop an interest.* One way is to discuss the course with someone who has taken it and enjoyed it. Also, a student who is interested in that subject area could probably give you ideas about why s/he is interested in the field and what can make the course more enjoyable for you. Another approach is to read magazine articles on assigned material, or watch a TV program or program segment on a study topic. At least, you can stay alert for interesting relationships between what you happened to read or see elsewhere and what you are studying.

(b) *During each study session, try to develop an interest in what you are doing.* Sometimes surveying or previewing the material will alert you to ideas and information of interest which will heighten your ability to concentrate and comprehend. You will usually benefit by trying to focus on the material's main points rather than by allowing yourself to get lost in the details. Looking for the general principles and broad generalizations in a chapter can often make it easier to concentrate because you know you are learning what is important.

(c) Some students have trouble concentrating on their work because they think about things they would rather be doing—their studies are not interesting enough for them at the time. One way to avoid such daydreaming is to *set aside time for the activities you particularly enjoy.* Then, when you do sit down to study, you will be less prone to begin thinking of other things you have already done or have plans to do. You will know your work is not keeping you from enjoyable activities; it is simply getting the attention it deserves.

(d) Another way to maintain interest while studying is to *arrange for variety.* That can mean studying for any one course for only an hour or so at a time, or by varying the types of activities included in a study session. You can read for an hour and then switch to writing. It helps to plan ahead for variety so you will not waste time trying to think up ways to provide it. (Huffman, 1992/93, pp. 313–314, based on Memory & Yoder, 1988)

Reading Selection 4

As you read the following passage about myth, fill in this graphic organizer:

Definition (What Myth Is):

Characteristics (Features of Myths):

Rationale (What Good Are Myths?):

A myth is a sacred story set in time and place outside history, describing in fiction form the fundamental truths of nature and human life. Mythology gives body to the invisible and eternal factors that are always part of life but don't appear in a literal, factual story. Most of the time, when we tell a story about our lives, we couch it in purely human terms. When was the last time you talked about monsters, angels, or demons when you were describing some strongly felt experience? Myth reaches beyond the personal to express an imagery reflective of archetypal issues that shape every human life. . . . In the past few years, a great deal of literature has appeared on the subject of mythology. The strong public response, I believe, has to do with our need for depth and substance in the way we imagine our experience. Mythology from around the world vividly explores the fundamental patterns and themes of human life as you find them anywhere on the globe. The imagery may be specific to the cultures in which the mythology arises, but the issues are universal. This is one of the values of mythology—its way of cutting through personal differences in order to get to the great themes of human experience. . . .

Mythology, for example, often presents a cosmology, a description of how the world came to be and how it is governed. It is important to be oriented, to have some imagination of the physical universe in which we live. That is why many mythologists have noted that even modern science, for all its factual validity, also gives us a cosmology, a mythology in the true sense of the word. . . .

Myth has the connotation of falsehood, as when we judge that an assumption about the way things are is "only" a myth. Myth may seem to be a flight of fancy because its imagery is often fantastic, with many gods and devils or impossible acts and unreal settings. But the fantastic elements in mythology are essential to the genre; they take us away from the realistic particulars of life to invisible factors that are nonetheless real. . . . Jung advised us to turn to traditional mythology in order to *amplify,* to see more clearly and hear more sharply the themes that are special to us. But the important thing is to realize that, although life seems to be a matter of literal causes and effects, in fact we are living out deep stories, often unconsciously.* (Moore, 1992, pp. 220–224)

---

* From *Care of the Soul* by Thomas Moore. Copyright 1992 by Thomas Moore. Reprinted by permission of HarperCollins Publishers, Inc.

Reading Selection 5

The following research summary discusses how college students can get more from lectures by self-questioning—asking themselves questions. Use the problem-solution graphic organizer in Figure 6.6 to take notes on the material. Then write a one-sentence summary of the author's main point.

For decades students in study skills courses have been taught procedures and formats to improve note taking from lectures. Hiller Spires at North Carolina State University has proposed that student comprehension of lecture material may be enhanced through direct instruction in comprehension monitoring through self-questioning. The comprehension monitoring includes self-generation of questions before, during, and after the lecture to help students set a purpose for listening, monitor concentration and comprehension, and evaluate comprehension of the content presented (Spires & Stone, 1989).

To better understand the impact of this comprehension monitoring procedure on the quality of student notes and on their comprehension of lecture material, Spires (1993) conducted an investigation with 99 college freshmen enrolled in a reading/learning skills course. The students were placed in one of three treatment groups. The first group received direct instruction in traditional note-taking skills plus the self-questioning procedure, the second group was taught note-taking skills plus the self-questioning procedure, and the third group served as a no-treatment control.

The group of students who learned the comprehension-monitoring strategy outperformed the other two groups on measures of the format and content of their lecture notes as well as on a measure of immediate comprehension. The performance of the note-taking skills-only group did exceed that of the control group. While Spires recognizes that additional research in this area needs to be conducted, these initial results suggest that when students know how to monitor their comprehension, they can benefit more fully from information presented in class.

References

Banks, C., McCarthy, M., & Rasool, J. (1993). *Reading and learning across the disciplines.* Belmont, CA: Wadsworth.

Bromley, K. D. (1988). *Language arts: Exploring connections.* Boston: Allyn & Bacon.

Brooks, C., & Warren, R. P. (1994). In W. Safire & L. Safir (Eds.), *Good advice on writing.* New York: Simon & Schuster.

Brown, R. M. (1994). In W. Safire & L. Safir (Eds.), *Good advice on writing.* New York: Simon & Schuster.

Covey, S. (1989). *The seven habits of highly effective people: Restoring the character ethic.* New York: Fireside/Simon & Schuster.

DeHaven, E. P. (1983). *Teaching and learning the language arts.* Boston: Little, Brown.

Funk, H., & Funk, G. D. (1989). Guidelines for developing listening skills. *The Reading Teacher, 42,* 660–663.

Hamp-Lyons, E. (1982). *Survey review of materials for teaching advanced listening and note-taking.* (ERIC Document Reproduction Service No. ED 225–359).

Huffman, L. E. (1992/93). 60-second synopses for better concentration. *Journal of Reading, 36*(4), 313–314.

Hunsaker, R. A. (1990). *Understanding and developing the skills of oral communication: Speaking and listening.* Englewood, CO: Morton.

Jalongo, M. R. (1991). *Strategies for developing listening skills* (Fastback 314). Bloomington, IL: Phi Delta Kappa.

Lundsteen, S. W. (1979). *Listening: Its impact at all levels on reading and the other language arts* (rev. ed.). Urbana, IL: National Council of Teachers of English.

Lunenfeld, M., & Lunenfeld, P. (1992). *College basics: How to start right and finish strong.* Buffalo, NY: Semester Press.

Memory, D. M., & Yoder, C. Y. (1988). Improving concentration in content classrooms. *Journal of Reading, 31,* 426–436.

Moore, T. (1992). *Care of the soul.* New York: HarperCollins.

Naylor, P. R. (1994). In W. Safire & L. Safir (Eds.), *Good advice on writing.* New York: Simon & Schuster.

O'Hair, M., & Wooden, S. (1988). Impact of listening skill development on college reading, notetaking, and study skills. In T. J. Betenbough & S. A. Biggs (Eds.), *Innovative learning strategies 1987-88: Eighth yearbook of the college reading improvement special interest group* (pp. 33–38). Newark, DE: International Reading Association.

O'Hair, M., Wooden, S., & O'Hair, D. (1987). Enhancement of listening skills as a prerequisite to improved study skill. *Journal of the International Listening Association, 1*(2).

Postman, N. (1982). *The disappearance of childhood.* New York: Delacourte.

Reiff, J. (1992). *What research says to the teacher: Learning styles.* Washington, DC: National Education Association.

Reynolds, M. C. (1992). *Reading for understanding.* Belmont, CA: Wadsworth.

Safire, W., & Safir, L. (Eds.). (1994). *Good advice on writing.* New York: Simon & Schuster.

Shepherd, J. F. (1988). *Reading skills for college study* (3rd ed.). Boston: Houghton Mifflin.

Smith, P. L., & Tompkins, G. E. (1988). Structured notetaking: A new strategy for content area readers. *Journal of Reading, 32,* 49.

Spargo, E. (1994). *The college student: Reading and study skills.* Providence, RI: Jamestown.

Spires, H. A. (1993). Learning from a lecture: Effects of comprehension monitoring. *Reading Research and Instruction, 32,* 19–30.

Spires, H. A., & Stone, D. (1989). Directed notetaking activity: A self-questioning approach. *Journal of Reading, 33,* 36–39.

Tuttle, G. E. (1988, March). *A study of listening across three situational variables.* Paper presented to the International Listening Association, Scottsdale, AZ.

Verderber, R., & Elder, A. (1976). *An analysis of student communication habits.* Unpublished study, University of Cincinnati.

Werner, E. (1975). A study of communication time. In A. Wolvin & C. Coakley (Eds.), *Listening.* Dubuque, IA: Brown.

Ziegler, I. (1994). In W. Safire & L. Safir (Eds.), *Good advice on writing.* New York: Simon & Schuster.

Participating in Class Discussions and Making Presentations

The ability to communicate effectively is important in every aspect of life—from school to marriage to almost any career you could undertake. . . . What you say and write can have a profound effect on you and the people around you. * (p. 21)

—Lori Beckman Johnson, *PC Novice Magazine*

---

* From "Finding the Right Word: Dictionaries, Thesauruses, and Quotations," by L. B. Johnson, 1994, *PC Novice, 5*, p. 21.

Prereading Questions

- How would you define class participation? List four types of speaking situations that you expect to be important to your college career and your professional career after college.

- What are your major concerns about making presentations in your college classes? Do you have any ideas about how to overcome the obstacles you may face?

- What makes a good speech good? What criteria are used to assess the overall effectiveness of speakers?

Assessing Prior Knowledge

What experiences have you had with public speaking in school or elsewhere? Have you ever presented a report in class? Been an active member of a student group? Accepted an award? Explained how to do something to an audience of less experienced individuals? Participated in a panel discussion or mock trial? Think about what you would like to do better when you speak before a group. What are your greatest concerns?

Vignette: Three Students Make a Class Presentation

Next week, Larissa will be making a presentation to her classmates on the paper that she wrote about changes in the American family for her "Introduction to Sociology" course. She finds the prospect of standing up in front of her peers intimidating and worries that she will make a mistake or look foolish.

Dara is reasonably confident that she can speak before a group because she had plenty of opportunities to practice public speaking while she was in 4-H—she even made it to the state-level competition. But she is unsure whether some of the things she has used in the past are considered appropriate in a college classroom. Of particular concern are the memory prompts, such as note cards, or the visual aids, such as posters, that she has used successfully before as a way to jog her memory and maintain audience attention.

Levon has been assigned to work with four other classmates to plan a group presentation, and he was elected as the leader. Just getting together for two meetings has been a problem because of everyone's different schedules, and now one of the group members is not doing his share of the work. Levon cannot decide how to deal with this problem, and the other group members have been complaining and expecting him to do something about it. No one wants to do the work *for* the negligent classmate, but no one wants to jeopardize his or her own grade, either.

Class Participation

As the vignette examples illustrate, students who are required to speak in class often have to resolve a number of issues, including coping with nervousness, preparing appropriately, and, sometimes, sharing responsibility. If you feel nervous about contributing in class during discussion times or toss and turn the night before a presentation, you are not alone. Studies report that worries about public speaking are listed among the top five concerns of American adults (Motley, 1988; Schaefer & Brashear, 1989). Knowing how to prepare for

Improvement in Action ⅢⅢ➡

Think about all the different speaking situations you might encounter, such as talking to a friend on the telephone, asking someone to dance, being interviewed for a job, or making a presentation to a class of 100 freshmen. Try to identify two types of speaking situations:

**Speaking Situations in Which
You Feel Confident**

**Speaking Situations in Which
You Feel Nervous**

What factors (e.g., group size, unfamiliarity with audience, importance of making a good impression) apparently contribute to your anxiety level? What factors seem to diminish your concerns about speaking? How can you make anxiety-producing speaking situations more like the ones in which you feel comfortable?

different types of college class participation situations can help you feel less self-conscious. Learning how to work with others in making group presentations is another fundamental skill, not only during college but also later on in virtually any profession. This is one reason that college students are required to make in-class presentations—their jobs after graduation will undoubtedly demand it. In this chapter, we offer you sound advice on how to participate more meaningfully in your college classes and master the skills of making effective presentations.

Improvement in Action ⅢⅢ➡

Think about all the classroom situations you have experienced during your school career. If you are like most people, sometimes you felt more comfortable participating, and sometimes you were more reluctant. Now think about the underlying reasons and organize those reasons into two categories:

Reasons I Did Not Participate   **Reasons I Did Participate**

What do your lists reveal about what you need to become a more active learner?

Barriers to Participation

Both our personal experience and studies conducted over the years show that only about 10% of college students voluntarily contribute in class. Many students say that they are afraid of looking foolish or asking a stupid question, so they sit in the back of the room, stare at the floor, and keep quiet. Large numbers of college students select silence as a "survival" strategy for several reasons. One reason is it seemed to work in high school:

> Jumping in to the free-for-all of college life takes getting used to. In high school, kids were what they wore, what they listened to, and, most important, who their friends were. If you did what was assigned and repeated what was taught, you got good grades. . . .
>
> Kids get the wrong signals in high school: only "dumb" people go for tutoring, only "wimps" drop classes, only "jerks" sit in the front row, and only a "teacher's pet" talks in class. That's way off base when it comes to college life. Students are happier when they jump in and take an active part. Accept the fact that people do fail courses and everyone needs all the help he or she can get. . . .
>
> When students solve their academic problems, they feel at home in the college environment. Worries about being unsophisticated fade as you learn to handle academics. Social life improves. There are hundreds and often thousands of people your age with similar goals floating around to provide a pool of new friends. Be proud of getting admitted to college. Only one in three high schoolers makes it as far as you have. . . . You deserve good grades, a full social life, and a strong start on your career. (Lunenfeld & Lunenfeld, 1992, p. 10)

When you feel anxious and self-conscious about speaking, particularly about speaking in front of your peers, you need to be aware that it is normal. If you are a young adult, it is also a stage that you are going through. Taken as a group, adolescents tend to be overly concerned about what their peers think of them. Young adults frequently have the feeling that all eyes are fixed on them and that those eyes are harshly judgmental of them whenever they speak. Believe it or not, this attitude is so common among adolescents that psychologists refer to it as the "imaginary audience"—the feeling of always being "on stage" (Elkind & Bowen, 1979). As psychologist Guy Lefrancois (1992) explains, one sign of maturity is overcoming this feeling of being "on stage."

BOX 7.3   ## *Improvement in Action* ⅢⅢ➡

Reread the preceding quote and list the incorrect assumptions that students fresh out of high school make about college. Now that you have been on the college scene, think of some additional assumptions about learning in college that you have found to be inaccurate or problematic. Compare the items you identified with those of the total class.

Assumptions in High School   **Assumptions in College**

The adolescent's imaginary audience is a collection of all who might be concerned with the adolescent's self and behavior. It is the *they* in expressions such as "they say . . ." or "they predict. . . ." Social psychologists inform us that each of us behaves as though "they" are watching and care. But the imaginary audiences of adults are much smaller, much less pervasive, and far less important than those of adolescents. According to Elkind, it is because of this imaginary audience to which the adolescent is continually reacting that young adolescents are often very self-conscious. It is also because of this same audience that many become so concerned about their hair, clothing and other aspects of physical appearance. It is as though adolescents believe that others are as deeply concerned about them as they themselves are and that others constantly judge them. (pp. 595–596)

Simply being aware that these feelings tend to diminish as you mature and gain experience can be of some comfort. If you think of participating in class as a sign of maturity (as many of your instructors do!), it might help you conquer the "imaginary audience" that interferes with active learning.

One of the most sensible ways to increase your confidence about participating in everyday class discussions is to read the assigned course material. If you have done the background reading and really tried to understand it, your effort will show. Then you will feel confident that you are asking good questions and can enter into the conversation without embarrassment.

Why Participate?

Students are often told to participate in class, but they are seldom told why. Actually, class participation offers several advantages:

1. **Participation enhances overall learning.** When you contribute in class, you stay alert and get involved. Even the best students can lose interest in a class if they never utter a word. Participating forces you to listen more carefully to others and really think about the topic being presented and discussed. It helps you master course material, for just as the Chinese proverb suggests, "I hear and I forget. I see and I remember. I do and I understand." Based on this piece of wisdom, it may not be that you have a poor memory at all. It may be that you need to become a more active learner. Give yourself the best chance at learning by speaking up in class!

2. **Participating regularly can improve your grades.** As any instructor can attest, students who do not attend class regularly or who look totally relaxed in the back of the room as they whisper funny remarks or write their homework for the next class are nearly always the same ones who are in a total panic at exam time or when midterm and final course grades are reported. Obviously, negligence like this has an adverse effect on academic performance. But participation can improve your grades in more subtle ways as well. If you feel that you are not the best writer, for example, making an effective presentation can compensate for a less than-perfect composition.

3. **Participation builds relationships with instructors and peers.** Yet another advantage of participating in class is that you will get to know your instructors and they will get to know you. Building these professional relationships with faculty is important when you need advice, additional help, or a job recommendation as you finish your program. By participating in class, you not only distinguish yourself from the crowd, you also work with ideas and remember them better than your classmates who remain silent all semester.

Successful students are very adept at "reading" the type of participation that the instructor seeks. Some faculty are much more open to sharing a personal experience than others, for example. Some prefer to present a lecture *followed* by a question-and-answer period. Still others teach almost entirely by raising questions. Particularly if you are being graded on class participation, find out how the instructor defines participation. To some instructors, class participation and class attendance are synonymous so that if you are consistently present, you are numbered among those who have participated. To other faculty, participation means frequent comments and questions during class discussion. To still others, it is based on the quality of formal presentations made in class that are rated using a checklist. Find out how each of your instructors defines and assesses participation. Be certain to look in the course syllabus to see how much importance is placed on participation, too. Speaking up and having a good attendance record can make the difference between an average grade and an excellent grade or, if the course is very difficult, between passing and having to repeat the course.

Types of Participation

College students have several important roles as speakers, including contributing in class, working in small groups, and making formal presentations to the class, either individually or in groups.

Contributing in Class

What, exactly, do instructors mean when they say that they expect you to contribute in class? At the minimum, they expect you to attend class, stay awake, and look alert. Most faculty also expect students to answer questions posed by the instructor or other students, make comments related to the topic under study, and ask questions—particularly those questions that reveal careful thinking about the subject matter or issues under discussion. Usually, faculty expect all three of these types of daily participation—answering questions, making comments, and asking questions—to be based on assigned and extra readings for the course. Unlike some of your previous experiences in which simply offering your personal opinion was often satisfactory, now the expectation is that you will *support* your opinions with what you are learning in the class. Generally speaking, unless a faculty member specifically asks for an account of personal experience (e.g., " Have any of you ever appeared on television?"), the instructor is probably more interested in your interpretation of the course material and what you are learning from your reading (e.g., "What are some of the most commonly used forms of nonverbal communication?").

The strategies that faculty use to encourage class participation vary considerably. Some faculty look down the class list or on a seating chart and randomly call on students to make certain that students are prepared for class. Some professors make class participation a key component of your grade and base it primarily on the quality of a major presen-

---

BOX 7.4   *Improvement in Action* ⅢⅢ➡

As you are walking into class with a friend, she says, "Let's sit way in the back. I like to keep a low profile in all my classes." You know that she was recently put on academic probation and is in danger of dropping out. Put the advice offered in this chapter thus far into your own words and try to convince her that more active class participation could improve her situation.

tation that you make to the total group. Other faculty give unannounced or "pop" quizzes as a way of encouraging regular attendance and finding out whether students are doing the required reading. Still other instructors simply equate class participation with attendance. At some universities, for example, an attendance policy is published in the undergraduate catalog. Then, if a student misses more than a certain number of classes during the semester, the instructor can lower the student's grade. Be certain to find out whether your college has an attendance policy and how it might affect your academic standing. Even if your institution does not have such a policy, one thing is clear: Students who are frequently absent and do not, at the very least, participate by showing up for class generally have poor grades. Make certain that you understand how each instructor defines class participation, and decide to be a participant rather than a nonparticipant.

Working in Small Groups

Another important way of contributing in class is through work in small groups. Increasingly, college faculty are asking students to work together in achieving a common goal. This practice, called *cooperative learning,* has much to recommend it. One rationale for collaborative work is that it helps students master not only the course content but also the interpersonal skills that are in such demand in the workplace. Group work can result in better overall quality and more in-depth projects as students pool their resources and share responsibility. By working together, they can "divide and conquer" more challenging and complex tasks. On the more practical side, group work can save instructional time. Instead of 40 presentations to schedule in a class of 40, for example, there would be just 10 presentations to schedule if students worked in groups of four. This approach would provide more time for each presentation and more class time for other learning activities.

For all these reasons, you will find that work in small groups is assigned in a wide variety of classes. You might be directed to apply course material to a case study in psychology class, to analyze samples of children's work in an education course, to peer edit others' writing in a composition course, or to discuss a piece of literature in groups using a set of prepared questions. Usually, the instructor will circulate around the room to listen in, answer questions, and informally assess each group's progress toward the goals set. Group work is not a time filler or a time to socialize. It is designed to help you meet the course objectives and gain mastery of course material. If you take it seriously, you will find that other students look to you to contribute meaningfully, and soon you will be developing leadership skills that will serve you well, not only in your career but throughout life.

Most small groups are asked to select a recorder (someone to take notes) and/or a reporter (someone to share highlights of the small group's discussion with the total class). Instead of avoiding these roles, volunteer. Your classmates will appreciate your willingness to accept the role of recorder or reporter, and your presentation skills will develop as a result. Additionally, your instructors will get to know you and remember that you have participated actively at grading time. Because participating in small-group activities and in-class discussions tends to be rather spontaneous and "ad-lib," these forms of class presentation are rather informal. There will also be times when you are expected to prepare thoroughly and make more formal presentations to the class, as the next section will describe.

Making Formal Presentations

The third key speaking role for college students is making a carefully preplanned in-class presentation, either individually or with members of a group. One of the most common mistakes in making a class presentation is to treat it like a presidential address by preparing a

Figure 7.1
**Presentations: What You
Need to Know Before
You Plan**

1. How much time should I plan for?
2. How formal/informal should the presentation be?
3. What kinds of visual aids are acceptable?
4. What resources (e.g., overhead projector, chart paper, videocassette player, etc.) are available?
5. What criteria will be use to assess my performance?

BOX 7.5   *Improvement in Action* ⅢⅢ➡

If you were free to choose the type of classroom participation that you would be graded on, which of the following options would you choose?

- Group activities with a group of four to six classmates
- A formal presentation to the entire class presented by you
- A formal presentation to the entire class presented with you as a member of a group or panel
- Individual comments and questions during regular class discussion
- A good attendance record

What does your choice reveal about your perceptions of your role as a participant?

---

lengthy speech and then attempting to memorize it or, worse yet, read it aloud. The most common type of formal presentation in a college class is a summary of a paper you have written. Once again, do not think of a presentation as a speech and try to memorize it or read every word. You will probably have no more than 5 or 10 minutes, and you certainly cannot read or say everything in your paper within that time. To plan an effective presentation, you need to get answers to all five questions listed in Figure 7.1 before you begin. If your instructor has neglected to give you this information, be certain to ask for further clarification before you begin planning your presentation.

Characteristics of Effective Presentations

According to the ancient Greeks, a good speech is composed of three equally important elements: ethos, pathos, and logos.

- **Ethos** refers to the speaker's sincerity, integrity, and credibility; it is the origin for the word *ethical*.
- **Pathos** refers to the human element, the "human interest" aspect that helps the listeners see how your information relates to their lives and the lives of others; it is the origin for the word *empathy*.
- **Logos** refers to the logic and persuasiveness of your argument; it is the origin for the word *logical*.

BOX 7.6   *Improvement in Action* ⦀▶

What is the most dynamic presentation or speech you have ever heard? The dullest? What makes an effective speech? An ineffective one? Compare your answers with the ABCs for an effective presenter in Figure 7.2.

Figure 7.2
ABCs for Effective Presenters

From *How to Make Presentations That Teach and Transform,* by R. J. Garmston and B. W. Wellman, 1992, Alexandria, VA: Association for Supervision and Curriculum Development. Copyright 1992 by ASCD. Adapted with permission.

Effective speakers know how to:

- **a**nticipate the questions that their **a**udience might have and **a**ddress them,
- **b**uild rapport with the audience and adapt the information to their needs,
- **c**ommunicate their depth of caring about a subject,
- **d**esign presentations to meet multiple learning objectives that are tailored to the audience,
- **e**ngage the audience in really working with the material,
- **f**ocus audience attention and accelerate learning through the use of examples,
- **g**ive their audiences the reinforcement of powerful visual aids to enhance the spoken message, and
- **h**elp their audiences maintain attention by using a variety of delivery strategies.

If you think about it, every outstanding speaker you have ever heard met the three requirements of ethos, pathos, and logos. Think, for example, of Martin Luther King, Jr.'s "I Have a Dream" speech, Winston Churchill's speech announcing England's decision to enter the war, Abraham Lincoln's Gettysburg Address, and Sojourner Truth's "Ain't I a Woman?" speech.

Think about the best presentations you have listened to, at school or church, on television, or at some public gathering. Perhaps you have watched an awards ceremony in which famous individuals made acceptance speeches. In the most successful of these speeches, the presenters convince the audience of their sincerity (ethos), evoke a response from the audience (pathos), and reveal careful thinking about their message (logos).

Topic Selection

After you know what is expected by your instructor and the general features of an effective presentation, you can focus on selecting a topic. If you have some choice about the topic, pick something that meets two criteria: a subject you care about *and* a subject that your audience—especially the evaluator(s) of your presentation—will also appreciate. Sometimes the topic of your presentation is entirely up to you. If this is the case, choose something that you know well (or want very much to know better) *and* care deeply about. Sometimes faculty give a list of topics from which to choose and pass it around the room. By the time it gets to you, few topics on the list may appeal to you. See whether you can negotiate the topic with the faculty member. She or he may not mind if two students investigate the same topic or even if they work together.

Sometimes you can investigate a particular aspect of a topic that you find more interesting. This is called narrowing or focusing your topic. Suppose, for example, "health care reform" appears on the list of acceptable topics. If you are an education major, you might want to investigate the impact of health care reform on young children. If you are studying to become a physical therapist, on the other hand, you might want to investigate the impact of health care reform on health care professionals. By narrowing the topic and applying it to your area of interest, you might discover a topic that meets the course requirements *and* builds your knowledge base in ways you find more interesting and valuable.

After you have selected your topic, you will need to investigate it further by going to the library. Most college and university libraries offer a short course on using the library or some type of orientation program. Take advantage of these opportunities to learn how to get information more easily. Most college and university libraries are "on line" so that you can access information via computer in the library or even elsewhere on campus. Take the initiative to get familiar with the library. Do not wait until the day the assignment is due and your nerves are frayed to begin learning how to access the information that you need. If you are calm, polite, and have given some thought to the specific type of information that you need, you will find that the reference librarians—those who specialize in locating information—can help you locate the most valuable information and save you hours of searching. For more detailed information on using the library, see Activity 42 in the Appendix.

Planning the Presentation

If you feel nervous about making a presentation, it is easy to become so preoccupied that you forget about the needs of your audience. Becoming more audience centered is a key to making effective presentations. Try to put yourself in the listener's place. What would attract your interest if you were in the audience? What questions did you have before you studied the topic? Try organizing some of your information around basic questions your audience would be likely to have.

Remember that all audiences come with several basic questions:

1. What is your topic?
2. Who are you and how did you become knowledgeable about this?
3. What facts, ideas, and skills can I acquire from listening?
4. How does this topic relate to me?
5. How can I apply this new information to my situation?

Figure 7.3 is an overview of the four types of audiences that you need to consider when planning your presentation (Garmston, 1997).

BOX 7.7 *Improvement in Action* ⫸

If you had to give an impromptu talk about a topic without preparing first, what subject would you select? What topic do you know so well, for example, that you could quickly organize your thoughts as you walk to the front of the room and then talk about it intelligently for 3 minutes? Why do you think you selected this particular subject for an impromptu speech? What steps can you take to make an assigned topic feel more like the one that you selected for your impromptu speech?

Figure 7.3
Meeting the Needs of Your Audiences

From *How to Make Presentations That Teach and Transform,* By R. J. Garmston and B. W. Wellman, 1992, Alexandria, VA: Association for Supervision and Curriculum Development. Copyright 1992 by ASCD. Adapted with permission.

Every effective presentation should address the needs of four audiences:

1. The professors who ask "What?" are seeking mastery and competence that allows them to perform new skills.

   ○ Engage them with facts

   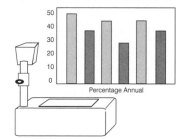

2. The friends who ask "So what?" are seeking personal involvement and interaction with other participants.

   ○ Attend to their feelings

3. The scientists who ask "Why?" are seeking understanding and the opportunity to reason about the information.

   ○ Involve them in formulating ideas

4. The inventors who ask "What if?" want to create, adapt, and reorganize information.

   ○ Get them involved in creative self-expression

   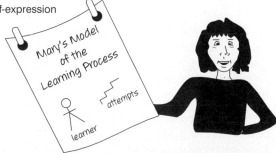

Introducing the Presentation

Get the audience involved right away. Some of the techniques that encourage audience involvement are described here:

1. **A set of questions**—When listeners are asked thought-provoking questions, they usually make more of commitment to listen and find out whether their answers were right. Rosa, a criminology student, began her presentation with "As we all know, eye witnesses to the same crime can see and describe the details of what they saw very differently. Therefore, skillful questioning is a basic skill for police officers. See whether you can answer these five questions about the recommended procedure for interviewing a witness. When you are finished, we will discuss the answers that I uncovered in my library research and the interview I conducted with a police officer."

2. **A real-life account**—When we hear about how an issue affected someone's life, it creates interest in the outcome. Jeff, a nursing major, is making a presentation on leukemia in his pediatric nursing class. He knows that his audience has a special interest in children, so he begins with an anecdote (a brief story) to get his listeners involved immediately. "This is a self-portrait drawn by Sheryll, a 7-year-old I cared for during my first clinical experience. About her picture, she said, 'My hair fell out. I don't think I'm getting better.'" Notice how this introduction establishes Jeff's *pathos* and emphasizes the human consequences of the disease before he gets into the facts and figures about leukemia.

3. **A show-of-hands survey**—One way to quickly get the group involved is to help them see how the topic relates to them and their concerns. When Larry gave a presentation on moral development in his psychology class, he began with this question: "If you knew that no speeding tickets could be issued on a designated day, how many of you would break the law by going over the speed limit?" By getting his audience to realize that they would have no compunctions about breaking the law, he can get them to think about their own morality and how their behavior is sometimes influenced more by fear of punishment than by a set of internalized standards.

4. **A startling fact or paradox**—Surprise is another element that gets the audience interested. When Brandon made a presentation on illiteracy in his "Teaching of Reading" class, for example, he told his audience that, according to the Book Industry Group, the average American reads less than one book per year. Then he presented a paradox—a situation that is puzzling and contradicts what we would expect. "How many books does the average American *teacher* read in a year?" The surprising answer—according to Feistritzer (1986)—is slightly more than one per year. After presenting this surprising introduction, Brandon moved into the major thesis of his presentation: that teachers need to be avid readers themselves if they expect children to read.

5. **A list of concerns generated by the group**—This strategy works particularly well with controversial issues or topics that are very much in the media. If you can safely assume that the audience is familiar with the topic, you can give them the opportunity to express their opinions and share their knowledge by simply listing their concerns. When Crystal made a presentation in her science class on preserving the rain forest, for example, she knew that many members of her audience already had some knowledge of and strong opinions about her topic. So she started by assessing their prior knowledge and asked, "What are some reasons that we should be concerned about the destruction of rain forests?" and created a list on an overhead transparency as people from the audience responded.

6. **Using a prop**—One dramatic type of introductory technique is the use of a concrete object or prop. A good example of this strategy occurred when former President Ronald Reagan used a dollar bill as a prop during his speech about the economy. In deciding whether to use a prop, try to analyze how formal the presentation has to be. If you are

in doubt about the appropriateness of a particular prop, check with the faculty member first. Hoff (1988) describes how, in one of the best speeches he ever heard, the speaker on the topic of diabetes made his point that the disease is not curable by giving himself the daily insulin injection that was necessary to maintain his well being. This was a very powerful way to capture the audience's attention and to meet the purpose of the presentation—to raise public awareness of the disease. For more on the use of concrete props, see Mooney and Noone's (1992) book on creating memorable speeches.

Whatever strategy you select, be certain that you are sensitive to your audience. It is also possible for a presentation to be insulting to the audience because of their race, gender, religious beliefs, or some specific situation. We once saw two students, one black and one white, work together on a poetry presentation. They had the idea of painting their faces for their presentation. The Caucasian student wore black face paint and the African-American student, white paint. Many members of the audience, including the professor, found this offensive—particularly since it was just a gimmick that went unexplained and had nothing whatsoever to do with their presentation. When you select your strategies for introducing a presentation, do not use anything that would be perceived as a way of manipulating the audience or anything that would make you less credible. The idea is for you to communicate that your intent is to be helpful and that you are well informed about your topic.

A Step-by-Step Guide to Effective Presentations

As you progress throughout your college career, you will probably be assigned to work with a group that makes a formal presentation to the entire class. Often, when students are given this assignment, they juggle their schedules, arrange a meeting, and accomplish very little because they are unsure about how to proceed. Remember that the primary objective of such a meeting is to determine who has responsibility for what. If you leave that meeting with a vague notion of what each person will contribute, your presentation will suffer. To illustrate how group planning *should* work, we will be going through the process that Carlene, Ed, Marsha, and Jose used to create an A+ presentation on the topic of memory for their educational psychology class. At their first meeting, they reviewed the instructor's requirements, shown in Figure 7.4.

Figure 7.4
Sample Presentation Assignment

Major Assignment—Educational Psychology

You are required to make a 10- to 15-minute group presentation on a topic discussed in your textbook. I will be sharing a videotaped example of an outstanding presentation from last year's class so that you will get a clearer idea of what is expected. After you complete your presentation, all members of the audience will assess your performance using the following criteria/evaluation form:

Evidence of planning and preparation	5	4	3	2	1
Accuracy and usefulness of content	5	4	3	2	1
Logic and organization of presentation	5	4	3	2	1
Quality and use of audiovisual materials	5	4	3	2	1
Opportunities for audience involvement	5	4	3	2	1

Comments:

At their first meeting, Carlene, Ed, Marsha, and Jose agreed to partition the responsibilities as outlined in Jose's notebook (see Figure 7.5).

On January 30, they meet again as scheduled and find that they have collected several excellent articles on improving memory. Following some discussion, they state their purpose as a question: How can we make the topic of memory meaningful for our audience of undergraduate students and still satisfy our instructor's expectations for covering the content?

Figure 7.5
Sample Planning Session Notes

1/21/98

Ed Psych Presentation

Due Date: February 7

Background Work

Library research: All will read and meet to compile findings on January 30.

Presentation Responsibilities

Setup: Marsha will put up posters.

Introductions (2 minutes): Carlene

Distribution of one-page summary (2 minutes): Carlene

Three memory techniques (2 minutes): Marsha highlights three memory techniques.

Memory and emotions (3 minutes): Ed discusses memory loss and early memories.

Distribution of bibliography and responses to Questions (3 minutes): Jose

Resource Materials

One-page summary (to be distributed to class): Carlene

Bibliography (also distributed to class): Jose

Visual aids (posters): Marsha

NEXT MEETING!!! JANUARY 30 right after class

BOX 7.8   *Improvement in Action* ⫸

Now that you have had the opportunity to think about making presentations in class, try to write down the sequence that you would follow in planning an effective presentation. Then compare your list with the one in Figure 7.5.

Carlene has been working on the introduction. She says that she will introduce each member of the group and recognize their contributions to the presentation. That way, their professor will know that they really did work together on it. Carlene also suggests that they introduce their topic with something like "We have all made some mistakes when our memories fail us. These errors can be embarrassing, such as forgetting someone's name just as you are about to introduce them. They might be expensive, like forgetting to fill your car with gas or checking the oil. Or, they might affect your immediate and long-term future, such as when you freeze up on an important test." The group approves of Carlene's introduction because it reveals her thinking about the topic, uses specific examples, and shows the audience how the topic relates to their lives.

Ed comments that they might want to hint at what is coming up later about memory aids by asking for a show of hands in response to the question "How many of you have used a post-it note on your computer, the bathroom mirror, or the dashboard of the car to remind yourself about something? This is just one strategy that psychologists suggest for improving memory. In the next 10 minutes, we will be sharing strategies for improving memory based on research by leading psychologists who specialize in the field. More specifically, we will be telling you about the three most widely recommended strategies for improving human memory that we found in our library research." The others agree that this would build interest and make the audience feel confident that the speaker will follow through with the commitment to be helpful. They also like the idea of getting the audience involved right away with a show of hands and reassuring them that they will stay within the allotted time.

Next, Marsha shares the poster that she created by using the largest-point type on her computer, cutting it out, and adhering it to a brightly colored piece of posterboard with a glue stick. The group is impressed with the professional look of this visual aid and feels certain that everyone will be able to read it well, even in the back of the room. Marsha says that she planned to introduce the poster with a statement like "I will describe three of the most widely recommended memory aids and offer a specific example for each one. This poster highlights each memory aid we will be describing. First, concrete prompts, like a string around the finger. Second, mnemonics, or memory aids, like "Every good boy does fine" for the musical scale. Third, visual imagery, using mental pictures to jog your memory, such as when you try to retrace every step you took before you lost your student ID card." The group members are pleased with Marsha's contribution. It is certain to help maintain attention and keep the listeners from getting confused as they take notes.

Ed shares some of the interesting ideas that he uncovered in his reading, including how disastrous it is to lose our memories. Ed plans to include some discussion of extreme memory loss, such as Alzheimer's disease and amnesia. Ed's great-grandmother is in a nursing home, and her condition has deteriorated to the extent that she no longer recognizes any of her family members. He plans to describe how tragic it is for his family to lose their great-grandma in this way. He also plans to talk about earliest memories and ask members of the audience to try to recall their first memory. According to research on the brain, these early memories are usually very vivid and rich in sensory impressions—sight, sound, touch, taste, and smell. Ed also plans to emphasize that, even if we have difficulty remembering our earliest memories and even if we eventually lose our memories, under ordinary circumstances, we can work to improve memory. The group likes the idea of looking briefly at extreme memory problems because this helps everyone realize how important our memories are to us. They think Ed's personal experience with his great-grandmother will help listeners identify with the subject and think about the emotional significance of memory.

In making their reports, each group member has located some good resources on the topic. Jose admits that he would rather "write more and talk less," so he offers to support the group by arranging all the best articles chronologically, typing the complete bibliographic information, writing a two-sentence summary or abstract for each one, and making

BOX 7.9

BOX 7.9   *Improvement in Action* ⫸

Use Figure 7.4 to create a "report card" for the group presentation on memory. How, specifically, did the group go about accomplishing each objective on the list? Start thinking about how you would share information on your major with the group, something that you will be doing later as a chapter assignment. How can you apply what you have learned in this chapter to a presentation about your major?

enough copies to distribute to the entire class before the question-and-answer period. The group feels that this feature will really impress their professor and all the members of the audience who seek facts. They give copies of articles that they found most helpful to Jose so that he can compile the information. After careful consideration, they decide that the one-page summary they planned may be unnecessary, now that they have the poster and Jose's material. They all agree to revise their original plan and delete the one-page summary.

The end of their presentation will be turned back to Carlene. She plans to conclude by saying, "To summarize, let's look again at these three methods on the chart that can be used to improve your memory and think about the examples that we began with. When you meet Mr. Fox, you will create a visual image of a red fox sitting on top of his head and now you can remember his name. Now if you are worried about forgetting to take your suit to the cleaners, you can use a concrete prompt like hanging it on the doorknob. And now, when you are studying for that important test, you can use a mnemonic device to trigger your memory, like the first letter of four key words in a list."

At the end of the presentation, it will be Jose's turn to explain how they developed the annotated bibliography and answer any questions the group might have. Jose will say, "As we investigated our topic, we uncovered several studies that made a significant contribution to an understanding of human memory. When we met to plan our presentation, I agreed to compile our work into this annotated bibliography. As you scan through the list, you will see that I have given the complete reference for each article and a brief abstract. You will also notice that the studies are arranged chronologically so that you can notice the major trends in the field. Are there any questions for us?"

Although Jose had been worried that someone would ask a question they could not answer, he found that because people were so interested in what they had to say and because their presentation was so thorough, the discussion afterward was actually enjoyable. One student said, "After you asked us to think about our earliest memory, I just wondered how far back people can go with their memories. My earliest memory is from when I was about 3. Does anybody have a memory from infancy?"

After the group actually gave their presentation, they received very positive feedback from their peers. The most frequently mentioned strengths were "interesting," "well organized," "good visuals," and "excellent resources." In his evaluative comments on the presentation evaluation form, the professor agreed. He wrote, "It's clear to me that all of you invested time in working to make this an informative and interesting presentation. The way that you shared responsibility is commendable. The idea of the annotated bibliography is excellent—I think I'll make it part of the assignment requirements from now on. Grade: A+"

One way to make your next presentation—group or individual—effective is to self-evaluate. If you can answer each question in Figure 7.6 in the affirmative, your next presentation is almost certain to be well received.

Figure 7.6
Self-Questioning As a Guide to Effective Presentations

From *Impact: A Guide to Public Speaking,* by J. H. Schaefer and M. A. Brashear, 1989, New York: Berkley Books. Copyright 1989. Adapted with permission.

1. Know your audience and let them know you.
   - Who is my audience?
   - What do they already know about my topic?
   - How can I communicate that I have thought deeply about my topic?
   - How can I let my audience know that my information has value for them?

2. Select a subject, purpose, and focus appropriate for the audience.
   - Why bring this audience and material together? (To persuade? Enlighten? Inform? Take action? Ponder? etc.)
   - How much do they care about this topic?
   - How formal or informal is the context?

3. Put yourself in the role of the participants.
   - What would make it interesting to me if I were in the audience?
   - What questions would I want answered?

4. Be well prepared and carefully planned, but spontaneous.
   - What is the best way to organize my message?
   - What strategies can I use to get the audience involved?

5. Organize your presentation as follows:
   - Begin with a thought-provoking experience that gets attention.
   - Preview main points using a visual aid.
   - Provide illustrative examples for key ideas, once again using audiovisuals as appropriate (but always be prepared for equipment malfunction).
   - Show the audience how what you are talking about benefits them, and provide for active audience involvement.
   - Stay within the time allotted.
   - Announce the ending, then sum up your purpose and ask the audience to take action.
   - Supply the participants with resource materials, such as a list of recommended readings.

6. Obtain evaluations of your session and revise as necessary.

Overcoming Nervousness

When college students are asked to list the things that are most unnerving about making a presentation to the class, they most often mention four things:

1. fear of forgetting what they were going to say,
2. appearing nervous and being judged harshly by the audience,
3. saying or doing something embarrassing, or
4. being unable to answer questions.

Now consider some strategies for counteracting those feelings.

Plan to Remember

In terms of remembering what you want to say, use the same techniques that most professional presenters use. Instead of trying to memorize everything, they think through their message, its basic components, and how to communicate the main ideas. That way, they can plan thoroughly but sound spontaneous. Experienced presenters use visual aids to communicate the important elements of their message to the audience and rely on those visual aids to assist them in remembering the main ideas. Figure 7.7 is an overview of memory aids commonly used by professional speakers.

Learn to Appear Calm

You can give the outward impression of confidence even when you are feeling very anxious. In terms of dealing with the physiological manifestations of nervousness, do what the experts do. If you are worried that your hands might shake, hold onto something such as your note cards, the podium, or the edge of the overhead projector. If you are concerned that your voice might break, bring a disposable cup and get a drink of water, then sip from it as inconspicuously as possible if you feel that your voice is about to quaver. Also, remember to *breathe*. Most of the time when your voice gives out, it is really your breath that gives out because when people are nervous, they tend to breathe in a very shallow way instead of breathing deeply. Try taking several deep breaths on your way to the front of the room. Also, when people feel anxious, they sometimes get a scowl on their faces. Professional presenters tell you to try to imagine that you are smelling something pleasant and replace that tortured look with a pleased one. If you feel uncomfortable making eye contact with your audience, don't look at the floor! You can give the impression of looking at your audience by scanning the back wall of the room. Or, you can find three or four people around the room who seem really interested and supportive and make eye contact with them.

Figure 7.7
Memory Aids to Use during a Presentation

Each of these examples relates to the previous discussion about the group presentation in educational psychology.

Note Cards

Jot down your major points on 3" × 5" cards. Be sure to number the cards in case you drop them!

1.	2.
Introduction	Show of hands
Memory fails	(e.g., post-it note)
• embarrassing (e.g., forget name)	NEXT. . .
• costly (e.g., ruin car)	
• affects future (e.g., fail test)	3. Strategies

Outline

Make an outline of your presentation to jog your memory. You may want to share it with the audience at the beginning on a poster or an overhead projector transparency.

> I. Three Memory Aids
>   A. Concrete props
>   B. Mnemonics
>   C. Visual imagery

Graphic Organizers

Try using a combination of sketches, flowcharts, words, and other symbols. Make it look like a gameboard that you follow from start to finish.

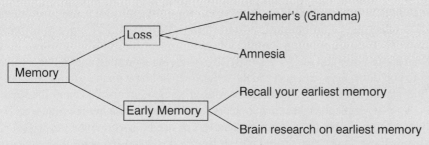

Overhead Transparency

Anything you type on a typewriter or computer can be made into a transparency at a print shop or on a laser printer. Use boldface print, a good ribbon, and at least 15-point size type. Remember that each transparency should contain just a few key phrases—don't clutter it up with too many details.

> **Memory**
> Introduction
> Three techniques
> Consequences of memory loss
> Earliest memories
> Bibliography/questions/evaluation

Figure 7.7
(continued)

Posters

Posters contain much of the same information as the transparencies. They can be propped up on the chalk ledge or taped up on the wall to help you remember your main points and share your message more effectively with the audience. Be sure to make the print large, neat, and dark enough so that everyone can see and read it easily. Remember that posters, like overhead transparencies, work best when you stick to the main points.

One-Page Summary

Make enough copies for everyone in the group to have their own, and use it yourself to remember everything you want to say. When using the one-page summary as a memory aid, try reprinting it for yourself triple-spaced with wide margins. Use the spaces and the margins to make notes for yourself about the examples you want to give.

In terms of coping with the psychological aspects of nervousness, try to keep your nervousness in perspective. As Verderben (1979) suggests, remember that a little nervousness helps you do your best, and that everyone else gets nervous too. Try to keep your focus on your message and your audience instead of yourself.

Handle Mistakes Gracefully

Do not allow yourself to get a major case of the "what ifs": What if I fall down? What if I lose my voice? What if there is a fire drill in the middle of my presentation? Of course, any of these things *could* happen but are very unlikely, so there is not much sense in worrying about them. Whenever you make an embarrassing blunder, just pause for a couple seconds, give a little smile, and go on. Do not feel pressured to say something clever or humorous. For example, when Bob was reporting on the increasing crime rates among the under-age 13 population in his criminology class, he gave the wrong statistic. He paused for a second and said, "Excuse me, I meant to say. . . ." and went on. Mistakes can simply be corrected, just as Bob did. They are not the end of the world.

What about virtual disasters? When Trish was giving a presentation in history class, she went to pull down the world map and the whole map holder with three maps on it pulled out of the wall and clattered to the floor. She paused, smiled, grabbed the map she needed, asked a couple of people to be her "map holders," and went on with her presentation. Trish certainly had bad luck, but no one thought any less of her or her presentation. In fact, she actually gained respect because she did not get flustered and showed grace under pressure. Of course, you will want to avoid mistakes whenever possible. But when they do occur, the effective presenter corrects them as soon as possible, maintains control over the situation, and keeps a sense of humor about it.

Field Questions Confidently

"What if someone asks me something and I don't know the answer?" This is often a major concern of presenters. One thing that you can do in this situation is to turn the question back to the group and save face with an "I did/I didn't" statement. For example, "I did read that (mention something that is related to the question), but I didn't come across any information on that particular aspect." Then you can turn the question back to the group: "Does anyone else happen to know more about this?" Usually, the instructor will help you out if you handle the situation skillfully instead of just saying, "I don't have any idea" or, worse yet, pretending that you know when you do not. You could also volunteer to find out the answer, saying something like, "It's an interesting point. Let me look into it further and get back to you on it." Then follow through by arriving at the next class meeting with a prepared answer. Figures 7.8 and 7.9 offer general and specific suggestions, respectively, on how to respond to questions.

Figure 7.8
General Suggestions for Responding to Questions
Adapted from Garmston and Wellman (1992).

1. Anticipate and answer the questions that you can foresee *during* your presentation rather than waiting for them to be raised afterward.

2. Make certain that you understand the question. Ask for clarification if necessary (e.g., "Are you saying that . . .?").

3. If there is a possibility that not everyone heard the question, paraphrase it before beginning your answer (e.g., "Gerri is wondering why . . .").

4. Try to "listen between the lines"—to the intent underlying a question rather than just the words.

5. Give a short reply if at all possible.

6. If a question will require a lengthy answer that may not be of general interest to the group, graciously suggest that you discuss it afterward (e.g., "That's an interesting idea, one that really looks at this issue from an artist's perspective. It also sounds like something that we can't discuss now because other presenters are waiting for their turn to speak. But I would be glad to talk with you about it after class.").

7. If someone asks a question that you cannot answer, use "I did/but I didn't" (e.g., "I did read about____, but I didn't run across anything that dealt specifically with_____."), turn the question to the group ("Did anyone else . . .?"), or offer to find out the answer ("I'll get back to you with that information at our next class.").

Figure 7.9
Specific Suggestions for Responding to Questions
From *How to Make Presentations That Teach and Transform,* by R. J. Garmston and B. W. Wellman, 1992, Alexandria, VA: Association for Supervision and Curriculum Development. Copyright © 1992 by ASCD. Adapted with permission.

Try to respond to questions and comments in ways that "match" the way the question was asked:

"Should we . . .?"
Calls for a yes/no
"Yes, you can and should form a study group because research with college students suggests that participation in these groups generally exerts a positive influence on academic achievement. . . "

"Are there other ways . . .?"
Calls for a list
"Three of the best strategies for combating illiteracy are . . ."

"Could you speak more about . . .?"
Calls for a short summary, followed by elaboration
"Yes, as I mentioned earlier, averages can be deceiving. Even though the *average* fitness level of Americans has increased, this may be more attributable to the extraordinarily high fitness levels of a small percentage of the population rather than to widespread improvement. In other words, a few fitness enthusiasts are pulling up the averages."

"I think this is just another . . ."
Comment is emotional—use feel-felt-found
Pause, then say something like, "Many people feel the way you do about poetry . . . I have felt this way too. And as I've read and thought about poetry more, I've found . . .

Figure 7.10
Speaker Evaluation Checklist

From *Impact: A Guide to Public Speaking,* by J. H. Schaefer and M. A. Brashear, 1989, New York: Berkley Books. Copyright 1989. Adapted with permission.

Preparation

Opening

_____ A strong, well-prepared beginning, powerful enough to attract audience attention.

Strategy

_____ The way the material is presented is relevant to the audience.

Closing

_____ A strong summary of key points and a clear "results" statement.

Compliance with Time

_____ Completes the presentation in the time allotted.

Credibility

Connection

_____ Uses eye contact and activities to encourage two-way communication.

Delivery

_____ Full inflection, natural word rate, pauses. Conversational style.

Intensity

_____ Demonstrates sincerity, enthusiasm, conviction. Appropriate vocal variety and volume.

Demeanor

Presence

_____ Appropriate dress, appearance, and grooming. Sets up and controls the physical surroundings to enhance the presentation.

Stance/Gestures

_____ Confident stance, smooth walking. Gestures in a natural way to support the verbal message.

Notes/Visuals

_____ Notes are unobtrusive. Visuals are well prepared and managed professionally.

Content

Analysis

_____ Approach to the subject is original, interesting. Central idea or objective is clear. Identifies appropriate outcomes for participants.

Material

_____ Provides sufficient facts, examples, illustrations, and opportunities for participation to support main points.

Organization

_____ Includes introduction, body, and conclusion. Good development of ideas, logical flow.

Evaluating Effectiveness

After your presentation is finished, it is only natural to wonder, How did it go? In some classes, your performance will be assessed by the instructor, by the students, or both, such as the example with Carlene, Ed, Jose, and Marsha's presentation on memory in Figure 7.4 or the evaluation checklist in Figure 7.10. Always use the constructive feedback from your listeners for self-improvement. Make notes about what went well, what went not as well, and ways to improve next time. Here is one student's journal entry and self-assessment after reading her classmates' comments:

> When the professor said that we had to make presentations on our majors, my first question was, "Do we have to stand up?" I don't know why this bothered me so much, but I just thought I would be more comfortable if I stayed in my seat. So I did. My presentation on veterinary medicine went pretty well. The things that were mentioned most frequently were: clear, expressive voice; good visual aids (I enlarged some interesting points from the Veterinary Medicine Program brochure on a copy machine and pasted them on posters); and interesting story (I told about how my interest in animals developed—I had 14 pets at one time when I was 8 years old). When I read the constructive criticism of the 27 people who listened to my presentation, practically every person mentioned that I should have stood up! Now that I see how many people prefer the speaker to stand up front, I guess I'll just go ahead and do it next time.

By using feedback from the audience, this student has already made plans for improving her next class presentation. Becoming an effective speaker is a project that is never really finished. Even those who make their living as training session presenters or go on the lecture circuit as keynote speakers are continually learning from their experiences with different audiences. Do what the professionals do—try to learn from each experience, maintain a positive attitude, and treat each presentation as an opportunity to improve the next time.

Special Situations

There are many other times when you will be called on to speak in class. Some of the more common class requirements/situations are reports on interviews, debates and panel discussions, and simulations or mock trials.

Conducting and Reporting on Interviews

Another type of speaking role, both in class and as an out-of-class assignment, is conducting interviews. Some guidelines for effective interviews are contained in Figure 7.11.

Listed in Figure 7.12 are the questions our students generated for Sterling White, an African-American student who struggled as an undergraduate but earned a graduate assistantship, completed a master's degree, and is now a public school teacher. The names of the students who formulated each question are listed afterward.

After you have conducted the interview, be certain to review any guidelines that your instructor has given for writing the interview. Generally speaking, you will want to do the following things:

- **Give some basic identifying information about the interviewee.** You should include age, gender, occupation, and reasons that this person was selected to be interviewed. Often when interviewing someone, it is best to preserve that individual's

Figure 7.11
Guidelines for Conducting Interviews

1. Be courteous in all correspondence and interaction with the interviewee. Arrange the interview at a convenient time for both of you.

2. Plan your questions in advance and send a copy to the interviewee several days in advance so that he or she has time to think them over.

3. As you write out the interview, try to avoid questions with yes/no or one word answers. Instead, develop questions that invite the interviewee to elaborate on his or her ideas. For example:

   Poor question: Do you like being a psychotherapist?

   Good question: What experiences and influences caused you to choose psychotherapy as a career?

4. Make plans for how you will record the interviewee's comments—through written notes, audiotape, videotape, etc. Be sure to get the individual's permission beforehand.

5. When the interviewee gives an answer that leaves questions unanswered, follow up with another question that probes more deeply into the issue.

   Question: How would you respond if . . . ?

   Answer: I would probably . . .

   Probe: Can you elaborate on this more and perhaps give a specific example?

6. If it is a face-to-face interview, arrive promptly; if it is a telephone interview, be sure to call at the agreed-on time.

7. If the total class is interviewing a guest speaker, try working on questions in groups, selecting the best ones, and then arranging them in a logical sequence.

anonymity and refer to them using a different name (pseudonym) or an initial (e.g., Ms. J.). This is particularly important if the person is being interviewed about a sensitive issue.

■ **Describe when and under what conditions the interview took place.** For example, "When I was home on spring break, I interviewed a teacher who was an enlisted man in the Navy and served in the Philippines in World War II. We talked for approximately 30 minutes."

■ **Type your questions and the interviewee's answers.** Some editing is permitted (such as omitting every "and, uh . . ."), but be very careful not to misquote or misrepresent what the person has said.

■ **Write a summary statement.** Explain your thoughts after you had a chance to reflect on the interview. What insights did you gain? What issues were raised? What did you learn from conducting the interview?

■ **Highlight the main points on your paper.** Select a few examples of your best questions and the interviewee's most interesting responses. Use this highlighted version of your interview to make your presentation in class.

Figure 7.12
Sample Interview Questions

1. Please tell us something about your background, such as where you were born, what it was like for you as a child, and the kind of family support you had for education.

2. What was your first year of college like? Was college what you expected it to be? Was it difficult to adapt? What was your grade point average after the first year? Did you finish your undergraduate program in 4 years? (Damian, Misty)

3. How did you decide on your major field? Did you ever change your major? (Shawn, Coleen, John, Vincent)

4. How did you cope with stress and social pressures? How did you manage your time? What do you recommend to us as college freshmen? (Nicole, Karma, Sean)

5. Please describe some of your major discouragements, times when you felt that no matter how hard you tried, you still would not succeed in college. (Melissa, Chris, Paul, Lisa)

6. What were the most successful experiences of your college career and the obstacles you had to overcome to achieve them? (Hubert, Iris, Michelle)

7. What made you decide to go on for your master's degree? Has anyone else in your family completed a graduate degree, or are you the first? (Claude, John, Mary)

8. Please describe some of the most significant people you have met throughout your college career and how they helped you. (Shawn, Coleen, John, Vincent)

BOX 7.12

BOX 7.12   *Improvement in Action* ⫸

Read a current newspaper or news magazine article and identify a controversial issue that elicits strong feelings from you. Write down some of the reasons for your ideas and opinions ("My Responses and Reasons for Those Responses"). Now imagine that you have been assigned to present a logical argument that takes the *opposite* side of this issue. Can you see the other side of the argument, even though you do not agree? Go back to the list of your responses and reasons. How can you argue *against* each one?

Debates and Panel Discussions

Debates are designed to highlight two opposing sides of a controversial issue (e.g., Democrats versus Republicans, abortion versus right to life). The goal is for each speaker to take a particular point of view and support it with a logical argument. The individuals engaged in the debate do not need to become angry or sarcastic. In fact, they may not even personally agree with the viewpoint they are arguing for! The purpose of the debate is to develop skill in presenting a persuasive, well-reasoned argument and to defend a particular viewpoint even if it differs from personally held beliefs. For example, in a music class, students have been asked to take the perspective of a musician who believes that classical music is the only good music, while other students have been assigned to argue that there are examples of quality music in jazz, rock, rap, polka, country music, and so forth. Even though the students assigned to the classical music side of the argument do not personally agree with that point of view, they can still argue for it. They argue that classical music has withstood the test of time. They argue that classical music is more difficult to play on an instrument, while many of the popular pieces of music are comparatively easy. They further argue that classical music is more universally known and accepted and that people all over the world study classical music, whereas other types of music are more limited to specific groups. As this example illustrates, the idea of a debate is to get practice in presenting a logical, persuasive argument.

In a panel discussion, the goal is to present several different perspectives on the same issue. In a panel discussion on toxic waste management, for example, an ecologist, a land developer, a nuclear plant manager, and a person who became ill from toxic waste buried on his property might all be asked to serve on the panel. During your college career, you might be asked to serve on a panel outside of class to present the student's point of view. One important thing to remember about panel discussions is that all panel members must have the opportunity to talk. Usually, this is accomplished by having a moderator who calls on each person at a predetermined time and lets each speaker know when her or his time is up. Therefore, it is absolutely imperative that you stay within the time allotted. If you do not, you will be cut off before you make your point or anger other members of the panel whose time you have taken. Most panel discussions are followed by a question-and-answer period with the audience.

Role Playing and Simulations

At other times during your college career, you will be asked to take on the role of another person. A good example of a simulation that involves role play is a mock trial. Obviously, it is not a real courtroom scene. Rather, it is a pretend courtroom scene in which you might be asked to take the role of a judge, lawyer, client, or witness. Usually, you are given some fairly specific instructions about how to play your role. At other times, you are expected to improvise based on what you have been reading and studying. A group of counseling majors, for example, might take on the role of professional counselor while other students take on the role of clients with various problems. When role playing and simulations are used appropriately, they give students some nonthreatening practice in applying basic principles they have learned to more lifelike situations and help prepare them for the real world.

Conclusion

When you learn to speak up in class and communicate with individuals and groups more effectively in a variety of contexts, you are making an important contribution to your interpersonal skills. Skill in speaking will serve you well, not only during college but also throughout your future. Every profession includes a set of expectations for speaking. If you want to be a health care professional, you will need to relate well with patients. If you are pursuing a career in business or journalism or computers, you will need to be persuasive as you present your ideas to others who are responsible for making decisions about what deserves financial support. If you want to be a teacher, you will have to learn to communicate clearly with children, parents, fellow teachers, and educational administrators. If you become a lawyer, your clients' well-being will depend on your communication skill. Whatever your career aspirations, it is important to remember that you *can* improve your speaking skills and that learning to make more effective presentations is important, not only during college but also throughout your professional career.

 Voices of Successful Students

"Everyone has a personal opinion—don't be afraid to speak up. Others are just as nervous when presenting themselves as you are or will be. Let others know what you think."

"I really hate giving presentations in class, but I am required to do so often in my major. Speaking in front of the class can help a lot of people who don't enjoy it. It did actually help me."

"Profs recognize and appreciate class participation. Often when grades are close, they remember who spoke. Do not be intimidated. You are paying for your education and should be an active participant in learning."

"Don't get nervous. Everyone goes through it, but just be prepared. Knowing the topic reduces nervousness."

"Whenever possible, participate in class discussions. It makes the lecture more interesting and also helps you retain information for later exams."

"Keep your eye on the audience, both the professor and the students. Don't read from your notes; know your material well enough to speak confidently."

"Class participation is a MUST! You learn so much when you participate. As far as presentations go, RELAX—everybody in that room wants to see you succeed."

"Try to say something in each class to establish your position in the group."

Extension Activities

Cooperative Learning Activity: The 60-Second Synopsis

1. Define the word *motivation*. With your group, brainstorm several things that enable a person to be *self-motivated*.
2. Read the speech that follows by Weaver (1991) entitled "Self-Motivation: 10 Techniques for Activating or Freeing the Spirit."* Highlight the main ideas.
3. Relate the suggestions on self-motivation to your personal experience. Can each one of the members of your group think of a time when they were entirely self-motivated? Jot down some ideas.
4. Formulate a plan for presenting this information, combined with brief examples from your experiences, in *60 seconds*. Make it interesting!
5. Make a presentation to the class. One group member can speak, or you can take turns. Add *interest* to your presentation by including *specific examples and testimonials*.
6. As each group reports, use a small piece of paper to provide a response. Tell the presenters what they did well. Give them *helpful, constructive feedback and suggestions* about how they might improve next time.
7. Create a diagram showing the processes you can use to build self-motivation, even when you feel very pressured and stressed.

Self-Motivation: 10 Techniques for Freeing the Spirit

Does it feel like you're being torn in all directions? Like you're getting stressed out? Like every teacher thinks his or her class is the *only* one you're taking? Like everything is coming down on you all at once, and you're not sure you can, or even want to, withstand the pressure? Do things feel like they are out of control? At least you know you're normal! Self-motivation is most likely to occur when you can successfully deal with the stresses in your life. Stress depletes both energy and motivation.

Professor Hans Selye, the world's foremost authority on human stress, defines stress as "the body's nonspe-

---
* From "Self-Motivation: 10 Techniques for Activating or Freeing the Spirit" by R. L. Weaver, 1991, *Vital Speeches of the Day, 57*, pp. 620–623. Published with the permission of Richard L. Weaver II, Department of Interpersonal Communication, Bowling Green State University, Bowling Green, OH 43401-0234, and *Vital Speeches of the Day.*

cific response to any demands placed on it, pleasant or not." We often recognize these nonspecific responses in a rapid pulse, increased blood pressure, frequent illness, unusual susceptibility to infection. Sometimes it appears as brooding, fuming, shouting, or even in increased use of alcohol, tobacco, or drugs. In some it's as severe as ulcers or a heart attack; in others, like one of my daughters (who takes after her dad in this), it's fingernail biting.

Often, what you need in times of stress is an electrical charge to boost your spirits, reinvigorate your emotions, and to reestablish balance in your life! The techniques that activate or free the spirit are precisely those techniques that you can use to eliminate—or at least reduce—the stress in your life. With the stress reduced, you are far more likely to be self-motivated—reinvigorated or charged up! At least you can regain some control.

What you need to know first is that stress is not always negative. Good stress occurs in life situations toward which you feel positively. I know, from my own personal experience, for example, that I chose this kind of work—being a professor—because the high-pressure schedule it demands seemed to be right for me. I *chose* to live under a fair degree of constant stress.

What you need to know second is that stress is individually determined. Meaning lies in us; thus, we are the ones who determine what is stressful. The useful part of this understanding is that if we determine it, then we can control it. We determine meaning! We are in control!

We all know *why* we stay in stressful situations. We stay in them for the rewards they offer, for approval, money, status, or self-esteem. Because we so often find ourselves in these stressful situations, what we need to do is to decide at various points in our life—*this* being one of them—are the rewards keeping ahead of the costs? Can we see a light at the end of the tunnel that is still worth pursuing? Often, the rewards or the goals are precisely what keep us going through life's little crises. Sometimes, of course, life's little crises look like gigantic catastrophes! But do you know what? If we didn't have any crises, what would we talk about? In many cases our crises, along with the weather, are the sum and substance of our conversations with others!

But we *can* develop strategies—or use specific techniques—to cope with stressful situations and thus rekindle the spark that ignites self-motivation. These techniques *can* alter the physiological impact that stress has on us, and they can reduce the harm that we do to ourselves and others in these situations.

What I want to talk about are some techniques for activating or freeing the spirit, but I want you to know that there is an underlying theme to my remarks. Self-motivation does not come from outside us. It can *only* come from inside. *Change must begin from within.* The key, then, to improvement and change is in recognizing and working with our individuality. What works for one person may not work for another. Also, for some people, it may involve the use of a number of techniques; for others just one may work. Some may have stress under control in ways not mentioned here at all. I will mention 10 techniques.

The **first technique** is to **recognize your own stress signals.** Stress can creep up on you insidiously—sometimes as the result of prolonged anxiety or even as a result of multiple causes. What if you're having troubles at home, then you're having some relationship problems, and maybe some small problems with a roommate, and *then* a couple of exams on top of that? Can you feel the pressure begin to mount?

Stress has its signals, but they may not always be as clear as you would wish. Practice monitoring yourself for the signs of unhealthy pressure. Common signs include irritability, sleeplessness (even when sleepy), rapid weight loss or gain, increased smoking or drinking, as mentioned before, little errors (physical or mental "dumb mistakes"), physical tension, nervous tics, or tightness of breath.

Last fall a student in one of my classes came in to talk to me about 3 weeks after the semester began. She recognized a number of these symptoms, and because she had had them before—to the extent of having to see a doctor—she realized that even though she knew she would enjoy the class, that she would get a great deal out of it, and that she *could* handle the workload, that it would be best for her, considering these early symptoms, to drop the class. And she did—*before* they became severe. We have to be wise in reading the signals. She carefully kept watch over her own stress signals, and she withdrew when they appeared—especially because she could easily anticipate the signals continuing and increasing in intensity. In this way, she did not exceed her normal, individual stress endurance. She was simply protecting herself!

The **second thing** we need to do—and this is especially important for students—is to **engage in exercise and practice good nutrition.** The two, of course, are related. I often get asked what keeps *me* going. This second technique takes on major importance in my life. Normally, my alarm goes off at 5:30 or 6:00 A.M. I get up and run through about 20 minutes of exercises. Then I run 3 miles; it takes me just under 30 minutes. And that starts my day! When I deliver a 9:30 A.M. lecture, I have already been up for hours!

Don't underestimate the importance of *exercise* to self-motivation. What happens to students is that many of them forget about exercise. Exercising the body keeps the mind sharp!

It used to be that I hated jogging; now, I look forward to it as an opportunity to plan my day, create ideas, and do some serious reflective thinking. You should know that exercise results in release of endorphins that have to do with confidence and self-esteem. It can make a *major* difference in your daily life. With more confidence and self-esteem, you will be more motivated.

Recently, I met an 80-year-old man who looked like 60. He told me his alarm goes off at 5. He gets up, exercises, rides a stationary bike, gets on a treadmill, uses a stairmaster, and then swims 10 lengths of a regula-tion-size pool. He said that he doesn't drink or smoke, and he feels like 50! That's *my* goal! We all have to get old, but *how* we decide to approach getting old makes all the difference. It's not the destination; it's the ride!

And don't forget the *nutrition.* Many students skip meals or only eat when they are hungry—and then not very well. We all have different patterns; but I can tell you this. If you stay away from junk food, eat regular meals of high quality, and make certain fresh fruits, fresh vegetables, and grains are well represented in your daily diet, you are far less likely to experience severe stress—and you will be more motivated as well! Good nutrition can play a major role in motivation.

Daily attention to health care can significantly decrease the effect of stress on both body and mind. Many of my campus meetings occur in the cafeterias. I watch students coming in for their first meal of the day and making a cheeseburger, fries, and a Coke their breakfast! This is horrendous! Breakfast is one of the most important meals of the day.

There is a **third technique,** too. If you are a person who stays unmotivated because of high levels of stress in your life, try to **locate the sources of dangerous stress in your life.** Take a look, first, at your personal relationships with family, employer or employees, friends, roommates, lovers, teachers, and strangers. Often, these forces will accumulate and create a negative stress reaction.

Second, take a look at your own personality. Are you making unreasonable demands on yourself? Do you, for example, insist on getting all A's? One of my friends who is in seminary became stressed out because of this demand on himself. When his wife pointed it out as unreasonable, and when he was able to see it as excessive and unnecessary, he was able to relax and better enjoy his classes.

There are other unreasonable demands you make on yourself. Do you like *never* making a mistake? Do you like never failing? You must learn to accept the possibility of failure without losing your sense of self-worth. Failing will not hurt your health; feeling like a failure will! Reinforce your sense of accomplishment, even in the face of failure, by recalling past achievements. Also, you can talk yourself through failures by:

- viewing failure as part of the process of exploring your world;
- accepting failure as a normal part of living;
- making note of the lessons to be learned and then moving on.

There are other unreasonable demands we make on ourselves, too. Do you like never being late? Do you like never being in the wrong? Often, you can minimize the stress of frustration and discover renewed enthusiasm and motivation by learning when to stop something, when to acknowledge that the aim is no longer worth fighting for, when to accept your own limitations, or when you are just plain being unreasonable with yourself! That's why constant self-monitoring is healthy. That's some of what I do when I jog. It gives me time to make some of those self-assessments.

Remember what we're doing here. We're trying to locate sources of dangerous stress in our lives. A third way to locate the sources of dangerous stress, in addition to looking at our relationships and looking at our own personality, is to look at our personal problems. For example, are you a person who carries grudges? Are you a person who dwells on past unpleasant experiences and incidents? What you may not realize is that carrying a grudge can deplete your naturally limited energy. For your own sake, and for the sake of finding renewed motivation, end unpleasant relationships and don't wallow in feelings of hostility, antagonism, or revenge. These deplete and destroy motivation.

What a lot of people don't realize is that worry is energy. When we worry, we *lose* energy. So when we stop worrying, we will have *increased* energy. I know this is easier said than done; however, if you recognize yourself involved in excessive worry, and you know this has a direct effect on your energy level—it wears you out!—you can begin to take specific steps to reduce the worry. Awareness is the first step to control!

What we need to do, and this is the **fourth technique** for activating or freeing the spirit, is to **turn energy into plans and action.** Think of stress as a kind of readiness in the extreme. It is an activation without release. So, when we take on the task at hand, however complex or frightening it might seem as we begin it—planning and then doing the necessary work greatly reduces stress. Not only will it get the work done, but it brings about relief and satisfaction as well.

Procrastination robs you of time, power, and freedom! And the consequences can be extreme: tension, conflict, self-criticism and depreciation, embarrassment, anxiety, guilt, panic, depression, physical exhaustion, even physical illness! This is *not* a speech on procrastination. But if this is the problem in your life that creates stress and robs you of motivation, let me tell you there are many good books on the subject. The response of most procrastinators to such a suggestion is, "Great. I'll read them later!"

Instead of believing that things are out of control and that you're helpless, you have to start by convincing yourself that you are *in* control and the day belongs to you. When you are *in* control, you are writing your own script and you are being proactive. But being proactive requires plans and actions.

Let me give you some quick time-management techniques here as part of plans and actions—the fourth technique for reducing stress.

- Do your most demanding work when you're fresh. Since reading is often tough (hard to stay awake through), make sure you do it when you're the freshest.
- Make double use of waiting time, driving time, walking across campus time, or time when you're doing routine tasks: read, write letters, listen to lectures that you've recorded, listen to notes and outlines that you've recorded, make schedules, do isometric exercises.
- Get up a half-hour earlier to gain some especially productive time.
- Go to bed earlier. Your lack of sleep robs you of quality time. You can't be self-motivated when you're half asleep!
- Control interruptions. Don't make phone calls when you're in the midst of important studying. Return calls later during your down time. Don't answer the door. Don't go wandering down the hall looking for someone to talk to.
- Organize your work area so you know where everything is, where everything belongs, and keep things in their place.
- Only deal with things once. Do it now! When you procrastinate, you will have this gnawing feeling of being fatigued and always behind. Procrastinating does *not* save you time or energy; it drains away *both* time and energy and leaves you with self-doubt and self-delusion. Memorize and repeat this motto: Action TNT—Action Today, Not Tomorrow! We need these little messages to motivate us.
- Finish what you start. Concentrate all your energy and intensity on the successful completion of your current major project. Completion builds energy and confidence.
- Limit your television viewing to mostly enlightening, educational, or special shows. STS—Stop the Soaps!

A **fifth technique** for activating the spirit is to **live in your own right way.** Some of us need speed and intensity. I, for example, would probably wither away and die under the limited stress of a quiet job or an isolated, do-nothing vacation! For me, because I am accustomed to high levels of activity, there is more stress in suddenly slowing down than in maintaining my usual frantic pace.

But no matter which way is your own right way, we all need *variety.* Variety offers diversions. Moving from one activity to another is more relaxing than complete rest. As a matter of fact, frustration often will follow swiftly when stimulation and challenge are removed from our lives.

The **sixth technique** is to **try to make whatever adjustments you need to make to unchangeable situations.** In other words, accept the givens; focus on your options. Although it makes sense to fight for your highest attainable goal, it does not make sense to waste your limited energy by resisting or fighting the inevitable. You don't have control over most of a course's assignments, requirements, or expectations, just like you don't have control over rush-hour traffic! So face it!

But in *every* situation, you have options. That is, you have opportunities to bring to bear your own unique personality. You have ways to be creative. You have room to offer your own insights. No matter the controls and regulations, no matter the rules and restrictions, the creative person will find ways to be creative. Rather than focusing on the givens, accept those. Focus on the options. Find ways to express the real you! Find places where you have freedom.

The **seventh technique** is to **start setting your own goals.** There is almost unbearable stress—and the resulting lack of motivation—when you try to live out the goals set for you by others. Friends, parents, relationship partners, advisers, and counselors all think they have some stock in *your* life. There is no harm in taking advice, but set your own goals. Over and over, I have witnessed renewed invigoration, a refreshed view of life and classes, and a rejuvenated spirit when students suddenly discover a major they really like and want to pursue. The major now is theirs; they have chosen it; they want to pursue it themselves—for themselves—no one else. Suddenly, they're in control!

And make your goals clear, specific, and achievable. I, personally, like doing things. But I like getting things done, too. Accomplishing, producing, and completing are so important, that I am continually setting new goals—but, believe me, they are ones I can accomplish.

The **eighth technique** is to **take direct action when called for.** Doing nothing is no substitute for doing what you feel you must. Let me explain. If you are confronted by a stressful situation that you can change, take direct action to eliminate the source of stress—even if it seems harder to do than accepting things as they are. There is no doubt that it is often hard to come right out and deal with a problem:

- like the choice of a major that isn't working out!
- a roommate who never picks anything up!
- a relationship partner who has become smothering!
- a friend who is demanding too much of your time and energy!

But when you weigh the problem against the stress it creates, it is even harder to live with the unrelieved stress!

The **ninth technique** is to learn and regularly practice **relaxation techniques.** When you get stressed out sometime, try sitting for 10 or 15 minutes and just concentrate on your breathing. Notice each breath as it comes in and goes out. It might even help if you count one as you exhale, then as you exhale again, count two, and so on until four. Then start counting all over again. This helps to focus your attention and regularizes your breathing. This has both a relaxing and cleansing effect.

Another common relaxation technique is to lie on the floor and progressively tense and relax all the muscles in your body. You can start with your feet and gradually work up to your jaw and eye muscles. Create a pleasant, relaxing scene in your imagination. Make it as vivid and detailed as possible. Visualize yourself in the scene, completely relaxed. If you can turn that scene on in your mind several times a day, especially when you feel tense, it will have a calming effect and give you renewed motivation.

The **tenth technique** for reducing stress and increasing self-motivation is to **find yourself a good support group.** When you feel necessary to others; when you have earned the goodwill and support of others; when you feel personal satisfaction in helping others; others offer a stabilizing effect that keeps us in touch, needed, and normal. Friends, family, relationship partners, classmates, fraternity brothers, or sorority sisters can serve as those who keep your life worthwhile.

Several things, now, should be clear to you. First, self-motivation is directly related to stress reduction. Second, stress is not always negative. Third, we are the makers of our own stress; thus, we *can* control it. Fourth, there are some useful, workable techniques for controlling it. We can create a great deal of distress for ourselves and others through our reluctance to make some all-out commitment to reducing stress and thus increasing our self-motivation. The real heroes are those who doggedly and joyfully work at becoming more loving and self-actualizing on a daily basis. There are no easy triumphs. Self-motivation is most likely to occur when we can successfully deal with the stresses in our lives. Your personal advance hinges on effort—your willingness to put into practice techniques for activating or freeing the spirit. (pp. 620–623)

Self-Improvement Strategy: Investigating Your Major

Use this project to enhance your presentation skills. All students will conduct an investigation to acquire more information about their chosen major field. The results of this investigation will be shared with the class in a 5- to 7-minute presentation.

The presentation will address the following points in any order the presenter chooses:

- Explain how you became interested in this profession. Identify any person who has served as a role model for you (e.g., family member, neighbor, teacher, friend, public figure).
- Use the college catalog to determine what you will be doing in your program over the next 4 years. Identify any learning experiences that sound particularly intriguing or particularly challenging. Are there any specialized areas within the field that appeal to you (i.e., a pediatric specialty in nursing, a personnel major in business, a secondary specialty in education)?
- What does the job market in this field look like right now? How might it change over the next 4 years? What is the average salary range? (The college placement office that assists students in finding jobs may be a good source for some of this information. Check the library for a recent article on employment trends in the field.)
- Identify several leading publications in the field and the names of three leaders in the field. You may want to ask a faculty member, briefly interview some students who are nearing the completion of the program, and/or consult several recently published textbooks on the topic.
- Include any other interesting information that you may come across in your investigation. Now that you know more about the major, are you still interested in pursuing it or have you changed your mind? If you have changed your mind, what other major or majors are you planning to investigate?

Additional Instructions

When you make your presentation to the class, be certain to get the students involved rather than lecturing them. Use materials such as flip charts, posters, overhead transparencies, and other visual aids to help you remember your main points and maintain your audience's attention and participation.

Final projects will be based on three criteria: (a) the amount of effort displayed in locating authoritative sources; (b) the quality of the information (free of errors, clear and concise, answers the questions posed); and (c) the overall effectiveness of the presentation (has a strong beginning such as an interesting fact, thought-provoking question, a real object used in the field, etc.; uses visual aids; gets other students actively involved).

Writing and Reflecting: Self-Assessment of Speaking Abilities

Using the speaker evaluation checklist in Figure 7.10, analyze your strengths and weaknesses as a speaker. In your journal, write responses to two questions:

- What are your strengths as a speaker? How did what you read in this chapter confirm these strengths?
- What have you learned from this chapter that will help counteract your weaknesses?

Reading Selections

Reading Selection 1

Read "Learning How to Learn" by Gordon (1990).* Using what you have learned in this chapter, outline a presentation that you could give on the topic of learning how to learn. Then create a memory aid to use in making your presentation (see Figure 7.7).

You know the feeling. You're reading a book, or attending a lecture, or listening to a panel discussion—and suddenly you're lost. No matter how you sweat and strain, you just don't get it. The subject is too amorphous. Your mind refuses to draw you a coherent picture of what it is that's being discussed. And even to the hazy extent that you do grasp it, you can't imagine how you or anyone else might use the information. How and when would you ever apply this concept, this model, this *whatever it is,* in the course of leading your life?

Your confusion could spring from any number of causes. Maybe you're unfamiliar with the terminology. Maybe you've missed an underlying premise, a key assumption. Maybe (here's a common one) the speaker or writer is explaining the subject badly. But there may be another explanation.

"One possibility is that there's really no subject there," says John Green, director of curriculum development for The Cedars, Inc., a training firm in Flint, MI. "People write and speak all the time about subjects that aren't subjects."

It's easy to suspect that this may be the case when the subject in question is "learning how to learn." If

you do suspect this—as I have—then you are the target reader for this article. Because this article will try to persuade you, the skeptic, that there *is* a real subject here.

As for those of you wondering what there is to be skeptical about in the first place. . . . Well, *look* at this concept: Learning as the object of its own verb? Learning as a generic activity, as a free-floating process, as a set of universally applied "skills"? Learning as a subject to study and teach, in the same sense that mechanical engineering and biology are subjects? And not just a subject to be taught to educators. Oh, no. And not just remedial "study skills" to be taught to people with learning disabilities or to 40-year-old high school dropouts who enroll in community college courses. No. Learning as a subject that everybody in the country ought to study, and soon. Even people with Ph.D.s.

Because of the ever-popular "accelerating pace of change," we've heard a great deal about this concept recently. Most of what we hear about it, though, comes in the form of stirring testimonials from highly placed sources ("The only man who is educated is the man who has learned how to learn," wrote psychologist Carl Rogers) or dire warnings ("The American education system is failing because it does not teach children how to learn, and American industry is failing because it hasn't tackled the job that schools failed to do," say all sorts of people).

It's a compelling idea. But it is rarely served with a lot of meat clinging to its bones.

What does it mean to learn how to learn? Even among those who would agree in spirit with Carl Rogers, there is no consensus that the best way to learn how to learn is to study learning, per se. What are we really talking about? Improving your ability to acquire new skills and knowledge? Boosting your intellectual confidence? Putting a keener edge on your mind? If so, then many people will argue that you should study Greek philosophy, study mathematics, study a foreign language, or study history. Learn *something,* for crying out loud, and "learning to learn" will take care of itself.

---

* From "Learning How to Learn," by J. Gordon, 1990, *Training, 27* (pp. 51–52). Reprinted with permission from the May 1990 issue of *Training* Magazine. Copyright 1990, Lakewood Publications, Minneapolis, MN. All rights reserved. Not for resale.

Actually, many opponents of that argument would concede that it is half right. Learning can and should be taught overtly, they say, but not necessarily in a class where the topic is learning. For instance, don't pull a group of corporate managers into a room to teach them "how to learn." Instead, pull them into a room to teach them strategic planning and draw their attention to the *process* of learning about strategic planning.

Still, the whole thing can look a bit like the chicken-or-the-egg argument over teaching children self-esteem. Is the kid doing poorly at math because she lacks self-esteem, or does she lack self-esteem because she's doing poorly at math? Either way, is the answer to try to teach her self-esteem, or to do a better job at teaching her math?

Similarly, if you want to train your mind, which serves your purpose better: 20 pages of Aristotle or 2,000 pages of "metacognition"?

This article will not try to answer that question. This article comes neither to praise the learning-to-learn concept nor to bury it. It comes simply to argue that learning really can be addressed as a discrete topic. Remedial study skills—how to take notes in class and whatnot—are not the only teachable skills involved. And while "teaching people how to learn" often turns out to be an umbrella expression for teaching all sorts of generic "enabling skills," it isn't always.

Let's begin with that last point.

Learning to Do . . . What?

"Learning is hard to sort out from a lot of other skills," says Green, who teaches workshops on the subject. . . .

Truer words were never spoken. Look into the literature on learning to learn, and you'll keep running into the same phenomenon. Whenever the discussion moves from the abstract to the concrete, you discover that a great many "learning skills" could be classified more precisely under different headings: problem solving, reading, communication skills, active listening, time management, goal setting, decision making, group dynamics, giving and receiving performance feedback—even teaching skills.

In fact, says Robert M. Smith in his 1982 text, *Learning How to Learn: Applied Theory for Adults,* "One model of 'essential life skills' equates knowledge of the problem-solving process with learning how to learn."

This is not to suggest that anything sneaky is going on. Obviously, your ability to communicate clearly, listen attentively, and think through problems in a logical manner will have a great deal to do with how quickly and easily you are able to learn any number of things. Learning certainly is one activity in which all of these abilities may be brought to bear. Learning can provide a rationale or an impetus for teaching them (Q: "Why should I take a course in problem solving?" A: "Because problem-solving skills are fundamental to learning new things, and you'll have to learn new things for as long as you live.").

Just the same, all of those skills also can be taught—and have been, for years—under many different banners. Can you teach goal setting in a class on "how to be a self-directed learner"? Sure you can. And when you do, you'll use examples relating to learning goals:

What, specifically, does the student want to learn about investing money in the stock market? Within what time frame does the student wish to learn it? How will the student decide whether he has achieved his goal?

Strictly speaking, though, the subject you're teaching there is goal setting, not learning. You could teach the same subject in a class on how to sell more widgets, using widget-related examples. By the same token, if we want children to be able to learn effectively, we should teach them to read. But we'd be teaching reading, not learning.

Reading, goal setting, problem solving, and so forth are enabling skills, and "learning to do new things" is just one of the activities they enable. We can call them learning skills, but we could as easily call them working skills or even living skills. Since we're being skeptics here, let's deny that to teach these things is the same as to "teach learning."

While we're being hard-nosed, let's declare ourselves impatient with that chunk of literature that deals with orienting people to "learning resources." This is where we are offered examples of "learning how to learn" wherein a librarian explains how to use the library, or a company keeps schedules of night-school courses offered by local community colleges.

If this is "teaching people how to learn," it is doing so in the same sense that directing little Johnny to the schoolhouse door is teaching him how to learn.

No, if we skeptics are going to agree that we can talk usefully about teaching learning itself, we need to draw some boundaries. Learning-as-a-subject cannot be synonymous with a collection of enabling skills. Learning also cannot be synonymous with consciousness, in the sense that our brains have no off-switch and are busy processing "new" information taken in by our senses every moment of every day. In other words, learning can't be something that everybody's doing all the time, the way sales trainers like to say that everybody's selling all the time. Learning must be something, as opposed to everything. It must be a specific sort of task.

Guess what? A lot of people in the learning-to-learn movement will tell you that if you think of learning as a particular sort of activity, as a task, as something you have to work at, then you have already taken the first giant step toward learning how to learn.

Metacognition and Study Skills

Metacognition is a term from cognitive psychology. Broadly, it means "thinking about thinking." It refers to your ability to monitor (pay conscious attention to) and control your thought processes—particularly, as far as educators are concerned, the processes you use when you're trying to learn about something. Writing in the *Performance Improvement Quarterly* in 1988, training consultant Ruth Colvin Park of Palos Verdes, CA, says metacognition also refers to "an individual's ability to accurately determine the goal of a given task, apply appropriate strategies to reach the goal, monitor progress toward the goal, and adjust strategies as necessary."

The key to it all, Clark says, is "comprehension monitoring." Metacognition implies a conscious awareness of what it is you're trying to learn, and how close to mastery you are at any given point. Other writers, talking about the same concept, refer to "self-regulatory skills" with which you monitor your own learning or evaluate, objectively, your ability to perform some task.

Nancy Dixon, associate professor of human resource development at George Washington University, offers an example. Suppose you're reading a magazine article. You come to a paragraph you don't understand. Do you *notice* that you don't understand? If so, what do you do? Do you stop, say, "Huh?" and read the paragraph again, striving for comprehension? Or do you just keep grinding on through the article?

"Asking yourself, 'Did I understand that?' is a metacognitive skill," Dixon says. If you reread the confusing paragraph, you're employing a metacognitive strategy. You are treating learning as a task, and you're taking an active approach to it instead of a passive one."

Remedial? Yes. "A lot of the metacognitive research comes from work with disabled people or people with at least mild learning disabilities," says Robert Smith, who is a professor of adult education at Northern Illinois University in De Kalb. He isn't crazy about the word *metacognition*. "It scares people," he says. "I like the term *self-monitoring*." Whatever you call it, the important thing is that "as you move through any educational experience, you're aware of what you ought to do next: Get out? Get help? Change strategies?"

Whether you are learning to play the stock market, play tennis, or play the ukelele, to metacognate your way through the experience is to be aware of learning as something you are *doing*, rather than as something being done to you by an instructor. "What we learn in school is how to be taught, not how to learn," asserts adult-learning theorist Malcolm Knowles.

The specific techniques that fall out of the metacognitive literature are mostly problem-solving skills (for example, how to break a large task into manageable subtasks and then decide which to tackle first, second, etc.), or "study skills." Examples? Read with a highlighter in your hand. Take notes while listening to a lecture. Read in bursts—that is, read for about 20 minutes then pause to reflect upon what you've read. Organize your life to make time to study. Don't read every textbook cover to cover; start with the index or the table of contents and find out what the book has to say about some particular topic that interests you.

The primary audience for training in these sorts of skills is "people who didn't do well in school," Dixon says. "Those of us who did well couldn't name the skills we're using, but we developed them—which is why we did well."

A big chunk of what is taught under the rubric "learning how to learn" boils down to a mixture of basic self-consciousness, enabling skills, study skills, and attitudinal/motivational adjustment (You can do it! You can learn!). The mixture can be geared toward traditional classroom learning situations, or collaborative "group learning," or independent, self-directed learning.

This brings us to one reason why the learning-to-learn concept can seem to possess, in John Green's phrase, an absence of mass. Enthusiasts tend to classify the information about learning how to learn according to categories such as classroom/group/self-directed. They rarely classify it as beginning/intermediate/advanced. An advocate will tell you that even people with Ph.D.s need to be taught how to learn. Then she'll start babbling about remedial study skills and Metacognition 101.

So there you'll be, perfectly happy to suppose that there are people in the world who ought to be taught these things—happy, indeed, to suppose that even a person with a doctorate might pick up *some* useful tidbit of information in such a course. (I haven't been quite fair in depicting metacognitive/study skills as entirely remedial.) But you'll be baffled by the assertion that everybody everywhere ought to drop everything and stampede into that class.

Most advocates, you see, don't really mean that Harvard graduates need to be taught to underline important points in a textbook. There's more to it.

Awareness II

"I never learned anything from a book or by listening," says management expert Peter Drucker. "I need to write, to do, to speak.

"Winston Churchill was a miserable student," Drucker continues, "because he only learned when he wrote." The "schoolmaster's" mistaken notion that everybody learns in the same way (i.e., by listening to the schoolmaster's lecture) "explains the obligatory 'school is awful for writers' tradition in European literature."

Gloria Gery, a consultant and computer-based training expert in Tolland, MA, says she never opens the manual that comes with a new household item, be it a VCR or a piece of computer software. Unlike her husband, who won't touch the thing until he has read and outlined the manual, she just starts tinkering. "My new microwave convection oven came with an instructional videotape," she says. "I'll die with that tape still shrink-wrapped."

Faced with a broad learning task, Gery says, "My style usually is immersion reading, followed by questioning experts, followed by variable manipulation." By variable manipulation, she means what is commonly called trial and error. Like with the oven.

Drucker and Gery have noticed things about themselves as learners that go well beyond noticing that they *are* learning, or that they don't understand a paragraph in a book, or that they can study better if it's quiet than if the radio is playing.

Gery, in fact, is equally definite about things she does not wish to learn: "On my tombstone it should say, 'She never learned how to program [computers].' I see no payoff there."

Gery says she has no idea how you'd teach people how to learn. "People already know how to learn; they're just not aware of their own tendencies. But I can see a huge advantage in making people aware of what works for them."

Another big chunk of the learning-to-learn literature deals with exactly that: making people aware of what works for them. There are a number of tests on the market that can build insight: Kolb's Learning Style Inventory, the Canfield Learning Style Inventory, the Productivity Environmental Preference Survey (PEPS), and others.

Each of these tests measures some different attributes, but as a group they can flag such things as: your sensory preferences when it comes to learning (kinesthetic, visual, auditory); your need for (or resistance to) structure and authority in a learning situation; your desire for competition vs. cooperation; whether you are most comfortable "splitting up" concepts into their component parts or "lumping" the parts together; whether you like to get the whole picture first and then the details, or get the details first and then build toward the big picture; and even the time of day when you're most comfortable straining your brain.

These are not things a run-of-the-mill Harvard grad would necessarily notice.

You don't put much stock in "personality" tests? Fine. Smith says he finds the Canfield most useful, but not because he's especially concerned with matters of validity or reliability. "I just use [tests like these] to build awareness," he says.

Look at it Gery's way: "Instruments alone aren't the answer," she says. "Sometimes I'm 'concrete-sequential,' sometimes I'm not. Simply knowing what [personal learning style] is your primary and what's backup isn't the skill. Knowing what to apply in which context is the skill." But that doesn't mean the style-indicator instruments aren't useful. They just "have to be linked to different contexts," she says.

Call it advanced awareness—Awareness II. Your deep-seated tendencies, your casual preferences, your most comfortable "style"—it's quite helpful to be aware of these things, according to those who advocate learning as a teachable subject.

Dixon, of George Washington University, pushes Awareness II in a different direction. She believes that the road to more effective learning passes through psychologist Chris Argyris' concept of critical reflection.

Critical reflection, in a nutshell, is a process by which we bring to conscious awareness some of the tacit assumptions that underlie our perceptions of the way things work. These assumptions influence the way we think about things. They influence the way we try to change things about ourselves and our surroundings. They influence the way we try to learn about things.

"Things" here can be anything from why we sold 10% fewer widgets last month to the meaning of life. If we drag our underlying assumptions to the surface and look at them, we can test to see if they're valid and to find out whether they're working for us or against us as we try to accomplish some goal.

Victoria Marsick, an assistant professor of adult education at Columbia University, sees the need for critical reflection this way: "People don't think very effectively. They act on conclusions and inferences that aren't appropriate to the situation. But there's no forum for them to take out their inferences and examine them."

The greatest amount of "pay dirt" in the learning-to-learn field "comes from getting people to discover the [faulty inferences] they've been stumbling over," Marsick says.

Dixon, Marsick, and others are investigating the possibility that entire companies may be able to mine that pay dirt. How? Well, you start with a process Argyris calls action science. Marry that to a method called action learning, in which small groups of critically reflective people meet over a period of months to solve organizational problems. . . .

But that leads to the subject of "the learning organization," which is a whole different kettle of fish. I'm not even going to try to persuade you that it's a real kettle, with real fish.

And if "learning to learn" still sounds fishy to you, exercise a different learning strategy: Find a better explainer. (pp. 51–62)

Reading Selection 2

Read the article about college sports programs cited here (Lederman, 1989).* Highlight, then list the major arguments. Then make a chart that summarizes the key points *and* opposing views ("Arguments for College Sports" and "Arguments against College Sports"). Can you think of any additional points that were not made in the essay? If so, add them to your chart. Now go back through your chart and add any personal experiences or news reports that you could use to further elaborate and defend your argument. For practice in presenting a logical argument, try this:

- If you are personally in favor of college sports programs, try to create an argument against them.
- If you are personally indifferent or opposed to college sports programs, try to create an argument for them.

The House Postsecondary Education Subcommittee heard conflicting testimony last week on the problems of college sports. Some witnesses said big-time intercollegiate athletics are plagued by major, systemic problems that will require fundamental reforms to correct. Others, including the executive director of the National Collegiate Athletic Association, said the vast majority of what goes on in intercollegiate sports is positive.

'Corrupting Influence of Money'

Critics at the hearing included Robert H. Atwell, president of the American Council on Education, and Frank Deford, a journalist and sports commentator, who argued that big-time sports, especially football and men's basketball, are rife with such problems as overcommercialization and what Mr. Atwell called the "corrupting and distorting influence of money."

Those concerns, said Mr. Atwell, "cast a shadow on the credibility of all colleges and universities.

"It's systemic, because it goes far beyond getting rid of the bad apples," he added.

---

* From "Congressional Panel Hears Conflicting Testimony About the Troubles of Big-Time College Sports," by D. Lederman, 1989, *The Chronicle of Higher Education, 35*, pp. A31–A32. Copyright 1989 by *The Chronicle of Higher Education*. Reprinted with permission.

To try to better the "basically unhealthy" enterprise, Mr. Atwell called, as he has frequently in the past, for an end to athletically related financial aid, for more institutional subsidy of athletics, for freshman ineligibility, for more sharing of revenues, and for severe cuts in the length of the playing seasons. He said he was speaking for himself and not for ACE's member institutions.

Richard D. Schultz, the executive director of the National Collegiate Athletic Association, acknowledged that big-time sports have some problems, but said the problems were limited to a few areas and institutions. He said the NCAA had taken many steps to punish wrongdoers and bolster academic standards.

"I take issue with those who would characterize the conduct of intercollegiate athletics today as disgraceful, out of control, or worse," said Mr. Schultz.

Rep. Pat Williams, a Montana Democrat who heads the postsecondary-education subcommittee, said at the start of the hearing that the panel had no specific legislation in mind as it began to explore the sports issues.

Objections to Proposed Legislation

The session's scattershot testimony did not seem to give panel members any clearer sense of what role, if any, the federal government might play in overseeing college sports.

Sen. Bill Bradley, Democrat of New Jersey, appeared before the subcommittee to make a pitch for pending House and Senate bills that would require colleges to make public the graduation rates of their athletes and other students.

Many in the higher-education establishment, including officials of the NCAA, have objected to the proposed legislation, known as the Student-Athlete Right to Know Act, as unwarranted federal intrusion. But the legislation seemed to have the general support of most of the lawmakers present at the hearing, including its two cosponsors in the house, Rep. Tom McMillen, Democrat of Maryland, and Rep. Ed Towns, a New York Democrat.

"The need for this is self-evident, the opposition to it is bewildering, and its inevitability is more or less certain," said Senator Bradley.

Opinions Offered on Many Subjects

Besides the graduation-rate issue, the subcommittee members heard opinions on such wide-ranging subjects as academic standards for incoming athletes, special admissions for athletes, sex discrimination, leadership by college presidents, and sports scholarships.

The quickness with which the testimony jumped from one subject to another may have served to obfuscate, rather than clarify, the issues.

Despite the range of views, there were some points on which most of the witnesses and lawmakers agreed:

- Public confidence in the integrity of intercollegiate athletics is declining because of a sense that colleges care more about winning than about educating athletes. Most of the witnesses agreed that higher education generally suffers by association.
- Although the distinction isn't always made, witnesses agreed, most of the problems in college athletics are limited to a few high-profile sports at about 200 of the nation's more than 3,000 institutions of higher education. Football and men's basketball in the NCAA's Division I are prime problem spots, they said, citing a study by the General Accounting Office that showed graduation rates for athletes in those sports lagging behind those of nonathletes.
- Efforts to clean up college sports should ideally be made mostly at the institutional level. College presidents and their governing boards, the witnesses said, must take responsibility for keeping their campus sports programs in perspective.

The witnesses disagreed about how well presidents have filled that role. Donna A. Lopiano, director of women's athletics at the University of Texas at Austin, called academic integrity a "matter of institutional will," and said that in that area there had been an "almost criminal" failure of educational leadership on some campuses.

Coaches Often Most Powerful

Mr. Williams noted that at many colleges, where coaches are often the most powerful people on campus, presidents risk their jobs when they take on the sports establishment. He wondered: "How realistic is it to assume that reforms can come from the president's office or that reforms can be made at the campus level at all?"

Mr. Atwell suggested that governing-board members needed to be more supportive of their presidents. "Too often trustees have been part of the problem, not part of the solution," he said.

Some of the lawmakers suggested that at the national level, the NCAA is spending too much time worrying about "minutiae," as George Miller, a California Democrat, put it, and not enough trying to make sure that athletes are not being exploited.

Mr. Schultz said the NCAA was taking steps to insure that athletes were treated like other students. He cited a certification plan that he has endorsed, which would impose penalties on institutions that have sports programs dramatically out of balance with academic programs on their campuses (*The Chronicle,* April 12 [1989]).

Other Witnesses Testify

The other witnesses and their basic messages were:

- Jefferson D. Farris, executive director of the National Association of Intercollegiate Athletics, who sought to distance the 500 or so college sports programs that his association oversees from the problem connected with big-time football and basketball.
- Sister Mary Alan Barszewski, athletics director at a Jersey City Catholic high school, who endorsed the Right to Know Act as a protection against ill-informed college choices by star high-school athletes.
- Mr. Deford, the editor-in-chief of a forthcoming national sports newspaper, who said the media had failed not by overemphasizing the negative in college sports, but by covering its "underside" too little.
- Ms. Lopiano, who called major college sports the "last bastion of white male chauvinists," who was

alone among the college representatives in welcoming federal intervention in such areas as preventing sexual and racial discrimination.

The committee will hold a second hearing on college sports this week. (pp. A31–A32)

Reading Selection 3

Read "Beyond Giving a Speech: Becoming a Poised, Polished Presenter" by Brash (1992).* Write a brief summary of the speech in your own words. Make certain that you are very precise in what you say so that the information remains completely accurate. You will be asked to read your abstract aloud in class in a small group and compare your abstract with those of some classmates. Your instructor will then provide you with a professionally written abstract so that you can improve your reporting skills. Compare and contrast your summary with the one written by a professional writer. In what ways was your report similar from the abstract? In what ways did it differ? Now try revising your summary.

I appreciate this opportunity to share some thoughts with you on the preparation and delivery of presentations. All of us in communications recognize that the further we advance in our profession, the greater our opportunities and requirements for giving presentations. We also recognize that it's wise to get experience: as *much* . . . as *soon* . . . as *often* as possible.

In addition, we can all benefit throughout our careers from taking public speaking courses and studying to improve our presentation skills.

Today I would like to focus on three main areas:

- Preparation, including content
- Delivery, and
- Use of visuals

Let's begin with preparation, which includes every aspect of effective presentation skills, such as deciding upon the objective, content development, delivery, and visual support.

It's important to identify our goal before we concentrate on the message, and we should begin by asking ourselves whether our objective is:

- To inform
- To persuade
- To inspire
- To motivate to action, or
- To entertain.

---

* From "Beyond Giving a Speech: Becoming a Polished, Poised Presenter," by P. W. Brash, 1992, *Vital Speeches of the Day, 59,* pp. 83–86. Copyright 1992. Reprinted with permission of Charles Parnell, executive speechwriter, Miller Brewing Co., and *Vital Speeches of the Day.*

Of course, the answer will depend largely upon the composition of the *audience*.

We should tailor every presentation to the *audience,* to the *occasion,* and to the *theme* of the meeting. This involves finding out as much as possible about the knowledge level of the audience and their interests. We should get to know them, talk with them, listen to them, and understand their needs. Only after we have carefully studied the *audience* are we ready to do research on the *topic*.

A classic example of someone who tailored his message to the audience and the occasion was Christopher Columbus.

Before Columbus met the King and Queen of Spain, navigational experts in both Portugal and Spain had already recommended against backing his rather unusual proposal to reach the Far East by sailing in the opposite direction—westward.

But Columbus understood the art of persuasion, of tailoring the message to the audience, and he knew how to put together an effective presentation. He knew, for example, that the Queen had a fervent desire to win more converts to her religion. So he made frequent references to the teeming masses of the Orient, just waiting to be converted.

Columbus learned that the Queen loved falcons and exotic birds, so he searched carefully through the accounts of Marco Polo's travels to the Orient and marked in the margin all references to those kingdoms where there were falcons and exotic birds.

He knew the King wanted Spain to expand Spain's commercial power, so he made frequent references to gold, spices, and other fabulous riches of the East.

All these points were worked into his presentation, which won the backing that resulted in the discovery of the New World.

While few of us are called on to make presentations where the stakes are quite that high, many of us *do* make presentations where a critical contract, approval of a major marketing program, or the fate of our own careers can hinge on the outcome.

Regardless of the nature of our presentation, we should begin by developing an **introduction** that gives the audience a clear understanding of what we are going to talk about and how we plan to proceed.

We might want to gain their attention with an unusual remark, story, surprising fact, or question.

We might want to tell them about important benefits they will receive—the way Columbus did.

The basic purpose of our introduction is to establish rapport with the audience and "tell them what we're going to tell them." Then we can spend the rest of the presentation actually telling them.

As part of tailoring our message to the audience, we should express it in simple English, avoiding acronyms, jargon, or specialized language.

We have a wealth of patterns to choose from when organizing the contents. Choices include chronological, spatial, topical, cause-effect or problem-situation, as well as several other alternatives. We should use the pattern that best enables us to give the audience a comprehensive picture of what we believe and feel about the subject.

Wherever possible, we should build our presentation around a few key ideas and feelings, not around facts. In today's world of information overload, 9-second sound bites, and short attention spans, audiences demand more than facts.

Television has helped create an impatient society, where audiences expect us to make our point simply and quickly. They are already saturated with facts. What they want is a comprehensive picture. If we can present it with clarity and enthusiasm, it will be more memorable and more likely to persuade them that what we are saying is worth considering.

In order to inject enthusiasm into our presentations, I believe that whenever possible, we should write each presentation with adrenalin pumping, with a high degree of excitement about the message we are sharing with the audience. The audience should feel that we cared enough to prepare the talk just for them. They must feel that our presentation is like a tailor-made suit, not one taken off the rack.

In addition to clarity and enthusiasm, we should seek opportunities to inject humor. That doesn't mean we have to tell jokes, or try to have people rolling in the aisles with laughter, but if there are any humorous aspects to our subject, we should make reference to them, even if all we are aiming for is a knowing smile or light laughter.

I believe the ideal length for a speech is about *20 minutes,* and we should know *10 times* more about the subject than we're able to say during that 20 minutes.

Having such a mastery of our material gives us credibility, the confidence to ad lib when appropriate, and the ability to answer questions with authority. It should be clear to the audience that we are brimming with information on the subject, that we are enthusiastic about it, and that only the limitations of time are preventing us from sharing even more exciting information and ideas with them.

I would caution that we should always resist the temptation to overstay our time limits in order to go into more detail. After all, it was Voltaire who warned that, "The secret of being a bore is to tell *everything.*"

How about **rehearsals?**

I spend as much time as needed to make sure my presentations run smoothly, even if it means working on them at home. If it's a major presentation, I rehearse.

Many people find it helpful to videotape themselves during rehearsal. It's one of the best ways to find out how believable you are.

If you decide to have a question and answer period, there are two major kinds of questions you may expect.

The first kind, a question of *policy* or *opinion,* is the easiest kind to handle—provided you are well versed in your subject.

The second is more likely to be a challenge to you. No matter how much you know about your subject, someone may ask you a *question of fact,* such as: "How many bushels of corn does your company buy each year from Wisconsin farmers?"

The worst thing to do is try to answer the question if you don't know the answer. The best is often, "Let me look into this further, and I'll get back to you."

Then make sure you actually do get back to them with an answer.

Another suggestion I would make about question and answer periods is that instead of ending your speech, and following it with questions, you should pause for questions at a suitable point before the conclusion of your speech.

This enables you to entertain however many questions you desire, then **conclude the speech using your prepared remarks.** This puts you in control of both the content and tone during those final critical minutes when the audience will be forming their lasting impressions of your presentation. It gives you the chance in your conclusion to drive home those essential points you want the audience to walk away with and leave a positive, upbeat final impression.

Now let's talk about **delivery.**

The importance of an effective delivery is understood by research showing that only 7% of the speaker's message is communicated by the spoken words. Fully *93%* of the message is dependent on the *quality of the delivery.*

This breaks down to *more than half—55%—*of a speaker's message coming across in *body language,* while *38%* is communicated through the *tone of voice.*

What this means is that your words are only a small part of your message. To an overwhelming degree, *you* are your message.

In fact, your speech really begins long before you reach the lectern, because your audience will start forming an opinion, based mostly on body language, as soon as they see you in the room. Research has shown that most people form an initial impression of others within *7 seconds* of meeting or seeing them.

In today's environment, one of the most important factors that will either promote or impede communication is how "likable" you are.

This quality is hard to define or teach, but the likable person generally projects an image of

- Optimism
- Concern for the welfare of other people
- Ability to see the opportunity in every difficulty
- Ability to handle stress
- Ability to laugh easily, especially at oneself
- Ability to perform at one's best in a crisis and to be humble in prosperity.

Knowing that you are being evaluated even before you go to the lectern, the best way to handle this is to smile and feel confident in yourself and your preparation.

You might remind yourself from time to time of Queen Victoria's remark when someone asked her about the consequences of a possible military defeat. She replied: "We are not interested in the possibilities of defeat."

For her, the possibilities of defeat did not exist. She understood that negative thinking leads to negative results, and *positive thinking helps create positive results.*

You must feel equally confident that your presentation will go well. That very confidence will help ensure that it does go well and that you will be perceived by the audience as both competent and confident.

You have every reason to be confident. After all, you are a likable person. You know your material. You've rehearsed as many times as necessary to master the material and feel comfortable with the flow of the words. You're ready . . . and it shows!

But no matter how much they rehearse, many people still get butterflies when they have to speak in public. What's the solution? Should you try to relax and get rid of the butterflies?

Paradoxically, I believe the answer is "No." The best way to handle the butterflies is *not* to try to relax completely. That would make you seem lifeless, inexpressive, and boring. Instead of getting rid of the butterflies, the best thing is to make them fly in formation.

This means that instead of worrying about being nervous, you can channel this nervous energy to your advantage for more *enthusiasm,* more *voice inflection,* and more *effective gestures.* As you channel your nervousness—which is a perfectly normal state of mind under the circumstances—it can actually help you come across to your audience as the knowledgeable, enthusiastic, interesting person you really are!

What about **posture?**

A natural, easy posture is best. The whole idea is to avoid any mannerisms or actions that distract the listener's attention from what you are saying. It helps to avoid stances and activities such as:

- Arms folded across the chest or clasped behind the back military style
- Hands on hip
- Arms down in front with hands folded below the waist
- Rocking back and forth, and
- Jingling items or crinkling paper in a pocket.

It's not necessary to focus too much on the mechanical aspects of delivery, but most speakers find they do best when energy and arm movements come naturally from their shoulders, not the elbows. You want to appear relaxed in movements, not stiff or wooden. It helps to stand firmly on both feet, without shifting your weight.

A very effective way to channel energy is through your voice. Taking *five* deep breaths before you begin talking forces your body to calm down and opens up your vocal passages so you can speak more effectively.

While you want to control your energy and your voice, you don't want to do it through speaking in a monotone, because monotones give rise to the adjective we all want to avoid—*monotonous.* Something that is monotonous is tiresome, because it is unvarying. What we want to achieve are *changes* in *inflection, tone,* and *volume.* For example, slow speakers can increase their impact by speeding up before delivering an important statement.

We should avoid nonwords or crutch words and phrases that fill in blank spaces and sometimes cause great distraction. They include:

- *Ah*—by far the worst offender. It's the most misused nonword in the English language. You can choose for yourself which word would be the worst punishment: 100 days of the ancient Chinese water torture, with its slow and endless "drip . . . drip . . . drip," or 100 days of listening to speeches by someone who uses "ah" every third or fourth word. Personally, I'd be tempted to choose the water every time.

We should also avoid:

- *Frankly* and
- *To be honest.*

These last two expressions serve no useful purpose, and they may backfire on you by raising the question of how frank or honest you have been in all the rest of your presentation, if, after several minutes of talking with the audience, you say *now* you are going to "frank" or "honest" with them.

Another important essential to good delivery is *eye contact.* It's best to maintain eye contact with an individual for *3-5* seconds or long enough to make a complete thought.

The speaker benefits from good eye contact. It keeps you as the center of attention and gives you feedback to see if your message is having its intended impact. You can tell if the audience is listening, confused, interested, bored, or disagreeing. If you're not getting the response you want, you can change your communication to get it.

Now let's talk briefly about **visual support.** Slides, overhead transparencies, and other visuals can be useful devices to perk up a presentation, as long as they're used responsibly and so long as they add clarity or impact to our ideas. But we shouldn't use visuals just for the sake of using them.

If we do use visuals, we should never deliver our presentation from them. The audience can read the slides too, and if we're looking at the screen, we lose eye contact.

We should always make sure the visuals have words large enough to read from the back of the room. It's best to have no more than *six* lines per slide or transparency, and have a "frame" of empty space around the words. It's also best to limit the text to just the key words, and use lists rather than sentences.

For greatest visibility, words on slides or flip charts should be in black, brown, dark blue, or dark green. Use red to highlight, underline, circle, box, or otherwise accent a main point.

We should darken the room to show projected visuals, but leave enough light to take notes.

Leaving the light turned up slightly also has the added benefit of helping prevent one of the most ego-challenging situations facing a speaker. There are few things that can do more to shake the faith you have in your own charisma than seeing one or two members of the audience . . . with eyes glazed over, valiantly waging an unequal, forlorn struggle . . . against the sandman.

If, on occasion, a member of the audience does nod off, don't let it devastate you. It doesn't necessarily mean you're a boring speaker.

You have to recognize that in any large audience there is always the possibility that you will have one or two people in whom "the spirit is willing, but the flesh is weak"—or where the flesh simply didn't have enough sleep the night before.

Meanwhile—to continue our discussion of visuals—in order to get the most benefit from them, it's always a good idea to rehearse with them. Make sure that all the slides are in the carousel in the proper order and that they show what you want. It's a good idea to number your transparencies in case you drop them and have to reassemble them quickly.

Plan your logistics, especially if you're giving a joint presentation. Know in advance the sequence of speakers, where each will stand, and how you will coordinate the slide show.

Manage your timing. Allow enough time for the audience to get settled and for questions.

And while I'm on the subject of questions, before I close, I'd like to pause now to answer any questions you may have.

I would **summarize** my main points by saying that a well-prepared and well-delivered presentation is characterized by:

- A clear goal
- An introduction that gains the attention of the audience and tells the audience what we are talking about
- A simple message tailored to the audience, occasion, and theme
- Humor, where appropriate
- A dynamic delivery based on our mastery of the subject matter, our confidence, and our enthusiasm for sharing ideas with the audience
- A conclusion that emphasizes our main points and leaves the audience with a positive feeling about themselves and the subject matter we have covered.

I would like to emphasize that the points I have covered are only a few of the many considerations we should keep in mind as we prepare a presentation.

Becoming a poised, polished presenter is a journey of a lifetime, and each time we do a presentation, we should learn something more about ourselves and our subject that will enable us to improve our performance the next time.

I wish each of you the very best of luck as you prepare and deliver your presentations. (pp. 83–86)

Reading Selection 4

Read and annotate Sarmadi's (1995) article on overcoming obstacles.* Create a graphic organizer based on your notes. Make certain that your organizer includes all of the author's major points.

---

* From "With Persistence Just About Any Obstacle Can Be Overcome," by C. Sarmadi, 1995, *Keys to Success, 2,* p. 15. Copyright 1995 by Prentice Hall, Inc. Reprinted with permission.

I remember learning in my Greek archeology class that one of the ancient Greek temples had the inscriptions, "Know Thyself" and "Nothing in Excess." These two cardinal rules which have remained basic since the dawn of civilization have helped me to grow just as much as they have helped the civilizations that took this advice. Being hearing impaired has provided its share of challenges; challenges that have strengthened my will power and enhanced my knowledge of my own abilities. My hearing loss forced me to push myself beyond my average ability and strive for maximum ability. For instance, the human body is normally given five senses. However, when one sense, such as hearing, is absent, the other senses grow stronger with more use and practice. Some may develop a keener sense of smell, sharper eye reflex, or a very sensitive sense of touch. In effect, challenges force you to "Know Thyself."

With every challenge I have overcome—from academics to athletics—I feel I have ascended on a higher plane of self-understanding. It truly gives one a feeling of power and satisfaction knowing what one is capable of. Persistence in the face of difficulty leads to the higher road. For me, the undying desire to learn more is a crucial element to overcoming challenges and limitations since "Knowledge is power," according to English philosopher Francis Bacon (1561–1626).

Another way that made it easier to know myself better was to emphasize my strengths more than my weaknesses. The advice of teachers and coaches has often been to work on improving your weaknesses first. Not for me, because when one starts spending so much time and effort on a weakness, the potential of their strengths could fade when they in fact could use more strengthening!

The second rule—"Nothing in Excess"—has been a great help in keeping emotional equilibrium and the key to being a well-balanced person. The challenge of this is learning the discipline of being able to say "No" at certain times to certain things. For me it has been a meaningful accomplishment to be able to strike the balance between social and nonsocial events, and it gives me the feeling of control over my life and behavior.

Excessive pride can be one's worst enemy; it is not only vain but it hinders one's personal progress. It would be ridiculous for me to be proud of my hearing loss; instead the pride stems from my accomplishments despite my hearing impairment. Pride without accomplishment to verify it is vanity.

My advice to all students is to maximize the use of services that universities provide, such as notetaking or counseling, and to remember that obstacles of any kind can be overcome . . . and that emotional obstacles are almost always easier to overcome than physical ones. (p. 15)

References

Brash, P. W. (1992, November). Beyond giving a speech: Becoming a polished, poised presenter. *Vital Speeches of the Day, 59*(3), 83–86.

Elkind, D., & Bowen, R. (1979). Imaginary audience behavior in children and adolescents. *Developmental Psychology, 15*(1), 38–44.

Feistritzer, C. E. (1986). *Profiles of teachers in the United States.* Washington, DC: National Center for Educational Information.

Garmston, R. J. (1997). *The presenter's fieldbook.* Norwood, MA: Christopher-Gordon.

Garmston, R. J., & Wellman, B. W. (1992). *How to make presentations that teach and transform.* Alexandria, VA: Association for Supervision and Curriculum Development.

Gordon, J. (1990). Learning how to learn. *Training, 27,* 51–62.

Hoff, S. (1988). *I can see you naked: A guide to fearless presentations.* Kansas City, MO: Andrews & McMeel.

Johnson, L. B. (1994). Finding the right word: Dictionaries, thesauruses, and quotations. *PC Novice, 5,* 21–23.

Lederman, D. (1989, May 24). Congressional panel hears conflicting testimony about the troubles of big-time college sports. *The Chronicle of Higher Education, 35*(37), A31–A32.

Lefrancois, G. (1992). *Of children: An introduction to child development.* Belmont, CA: Wadsworth.

Lunenfeld, M., & Lunenfeld, P. (1992). *College basics: How to start right and finish strong.* Buffalo, NY: Semester Press.

Mooney, W., & Noone, D. J. (1992). *ASAP: The fastest way to create a memorable speech.* Hauppauge, NY: Barron's Educational Series.

Motley, M. T. (1988). Taking the terror out of talk. *Psychology Today, 22*(1), 46–49.

O'Connor, J. (1992). Dealing with performance anxiety. *Anchor Point, 6*(5), 30–34.

Sarmadi, C. (1995). With persistence just about any obstacle can be overcome. *Keys to Success, 2*(1), 15.

Schaefer, J. H., & Brashear, M. A. (1989). *Impact: A guide to public speaking.* New York: Berkley Books.

Verderben, R. F. (1979). *The challenge of effective speaking* (4th ed.). Belmont, CA: Wadsworth.

Weaver, R. L. (1991, August). Self-motivation: 10 techniques for activating or freeing the spirit. *Vital Speeches of the Day, 57*(20), 620–623.

Prereading Questions

- How do you usually prepare for a test?

- What are some specific test-taking strategies you have learned?

- What can you do after receiving a poor grade on a test?

- What action can you take when your grades begin to fall?

- Why is it important to monitor your own progress in a course?

Assessing Prior Knowledge

Reread Ellis's (1984) quotation at the beginning of this chapter to become more familiar with it. Then, close your eyes and imagine how you would feel walking on a railroad track. Now think about how you would feel walking on that track if it were high above the ground. Can you imagine being so well prepared for taking tests that you feel as if that track is lowered to the ground? By drawing on your knowledge of test taking and combining it with information in this chapter, you should feel confident in your ability to score well on tests. You should also be able to set some goals and evaluate your progress toward those goals throughout the semester to monitor your growth as a student.

Vignette: The Test

Students have different approaches to preparing for tests. Neither Lozetta, Marla, nor Jerome has an approach that leads to success on a test.

Lozetta sees the professor in the course in which she was enrolled last summer. "I had my first big test," she says as they stand in the cafeteria line.

"How did you do?" the professor asks.

"Not good. I got a 67%."

"How did that happen?" the professor asks.

Lozetta replies, "I didn't study. I just don't do well on tests."

Lozetta didn't prepare for the test. She is resigned to the fact that she does not do well on tests.

Marla is studying for a test that will undoubtedly determine her grade for the course. She is right between a B and C, and this grade will decide whether she meets the 2.0 overall grade point average requirement to continue in her major. In her textbook for the course, Marla has highlighted practically every word—every page is a blur of pink and yellow stripes, making it virtually impossible to sort out information that is important to study for a test. Although Marla clearly invested time in working with her textbook, her efforts were not focused and therefore did not prepare her for the test.

Jerome's situation is complicated by the fact that he cuts class regularly. He tries to study for the exams, but his notes are incomplete, and he is unable to integrate information from lectures and the text. In addition, Jerome lacks information about the test that the professor has given in class. He finds out later that the professor had been quite specific about what to study and that most other students thought the same test that Jerome nearly failed was easy.

How could Lozetta, Marla, and Jerome be helped? Think about your response to this question in Box 8.1.

BOX 8.1 *Improvement in Action* ⅢⅢ➡

What suggestions could you give to Lozetta, Marla, and Jerome who are struggling with studying for tests?

Suggest five study strategies for Lozetta who did not study and does not take tests well.

How can Marla improve her highlighting technique to make it more effective?

What would you say to Jerome to convince him of the importance of going to class?

Preparation for Test Taking

Preparation for test taking starts when the course begins. Study the syllabus to find out when tests will be given and projects due. When you establish your calendar for the semester, note the time frame for these tests and projects. Check your calendar daily to review the requirements.

If you use the critical thinking, reading, writing, and listening strategies presented in this book, you will have a good foundation to work toward your goal of being successful on exams. Applying what you have learned thus far is a step in the right direction. Think of tests as learning experiences (McWhorter, 1998). Frequent quizzes force you to keep up with assigned reading. Study helps you relate concepts and store information in long-term memory. In order to "ace" tests, additional strategies, such as preparing mentally for tests and knowing how to study for and take different types of tests, are equally important.

Of course, reviewing for tests is not synonymous with cramming. Cramming is doing a massive study session at the last minute—the day or evening before the test. This procedure will enable you to acquire *some* of the necessary information, but it does not provide for complete preparation or later recall. In fact, if cramming continues through the night, it may be the cause of poor test performance. A student who pulls an "all-nighter" is not as alert for test taking as one who is well rested. In fact, we have known students who were so exhausted from studying all night that they could barely stay awake during the test.

Nevertheless, if occasionally you get into a bind and need to cram for an exam, there is a general strategy for cramming. This strategy will work, of course, only if you have completed assignments and attended class, so you have some knowledge of course content. There is no real way to pack a semester or half of a semester's learning into one marathon study session. But under difficult circumstances when you need to "speed study," select some content that you think is important and focus your study on that content. What is important in cramming is to know some course content well and to avoid just "surveying" all of the content to be covered by the test. Be aware, however, that you are likely to forget 80% of the material you cram within a week or two, so you will have to relearn it for any subsequent tests you have to take on the material.

Far better than cramming is to begin a systematic review of reading material and class notes several days to a week before the exam, depending on the comprehensiveness of the exam. Be sure to consider time parameters when planning your study time. You may have outside obligations, such as a job, family responsibilities, or time spent commuting to campus. For a quiz, you should begin to review 2 days in advance. For a comprehensive exam, such as a final exam, begin reviewing a week ahead of time. Some of this review might be done in your study group.

How do you know what is important to review? You have a massive amount of material, especially if the test is a midterm or final examination. Trying to determine which information warrants the most attention is often mind-boggling. Some guidelines are described in the following sections.

Matching Study to Instructor's Approach

Professor Eiseman gives a daily five-point quiz. Professor Craig gives a weekly 10-item quiz on each chapter of the text. Professor Ouyang gives midterm and final examinations only. Professor Hernandez gives just one examination, a final that covers content for the entire course. Each of these situations calls for a different study strategy. Studying in this context assumes that you are familiar with the information because you have prepared for each class. How would you prepare for the tests listed in Box 8.2?

BOX 8.2   *Improvement in Action* ⅢⅢ➡

What strategies would you use to prepare for these tests?

■ A five-item daily quiz

■ A 10-item weekly quiz

■ A midterm and a final examination (two major exams in the course)

■ A final examination (one major exam in the course)

How do your strategies differ?

In reviewing for Professors Eiseman's and Craig's quizzes, you may find reviewing highlighted notes, the chapter summary, and class notes to be sufficient. In Professor Ouyang's class, in which he gives just midterm and final exams, students will probably find it necessary to spend considerable time reviewing all course materials, memorizing key concepts. And, in the last case, Professor Hernandez's final examination only, students might find it most helpful to prepare note cards with key concepts, identify major sections in the text and notebook with tabs, and periodically schedule reviews throughout the semester. Now, return to Box 8.2. Compare your approaches for preparing for the exams with those that were suggested. You may decide to add some of the suggested approaches to your repertoire. Remember, for more comprehensive exams, such as a final exam that covers content for the entire semester, you must begin preparation well in advance of the exam.

Students need to focus on what is emphasized in the course. Most instructors stress the concepts they consider to be most important during lectures or small-group work. For some professors, class notes are a way of elaborating on what is important in the book. Other instructors will lecture primarily on information that is not found in the textbook and hold students responsible for understanding the information in the textbook. This approach leaves the decision making on the importance of information in the text to the student. In situations like this, focus on the information that the author of the textbook deems important, which you can determine by concentrating on the author's major topics, chapter objectives, and review questions.

Often, the syllabus will indicate the content (chapters, class notes, films, etc.) and format (multiple-choice, essay, etc.) of tests. As the time for the test approaches, the instructor may give additional information about the emphasis, content, and types of questions. This gives students an opportunity to ask questions for greater clarification. At times, professors can be really specific, giving hints about the test with a comment like, "Be sure to study the overview on page 137." There is a real bonus for being in class on that day. If the professor does not review test content, ask questions at the beginning or end of class, or make an appointment to discuss the information.

Matching Study to Test Type

When you note that a comprehensive test like a midterm or final examination is scheduled, establish a plan of study for each day. This type of test calls for more time than a review the night before. Set aside a number of hours that you need to be ready for the test. This could mean working backward from the test date to decide how many study sessions you need to be prepared. Determine which aspects of the course to study at each session. You may want to study the material that is most difficult for you first, so you give yourself ample time to understand it. Assemble all of the materials that you will need for study. Decide how you will spend the time. Will you review reading and class notes? You may map ideas as a strategy for recall. Repetition is an important memory aid. Identify the most important notes, and, using key words, commit those ideas to memory. During the test, these key words can be used to recall major ideas.

Test items are broadly categorized as either "objective" or "essay." An objective item has one right answer that can be checked using a key. Essay exam items are more subjective— they have many possible answers, different degrees of correctness, and even though an instructor has criteria for evaluating responses, more individual appraisal of each response is required. Subjective essay exams also differ in terms of what they require of you, the test taker.

You will need to prepare differently for objective tests, such as sentence completion, multiple-choice, true/false, and matching tests. On an objective test you need to *recall* information and, in the case of multiple-choice and matching items, simply *recognize* information. True/false tests, on the other hand, require you to make a judgment on the accuracy of information. A thorough knowledge of the content area will enable you to recognize and select correct answers for objective tests.

Preparing for essay exams is decidedly different preparation than for objective exams. In contrast, essay exams require you to reconstruct knowledge—that is, recall information that you have learned and manipulate that information using such processes as comparing, contrasting, or critiquing. As you study, you will need to predict the type of question(s) that your instructor might ask. Refer to Chapter 9, "Writing Effectively at the College Level," to explore all of the types of essay questions that might be asked. Some of those types of questions will be explored further in approaches to answering essay questions in this chapter.

But regardless of the type of exam item, essay or objective, you must be prepared to score well. By focusing on the way that you anticipate using the information, you can prepare more efficiently and effectively for any type of test. For the essay exam, you will need to reconstruct information—that is, recall sufficient information to write a coherent answer. You might practice for the essay exam by outlining or mapping information on topics you anticipate being on the exam. You could compare several potential essay questions and then answer them based on what you think the instructor feels is important. Try to weave in key vocabulary words in your answers whenever possible. For objective-type exams, you need to recall, recognize, and judge the accuracy of information. To prepare for these exams, you should use memory techniques to learn content. You might think that less preparation is needed for the objective-type exam. To earn a high score, you need to spend as much time as you would preparing for an essay exam.

Some instructors give unannounced or pop quizzes. There is no better way to be prepared for these than to be prepared for class each day. In fact, that is the reason that pop quizzes are given: to prevent students from coasting along with difficult material instead of studying every day. Preparing for pop quizzes means studying the required textbook, library material, and class notes. Failing one unannounced quiz may not substantially affect your grade, unless the quiz is worth a considerable number of points. However, repeatedly failing pop quizzes will lower your final grade. Failure on unannounced quizzes also indicates to the instructor that you are not prepared for class. If your instructor allows you to miss just one quiz all semester, it is important not to "use up" your one missed quiz too readily. Push yourself to go to class when you feel like missing because you are tired, busy, or have a cold. Expect that one day you may really be too ill to attend class, have mechanical difficulties like the car breaking down, or have a friend or family member who desperately needs you in a crisis. Do not depend on classes being canceled for poor weather conditions. Unlike high schools, colleges and universities rarely, if ever, close due to the weather, unless a meteorological disaster strikes. University officials assume that most students can manage to get to class. So, carefully guard your "free" pop quiz—chances are you will really need that cushion later.

Mentally Preparing for Tests

Preparing for quizzes and exams by studying is important; however, mental preparation is also important. Some students suffer from test anxiety. Pauk (1993) notes that there is really only one cure for text anxiety: preparing for the exam. Preparation involves more than reviewing the night before the exam. Preparation begins the first day of class and each sequential class. Attend class and take thorough lecture notes. Read and study assignments. As the course progresses, take advantage of opportunities for tutoring on campus if you need additional help. Join a study group, as described in Chapter 5. Find out as much as possible about the test from the syllabus, the instructor, or students who have had the class with your instructor.

Your attitude and expectations will influence your performance. "Test anxious students often sabotage their own efforts by mentally preparing themselves for failure. Think positively. Your attitude will influence how you do on an exam. And a positive attitude begins with your feeling of preparedness" (Pauk, 1984, pp. 202, 217). Everyone experiences mild anxiety at test time. A little anxiety will actually enhance performance, but a high degree of anxiety will interfere with performance (Maddox, 1963).

You can reduce anxiety and get off to a good start in class by doing well on the first test. Shaughnessy (1990) notes that it is particularly important to study thoroughly for the first test. In doing this, you will avoid having to be concerned all semester about making up for your initial low grade if you do not do well.

Some students feel more confident in taking exams and are test-wise. Others routinely say, "I know much more than what my test grade shows. I don't test well. No matter how I approach the exam, I don't get a high score." With which of these comments and the comments in Box 8.3 do you identify most strongly?

In addition to careful planning for review of information and anticipation of test questions, the following strategies should help you approach tests with more confidence.

BOX 8.3   *Improvement in Action* ⅢⅢ➡

Do you identify with any of these comments about tests? If so, why?

- "I freeze up when the test is put before me."

- "My mind goes blank when I begin the test."

- "I do not do well on true/false tests. I think I read too much into the questions."

- "When taking a multiple-choice test, I never know when to choose *all of the above*."

- "When the test calls for filling in the blank with a word or phrase, I never seem to be able to figure out what fits in there—even if I studied."

- "On essay tests, I am never sure if I have interpreted the question correctly."

General Approaches to Test Taking

Some general approaches to exams can ease your anxiety and help you get off to a good start. Be sure to bring the tools of test taking with you to the exam. These could include well-sharpened pencils, erasers, pens, a "blue book" for an essay test, a watch (in case there is not a clock in the room), and scratch paper, if it is permitted. Special area tests may require other tools: math and science—a calculator, ruler, protractor, or periodic table; foreign language—translator's dictionary (Gall, Gall, Jacobsen, & Bullock, 1990). Be certain to find out which tools are permitted—some instructors will let you use a dictionary, for example.

Arrive early for the test so that you will be there for the initial test directions. While you are waiting for directions, skim the test to get a sense of the instructor's expectations. Your professor may request that you do not write on the test, just on the answer sheet. Determine where you are to write your answers and write your name on all pages on which you are permitted to write. You may be asked to write them directly on the test copy, to fill in small circles or "bubbles" on a computer scoring sheet, or to write your essay on composition paper or in a small book specifically for that purpose called a "blue book." Note that you may need a number two pencil for a bubble sheet. If the appropriate pencil is not used, the answers will not be counted accurately. If you are not sure where all answers should be recorded, wait for further instructions and an opportunity to ask questions.

Do not begin taking the test until oral directions are given. Some instructors will read directions to you and ask for questions that the class may have. They may draw attention to specific typographical errors or misprints. Your instructor may remind the class that you have to answer only two of four questions and emphasize the point value of the test items. The instructor may add oral instructions that are not written on the test copy. Sometimes these will be put on the board. It is crucial that you attend closely to this initial information. Not following directions can cost you points. Your efforts to know course material will be diminished because of the point loss for not following directions. A faculty member we know, for instance, printed the test on both sides of the paper to conserve paper. A student who arrived late did not hear this direction and, as a result, neglected to answer half of the test! As this example points out, only after you have given thorough attention to directions are you ready to begin the test.

Before answering any questions, you may want to use a technique, called the "splash-down method," that will help you recall information (Standley, 1987). Using the back of the test or scratch paper, quickly (no more than 1 to 2 minutes) write words, phrases, mnemonics, or anything that you know will later jog your memory. Doing this also helps ease tension.

Begin the test by answering the question that has the greatest point value. Then, proceed to the question with the second greatest number of points. The procedure will enable you to focus on questions that will earn the most credit for you. As you work, you may want to skip over items that are overwhelming and return to them later. Answering the easy high-point questions first will give you a sense of confidence.

Concentration and attention to the task are key. Focus all of your attention on the test. For now, try to put aside any issues other than the test that are consuming your thoughts. Try to stay focused and avoid any distractions in the room. This may mean that you will need to request a change of seat if the location of your seat is not comfortable or conducive to concentration. For example, some rooms are adjacent to other classrooms where students are engaged in group activities, and hearing their conversations can be distracting.

Use all of the time for the test. No points are gained for a rapid finish since few tests at the college level are timed. Monitor your time so that your pace will allow you to finish in the time allotted. This is especially crucial if the test is limited to one class period. After you have finished, reread the questions and review your answers. Always check your answers, but do not change them unless you are reasonably certain that you have made an error and your original answer is incorrect. Do not be concerned that some students are leaving the test before the period is over. Research shows that there is no relationship between high scores and the time to complete the test (Smith, 1989). In all our years of teaching at the college level, we have never heard a student say, "I wish I had left earlier instead of taking the time to check my answers," but many, many times we have heard, "That was a stupid mistake and it affected my grade. I wish I had taken the time to check the answers."

Strategies for Taking Specific Types of Tests

These general points for approaching test taking are important; however, additional strategies are needed to answer specific question types, such as essay, sentence completion and short answer, multiple-choice, true/false, and matching questions.

Essay Tests

For an essay test, you often have to purchase a blue book from the bookstore or provide your own paper. If you provide your own paper, take standard 8 1/2" × 11" composition paper to the exam. For the best appearance, make sure that you do not use paper that you tear from a notebook that leaves the edges ragged. The choice of paper and your handwriting will be the first impression the instructor has of your work.

Instructors have many papers to read. Legible handwriting is important to earn the maximum number of points. If your answer or any part of it cannot be read, your instructor will ignore it, and you will lose points even though you mastered the material.

The first step in the approach to answering an essay question is to focus carefully on the type of answer that the instructor requests. Some types of questions are easier than others. For example, if you are asked to *define, describe, list,* or *outline,* your task will be relatively simple. These terms are familiar ones and rather straightforward. However, other types of essay questions are considered more intellectually challenging because these questions require more integration of thought. Some of these higher-level essay questions ask you to *compare and contrast, critique, summarize,* and *apply.* Familiarity with these terms is essential. Figure 9.3 in the next chapter defines these terms and others.

We cannot emphasize enough that you need to read the essay question carefully and interpret it correctly. Begin by preparing a brief outline or map of your answer. Prewriting is important in all writing situations, especially under pressure. This outline or map could be so abbreviated that another person may not be able to make sense of it because of the abbreviations that you use. Outlining or mapping may seem as if it is wasting valuable writing time, but it serves two purposes:

1. It focuses your thoughts.
2. Once you have outlined or mapped, you can reread the question to make sure that you are interpreting it correctly.

Once you begin writing, it is also a good idea to reread the question periodically to make sure that you are answering the question asked. Some essay questions contain more than one question. Be sure you answer every question asked. Students often answer the first part of a question and do not look back at the question, forgetting to answer the other parts of the question—losing many points in the process. A good idea is to underline the question words in the essay.

Read the partial essay answer to this comparison and contrast question, "Compare and contrast the applications of a database and spreadsheet." Notice how the student began the essay with an introductory statement and then explained how the database and spreadsheet are alike and different.

Spreadsheets and databases have some similarities, but they are more different than they are alike.

Similarities　They are similar in the following ways. First, both are available in computer software programs as a means of organizing information. Both need alphabetic data to organize the information that will be stored. This means that the individual using the database or spreadsheet must organize the material before entering it in the computer. This organization saves steps so you do not need to make changes in the format later. Data are entered into both spreadsheets and databases and can be manipulated—that is, sorted or calculated if the data are numbers. . . .

Differences　In contrast, spreadsheets and databases are different in their intended use. Spreadsheets are worksheets for numerical information. Each time new information is entered into the spreadsheet, the spreadsheet can be recalculated to reflect the additional numerical information. For example, if a professor keeps grades on a spreadsheet, each time the scores from a quiz are entered into the computer, the spreadsheet can be recalculated to reflect the current percentages the students have earned.

Databases can be used to calculate data; however, they are not able to handle the volume of numeric information or the higher-level calculations that the spreadsheet can. The database is best for information that can be sorted or reorganized in various ways. For example, if you were keeping a list of addresses on a database, you might want to print a list of addresses, sort them in ascending ZIP code order for bulk mailing, or identify all individuals from a particular town. The database could do this with ease. . . .

It is clear that both spreadsheets and databases have specific uses and, yet, are somewhat related.

In the essay on spreadsheets and databases, note the subtitles that have been inserted for ease in reading. Most professors appreciate this type of organization that makes reading easier, even though they do not specifically ask for it.

The student added a concluding sentence for the essay. This sentence wraps things up and signals to the instructor that you finished the answer. The concluding sentence refers back to the main idea—that is, the introductory statement in the essay. Recall in the answer to the question on spreadsheets and databases, the introductory sentence was "Spreadsheets and databases have some similarities, but they are more different than they are alike"; the concluding sentence was "It is clear that both spreadsheets and databases have specific uses and, yet, are somewhat related." Both the first and last sentences are related.

To write an introductory statement, take part of the question and turn it into a sentence. This statement can serve as the introductory main idea sentence for the answer. Read the question in Figure 8.1. Then, in Box 8.4, write introductory sentences for the answer.

Look at another type of essay question. The question in Figure 8.2 is from a criminology test. As you can see from the beginning of the student's response to the gun amnesty question, she seems to be off to a good start. Note how she strengthens her position with evidence from an article she had read. Having support for answers is essential and often overlooked by students. Often, the professor will write a comment like, "You did not use readings to support your argument." What they are asking for is what this student did—to refer *specifically* to the textbook, lecture notes, or supplemental reading that supports a particular point. It is a good idea, also, to use new vocabulary introduced in the course in the essay answer, if possible.

Success on all essay questions depends on not only the student's knowledge base but also the correct interpretation of the question. Review the meaning of the essay descriptive words so you are prepared for your essay test. If you have some doubt as to the interpretation that the instructor wants, ask when initial instructions for the test are being given or as you prepare to outline or map your answer in preparation for writing. Find out, too, if you

Figure 8.1
American Politics Essay Examination

Applying course content and knowledge from your reading, answer the following question. Present both sides of the argument.

Should fund raising for political campaigns be regulated by legislation?

BOX 8.4   *Improvement in Action* ▌▌▌➡

Write introductory statements for an answer to the essay question in Figure 8.1. You should include two statements, one for each argument that you would present. Compare your sentences with those of a classmate.

Figure 8.2
Introduction to Criminology Weekly Quiz

Read the question carefully, and write your answer legibly. Be sure you answer the question that is asked. Your answer will be judged on your knowledge of course content and completeness.

1. *Critique the gun amnesty program in which individuals who own illegal types of guns are able to turn them in to the police with no charges filed against them. (5 points)*

Student Response:

The gun amnesty program is ineffective in many ways. The period for surrendering the gun is specified so that illegal guns cannot be turned in at all times. This period of amnesty may encourage some individuals to surrender guns, but many illegal guns are still in circulation. It is just a drop in a bucket. This point was brought out clearly in an article, "Effective Gun Control" in the October issue . . .

are permitted to ask the instructor for clarification on test items during the test. Some instructors are very willing to help you understand the question better—as long as you do not expect them to give you the answer. If you are concerned that other students will be distracted or you will be overheard, take your test paper up with you and write your question for a simple, quick response in the margin, and the instructor can say yes or no or write a reply.

One last issue concerns the mechanical aspects of language. Be sure to ask whether correct spelling "counts." Ask also about the mechanics of writing, such as punctuation and capitalization. Find out if you are permitted to use a dictionary or thesaurus.

Stay focused on the question and answer it succinctly. A longer essay will not earn a higher grade if the response is not of the quality expected. Remember, "Your paper will be read, not weighed. Wordy, overlong answers weaken your performance" (Spargo, 1994, p. 200).

Sentence Completion and Short-Answer Tests

Two other types of questions for which you must furnish the answer are sentence completion and short answer. Examples of these appear in Figure 8.3.

Sentence Completion

The sentence completion question is easier than the essay question because there is no need to organize your thoughts for writing. You need only to write the missing word or phrase. The instructor usually insists on a specific word or phrase. Four helpful hints in answering sentence completion or fill-in-the-blank questions follow:

1. Focus on the key words in each sentence. In Figure 8.3, notice the key phrases in the two sentence completion questions. They are *measure of central tendency* and *occurs most frequently* for question 1. For question 2, the key words are *easy test, students did well,* and *distribution of scores.*

2. Disregard the size of the blank in the sentence. Many instructors will have a standard-sized line length for answers regardless of the length of the answer. You may

Figure 8.3
Educational Measurement Quiz 1

Sentence Completion

Complete each sentence by writing the correct word or words on the corresponding blank on the separate answer sheet. Spell correctly for maximum credit. Each item is worth one (1) point. A 5-point bonus will be given if all correct answers are spelled accurately.

1. The measure of central tendency referring to the score that occurs most frequently is the _____.

2. If you gave an easy test and most students did well, the distribution of scores would be _____.

Short Answer

Define the following terms. Each correctly defined term is worth one (1) point.

1. mean score
2. median score

---

be instructed to write your answer on another piece of paper. If so, the blank may be very short; perhaps, three (____) or five (_____) spaces. In Figure 8.3, the blanks in the sentence completion questions are the same size, so there is no indication of the length of the response expected. The correct answers to questions 1 and 2 are *mode* and *skewed*.

3. Make sure that the answer is grammatically correct when the sentence is completed. Note in Figure 8.3, the answers *mode* and *skewed* are grammatically correct.

4. Check your spelling—often these blanks call for specialized vocabulary words and their definitions, so knowing the correct spelling is important. Sometimes, you can copy correct spelling from another part of the test.

Short-Answer Questions

The short-answer question may require a phrase, such as a definition for vocabulary as shown in Figure 8.3, or a sentence or two of explanation. The correct answers for the short-answer questions are (1) mean score—*arithmetic average of a set of scores;* (2) median score—*the middle score of a set of scores arranged in ascending or descending order.* The instructor could have asked for examples of mean and median scores.

Sometimes a short-answer question will call for a description or explanation. For example, the item "Briefly describe the effects of auto emissions on the pollution index" calls for a description. You would write a short paragraph to respond to this question.

Study guides that accompany the text often have practice items like these.

Multiple-Choice, True/False, and Matching Tests

Unlike short-answer and completion questions in which you recall and compose an answer, multiple-choice, true/false, and matching items require you to *recognize* correct answers among incorrect answers.

Multiple-Choice Questions

When you begin a section of multiple-choice questions, as in other types of questions, read the directions carefully. You may be directed to choose the best answer or more than one answer.

By eliminating incorrect answers, you can determine the correct answer. The multiple-choice question calls for elimination of some or all answers (*none of the above*) or acceptance of all answers (*all of the above*). In other questions, you may be asked to identify the incorrect answer (*all of the following except*).

You can approach a multiple-choice test in three ways; all of them are appropriate:

1. Start at the first question and keep going, question by question, until you reach the end, never leaving a question until you have either answered it fully or made an educated guess.

2. Answer every *easy* question first—the ones you know the answers to without thinking at all or those requiring the simplest calculations—then go back and do the harder ones.

3. Answer the *hardest* questions first, then go back and do the easy ones.* (Fry, 1994, p. 105)

---

* From *"Ace" Any Test* (2nd ed., p. 105), by R. Fry, 1994, Hawthorne, NJ: Career. Copyright 1994 by Career Press Inc. Reprinted by permission.

You must determine which approach suits your style and best use of the time allotted for the test. Assess these approaches in Box 8.5.

Another important consideration in taking multiple-choice tests is the amount of time that you can spend on each item. Often tests are composed of sets of different types of questions, so pacing yourself is a little more difficult than if the questions are all of one type. But suppose you have a test with 50 multiple-choice questions and 1 hour in which to complete the test. This would give you approximately 1 minute per question; however, not all questions will take the same amount of time. Some may be harder and others easier. In addition, you must spend extra time considering the options for some items. Of course, you want to allow time to review your answers before turning in your test.

One approach to answering multiple-choice questions is to read the stem or the initial part of the question along with each option as if you were reading a true/false statement. If the statement reads true, consider it; if it reads false, eliminate it. If the statement reads true, note it but continue to read the other options along with the stem of the question. If at least two of the options are correct, mark *all of the above* as the correct answer. See Figure 8.4 for an example in which *all of the above* is a correct answer. You would probably know that answers a. and b. are correct so you would choose *all of the above*. If one option does not correctly complete the stem of the question, *all of the above* would not be a good choice.

Another approach to answering multiple-choice questions is to guess before selecting the answer (Kesselman-Turkel & Peterson, 1981). This strategy requires you to cover

---

BOX 8.5   *Improvement in Action* ⅢⅢ➡

Evaluate the three approaches to a multiple-choice test by completing the chart here:

Approaches to Multiple-Choice Tests		
Approaches	**Advantages**	**Possible Disadvantages**
Answer all questions in order of presentation		
Answer easiest questions first		
Answer hardest questions first		

Figure 8.4
A Multiple-Choice Question

1. TV cable service offers
   a. variations in the cost of service.
   b. access to channels specific to local areas.
   c. access to broadcast stations and premium cable stations.
   d. all of the above.

the answers, read the question, make a guess, and then look at the answers. Select the option that is closest to your guess. When using this approach, always be sure to read every answer before making your final selection.

Sometimes you have no idea as to which answer is correct in a multiple-choice item. Ellis (1984) suggests these approaches to this dilemma: (a) If two answers or quantities are similar, choose one of these answers; and (b) if numerical answers represent a range of answers (such as 2, 10, 35, 40, 65), choose one in the middle. If all else fails and there is no penalty for guessing, make an educated guess. You will know whether there is a penalty for guessing if the instructor tells you or the penalty is written in the directions. A test with a penalty for guessing may award you two points for every correct answer and subtract one point for every answer that is incorrect. You have to make the decision as to how confident you feel in answering each item when there is a penalty for guessing.

True/False Questions

Often, tests will contain a combination of multiple-choice and true/false items. A multiple choice test gives you a 25 percent chance of selecting the correct answer (assuming there are four possible answers). However, a true/false test increases your chances to 50 percent (Brown & Miller, 1996). Approach true/false tests as you would other tests: Read the directions carefully and decide which approach you prefer. You could answer all questions in sequence, focus on the hard questions first, or begin with the easy questions. If *any* part of the statement is false, mark the item *false*. For example, the following true/false statement has a false component: "To be classified as a mammal, an animal must live on land, be warm-blooded, and have hair." Living on land is not characteristic of a mammal, so the statement is false even though it is true that an animal must be warm-blooded and have hair to be classified as a mammal.

Other indicators of false statements are the use of absolutes indicated by words such as *always, never, every, only,* and *none*. For example, the following true/false statements would be marked false because of the qualifiers that indicate there are no exceptions:

A jury never reaches an impasse.

Taxation always leads to uprisings, such as the Boston Tea Party.

In contrast, words that limit the applicability of a statement such as *often, usually, rarely, sometimes,* or *generally speaking* may indicate that the statement is true (Jensen, 1979). For example, the following true/false statements would be marked *true* because of the clues given by the words that limit applicability:

Generally speaking, the thicker the book, the more expensive it is.

Usually, the prospective buyer of a new automobile does not need to accept the first price quoted.

If you absolutely do not know the answer and there is no penalty for guessing, mark the statement true. Many instructors write more true statements because they want the student to leave the test with accurate information.

Matching Questions

Test items that require the test taker to match items assess recognition of important words and concepts. Matching is often used with new vocabulary, for example. Items to be matched may appear in two columns with the same or a different number of items. Uneven

Figure 8.5
Matching-Type Items

Match each grade on the left with its descriptor on the right by writing the letter of the correct answer on the blank. You may not use all the definitions. Each item is worth (1) point.

_____ A   **a.** indicates good work

_____ F   **b.** most desirable grade

_____ B   **c.** indicates average work

            d. indicates failing work

numbers of items are more difficult because items that do not apply must be eliminated. On this type of question, you probably want to begin by matching the items of which you are certain. Mark off these and then try to match the items of which you are uncertain. Figure 8.5 gives an example of matching-type questions.

Other strategies for matching-type items depend on circumstances such as the number of items in the matching set and whether answers can be used more than once. *Be sure to ask the instructor whether matching items can be used more than once.* These circumstances require you to mark items carefully so you can account for answers that you have used. Also, if you are debating about whether an item in a sequence, such as the stages in child development, belongs in blank 3 or 4, you can put it in *both* places to increase your chances of getting it right on at least one of the items. This strategy may not work if answers are to be recorded on a bubble sheet for computer scoring. Usually, items that are double-marked will be eliminated when they are scored. Once again, this is a question to ask your professor.

On all of these types of questions, be cautious in changing your answer unless you are sure you have erred. If you recall some information that indicates your original answer is wrong or if you misread the question, then change your answer. Otherwise, stick with your original answer. Studies show that first answers have a better chance of being correct.

The Open-Book Exam

The open-book exam may contain a variety of types of questions. Often, this kind of exam will be in essay format. At first consideration, the open-book or open-notes test sounds easy. Your first inclination may be to go to the open-book test unprepared—after all, you can refer to your book or notes if you do not know the answer. But organization is the key to success on such an exam, and being organized requires careful preparation. You will need to locate information and respond in a limited period of time. Become familiar with the location of information. Use post-it notes to tab pages of the information you consider to be most important. Prepare note cards containing important concepts. Study for the test as if you were going to take the test without your book or notes. That is, become very familiar with the information. When the test is given, work quickly locating information you need. It is especially important to monitor the time and not get caught up in the myriad of information that you have available in your book and notes.

Another variation of the open-book test is the take-home essay exam. Usually, take-home tests are used in upper-level undergraduate courses or graduate school. Actually, a take-home essay exam is just like writing a paper for class, except that there usually is a *very* short time limit of just a week or so. Things to remember with this sort of test are (a) apply everything you know about answering essay questions; (b) get started right away,

Figure 8.6
Evaluation of Your Study Group

Address each question in your study group. Modify the questions to evaluate your study group if you are interacting using technology. If the answer to any question is no, discussion should focus on how to resolve the issues.

1. Do all group members regularly attend the sessions?
2. Does each group member contribute to the sessions, including coming prepared to the sessions?
3. Are relationships between and among group members such that the group is productive?
4. Is the group meeting frequently enough? Too often? Should the schedule be adjusted?
5. Are all members of the study group assuming responsibility for leadership during sessions?
6. Is the full study session being used for study, or are conversations about social events and issues consuming study time?

because time is very limited; and (c) polish and edit your answer until it is practically flawless from a mechanical aspect. Remember that instructors usually give this type of exam because they want to see your best writing rather than your extemporaneous writing.

Self-Evaluation of Your Study Group

Recall in Chapter 5 that study group procedures were discussed. Assessing the effectiveness of your study group needs to be done one or two times during the semester to keep the group functioning well. Your exam results are a way to judge the effectiveness of your study group and provide an opportunity for self-evaluation.

One way to prepare for quizzes and exams is by reviewing with your study group. Once you have arrived at the point of the first test in the class, your group will have completed what might be termed a cycle of study. It is probably a good time to evaluate how well the group is functioning and make any adjustments based on the evaluation. Scheduling a session for evaluation when your group could concentrate on just that task is valuable. Evaluation questions that you could address during this session to enable you to fine-tune your study sessions are contained in Figure 8.6.

Periodic evaluation of the work of the study group should be built in when the study group is formed. If members of the group can be open and honest with each other during evaluation sessions, the group should operate smoothly.

Evaluating Progress

So far in this chapter we have discussed methods of preparing yourself for the different types of college exams you will encounter. By implementing these suggestions, you will be prepared. You will know how to determine what content will be evaluated on the test and how to choose the best strategies for tackling individual questions.

Unfortunately, this does not guarantee that you will do well on all the tests you take in college. No college student does brilliantly on every exam he or she takes, no matter how well prepared. Brilliant students do exist, but the "superstudent" who is always organized, has an excellent memory, and never suffers from anxiety or self-doubt is just a myth. Comparing yourself to this image is dangerous because it sets you up for failure and results in a poor attitude toward study (Barnes, 1992).

Successful students do have some similarities, however. They (a) learn from the mistakes they make on exams, (b) monitor their progress, and (c) seek help when necessary.

Test Recovery

After hours and hours of study, the test is finally over. You walk out of the room mentally and physically exhausted. If you prepared thoroughly for the test, this will be a good feeling, knowing that you have been mentally challenged and demonstrated your understanding to the best of your abilities. You will not feel this way after every test, however, even if you did prepare thoroughly.

Examine Box 8.6 and see what you did when you received a grade that did not meet your expectations.

Some of these behaviors—such as blaming your instructor, throwing your test away, or blaming the grade on the format of the test—can be detrimental to your test-taking success. If you looked the test over carefully as the professor discussed it, looked up the information in your notes, or talked with the professor after the class, you already have some good posttest habits. Conferring with students after the exam also has its advantages. It gives you the opportunity to infer which questions you answered correctly and which you may have missed. Remember that conferring with others who did poorly just to vent your

---

BOX 8.6   *Improvement in Action* ‖⟶

Take a minute to think about the last time you earned a poor test grade, either in high school or college. After receiving your grade, what did you do? Circle all the responses that apply:

1. Exercised to burn off steam
2. Withdrew from the class
3. Blamed your poor grade on the instructor
4. Inquired about a tutor
5. Compared your score with that of the other students in the class
6. Threw the test away
7. Looked at your paper carefully either during or after the class
8. Immediately looked up the information you were not sure about in your notes or textbook
9. Talked with friends in the class immediately afterward about the answers they got on the exam
10. Felt you would have done better on the test had it been a different format (such as essay rather than multiple-choice)
11. Made an appointment to go over the test with the instructor

resentment is counterproductive. If most of the other members of the class did better than you did, do not dwell on this situation too much, since you may begin to feel inadequate. Inquiring about a tutor and withdrawing from a class in which you failed a major exam are also viable options. Withdrawing from a class should not be considered until after you have discussed the matter with your advisor. Exercising can be a positive way to forget about the test until you are ready to concentrate on how to improve your performance. All of these reactions to receiving a poor test grade are normal, and you have probably responded in a variety of ways over the years. The next portion of the chapter will help you analyze your test performance and closely monitor your academic progress.

Whatever the outcome of the test, whether you feel you did well or not, immediately after taking a test is the time to relax and give yourself a break for taking another small step toward college graduation. Until you are ready to focus on your studies again, spend some "down time" getting together with friends, going to a movie, or catching up on some needed sleep. Whatever option you choose, do not dwell too much on the experience if you believe you did poorly. Learn a lesson from your experience, and resolve to take positive action to improve your next exam score. As. Dr. Zonnya states in her book that discusses turning defeats into triumphs, "The only time you really fail is when you fail to learn" (Zonnya, 1995, p. 90).

Receiving Your Grade

Getting a test or quiz back with an A or B is a tremendous feeling. You not only feel that you are acquiring knowledge and skills but also that you are able to demonstrate this understanding to others. Receiving a poor test grade, on the other hand, can be an overwhelming disappointment, especially when you feel you studied carefully for the test. A test grade below what you expected can be even a bigger blow, if you were confident that you did well immediately following the exam. What went wrong?

The first step in preparing for the next test is figuring out what went wrong on the last one. A natural tendency at this point is to give up and blame it on something—a tough professor, your ineptitude as a test taker, the duration of the test, the format of the test, your illness that day, or the personal problem you were trying to resolve. Yet it is imperative that you accept responsibility for *your* test scores. You alone can learn from your mistakes and work toward improving your next test grade.

Learning From Mistakes

You need to move beyond being dissatisfied with your test score to examining your mistakes so that you do not make them again. When deciding how to improve test scores in the future, your latest paper becomes your "textbook"—you need to study it to figure out *how* you made those mistakes. That way, you can gain a better understanding of your test-taking abilities.

Going over the test in class is an opportunity to see what type of performance the professor was expecting to see. Sometimes this is not possible—either the tests are distributed at the end of the class period, or the test scores are posted, usually outside the classroom or the instructor's office. If you are too upset to examine the test when you first receive the score, go for a walk or engage in some other physical activity to clear your mind so you can evaluate your grade at a later time. If the instructor does not go over the exam in class, make an appointment so you can look at it together. A copy of the test (not just the answer sheet) and the answer key should be made available to you. If the instructor will not allow you to take the test with you, ask if you can look it over while remaining in or near the instructor's office. This is certainly not the best situation for you, but many instructors are strict about not letting copies of tests out of their view. Understandably, if he or she pulls the questions from a larger bank of questions, it would be imprudent to allow students to take copies of the exams with them.

Analyzing Your Performance

You can probably remember times you sat half-listening as teachers gave back a test and went over it, vowing to yourself that you will study "harder" next time. Most students think it is simply a matter of time, that logging more study hours results in higher grades. Successful students know that getting better grades means more than just sitting in front of the books for longer periods of time. You may need to improve your note-taking skills, study strategies, or reading behaviors. Successful students also know that examining a corrected copy of the test they "bombed" can be very beneficial in earning a better grade on tests to come. The following strategies for analyzing your test performance, highlighted in Figure 8.7, can help you do just that.

1. **Read all comments written by the professor carefully.** A professor's handwriting may be hard to read, especially if the professor has had large quantities of papers to read. If you cannot decipher or do not understand a particular comment, ask the professor to interpret or clarify the comment. Think about how to apply the comments to the next exam. Going over the test in class is an opportunity to see what kind of performance the professor was expecting. Examine the typical professor comments and what these comments mean in Figure 8.8. Think about how to apply the comments to improving your next exam by completing Box 8.7.

2. **Be prepared to listen carefully and take notes.** When the time comes to go over the exam, get prepared to look carefully at your test. Have your notebook handy so that you can write down questions you want to look over again later, comments that the professor makes about the criteria for assessing responses, and information that you did not know at the time of the test.

3. **Check all of the wrong answers to make sure they are truly wrong.** Instructors are human, and they may have made a mistake on the answer key. If so, your answer may have accidentally been marked wrong. Be sure to speak up if this is the case. If a majority of the students get a question wrong, the instructor may see that the question had a clarity problem and might even give you credit for that question.

Figure 8.7
Strategies for Analyzing Your Test Performance

Students who analyze their test scores to understand why they earned the grade they did

- read all comments written by the professor,
- are prepared to listen carefully and take notes when going over the test,
- check the wrong answers to make sure they are truly wrong,
- adjust study habits,
- speak up when they don't understand how the correct answer was obtained,
- save questions that don't pertain to the whole class until the end of class, and
- don't waste time trying to earn more points questioning every detail of how the test was scored.

4. Try to understand why you got a question wrong. Use the analysis sheet in Figure 8.9 to help you determine this. This analysis sheet is also in the Appendix at the end of this chapter so you can make copies for each of your exams. By completing the analysis sheet, you can learn many things about yourself and the way you perform on tests. To use the sheet, fill out the first block of the sheet *the day you take the exam*. This way, the circumstances of the test will still be fresh in your mind. How long was the exam? You may find that your performance diminished as you got closer to the end. Write down your predicted grade so you will become keener about judging your performance. Did you find that several weeks went by between taking the exam and getting it back? Making adjustments is much easier if you get your exam back shortly after you take it. You may also want to jot down on the back of your sheet those items that are still bothering you after the test. Make notes if you were unable to find the information after the test as a reminder to address this when going over the test. Then fill out the question profile. This can give you some insight into the types of questions you are missing. Also write down the instructor's as well as your own thoughts in reference to those questions. The bottom part of the sheet allows you to formulate a plan for action.

5. Adjust your study habits accordingly. If you find that you lost the majority of points on the essay part of the exam, go back and reread the section in this chapter on taking essay exams. If you find that most of your errors were careless mistakes, make a conscientious effort to read the directions carefully and make sure you are addressing what the question asks. If you are misinterpreting many of the questions, it may be useful to join a study group to make certain you are interpreting the information the same way as the other students in the class.

Figure 8.8
Professor Comments and What They Mean

Professor's Comment	What it Means
Expand your answer Not enough detail Not enough support	Make a statement and then support it. Include specific information from lecture, the text, or other class materials.
Not clear What does this mean?	What you have said has not been presented in a coherent, logical way.
Read the question See format	You haven't followed the directions or did not answer the entire question.
Watch spelling and grammar	Many professors will not mention this before a test. They expect you are demonstrating your best professional effort.

BOX 8.7   *Improvement in Action* ⏵

Think of some of the comments you see on your tests and papers. What instructor comments are most common? What have you learned in this chapter that will help address these flaws in your work?

Figure 8.9
Posttest Analysis Sheet

Name_____   Date of exam_____
                                 Date exam was returned_____
Course_____   Predicted grade_____
                                 Actual grade_____

Days and times of study_____
Test duration_____
Percentage of course grade the test is worth_____

Question Profile			Reason That Question Was Wrong			
Question Missed	Points Earned	Type	Careless-ness	Material Unfamiliar	Mis-interpreted	Not Complete
1	$\frac{0}{3}$	M.C.	*			
8	$\frac{0}{3}$	M.C.		*		
13	$\frac{0}{3}$	M.C.	*			
14	$\frac{0}{3}$	T/F			*	
18	$\frac{5}{10}$	COM		*		
20	$\frac{18}{25}$	ESS				*

*M.C., multiple choice; T/F, true/false; COM, completion; ESS, essay.

Questions that I answered incorrectly and want to investigate further:

Professor comments:

My comments: *Most of the items I went back and changed were incorrect.*

Improvement plan: *Next time I'll stick with my first answer and try not to read too much into the question.*

BOX 8.8   *Improvement in Action* ▮▮▮➡

Use Figures 8.8 and 8.9 to analyze a test from one of your other classes. Bring your test and the completed posttest analysis sheet to class for discussion.

6. Do not be afraid to speak up when you do not understand how the correct answer was obtained. If the answer was explained by the instructor, but how the correct answer was obtained is still not clear, speak up. Other students in the class may still be confused too. It is important not to be defensive or hostile when speaking to your instructor. Remember why you are speaking up: You want to enlist help and persuade him or her to see your point of view.

7. Save questions that pertain only to your individual test or response until the end of class. Course time is valuable. If your question does not pertain to the whole class, do not waste the time of the other students by pursuing something that is unique to your paper. Making sure that the instructor explains the criteria for getting all possible points on an essay *is* important to the whole class. Trying to show the instructor where you thought you had addressed that point in *your* essay is *not*. If students question every detail of how a test was scored, they are not focused on the purpose of taking class time to go over the test, which is to clarify misunderstandings and learn from mistakes.

8. Do not be a student who tries to get more points on a test by questioning every detail of how each question was scored. Fry (1994) suggests not making a nuisance of yourself by challenging everything in class, waving your hand, and begging for points. Instead, concentrate on the answers you clearly got wrong. "Even a semi-alert student evaluating his or her own exam can grab a couple of extra points and those points can move you up a letter grade" (Fry, 1994, p. 113). If the question was ambiguous and your answer could arguably be correct, present your point of view. It helps to strengthen your position if some of the other class members chose the same answer. Be calm and diplomatic. Present a logical, coherent argument for an answer you believe to be correct. For example, present proof from your text or quote what you wrote in your notes.

There is a possibility that you took the necessary steps in preparation for studying and that the instructor is partially responsible for low student scores. The test could have been too long for the time allotted, the material on the test may not have been emphasized in class, or the questions might not have been written clearly. What should you do if this occurs? Actually there are several solutions, including trying to get more accurate expectations from the professor. Encourage the professor to discuss the format of the exam as well as the content that will be emphasized. Figure 8.7 describes strategies for evaluating your exam performance.

Keeping a Grade in Perspective

"The good test does only these things: assesses what you have been taught, provides a realistic challenge relative to other students at your level, and provides feedback to you to modify or maintain your performance" (Monte, 1990, p. 107). These tests will not measure intuition, creativity, people skills, or entrepreneurial potential (Combs, 1994). Say you have earned a poor grade on a test in one of your courses, maybe even failed. Although a failing grade is serious and tells you that you need to take a closer look at how you are preparing for tests, keep this in perspective. This is just one test. You will be taking lots of tests during your college career, and you will not do well on all of them. There is no need to question your abilities as a college student yet.

Monte (1990) describes how grades have different meanings for different individuals. One school of thought is that grades (and the grief they cause) are basically unfair and a subjective indicator of a student's worth.

Part of this is true. No grade is a reflection of a student's worth. Ever. On the whole though, grades do reflect fairly well a student's level of achievement relative to others in the same class. No matter what the grade—good, poor, or mediocre, it tells nothing about that student's worth, humanity, or goodness. But grades say a lot about the student's level of academic achievement, effort and performance.* (p. 15)

Monte continues by saying that students sometimes protect their self-esteem by saying college grades are not important. He compares college tests with a thermometer, illustrating how the grade is not important any more than a thermometer that records your fever is important. Both instruments are used to monitor your condition at a particular time. If there is a problem, these instruments will indicate this, and treatment can be administered. Tests certainly are not *just* for identifying problems. They should document growth, maturity, and achievement.

Just as it is important to realize that a test will never be a measure of you as a person, it is also important to understand the impact these grades, as a whole, will have on your life after college. Grades do serve the function of differentiating among poor, average, and superior students. Generally, higher levels of effort mean higher grades. This can translate into more effort and higher achievement in the workplace after college.

When major corporations recruit, when graduate schools and professional schools screen candidates for admission, and when potential employers who require a college degree interview prospective trainees, you'd better believe they review a person's grades. You are in college to *earn* high grades not just to get a grade but to get a grade that is a measure of what you learned. (Monte, 1990, p. 16)

Chickering and Schlossberg (1995) have also explored the value of tests: "Many exams and tests are flawed; few assess the full range of knowledge and competence that are required. But they are here to stay. Their efficiency and objectivity, relative to other forms of evaluation, make them useful tools for many decisions involving human competence" (p. 183). Tests can be significant opportunities for learning. Good tests serve as markers of progress and encourage students to assimilate and integrate information learned previously.

Grades are external measures of how you are doing in comparison to the rest of the class, but they should not be the only measure you use to determine how well you are doing in a course. More important than any grade you will earn is how *you* feel you are doing in the course. A grade may not reflect the inner satisfaction you have in getting a C in your first statistics course, after battling a real fear of math during high school. Perhaps you e-mail a friend who lives in Germany and have decided to choose German I as an elective, even though you have no previous experience with this language. The students in the class may have more experience than you do, which may put you at a disadvantage when it comes to your grade. This will not matter to you if your personal objective—being able to use some German words and basic elements of conversation—is met by the end of the semester. Conversely, an A will mean little to you if it was an exceptionally easy course in which everyone got an A. That "blanket A" is meaningless if you have not learned anything and know that you did not really deserve it. Ultimately, what counts is how you feel you have progressed toward becoming a more educated person. That impression should be the basis for your final evaluation. Examine how others feel about this issue by completing the tasks in Box 8.9.

Monitoring Your Progress

Have you ever reached the end of the grading period with no idea of how you are doing in a class? If so, this is a habit that needs to be changed. Think back to competitions you have been involved with in the past. In order to know whether you were a contender for a cham-

---

* From *Merlin the Sorcerer's Guide to Survival in College* (p. 15), by C. F. Monte, 1990, Belmont, CA: Wadsworth. Copyright 1990 by Wadsworth Publishing Co. Reprinted by permission.

pionship in any of the competitions you participated in, you evaluated each step of your progress along the way. You did not just get to the final level of competition and say, "How about that—we're in the championships. I wonder how that happened!"

Take a look at the following example:

Tracy has been practicing diligently for a spot on the university gymnastics team. She was a member of her high school team. At the beginning of the year, her floor routine was a definite strength, and her coach suggested she work on her weaker area, the uneven parallel bars. He said that this would make her a better all-around team member and increase her chances of joining a college team. She knew this would be a real challenge, since she was not fond of the parallel bars. In a competition the previous year, she had taken a bad fall that had shaken her up quite a bit, injured her left arm, and kept her out of gymnastics for 5 weeks. But she knew her coach was right. She went home that night and formulated a plan for developing her routine.

First, she would watch some videotapes of routines on the bars. Next, she would start out slowly and begin a series of specific flexibility exercises that would prepare her muscles. Then, she would begin systematically practicing for the first meet.

Tracy was pleased with her routine by the time the first meet came. The scoring had changed slightly from the last time she had competed, and she finished with a score of 4 out of 10, a disappointing outcome. The following day, she watched a tape of her performance and compared it with those of other gymnasts in that competition. She saw that she had a poor dismount, which accounted for a penalty, and that her routine was not nearly as complex as the other competitors'. The next week she specifically worked on dismounting and included a few new moves.

At the next competition, she did much better, earning a score of 7. She continued to evaluate her performance after each competition and, halfway through the year, realized that she and the team had a chance at the regional championship. She asked to have her hours cut back at the deli where she worked part-time so that she could spend more time practicing with two other team members. They critiqued each others' performance and gave each other positive reinforcement that helped boost their confidence. As a result of their team effort, Tracy and her teammates won the championship.

Just as Tracy worked toward achieving her goal by making small adjustments and carefully monitoring her progress, successful students monitor their grades and understand that higher grades are often the consequence of making small adjustments. It might mean studying more, improving communication with the instructor, identifying areas of weakness in test-taking strategies, and making high grades a priority. You too can attain higher grades just as you have attained other goals throughout your lifetime (refer to Box 8.10).

Monitoring Your Grade

Just as you continually monitor and modify your plan when participating in challenging events, the grade you are earning must come under close scrutiny.

In *How to Get the Most Out of College,* Chickering and Schlossberg (1995) state, "Teaching and learning in college typically suffer because we are unsophisticated about evaluation and underestimate the importance of frequent and thoughtful feedback" (p. 221). In order to modify and plan approaches to study, and ultimately improve a course grade, it is necessary to receive frequent feedback. Courses in which the instructor uses only a midterm and a final as the exclusive means of evaluation often cause students to feel uncomfortable, and rightly so. Most students prefer to have many and varied assignments so that they can keep a check on their progress and demonstrate their strengths.

Unfortunately, many courses do offer only a midterm and a final. What should you do in this situation? The key is to be as prepared as possible for the tests. This means making sure you ask the instructor for specific information concerning each test, such as, How many questions will there be? What type? What point value will those questions have? What specific information will be included?

If you are not being formally evaluated except for the midterm and final, you will have to be responsible for your own informal evaluation throughout the semester. Some ways to do this include:

- periodically making lists of new vocabulary you come across in your readings,
- asking questions about assigned readings,
- identifying and listing main ideas from your reading,
- forming a study group so that you can evaluate each other informally, and
- constructing graphic organizers from what you read.

Occasionally, instructors will give you another chance to master a difficult task. If you have the opportunity to redo an assignment or retake an exam, do not pass it up, even if it means adjusting your immediate schedule to include the additional hours it will take. Rewriting an important paper that is worth a third of your grade, for example, can dramatically affect your overall course grade.

At any given time during the semester, you should know where you stand in the course. This will take some organization on your part. First, look at the course syllabus. The syllabus should list all the assignments, quizzes, and tests you will be responsible for. It should indicate how many points or what percentage of your grade each is worth and explain the grade computation procedures.

Second, read the syllabus to see what other factors enter into the calculation of your final grade, such as participating in class, attending special lectures or functions on campus, and attending class. At some universities attendance is mandatory; at others it's not, so

Figure 8.10
Guidelines for Monitoring a Course Grade

For each of your courses, monitor your grade by following these guidelines:

- Examine the course syllabus and list the assignments, quizzes, and tests for which you'll be responsible.
- Read the syllabus to see what other factors enter into the calculation of your grade such as attendance, class participation, keeping a journal, and so forth.
- In your course notebook, organize a place where you can record your score for each test or assignment.
- Check your progress regularly.
- Periodically write down your feelings about your progress in a personal journal.

Figure 8.11
Sample Student Grades for General Psychology Course

Tests and Assignments	Possible Points	Points Earned
Exam I	100	73
Exam II	100	84
Personality Inventory (Assign. 1)	50	43
Television Profile (Assign. 2)	50	50
Exam III	100	—
Paper	100	—

make sure you are aware of what the policy is at your college. If it is mandatory and the minimum is not met, you can fail the course even if you complete the assignments and tasks and do well on the tests. Regardless of what the policy is at your university, missing class sessions can only be detrimental to your grade.

Third, in your course notebook, organize a place where you can record each test score or assignment grade. List these items in the first column. In the second column, indicate the number of possible points or the percentage of the total grade it is worth. Entitle the third column "Points Earned" or "Percentage Earned." It is also important to know what the grading scale is, which should be indicated on the syllabus. Figure 8.10 summarizes these guidelines. Examine Angelo's grades for his General Psychology course, and calculate his score in Figure 8.11 to practice monitoring your grade. The professor grades using a "straight" percentage, which means 90%–100% = A, 80%–89% = B, 70%–79%= C, and so forth.

The total number of possible points is 500. By calculating 90% of 500, you can determine that to get an A in the course, you must earn 450 points. Angelo has earned 250 points so far, but he still has two assignments to complete. If Angelo earns 100 points on the third exam *and* scores 100 points on his paper, he will earn an A for the course, even though he got a C on his first exam and a B on his second exam. He has done very well on his assignments and has continued to improve his test scores, but he still feels getting an A would be difficult. Now, because Angelo sees how close he is to an A, he remembers that the professor told the class about an opportunity for extra credit and makes a note to check into it.

Fourth, check your progress in each of your courses periodically. You may do this at weekly, biweekly, or monthly intervals. Less frequent monitoring may not allow you enough time to give extra attention to a given course. Put dates on your calendar to remind yourself to check your progress during the semester. Set a time to evaluate your progress and examine your long-range goals. It is a good feeling to know you are making progress on achieving your goals.

Fifth, periodically write down your feelings in a personal journal. Writing about and reflecting on your academic life can also enable you to monitor your progress. You may gain insight into how you learn best and how you actually feel about that learning. McMahan (1996) suggests that when you find yourself in a situation that gives you problems, address these questions: What were your initial reactions? What did you do right? What might you have done differently? Examine this excerpt from Choa Ti's journal:

> I'm so disappointed. I got a Calculus test back today and I got a C. I studied my brains out for that test, and really thought I knew the material. I put much more time into studying than I have in the past. I do feel like I am getting it though, even if I do struggle, it is making sense. Maybe I'll see if I can get a tutor to help me before the next test.

Through writing and reflecting, Choa Ti has come to understand the intrinsic value of learning by realizing that grades are not everything. By writing how she feels about her progress, she is able to look back and see how she felt at a particular time and use this experience to guide her in the future.

Another aspect of your course grade may be the participation component. Do not overlook the importance of participation. It can account for as much as 10% of your grade in some courses, especially when you get into your upper-level courses. Instructors are looking for students who are not only physically there but mentally engaged in that day's activities. Make sure you are contributing to the course by volunteering answers and asking questions when the instructor encourages this. As mentioned in previous chapters, be prepared for class by reading assignments and reviewing notes from the previous class.

Good teachers also look for nonverbal feedback from their students. Looking attentive by making eye contact with the instructor, smiling when he or she relates a personal anecdote, or nodding in agreement gives the instructor the feeling that you are actively listening. At the same time, students who are yawning, looking out the window, whispering comments to a classmate, or appearing distracted by something going on outside do not seem to be interested in what the instructor is saying.

How can this behavior affect your grade? Take a look at the situation described in Box 8.11.

The opinion that an instructor is forming of you influences the grade you will receive in the class and may even continue beyond this point if you ask that person for a letter of recommendation, or have that person as the instructor for another course, or work with the instructor later as your supervisor for an internship. If you are often involved in behavior that indicates you are not giving the instructor your full attention, more than likely that instructor will be less willing to give you extra attention when you need it. If your grade is borderline, say, right between a B and a C, the instructor is more likely to give the student who has been attentive the benefit of the doubt. Make sure that you are projecting the image of a student who wants to learn the subject matter being taught and is willing to put forth the effort needed. Slouching in your seat, putting your head down on your desk, groaning when activities are explained—all of these behaviors will be unappreciated by your instructors and cause them to wonder whether you are a serious student.

If you are looking for ways to improve your grade, extra credit may be a possibility. Unless you have earned all A's on all your papers, tests, and projects, it is always a good idea to take advantage of the extra points. Very often these extra-credit assignments are a good application of what you are learning in class. In an art history class, for example, a

In a small lecture hall, students are listening to a zoology lecture. Kazi is falling asleep because he stayed up late the night before studying for an exam in another course. Clyde is asking the person behind him about the statement the professor just made, to make sure he wrote it down correctly. Benita is talking to her friend beside her about what might be on the upcoming test, and they are occasionally snickering as they interject their own humor into some of the proposed questions. Carrie is closing her eyes in an attempt to visualize the terms on the overhead and trying to make up a mnemonic device for remembering them.

Determine which students are trying to positively affect their learning during the lecture. Identify what they are doing that demonstrates that they are trying to become better students. Next, view the situation from the professor's perspective and write some ideas about what he or she would think. Are these perspectives the same or different? Be prepared to discuss this in class.

professor may ask for volunteers to help collect data in a local neighborhood, interviewing residents and recording the architectural features of homes from the early 19th century. Or, an instructor may award extra-credit points for attending a lecture of a prominent person who is speaking on campus. These experiences not only provide you with additional points but enlarge your intellectual experience. Extra credit may also serve as "insurance" in case you miss an unannounced quiz or do not perform up to your expectations on a paper.

Monitoring the Semester

You need to monitor not only your individual courses but also how your semester is going as a whole. Knowing where you stand in each of your courses will enable you to adjust your academic activities so that you will feel prepared when it comes time for finals. Scharf-Hunt and Hait (1990) offer suggestions for goal setting that can be applied to your semester evaluation of progress.

1. **State your present situation.** You may observe, for example, that you have too many C's this semester.

2. **Write a reasonable statement of your goal or objective.** Check back with the goals you wrote in Chapter 3. Maybe you stated that you wanted to have a 3.0 by the end of the semester.

3. **Identify what you need to do to reach your semester goal.** What will you do to change? Perhaps you need to allot more time for studying Spanish and take your papers over to the writing center before turning them in. Ask yourself, "Did this paper or assignment get me where I want to be? If not, why not? Did I plan the wrong action? Was my failure a result of inadequate planning? Or did I set the wrong goals?"

You may need to reexamine study habits. What are you doing during your study time? Perhaps you need to interact more thoroughly with the material. Are you just reading "over" the information? Refer back to Chapters 4 and 5 if you suspect this may be a problem.

As you evaluate, you may find that your study partner does not seem to be helping and is often distracted with socializing in the library. As a result, you may decide to find another study partner. You may find that making an appointment before the exam with the professor has really proved to be helpful. She or he knows you as an individual in this large,

Figure 8.12
Guidelines for Monitoring Your Semester

The following suggestions adapted from Scharf-Hunt and Hait (1990) will be helpful in determining where you stand during the semester and will enable you to implement a plan of action.

1. State your present situation.
2. Examine the goal statements you previously designed.
3. Identify what you need to do to reach your semester goal.
4. Write down a time frame for when you will complete the steps you have identified.
5. Decide at which point you will review your progress.

BOX 8.12 *Improvement in Action* ⅢⅢ➡

Think about a situation in your life when you followed the goal-monitoring system in Figure 8.12. The example you select can be school related or not—something like getting a summer job or buying a car, for instance. Or it could be an academic goal, such as getting a scholarship. Be specific about your plan of action.

lecture class and has given you some ideas on specific topics to examine in preparing for the essay portions of the exams.

4. Indicate on your list of "things to do" or calendar when you will complete the steps you have identified. Perhaps after looking at your calendar you decide to study for Spanish on Tuesday and Thursday mornings, rather than Thursday night. You may make appointments at the writing center 1 week before your major papers are due.

5. Decide at which points you will review your progress. As mentioned in the previous section, regular periods of evaluation are necessary. You may decide to check your progress every week or two. Once or twice per semester is not enough to truly identify and modify the progress you will make during the semester. These evaluation checks can be indicated on your calendar. These suggestions are summarized in Figure 8.12.

When finals are approaching, you will want to know exactly where you stand in each of your courses. It is a good idea to check with your instructors to make sure the scores you have recorded and the instructor's scores are the same. When you know your grade in each of your courses, you can then determine how and when to study for your final exams. If you know you have a solid A in botany, it may be beneficial to devote more effort and time to your anthropology course where your grade is between a B and a C. Studying the textbook and meeting with the instructor during office hours to get some additional guidance might have a more positive influence on your overall grade point average.

Seeking Help When Necessary

You should not feel alone in your quest to earn good grades. Your family, friends, and instructors want you to succeed. Other people can be instrumental in your success, too, and you should know them, or at least know who they are, so that they can be of service if you need them.

Figure 8.13

Figure 8.13
People You Need To Know

- **Your advisor** the person who oversees your program of study. He or she has your academic record and makes sure you do everything you need to in order to graduate.
- **The chairperson of your department** takes care of scheduling difficulties, course substitutions, program changes and personal problems students may have
- **The dean** the highest ranking administrator in your college who makes final decisions concerning graduation and makes sure state regulations are followed

People You Need to Know

Your academic adviser is your most important college contact. An academic adviser is the person who will help you plan your program of college study. This person holds your cumulative folder with all your important forms such as copies of your grade reports, letters of acceptance into specific areas of study, letters from the dean, and other significant records. You should also have copies of all the documentation in the file and keep it in a separate folder so that you can access your records if you need them. It is worth your time to develop a relationship with your adviser so that he or she knows you are a responsible student. Make an appointment to discuss your progress and plan your schedule with your academic adviser at least once per semester.

The chairperson of your department is someone else you should know. This person manages your program of study at the department level. He or she takes care of scheduling, making course substitutions, and keeping faculty informed of what is happening at the university level. He or she may also teach courses in the department. This person can help you if you are having a problem scheduling a course you need, have a personal problem that has interrupted your semester, or need to manage departmental paperwork. The departmental chairperson also handles "special dispensations" such as transfer credit and course exemptions. Making an effort to meet the chairperson will make you feel more comfortable when you need this person's help with a problem.

The dean is a person who oversees the college that includes your major. He or she is the highest-ranking administrator in your college and makes decisions that affect all the departments in a particular college, including the requirements toward a degree for your major. For instance, if you are a mathematics major, your dean might be in charge of the College of Natural Science and Mathematics. This person is also responsible for guiding the college in meeting state regulations and national standards for program quality. Although you may not necessarily need to make an appointment to see the dean, you should at least know who this person is. These people are highlighted in Figure 8.13.

All of these people are there to help you have a successful college career. They are also there to see that the academic integrity of the university is upheld, meaning that if you are not doing well academically, they must enforce the rules of the college. For example, say you need to have a 2.5 grade point average to take courses within your major, but you have not attained a 2.5. Your academic adviser, departmental chairperson, and college dean are not going to help you enroll in a course within your major. Why? Because it is your responsibility to earn a 2.5, and they must consistently enforce the rules. It is not their job to "give you a break." They *will* help you decide what courses you want to repeat to raise your GPA and will provide you with the signed paperwork so that you can improve your overall grade point average.

There are certain ramifications for not doing well academically. If you fall below a certain grade point average, you may be placed on academic probation. Usually if you do not improve your grades over a certain period of time, you are automatically dismissed from the university. Students who are negligent are often surprised when the college personnel who have tried to support them enforce academic policies by dismissing them from the university, but this is a necessary function of university administrators. If they permit everyone who is performing poorly to stay in college, the university's reputation will suffer, and the degrees awarded will be meaningless.

On the other hand, if your grade point average is high—usually 3.0 or higher—you will be on the dean's list, an academic honor of recognition. Students attempting to earn grades high enough to merit the dean's list can look at their total semester rather than focusing on just one class. It motivates them to work harder in classes they may not enjoy, just so their grade point average is not pulled down.

By using the strategies suggested in this chapter, you are demonstrating that you are an active learner who uses tests as a means of improving your abilities as a college student and who has control over your grades.

Think about the number of exams you will take as a college student. If you average three exams per semester, say, in five classes, that is 15 exams per semester. Multiply that by eight semesters in 4 years—that equals 120 exams! Take action now to make your experiences with tests more positive.

 ## *Voices of Successful Students*

"Make sure you understand the material as it's being presented in the class. Don't be afraid to ask the professor questions if you don't understand."

"Prepare up until the night before a test, then the night before, go over the material once, then relax and get to bed at a decent hour. There's no sense in cramming since that way, you only learn for the short term."

"Look at the material you are responsible for and guess what the essay questions might be. Then, spend some time writing out the answer to the questions you anticipate."

"Take 5-minute study breaks every 45 minutes to keep you on task."

"I get easily distracted, so I find it helpful to study very early in the morning, before most people are awake, when I have a test coming up."

"I went to class as much as possible, kept up on the readings, both textbooks and professional journals, studied at least 2 days in advance for exams, gave myself rewards for studying and doing well. My rewards included going out with friends, a yogurt waffle cone, and time to myself."

"Review your notes after each class. This way, you won't feel so overwhelmed when exam time comes."

"Make a schedule of each day and use your time wisely. Study using the two-to-one rule: For every hour you are in class, you should study for 2 hours on that subject."

"I treat every class as if we were going to be given a quiz at the end—therefore, I have to know the material. I concentrate on good note taking during class."

"Always keep a written record yourself on the grades, scores, points, or percentages you get in each class."

"Don't be afraid to meet with professors if you have a question about your grades or questions about an exam—they are human and can make mistakes, too!"

Cooperative Learning Activity: What Would You Do?

In small groups, examine the following situations and decide what action you should take. After all the situations have rotated among the groups, discuss with the class what you decided.

Situation 1

A professor has written a large question mark next to a response you gave for an essay question, and you only got half credit for it. What would you do?

Situation 2

Over the weekend you find that you are snowed in at a friend's house and you have a major exam on Tuesday. You do not have your book or notebook for studying, since you thought you would be back Sunday night and have plenty of time. It is Sunday morning and it's still snowing. What do you do?

Situation 3

You get together with some people from your class 3 days before the exam. As you listen to the other students, you feel like you are studying for a completely different test! They wrote things in their notes that you do not have; they have terms memorized that you did not expect to be on the test and therefore did not study. Your classmates also seem to be able to jump in with examples and references that are unfamiliar to you. You feel your palms begin to sweat and start to panic. What should you do?

Situation 4

While preparing for a test, you notice a friend of yours has prepared a "cheat sheet" and plans on using it, boasting that the gullible professor will never catch her. She claims that there is no sense in memorizing this "junk" when she is never going to use it

again. Your friend asks you whether you want to sit in the back with her. What do you do?

Situation 5

A friend has just gotten a 41% on her first microbiology test. She is in tears. Between this and the homesickness she has been feeling, she is seriously considering quitting school. What would you do?

Situation 6

An upperclassman you admire tells you that he cannot finish his lab work for a physics course. He wants you to do the experiment and let him copy it. If you help him this time, he promises to do one of the experiments for you later on and let you copy his. "It's not cheating—it's just divide and conquer," he explains. What would you do?

Self-Improvement Strategy: Monitoring Your Grades

Begin monitoring your grades in each of your classes today. Make an appointment with each of your instructors at the midterm to discuss your progress, even if you are doing well in the course. Check the scores you have recorded with the instructor's scores, discuss what grade you would like to earn by the end of the course, and plan your strategies to attain your goal using Figure 8.11.

Writing and Reflecting: Preparing for Your Next Test

You will be taking approximately 120 tests during your college career. This chapter offers many suggestions for improving your test scores. Develop three specific ideas that you are going to try when preparing for your next test. Be specific. After the tests, reflect on how the ideas worked, and use this as a means of preparing for future tests.

Reading Selections

Reading Selection 1

Test scores are often analyzed to see whether a significant change has taken place because of some treatment. You may be familiar with some basic concepts of research that you have read in newspapers, such as batting averages, political polls, or Nielsen ratings. Read the following excerpt describing "Measures of Central Tendencies" by Ary, Jacobs, and Razavieh (1990).* After you have completed the reading, invent a research problem that could be in your discipline. Then, fabricate a list of numbers and identify the mean, median, and mode. For example, you could list 10 scores that students might earn on a pop quiz or predict the number of hours that entrants in a dance marathon were able to continue in the competition.

Measures of Central Tendency

A convenient way of summarizing data is to find a single index that can represent a whole set of measures. For example, finding a single score that can give an indication of the performance of a group of 300 students on an IQ test would be useful for comparative purposes. In statistics three indices are available for such use. They are called measures of central tendency, or averages. To most laymen, the term average means the sum of the scores divided by the number of scores. To a statistician the average can be this measure, known as the mean, or one of the other two measures of central tendency, known as the mode and the median. Each of these three can serve as an index to represent a group as a whole.

The mode is that value in a distribution that occurs most frequently. It is the simplest to find of the three measures of central tendency because it is determined by inspection rather than by computation. Given the distribution of scores: 14, 16, 16, 17, 18, 19, 19, 19, 21, 22, one can readily see that the mode of this distribution is 19, because it is the most frequent score.

The median is defined as that point in a distribution of measures below which 50 percent of the cases lie (which means that the other 50 percent will be above this point). For example, given the distribution of scores 14, 16, 16, 17, 18, 19, 19, 19, 21, 22, the point below which 50 percent of the cases fall is halfway between 18 and 19. Thus the median is 18.5. To find this value we first placed the 10 scores of the distribution in rank order and then found the point below which one half of the scores lie.

The most widely used measure of central tendency is the mean, which is popularly known as the average or arithmetical average. It is the sum of all the values in a distribution divided by the number of cases. Given the scores 112, 121, 115, 101, 119, 109, 100, we find that the total is 777. Since there are 7 scores, we divide this number by seven, and find the mean score to be 111. Note that it is not necessary to arrange the numbers in a different order to calculate the mean. (p. 127)

Reading Selection 2

Read this selection on disposing solid waste by Macionis (1995).* Prepare for an essay test in which you would be required to answer the following question: "Without using the text, outline the problems with solid waste disposal as if you were preparing to give a presentation to a community organization on this topic."

Solid Waste: The "Disposable Society"

As an interesting exercise, carry a trash bag over the course of a single day and collect all the materials you throw away. Most people would be surprised to find that the average person in the United States would almost fill the bag with several pounds of paper, metal, plastic, and other disposable materials. For the country as a whole, about 1 billion pounds of solid waste are generated *each and every day.*

It is easy to see why the United States has been dubbed a *disposable society.* Not only are we materially rich, but ours is a culture that values convenience. As a result, we consume more products than virtually any society in the world, and we purchase much of it with a great deal of packaging. The most commonly cited case is fast food, served with cardboard, plastic, and styrofoam containers that are thrown away within minutes. But countless other products—from film to fishhooks—are sold with excessive packaging for the purpose of making the product more attractive to the customer (or harder to shoplift).

Consider, too, that manufacturers market soft drinks, beer, and fruit juices in aluminum cans, glass jars, or plastic containers, which not only consume finite resources but also generate solid waste. Then there are countless items intentionally designed to be disposable. A walk through any local supermarket reveals shelves filled with pens, razors, flashlights, batteries, and even cameras intended to be used once and dropped in the nearest trash can. Other products—from light bulbs to automobiles—are designed to have a limited useful life, and then be-

---

* From *Introduction to Research in Education* (4th ed., p. 127), by Donald Ary, Lucy Chester Jacobs, and Asghar Razavieh. Copyright 1990 by Holt, Rinehart and Winston, Inc. Reprinted by permission of the publisher.

* From John J. Macionis, *Sociology* (5th ed., p. 598). Copyright 1995. Reprinted by permission of Prentice Hall, Inc., Upper Saddle River, NJ.

come unwanted junk. As Paul H. Connett (1992:101) points out, even the words we used to describe what we throw away—*waste, litter, trash, refuse, garbage, rubbish*—reveal how little we value what we cannot immediately use and how we quickly try to push it out of sight and out of mind.

Living in a "disposable society" means that the average person in the United States consumes 50 times more steel, 170 times more newspaper, 250 times more gasoline, and 300 times more plastic each year than the typical individual in India (Miller, 1992). Just as this high level of consumption means that members of our society use a disproportionate share of the planet's natural resources, so it also means that we contribute the lion's share of the world's refuse.

We like to say that we "throw things away." But the 80 percent of our solid waste that is not burned or recycled does not "go away"; rather, it ends up in landfills. The practice of using landfills, originally intended to improve sanitation, is now associated with several threats to the natural environment.

First, the sheer volume of discarded material is literally filling landfills up all across the country. Especially in large cities like New York, there is simply little room left for disposing of trash. Second, material placed in landfills contributes to water pollution. Although, in most jurisdictions, law now regulates what can be placed in a landfill, the Environmental Protection Agency has identified thirty thousand dump sites across the United States containing hazardous materials that are polluting water both above and below the ground. Third, what goes into landfills all too often stays there—sometimes for centuries. Tens of millions of tires, diapers, and other items that we bury in landfills each year do not readily decompose and will become an unwelcome legacy for future generations.

Fifty years ago, it was common practice for manufacturing plants to dispose of all types of hazardous waste simply by dumping them in a woods or pouring them in a stream. Today, laws in most states provide stiff penalties for such actions, but enforcement has been lax. The problem of solid waste includes both the waste products of manufacturing and the solid waste each of us generates daily. To cope with its sheer volume, environmentalists argue that we must turn "waste" into a resource, one that will benefit, rather than burden, future generations. One such strategy that has caught on throughout the country is *recycling*, programs to reuse resources we would otherwise discard as "waste." . . .

Finally, the oceans also have long served as a vast dumping ground for all kinds of waste; no one can calculate how much. Solid waste pollutes water, and polluted water kills fish or renders them dangerous to eat. Ocean dumping also spoils a source of beauty and recreational pleasure. Perhaps most dramatically, in recent years the news media have reported large amounts of trash (including toxic materials and dangerous items like syringes) washing up on the shores of both coasts of the United States. (p. 598)

Reading Selection 3

Read the following selection on the Berlin Wall by Kagan, Ozment, and Turner (1995).* Prepare for a take-home exam in which you will be required to answer the following question: "Trace the events surrounding the building and removing of the Berlin Wall. What effects did these actions have on East and West Germany? List resources, such as a video, that you might use to support your answer, if you had this assignment."

The Breach of the Berlin Wall and German Reunification

No part of Europe had so come to symbolize the tensions of the Cold War as the divided Germanies. The Berlin Wall had been erected in 1961 to halt the outflow of the East Germans to the West. In the autumn of 1989, as tens of thousands of East Germans moved into West Germany through Hungary and then Austria, popular demonstrations erupted in many German cities. The most important demonstrations occurred in Leipzig. The streets filled with people demanding democracy and an end to Communist Party rule.

Adding to the pressure of the popular demonstrations, Gorbachev told the leaders of the East German Communist Party that the Soviet Union would no longer support them. With startling swiftness, the Communist leaders of the East German government, including Premier Erich Honecker (b. 1912), resigned, making way for a younger generation of Communist Party leaders. These new leaders, who remained in office for only a matter of weeks, promised political and economic reform. They convinced few East Germans, however, and the emigration to the West continued. In November 1989, in one of the most emotional moments in European history since 1945, the government of East Germany ordered the opening of the Berlin Wall. That week, tens of thousands of East Berliners crossed into West Berlin to celebrate, to visit families, and to shop with money provided by the West German government. Shortly thereafter, free travel began between East and West Germany. . . .

Further political change occurred in East Germany. For all intents, the Communist Party had become thoroughly discredited. Enormous corruption among party officials was exposed. The East German Communist Party changed its name and claimed that henceforth it would be a social democratic party. Free elections in 1990 brought into the East German Parliament a conservative majority that sought rapid unification with West Germany.

The revolution in East Germany, more than those elsewhere in Europe, had broad ramifications for international relations. Within days of the first dramatic events in East Germany, the issue of reunification of the Germanies confronted West Germany and the other Western nations. Helmut Kohl (b. 1930), the Chancellor of West Germany, proposed a tentative plan for reunification. Late in 1989 the ministers of the European

---

* From D. Kagan, S. Ozment, and F. M. Turner, *The Western Heritage* (5th ed., p. 1182). Copyright 1995. Reprinted by permission of Prentice Hall, Inc., Upper Saddle River, NJ.

Economic Community accepted in principle the unification of Germany. By February 1990, some form of re-unification had become a foregone conclusion, accepted by the United States, the Soviet Union, Great Britain, and France.

In the closing months of 1989 and the opening weeks of 1990, it became clear that the citizens of the two Germanies were determined to reunify. With the collapse of Communist Party government in East Germany, there was no longer a viable distinction between the two Germanies. With the Communists in confusion, the forces of national self-determination came to the fore. The rapidity of German reunification, however, was to sow the seeds of new problems. (p. 1182)

Reading Selection 4

Read this selection on population growth in the United States by Fisher (1995).* Anticipate what a professor might ask on a test, and prepare for it by writing five true/false questions and three multiple-choice questions based on the content of the selection. Exchange questions with a classmate, and answer each other's questions.

Population Growth in the United States

The rapid population growth experienced by the United States after 1800 was a response to high birthrates, declining mortality, and *immigration,* the movement of people into a country of which they are not native residents. Although exact figures are not available, birthrates and death rates in the early nineteenth century may have exceeded 5 percent and 2 percent per year, respectively. A century later (during the Depression of the 1930s) the birthrate had decreased to 1.8 percent per year, but it rose sharply after World War II, possibly to compensate for wartime delays in family growth and to respond to postwar economic prosperity. During the *baby boom* of 1946 to 1965, the birthrate reached a new high of 2.7 percent per year. But then came a *birth dearth,* as the birthrate dipped to a historic low of 1.46 percent per year during the mid-1970s. When the baby boomers themselves reached childbearing age, a very modest upturn took place, and by the early 1990s the birthrate was just slightly above 1.6 percent. . . . Because of the increased population, that rate represents nearly 4.1 million births per year, not so different from the 4.3 million at the peak of the baby boom.

The declining population growth rate of the past century has not been in exact correspondence with changes in birthrates. Reduced mortality rates have also had an effect. The decline in infant mortality and the extension of life expectancy beyond seventy years mean that more people are alive at any given time.

Immigration has been another important factor in the growth of the United States. More than 50 million people have immigrated to the United States since 1820. Those immigrants not only enlarged the population as they came but also increased the base for future growth. Legal immigration during the 1970s and much of the 1980s has been at the rate of about 600,000 persons a year and accounted for about 26 percent of the population growth during the 1980s. Recent rates have increased sharply, however, to nearly 1.8 million in the early 1990s. The precise extent of illegal immigration is not known but is considered to be substantial.

Even though the rate of population growth has declined from more than 3 percent per year in the early nineteenth century to approximately 1 percent per year in the late 1980s, the increments in population are not small. By virtue of both the natural rate of increase and legal immigration, the United States continues to grow by more than 2 million people per year. (p. 127)

Reading Selection 5

Read the following excerpt from Daniel Goleman's popular book, *Emotional Intelligence* (1995)*. Summarize what you think the author is trying to say in one or two paragraphs, then relate any personal experiences you may have had when you felt you were in a hopeless situation.

Pandora's Box and Pollyanna: The Power of Positive Thinking

College students were posed the following hypothetical situation:

> Although you set your goal of getting a B, when your first exam score, worth 30% of your final grade is returned, you received a D. It is now one week after you have learned about the D grade. What do you do?

Hope made all the difference. The response by students with high levels of hope was to work harder and think of a range of things they might try that could bolster their final grade. Students with moderate levels of hope thought of several ways they might up their grade, but had far less determination to pursue them. And, understandably, students with low levels of hope gave up on both counts, demoralized.

The question is not just theoretical, however. When C. R. Snyder, the University of Kansas psychologist who did this study, compared the actual academic achievement of freshman students high and low on hope, he discovered that hope was a better predictor of their first semester grades than were their scores on the SAT, a test supposedly able to predict how students will fare in college (and highly correlated with IQ). Again, given

* From James S. Fisher, *Geography and Development: A World Regional Approach* (5th ed., p. 127). Copyright 1995. Reprinted by permission of Prentice Hall, Inc., Upper Saddle River, NJ.

* From *Emotional Intelligence* by Daniel Goleman. © 1995 by Daniel Goleman. Used by permission of Bantam Books, a division of Bantam Doubleday Dell Publishing Group, Inc.

roughly the same range of intellectual abilities, emotional aptitudes make critical difference.

Snyder's explanation: "Students with high hope set themselves higher goals and know how to work hard to attain them. When you compare students of equivalent intellectual aptitude on their academic achievements, what sets them apart is hope."

As the familiar legend has it, Pandora, a princess of ancient Greece, was given a gift, a mysterious box, by gods jealous of her beauty. She was told she must never open the gift. But one day, overcome by curiosity and temptation, Pandora lifted the lid to peek in, letting loose in the world a grand afflictions - disease, malaise, madness. But a compassionate god let her close the box just in time to capture the one antidote that makes life's misery bearable: hope.

Hope, modern researchers are finding, does more than offer a bit of solace amid affliction; it plays a surprisingly potent role in life, offering an advantage in realms as diverse as school achievement and bearing up in onerous jobs. Hope, in a technical sense, is more than the sunny view that everything will turn out all right. Snyder defines it with more specificity as "believing you have both the will and the way to accomplish your goals, whatever they may be."

People tend to differ in general degree to which they have hope in this sense. Some typically think of themselves as able to get out of a jam or find ways to solve problems, while others simply do not see themselves as having the energy, ability, or means to accomplish their goals. People with high levels of hope, Snyder finds, share certain traits, among them being able to motivate themselves, feeling resourceful enough to find ways to accomplish their objectives, reassuring themselves when in a tight spot that things will get better, being flexible enough to find different ways to get to their goals or to switch goals if one becomes impossible, and having the sense to break down a formidable task into smaller, manageable pieces.

From the perspective of emotional intelligence, having hope means that one will not give in to overwhelming anxiety, a defeatist attitude, or depression in the face of difficult challenges or setbacks. Indeed, people who are hopeful evidence less depression than others as they maneuver through life in pursuit of their goals, are less anxious in general, and have fewer emotional distresses.

References

Ary, D., Jacobs, L. C., & Razavieh, A. (1990). *Introduction to research in education.* Fort Worth, TX: Holt, Rinehart & Winston.

Barnes, R. (1992). *Successful study for degrees.* New York: Routledge.

Brown, S. A., & Miller, D. A. (1996). *The active learner: Successful study strategies* (2nd ed.). Los Angeles: Roxbury.

Chickering, A. W., & Schlossberg, N. K. (1995). *How to get the most out of college.* Boston: Allyn & Bacon.

Combs, P. (1994). *Major in success.* Berkeley, CA: Ten Speed Press.

Ellis, D. B. (1984). *Becoming a master student* (4th ed.). Rapid City, SD: College Survival.

Fisher, J. S. (Ed.). (1995). *Geography & development: A world regional approach* (5th ed.). Upper Saddle River, NJ: Prentice Hall.

Fry, R. (1994). *"Ace" any test* (2nd ed.). Hawthorne, NJ: Career.

Gall, M. D., Gall, J. P., Jacobsen, D. R., & Bullock, T. L. (1990). *Tools for learning: A guide to teaching study skills.* Alexandria, VA: Association for Supervision and Curriculum Development.

Goleman, D. (1995). *Emotional intelligence: Why it can matter more than IQ.* New York: Bantam.

Jensen, E. (1979). *You can succeed: The ultimate study guide for students.* New York: Barron.

Kagan, D., Ozment, S., & Turner, F. M. (1995). *The western heritage* (5th ed.). Upper Saddle River, NJ: Prentice Hall.

Kesselman-Turkel, J., & Peterson, F. (1981). *Test-taking strategies.* Chicago: Contemporary Books.

Macionis, J. J. (1995). *Sociology* (5th ed.). Upper Saddle River, NJ: Prentice Hall.

Maddox, H. (1963). *How to study.* London: Fawcett Premier.

McMahan, I. (1996). *Get It Done.* New York: Avon.

McWhorter, K. (1998). *College reading and study skills* (7th ed.). New York: Longman.

Monte, C. F. (1990). *Merlin the sorcerer's guide to survival in college.* Belmont, CA: Wadsworth.

Pauk, W. (1984). *How to study in college* (3rd ed.). Boston: Houghton Mifflin.

Pauk, W. (1993). *How to study in college* (5th ed.). Boston: Houghton Mifflin.

Scharf-Hunt, D., & Hait, P. (1990). *Studying smart.* New York: HarperPerennial.

Shaughnessy, M. P. (1990). *How to learn more in less time.* Portales: Eastern New Mexico University. (ERIC Document Reproduction Service No. ED 322 985).

Smith, B. (1989). *Bridging the gap: College reading* (3rd ed.). Glenview, IL: Scott, Foresman.

Spargo, E. (1994). *The college student: Reading and study skills* (4th ed.). Providence, RI: Jamestown.

Standley, K. E. (1987). *How to study.* Palo Alto, CA: Seymour.

Zonnya. (1995). *Get Off Your Yo Yo!* New York: St. Martins.

CHAPTER APPENDIX

Posttest Analysis Sheet

Name_____   Date of exam_____

                                     Date exam was returned_____

Course_____   Predicted grade_____

                                     Actual grade_____

Days and times of study_____

Test duration_____

Percentage of course grade the test is worth_____

Question Profile			Reason That Question Was Wrong			
Question Missed	Points Earned	Type	Careless-ness	Material Unfamiliar	Mis-interpreted	Not Complete
1	⅔	M.C.	*			
8	⅔	M.C.		*		
13	⅔	M.C.	*			
14	⅔	T/F			*	
18	⁵⁄₁₀	COM		*		
20	¹⁸⁄₂₅	ESS				*

*M.C., multiple choice; T/F, true/false; COM, completion; ESS, essay.

Questions that I answered incorrectly and want to investigate further:

Professor comments:

My comments: *Most of the items I went back and changed were incorrect.*

Improvement plan: *Next time I'll stick with my first answer and try not to read too much into the question.*

Writing Effectively at the College Level

Being educated means being skillful with language—able to control language instead of being controlled by it, confident that you can speak or write effectively instead of feeling terrified. When successful people explain how they rose to the top, they often emphasize their skills as communicators. . . . Writing, private or public, . . . is really about you, about the richness of your life lived in language, about the fullness of your participation in your community and in your culture, about the effectiveness of your efforts to achieve change. The person attuned to the infinite creativity of language leads a richer life. So can you.* (p. 175)

—J. N. Gardner and A. J. Jewler

* From *Your College Experience: Strategies for Success* (p. 175), by J. N. Gardner and A. J. Jewler, 1992, Belmont, CA: Wadsworth.

Prereading Questions

- What process do you currently use to write a paper?

- What are some typical college-level writing assignments and appropriate ways of responding to them?

- What is plagiarism, and why is it considered to be the worst mistake in college writing?

- If you could change your writing in any way, what is the first thing that you would want to improve?

Assessing Prior Knowledge

By the time they enter college, most students have written at least one major report or research paper. Think about an important writing assignment that you completed in high school or on the job. What did you learn about yourself as a writer in the process of writing that paper? Writing papers is expected in many of your college courses. Do you dread this, or do you look forward to it? Make a list of some things that you would like to improve in your writing. How did you decide what to put on your list?

Vignette: Three Students at the Writing Center

Three college students are at their college writing center completing similar assignments for different college courses. In every instance, the students are required to investigate a contemporary issue, locate reference materials on the topic, and write a four- to five-page paper with a bibliography that includes at least six different sources.

Aarika has known since September that she has an important writing assignment due in art history. Not that she has not thought about it—quite the contrary. It has been on her mind frequently because she lacks confidence in her writing skills. But each time that she sits down to write, she cannot decide where or how to begin. Aarika's attempts to get started on her paper usually result in several pieces of wadded-up paper and a sigh of frustration.

Duane's experience with writing is equally frustrating yet dramatically different. His teacher for a college composition course is requiring all students to maintain a writing folder and to revise the same piece of writing several times, based on peers' and the instructor's comments, suggestions, and questions. Whereas Aarika feels that she cannot get started writing, Duane feels that he will never get finished.

In contrast to these other two freshmen, Victor has neither worried about nor worked on his assignment for Philosophy 101. The night before the paper is due, he decides to look at the books that the professor put on reserve at the library. Because he and many other classmates have put off their writing until the last minute, Victor wastes even more time waiting for his turn to use the material. After he finally gets his hands on it, he panics. He has never read anything so confusing—it is almost as if it were written in a foreign language! Victor decides that the only safe route is to do what he did in high school. He looks up several key ideas in the dictionary and in the encyclopedia, and then he copies lengthy quotations from various sources. Unfortunately, Victor commits the most costly writing mistake a college student can make. Because he fails to give the authors appropriate credit in the text of his paper, he is guilty of plagiarism.

The grades of these three students clearly reflect the quality of their effort. On Victor's paper, the professor writes, "Learn to use *authoritative sources* in your written assignments and follow instructions. Your paper was to have a minimum of six different references that were appropriately cited. When you quote someone else's words, you *must* use quotation marks, include the author's name, and indicate the page number on which those words appeared. Plagiarized. F." Aarika ultimately manages to produce a passable paper, but because she was rushed, she did not bother to proofread, to ask someone else to read it, or to use the spell-checking feature on the word-processing program. The professor writes on her paper, "Even though the *content* of your paper was acceptable and merited a B, the numerous mechanical errors on your paper have lowered your grade substantially. Next time, proofread carefully. C−." Of the three students, only Duane was successful in attaining an A on his paper. At times, he was weary of revising the same piece of writing, but he now recognizes how real writers write and has gained important insights into how that process works for him.

This chapter on writing will provide you with basic information about college writing, including the writing process, typical types of college writing assignments, appropriate use of reference materials, and stages in the writing process.

BOX 9.1   **Improvement in Action** ⅢⅢ➡

Which of these students did you identify most strongly with—Victor, Aarika, or Duane? Why?

Make a list of the assets and liabilities that you bring to the task of writing:

Assets/Strengths   **Liabilities/Weaknesses**

As you read this chapter, search for suggestions that will enable you to capitalize on your strengths and counteract your weaknesses.

Understanding Writing

Many freshmen in college reading and study skills courses equate writing with grammar, spelling, punctuation, and word processing. But this assumption is clearly incorrect. Although the mechanical aspect of language—its correctness—is important for the final draft, it is the quality of thinking behind the words on paper that is most important. That is why college courses on writing are called *composition,* because a writer uses words to compose a paper just as a musician uses musical notes to compose a piece of music. In recent years, the study of writing has contributed greatly to understanding the interrelationship between thinking and writing. Leading researcher and feminist Mary Belenky has noted that, "In a world that is going to need everybody functioning as active thinkers, not just the privileged few, writing as a way to thinking should be taught to everyone" (Ashton-Jones & Thomas, 1990, p. 291).

If writing truly is "thinking on paper," consider what it means when a student says, "I'm just not good at writing." Does the student mean to say that he or she cannot think clearly or well? Probably not. It would probably be more accurate to say that he or she has discovered that writing is difficult and has not developed the confidence and skills to surmount those difficulties. We find that the students who are most convinced that they can-

---

BOX 9.2   *Improvement in Action* Ⅲ➡

Have you ever rewritten a paper more than once or twice? If you have not, you have not really tried to write well. Think about a particular hobby or activity that you enjoy, such as sports, crafts, music, and so forth. Make a list of the strategies you have used to improve your performance in that activity:

Now make a list of the things that you have done to improve your writing:

How do the lists compare? Remember that writing well takes just as much effort as doing other things well, such as playing basketball, learning a new language, or playing a musical instrument.

not write are usually the same students who admit to writing an assignment in 15 minutes and not taking the time to revise. An analogy to a physical skill helps illustrate why time and effort devoted to the improvement of writing are so essential. Nobody expects to become a track star by ambling around the track a few times, yet many students with a record of writing difficulties expect an A+ paper to appear miraculously on the computer screen as they type. Not every writer is expected to publish a poem, article, or book. But all college students need to attain a level of writing proficiency that will enable them to achieve their academic and professional goals.

As a first step in improving your writing, try to be more realistic about writing well. Although it is true that writers become more efficient as they gain confidence, increase their skill, and practice writing for different purposes, the fact remains that even the most widely published authors revise their manuscripts a dozen times or more. (This chapter, for example, was rewritten 16 times, and we are all professors with doctoral degrees!) So before you say, "I'm not a writer," remember that people who call themselves writers devote extraordinary time and effort to building their competence and polishing their work, just like that track star who practices regularly.

Distinguishing Features of Writing

What is your understanding of the writing process? Here is how an 18-year-old freshman in Rico's (1991) class explained her new perspective after completing a course on writing:

> Writing is discovering and uncovering what goes on inside of you. What you remember. What you forgot. Writing is revealing yourself to yourself in the same way that you become intimate with someone who was once a stranger. Writing is difficult because it depends on exposure of yourself to the one who thinks most critically of you—yourself. Writing is bizarre when it is finished and you step back and say, "Did I write that?!" Writing is selfish because it can be what you most care about, and others may not understand. Writing is fun because you finally use one of the seldom-tapped resources of your mind. Writing is necessary. (p. 19)

The following is a discussion of some of the most basic and important assumptions that you need to make about college composition.

Writing Assumption 1: Writing Is, First and Foremost, Communication

Consider the case of the undergraduate who wrote a completely mystifying essay for his history professor. When the professor asked him to read a paragraph about the Magna Carta from his paper and interpret it, the student stated it simply and cleared up the confusion. "Well, why didn't you just write it that way in the first place?" the professor asked. "I guess I wanted to impress you by using a lot of big words," the student replied. This is frequently a concern of students—sounding intelligent. Although your writing for a course assignment should have a more formal tone than that of a friendly letter, you can also go too far in the other direction, as this student did, and fail to make sense because you are using words you do not understand.

This does not mean that you should keep writing the way you did before you entered college, however. Rather, you should strive to use the new, professional vocabulary you are acquiring during college study when you write. Your instructors will, to some extent, base their evaluation of your mastery of the course content on your ability to use and understand the terminology associated with the field.

BOX 9.3

Now that you have read one student's ideas about writing, what are your ideas? How would you define written composition? Compare and contrast your view of writing with that of the student just described. How did you acquire your view of writing? What negative and positive influences have shaped your perspective?

My Ideas about Writing   **Sources for Those Ideas**

Consider, for example, the situation of two students in an educational psychology class. Their professor has asked them to define and explain the term *surrogate* in their papers. Surrogates are people or objects that "stand in" for someone else. A surrogate parent, for example, is a person or thing who takes over some of the key responsibilities of the biological parent, such as a legal guardian who sees to it that the child is provided for. In studies conducted with primates by the Harlows, a husband-and-wife research team, their purpose was to investigate the effects of various types of surrogates on the behavior of infant monkeys. Real, live monkeys were used as substitutes in some of the research. In other studies, wire mesh shapes that had "eyes" and sometimes were covered with cloth or gave milk through a bottle were used as surrogates for the mother monkeys.

Their professor asked about the term *surrogate* and the Harlows' research on a test. She wanted students to "Define and explain surrogates as they relate to the field of psychology. Use your readings to support your ideas. Be certain to respond in a way that reflects your knowledge of the field of psychology." Here were two of the answers that the faculty member read. Which one, Kate or Terrell, did a better job of using a professional vocabulary?

> **Kate's answer:** In the stuff we read for class, it talked about how baby monkeys who don't get to see their mothers would hang on to these shapes made out of wire and cloth. The baby monkeys acted toward the shapes like they would have to their mothers.

> **Terrell's answer:** According to the research summary in the text, infant monkeys who were isolated from their real mothers formed emotional attachments with wire mesh and terry cloth shapes. An object that takes the place of someone else—in this case, the wire mesh "mother"—is referred to as a *surrogate* because it functions as a substitute for the real parent.

In comparing the two examples, you can easily see why the second example would be preferred. The student uses the new vocabulary (e.g., *emotional attachment, surrogate*), cites evidence to support the statements made ("According to the research summary in the text . . ."), and seems to be more familiar with the material.

One way to check your comprehension of a new vocabulary word is to write a sentence in which nothing other than the new word would fit. Here is an example of what we mean:

Poor use of new vocabulary: "Distance learning is an important educational tool."

Note that hundreds of words could fit into this very generic sentence. It does nothing to explain the meaning of the word in context.

Good use of new vocabulary: "In distance learning, advanced, interactive television technology is used to overcome barriers of time and distance. The most common application of distance learning is to gather groups of learners together so that they can see, hear, and discuss ideas with an expert without the added time, expense, and inconvenience of traveling away from their workplaces."

In the second example, the writer demonstrates an understanding of the terminology by defining the vocabulary in the first sentence and following it up with an example. Always strive to communicate your understanding of the terminology associated with various fields of study in your writing—it will dramatically improve instructors' evaluation of your work.

Writing Assumption 2: Writing Begins by Putting Your Critical Side on Hold

Within each one of us are a harshly judgmental critic and a creative, free spirit. Too many college students begin a writing assignment by attempting to satisfy the critic. They struggle mightily to achieve the perfect opening line or first paragraph, assuming that everything will fall into place if only they can "get the words right" at the beginning. Professional writers take a very different approach. At the beginning of the composing process, they put their critical side on hold. During the first try at composing their papers, professional writers do not worry about errors or evaluate what they have written. Their goal, initially, is simply to get some ideas down on paper, ideas that are admittedly tentative and need revision, but a place to begin, nevertheless. This process of reserving judgment and just forging ahead is called *freewriting* because the writer does not allow him- or herself to be stalled by worries about style, form, and correctness—at least not at first. The goal is to put thoughts down on paper, gradually revising and refining a piece of writing until it is clear, concise, and error-free.

Beginning a paper is analogous to quickly cleaning up a living room after a wild party. You do not make a careful plan; you simply begin. This is not the time to be arranging flowers in a vase on the table. The table needs to be put back in place first. You save the refinements for later and focus instead on the most pressing issues, such as clearing a path so that you can begin to work. You do not stop to pick up a piece of lint on the carpet. You can take care of that later. You accept the fact that this is a big mess and focus on big things. At the beginning, writing is like that "disaster area" room: extraordinarily messy and in need of a big-picture perspective. Not that those little things will be ignored. Rather, you will worry about them later, when it is more appropriate.

Robert Louis Stevenson is credited with saying, "When I say writing, oh, believe me, it is chiefly rewriting that I have in mind." Revision is the essence of good writing. Each time writers revise, they work with the words until the writing is clearer, more concise, better organized, and more powerful. One of the great advantages of writing is the fact that we have the opportunity to correct errors ahead of time.

Writing Assumption 3: Writing Is a Craft

Practically every piece of writing is flawed in some ways, even writing that is published and celebrated as excellent. If you interview the authors of those manuscripts, they will usually say that there are portions of the book or article that they still are not quite satisfied with. College students who doubt their writing ability are even more critical of their work. Many have had the humbling experience of seeing their writing mistakes pointed out repeatedly by teachers, even in red ink. These students also operate on the assumption that writing ability is more innate than learned and that professional writers are people for whom writing is virtually effortless. It isn't.

In much the same way that a woodworker or an ice skater masters the craft, good writing is carefully crafted. As writers gain confidence and acquire new skills, their writing improves. With each success, they take on new challenges until the final result *appears* effortless, just as the master woodworker's hands seem to fashion wood easily or the practiced skater glides smoothly around on the ice. But at the beginning, the inexperienced writer, like any inexperienced craftsperson, is awkward and halting. It takes considerable effort to make a piece of writing flow, but even students who have serious doubts about their abilities can make remarkable progress by getting feedback on their writing and revising on the basis of that feedback. Many colleges have writing centers where more experienced writers assist less experienced writers, yet students are often reluctant to use these support systems. They think that asking for help with writing is a way of saying "I'm stupid" or cheating. Instead, college students need to think of college writing as an apprenticeship, a craft that is best learned with the expert guidance of craftspersons or coaches who are experienced writers themselves.

Take, for example, the story of a student in one of our college reading courses. When the professor complimented her on a paper she had written and revised several times, she confided, "Nobody ever liked my writing before." The next year, she was hired as a work-study student in the Art Department. Her job? To write advertising copy for the many cultural events sponsored by the department. When she started college, she thought writing was her weakness, but it turned out to be a strength *because she treated it as a craft instead of as an inborn ability*. This crafting aspect of writing is so basic that writers are sometimes referred to as "wordsmiths"—people who bend and shape words into writing just as a blacksmith crafts implements and horseshoes from metal. Figure 9.1 gives some students' opinions on how writers can improve their writing.

Writing Assumption 4: Writing Is More Than Speech Written Down

Have you ever been in the midst of writing something and thought, "Hey! I never thought of this before. It just occurred to me as I was writing." That is because when we write, we are not simply transcribing spoken words or inner speech into written form (Murray, 1990). Writing is thinking. Anyone who can think clearly can write clearly (Zinsser, 1990). But if your thinking is muddled, writing will seem like a hopeless endeavor. Good writers have acquired techniques for sorting out their thinking.

Figure 9.1
How to Improve Your Writing
Adapted from Bloom (1991).

Lynn Bloom's (1991) writing class offers the following suggestions:

- "Writers read a lot and pick up vocabulary and sentence patterns, a sense of style, as they read."
- "Writers learn from reading aloud, from paying attention to the sound."
- "They learn from writing and revising work that really means something to them, and from submitting multiple drafts for portfolio grading."
- "Writers learn from reading their works to each other."
- "Writers learn from teachers who write, who are part of a group of writers."

Improvement in Action ⫸

Think back on the section you just read about the basic assumptions about writing. Was there any information that surprised you? Make a list of the suggestions included in this section that you have not tried previously. Use at least one of the suggestions on your next writing assignment. Then assess the results of this change on your writing habits and make some notes for discussion here:

At some point in your school career, somebody has probably told you to use an outline to organize your writing. Yet even the most proficient writers often say that while it is easy to write the outline *after* they have finished a paper, it is often extremely difficult beforehand, while their thinking is not completely clarified. Try experimenting with some of the graphic organizers that you used in note taking as a way of organizing your thoughts before you begin to write. Think of this first stage in writing as playing with ideas instead of a firm commitment to a particular organizational pattern. If you are very adept at using a word processor, you might find that using the cut-and-paste option and moving text around when clusters of ideas begin to emerge is your best way of getting organized. For other people, individual ideas on separate pieces of paper or note cards that can be physically and visually rearranged are the best organizational strategy. Actually, the note cards approach is much like the shopping list approach to note taking because you begin with a disorganized group of ideas and put them into categories. You may even find that a combination of these strategies works best for you—maybe using a graphic organizer sketched out on paper at first and then going to the computer as a second step. Continue to experiment with different strategies until you find your best way to write a particular paper.

Writing Assumption 5: Writing Is a Complex Mental Activity

When we write, our brains are barraged by messages. Almost simultaneously, the brain can give an idea, send off a signal that a word is misspelled, cause us to wonder whether this is what the professor really wants, and suggest going back to reread notes. Writing is difficult because it puts the brain on full-time circuitry overload. We start to feel overwhelmed like a newly hired fast-food restaurant worker at a backed-up drive-through window during lunchtime. One solution is to sort out these conflicting messages and deal with them one at a time. Begin simply by getting ideas down on paper. As mentioned earlier, do not start by worrying about spelling, punctuation, grammar, or correctness. Just write and keep on writing. If you begin writing early and edit your writing for different things at various times, writing will not seem like such a frustrating task. You can begin by focusing primarily on ideas, for example; then move to an emphasis on organizing those ideas; next concentrate on the accuracy of the content; then make your message clearer and more readable; and, finally, focus on the grammar, spelling, and typographical errors. By selecting a focus area for your revision efforts rather than trying to correct everything at the same time, you can learn to be a more efficient and confident writer.

How to Succeed in College Writing

You can succeed in college writing by following all of the keys to success in Figure 9.2. Each one of these success keys in writing is discussed in the sections that follow.

Writing Success Key 1: Determine the Purpose for the Assignment

One common complaint of faculty is that students fail to differentiate among some of the most common purposes for writing. Some of the specific writing tasks that are required of students on papers and on essay exams are described in Figure 9.3.

Writing Success Key 2: Begin Early

The importance of gradual, thorough preparation for a major writing assignment cannot be overestimated. If you begin to write a paper and return to it a few days later, many of the errors and awkward sentences will be much more apparent than they were previously. In other words, you can begin to edit your own work—but only if you give yourself time. Some peer tutors, graduate assistants, and college faculty are willing to give you feedback on outlines or initial drafts of your paper. If so, take advantage of this opportunity to obtain additional guidance as you prepare your paper.

Beginning early offers another advantage: The lines at the writing center, library, and copying center are usually much longer at the end of the semester. If you start early, you avoid the end-of-semester rush and the increased likelihood that equipment will malfunction or be in use when you get there. You will have more free time at the beginning of the school term, so it is imperative to *work ahead!* Many students do not use this time and feel very confident that they are keeping pace with all of their course requirements, only to panic at midterm or the end of the semester or quarter. In our own experience with college freshmen, most begin with great determination and enthusiasm. By midterm, many are feeling overwhelmed. Some "lose their good grades" during the last 2 or 3 weeks—even during the

Figure 9.2
Keys to Success in College Writing

- Determine the purpose and audience for your paper before you begin writing.
- Start writing early so that there is time to revise several times and edit.
- Develop a workable note-taking strategy.
- Use the work of others appropriately by citing and referencing any sources that you consult in preparing your paper. Never present someone else's work as your own.
- Follow each professor's instructions carefully.
- Be flexible and learn to revise—get an experienced writer to read and critique your paper.
- Even after you think you are finished, read your paper two more times.

Figure 9.3
Terminology Used in Writing Assignments

Each of the terms defined here is commonly found in professors' instructions for writing essays or papers. If you have any question about what is expected in a written assignment, always ask the instructor. Make certain that you clearly understand expectations for a piece of writing *before* you invest all that time and effort in writing it.

Summarize—to restate material briefly, "boiling it down" to the essentials while still capturing all of the important features (Banks, McCarthy, & Rasool, 1993).

Synthesize—to combine pieces of information from various sources into a coherent whole.

Compare—to analyze the distinguishing features of two or more things, then explain how they are alike or how they are different and describe details that document those similarities/differences.

Contrast—to analyze the features of two or more things and explain how they differ.

Evaluate or critique—to assess the quality of the thinking behind a statement or a line of reasoning, to "look for holes" in the logic of an argument.

Take a position and defend or support—to approach a writing task as if in a debate, adopt a particular point of view, and then to move beyond pure opinion by providing specific details and evidence to support that particular perspective.

Apply—to use what you know or have read in one situation to interpret another. Students are often directed on an essay test, for example, to "use what you have been learning in this class" or "apply your readings" when responding to the question.

last 2 or 3 days. Planning ahead also avoids some of the most frustrating barriers to success—like a storm blowing out the electricity on the one night you allotted to enter and print out your paper on the computer or having the ribbon go out on the printer when none of the office supply stores are open.

Writing Success Key 3: Take Good Notes

Vinnie has been working on an important paper for a comparative religions course. He knows that he needs at least a B in the class to remain in academic good standing, so he makes a commitment to work at the library at least once a week for 2 hours over the next 7 weeks of the semester. The only problem is that Vinnie has no organization to his notes on what he has been reading. Some of his notes are in the back of notebooks for various classes; some are on cards; others are on loose pieces of paper stuffed in his backpack. Some of the information he needs to include, such as the date or page number, is missing. When the time arrives to write his paper, Vinnie finds that he has to do quite a bit of searching through all of his papers and backtracking at the library in order to actually produce the completed paper. He vows to be better organized next time. What could he have done to avoid these problems?

First, Vinnie needs a better strategy for taking notes. He must keep all his notes for the paper in one place, such as an expandable folder or on one file on a computer disk (always with a back-up copy, disk *and* paper). Second, Vinnie has to realize that any time he reads something useful at the library, he needs to record not only the helpful information but also the source of that information. Figure 9.4 describes some useful ways of taking notes on written material.

Figure 9.4
How to Take Notes at the Library

Sample Bibliography Cards

Preparing your bibliography cards in advance makes referencing during note taking easier. When taking notes for your paper on a note card or page, you simply need to make a quick reference to the source by identifying the author's last name or a key word in the title of the book or article.

Book:

Harvey Weiner and Charles Bazerman

All of Us: A Multicultural Skills Handbook (2nd ed.) Boston, MA: Houghton Mifflin, 1994

Article:

Nancy G. Lee and Judith C. Neal

"Reading Rescue: Intervention for a Student 'At Promise' " *Journal of Reading 36(4),* December 1992, pp. 276–282

Notes:

- Use index cards to record all of the bibliographic information.
- Print out the abstracts (short summaries) of the article on the library computer, cut them apart, and staple them to the front of 5" × 8" notecards. After reading the article, put your handwritten notes on the back of the card. Remember to include the page number for any direct quotations.
- Make a photocopy of the article (make sure you have volume number, and date) or book chapter (make sure you have author's name, book title, city, state, and publisher). If you have printed an abstract, staple it to the photocopy.
- Download information from the computer onto a disk and print it out at the computer center or on your personal computer.
- Take your laptop computer to the library and type in the information as you read. Be certain to save frequently, make a back-up copy of your disk, and print out a paper copy as soon as possible.
- Prepare your note cards in the same style that you will be using to type your reference list.

Writing Success Key 4: Document Sources and Avoid Plagiarism

When you were in high school, you probably wrote a research paper that required you to use the encyclopedia and other reference tools from the library. If you were like most high school students, you came very close to copying the material from those sources. *In college, this practice is completely unacceptable.* You will be expected to consult the writings of leading authorities in various fields (rather than the encyclopedia), and you must be particularly careful about how you use their work. As Victor's experience in the opening vignette illustrated, the improper use of published material has serious consequences, not only for your grade on the paper but also for your performance in the course. It could even jeopardize your college career. The foremost rule to remember is that using material from a published source is permissible only if it meets *both* of the following conditions:

1. The material copied is a small fraction of the work—for example, no more than a short paragraph from any single article or no more than two total paragraphs from any one book.

2. *Any* material that was not written by you or is not *your own thinking* is clearly identified in your paper and reported with appropriate citation.

Figure 9.5
Knowing What to Document

From *The Holt Handbook* (3rd ed., pp. 597–598), by L. G. Kirszner and S. R. Mandell, 1992, Orlando, FL: Holt, Rinehart & Winston. Copyright 1992 by Holt, Rinehart & Winston. Adapted by permission.

You must:

- always keep another writer's words and ideas distinct from your own in your writing;
- acknowledge the source of any material that you quote directly, both in the body of the paper and in the reference list at the end of the paper;
- document material that is paraphrased or summarized from another source or sources;
- always cite the original source for opinions, conclusions, statistics, and so forth;
- document any information that is not widely known or open to dispute; and
- document any tables, charts, graphs, or statistics taken from a source.

Citation means that the author's name, the date the work was published, the title of the book or article and journal is supplied, and the page number(s) that you consulted are recorded and typed into your assignment. The obligation to cite sources applies when you are *paraphrasing* (putting someone else's ideas into your own words) as well as when you are *quoting* someone verbatim (word for word). Whenever you are using someone else's ideas and material, you must "give credit where credit is due." This conscientious effort to make sure that another person's ideas and words are not represented as your own is referred to as *documentation*. Figure 9.5 is an overview of what must be documented.

Usually, if students plagiarize material in the ways we have just explained, it is because they are unclear about these procedures. There are, however, much more deliberate and intentional forms of plagiarism, ones that usually result in school dismissal if they are discovered. One example is the student who pays someone else to write a paper for an assignment or who resubmits a paper that was written by someone who took the class previously. Another is a student who deliberately copies large sections of material from a published work. These students are usually surprised when their unethical behavior is discovered. But they forget that in most instances, the instructor has already seen examples of their writing style. If it is suddenly, dramatically better, it raises suspicion. As far as copying from published works is concerned, students forget that college faculty are usually avid readers of books and articles in their fields. So most faculty can spot a forgery based on their familiarity with published material. Remember also that to a considerable extent, faculty are the ones who write what is published in professional journals so they regard published material as personal property—and are about as unsympathetic toward plagiarism as you would be if someone took your car or CD player without asking first. Figure 9.6 offers some useful guidelines for avoiding plagiarism. Plagiarism is one of the worst mistakes that you can make in college writing.

Always take careful notes on any written material that you use. Every time you read something related to your topic, make certain that you write down the author's complete name and the complete name of the article, book chapter, or book. Also write down the specific page number for any quoted material.

- For an article, write down the title of the journal, the month and year it was published, the volume and the number (these are usually on the inside cover), and the inclusive page numbers on which the article appears (for example, pp. 19–27).

- For a book, you need the title, city and state where it was published, the publishing company's name, and the year it was published. If you are referring to a chapter from an edited book (meaning that various authors wrote the chapters), you will

BOX 9.5   *Improvement in Action* ⫸

Look again at the quotation at the beginning of this chapter on page 199. Using the criteria from Figure 9.5, decide which of the following excerpts from student papers would be plagiarized versions of the quote:

■ **Paper 1:** Skill with language, both spoken and written, is one characteristic of an educated person.

■ **Paper 2:** People who are educated are skillful communicators and use their knowledge of language, both spoken and written, to help them in their personal and professional lives (Gardner & Jewler, 1992).

■ **Paper 3:** The term *educated,* as defined by Gardner and Jewler (1992), means efficiency in using the communication skills of speaking and writing to foster growth and change in both the public and private sectors of life.

■ **Paper 4:** One can either control language or be controlled by it. Educated people continually strive to improve their skills as communicators so that they can control language and become more successful.

If you answered that plagiarism occurs in papers 1 and 4, you were correct. Paper 1 is an example of paraphrasing, of putting someone else's ideas into your own words. It requires in-text citation, like this: (Gardner & Jewler, 1992). Why? Because those ideas did not originate with the student who put them into the paper. Papers 2 and 3 are *not* plagiarized because both of them cite the source of the ideas in the paper. When your instructors see the names and dates typed into your paper, they know that you are giving credit to the people whose work you consulted. Paper 4 is an even more blatant example of plagiarism because it is even closer to the original quotation than paper 1. It too could be corrected by simply including the name and date for the source that was used.

Figure 9.6
Guidelines for Avoiding Plagiarism
From *The Holt Handbook* (3rd ed., pp. 593–594), by L. G. Kirszner and S. R. Mandell, 1992, Orlando, FL: Holt, Rinehart & Winston. Copyright 1992 by Holt, Rinehart & Winston. Used by permission.

- In your notes, make certain that you have *recorded information from your sources carefully and accurately.*
- In your notes, *put all words taken from outside sources inside circled quotation marks, and enclose your own comments in brackets.*
- In your paper, *differentiate your ideas from those of your sources* by clearly introducing borrowed material with the author's name and by ending with documentation.
- In your paper, *enclose all direct quotations* within quotation marks and cite the source of any paraphrased or summarized material.
- In your finished paper, *review paraphrases and summaries* to make certain that they are in your own words and that any words and phrases from the original are quoted.
- Always document *direct quotations and all paraphrases and summaries* in your paper and in your reference list at the end of the paper.
- Always document *facts that are open to dispute or are not common knowledge.*
- Always document *opinions, conclusions, figures, tables, graphs, and charts* taken from a source.

also need to write down the inclusive page numbers (for example, pp. 45–56) of the chapter. Also note the name(s) of the editor for an edited book.

Writing Success Key 5: Follow Instructions

Many faculty provide specific instructions about how to prepare a paper for their classes. It seems obvious that a student would follow these directions, but these guidelines are often discussed very early in the semester. They may be mixed in with class notes or attached to the syllabus. Students who are rushing to complete their assignment at the last minute are especially susceptible to forgetting to reread and follow the specific instructions prepared by the instructor.

Typically, these instructions require you to

- consult various readings from the library and take notes on what you read;
- cite a minimum number of references, not only at the conclusion of the paper in a bibliography but also throughout the paper to document the work of others; and
- use a very specific style of documenting others' work.

Different fields of study often have different ways of referencing consulted materials. Three main types or styles of referencing can be used, so be sure to know which style your instructor is requiring. This book, for example, uses American Psychological Association (APA) style, as do most psychological and educational publications. Look at the references at the end of any chapter in this book, and you will see what APA style looks like. Additionally, you can see examples of in-text citations using APA style in the body of each chapter. The two other most commonly used referencing styles are those developed by the Modern Language Association (MLA) and the *Chicago Manual of Style* (CMS). See the Appendix at the end of this chapter for specific examples of APA, MLA, and CMS styles. Most college libraries will have all of these style manuals available at the reference desk for your use. There are also handbooks that show you the basics of how to use each style, such as *The Holt Handbook* (Kirszner & Mandell, 1992). Some instructors will distribute guidelines. Others will allow you to use the referencing style that is used in your major field. When in doubt, check to see how material is documented in the materials that you are reading for the class—your textbook, the articles you are reading, and so forth. Whatever style you use, make sure it is the one required and use it consistently. This is yet another way that a tutor or writing center staff can be of assistance—by helping you meet the referencing style requirements without making errors.

Writing Success Key 6: Be Flexible and Learn to Revise

One of the college writer's greatest enemies is panic, the feeling of pressure to produce a top-quality paper on the first attempt. All of us who try to write are familiar with that feeling of a knot in the stomach as we stare at the blank paper or computer screen and grow frustrated or angry as we keep trying to compose the perfect first line. But who says that the first line is the only place to begin? Maybe it would be easier to start in the middle or write the ending first! Writing is not some neat, orderly series of steps; it is a gradual and recursive process. The word *recursive* means literally to rerun. When we say that the writing process is recursive, we mean that you can move around among tasks as the need arises.

Suppose, for example, that you thought of another important point that could be made in your paper. You may find a trip back to the library to get a statistic that backs up your argument is just what is needed, even though the paper is nearly finished. Likewise, you might find that when you are not making much progress writing, it is a good time to take a break and work on some aspect of your paper that you would normally do at the end, such as typing the cover sheet or beginning to type your reference list. Good writers learn to be more flexible in their thinking rather than punishing themselves because the words don't come out right on the first, second, or third attempt. Effective college writers actually *expect* their writing to be bad—at first, that is. They systematically attack the problems until their papers clearly reflect what they are thinking. One strategy for improving writing is to examine some basic building blocks of writing—basic formats for writing a paragraph, developing a thesis statement, and composing a longer paper.

Basic Writing Structures

Another source of support for your writing is working with some basic formats for writing paragraphs and papers.

Writing Paragraphs

One way to gain control over the mental chaos sometimes created by writing is to use some basic formulas or structures as guides. At some point in your school career, someone has probably instructed you on how to write a paragraph. The question is, did you ever really understand what they were trying to tell you? Until you actually produce a paragraph in standard form, it is hard to see what their advice means.

One strategy that we have used successfully with students is what we call "the package paragraph." Think for a moment about wrapping a very special, fragile gift to be delivered through the mail. Consider the basic steps you would follow in preparing that package. Figure 9.7 summarizes those steps and how they relate to writing a paragraph.

Developing a Thesis

Whenever you attempt to write a paper in college, you will need to focus your ideas around a central statement. This statement, called a *thesis statement,* usually appears in your first paragraph and performs three very useful functions:

1. It identifies your topic.
2. It narrows your topic and focuses the reader's attention on the particular aspect you will be discussing.
3. It makes a clear statement about the point of view or perspective you will be taking on the topic (Kirszner & Mandell, 1992).

Figure 9.8 shows an example from a student paper on fraternity and sorority pledging practices.

Figure 9.7
The Package Paragraph

When you write a paragraph, imagine that you are getting a package ready to mail at the post office.

Step 1: Choose a container. I have to think about the item as a whole—what box will it fit in?

Writing analogy: What is this paragraph going to be about, generally speaking? What sentence "fits," so that it is neither too "small" (narrow) or "large" (broad)?

Step 2: Arrange the contents. I have to decide what to use to support the item and keep it secure.

Writing analogy: What evidence and examples do I have to support and verify my first sentence?

Step 3: Send it. I have to address the package and direct it to its destination.

Writing analogy: How can I tie it all together—beginning, middle, and end—and send it on its way?

Now look at a paragraph that follows the "package" pattern: One of the ironies of teaching writing is that most teachers give of their expertise when the student needs it the least. They give a lot of help before the student starts to write and after the student has written, but too little during the process. Once the student has done a rough draft and has freely committed himself to doing a revision, he then truly needs a teacher's help. (Clark, 1975, p. 68)

BOX 9.7   *Improvement in Action* ⫸

What is the best piece of writing that you ever did? The worst? In what ways did your writing process for your best writing differ from the process you used for your worst writing? In what ways were the two similar? Create a Venn diagram that compares/contrasts the two. Then write a package paragraph using the information from your Venn diagram:

Begin with a suitable container: ("In comparing my best and worst writing, my general conclusion was that . . . ")

Select the contents: ("Differences in my best and worst writing included . . . ," "Similarities in my best and worst writing were . . .")

Wrap it up: ("To summarize, my best writing occurs when . . . , while my worst writing occurs when . . .")

BOX 9.8   *Improvement in Action* ⅠⅠⅠⅠ➡

Try this experiment. Rewrite your paragraph from Box 9.7 using Figure 9.7, the package paragraph, as a guide. Give both paragraphs to someone to read. Ask them which one they understood better and which one they generally preferred and why. Be prepared to report to the class on your findings.

Figure 9.8
Developing a Thesis
Adapted from Kirszner and Mandell (1992).

1. Select a topic.
Fraternities and sororities.

2. Narrow your topic; make it more specific.
Pledging practices in fraternities and sororities.

3. Take a perspective on the issue.
Personal injury can result from pledging activities.

4. Make an announcement.
This paper will . . .

Sample Introductory Paragraph with Thesis Statement

Topic
Fraternities and sororities are a part of life on most college and university campuses.

Narrowing
In order to join these organizations, college freshmen typically engage in a variety of silly and embarrassing activities, something that is supposed to prove their worth as pledges and to be all in good fun.

Position
But what about pledge experiences that are no longer fun, experiences that become dangerous or destructive, resulting in injury or even death for the person who pledges?

Announcement
This paper will examine the negative side of fraternity and sorority pledging by examining the consequences for the individual pledge, for the organizations involved, and the effects on university policies.

Notice how the introductory paragraph that includes a thesis statement is clear, concise, and sets the reader's expectations for what is to follow. Be sure to use this thesis statement writing strategy in all of your important papers.

Writing Structures for Papers

Naturally, the type of writing task affects your writing strategy too. Your style and strategies will differ when you are writing about a personal experience in your journal versus when you are preparing a lengthy research paper with numerous references, for example.

Writing a Major Paper, Step by Step

Often, the sequence of the process in writing a college paper follows the basic progression outlined here.

1. **Select a topic.** When students are assigned to write a paper, faculty have different ways of determining what students will write about. Some faculty assign the same basic topic to all students. Other faculty circulate a list of possible topics and allow students to choose from that list. Still other faculty give you a free choice of topics. For students who are unaccustomed to making their own decisions about a topic, this last way of approaching the selection of a subject is often problematic. If you are completely new to a field, how do you decide what to write about? As a start, try skimming through your textbook's table of contents. After you find something that looks interesting, turn to that chapter and skim through the headings and subheadings. Write down two or three possibilities, then ask your professor which ones he or she would recommend.

2. **Complete your background reading and prepare notes.** How do you get started in searching for information? One of the best ways is to look through the bibliography of your textbook and the list of recommended readings prepared by your instructor (usually attached to the course syllabus). This approach will give you an idea about which authors, journals, and books to consult. Many faculty put readings on reserve at the library; do not forget to consult these also.

After you have located some books and articles from leaders in the field, you can use their work to lead you to other high-quality sources. Examine the sources that *they* consulted before writing *their* book or article, which are listed as references at the end of the publication. Conducting library research in this way is like finding the thread that will help you unravel the mysteries that new fields present. If you begin with a source recommended by your instructor, it will help you locate more of the best sources, read them, and enable you to become a "quick study" in the subject.

To get the very latest information, you will need to conduct a search at the library. Most modern libraries have a computerized system that enables you to identify your topic and search using key words. Ask the reference librarian at your college library to help you with this process. Sometimes you can download information onto a disk and print it at the computer center or on a personal computer. Often, these printouts will contain all the bibliographic information and an abstract (brief summary) of the article. By reading the abstracts, you can decide whether that particular article will be useful and save some time by reading only those articles that sound the most promising.

Whatever method you use to search, be sure to record all of the pertinent information for the bibliography. If you do not get this information at the outset, you will have to go back to the library later to look it up, so try to be efficient.

3. **Reread the information about how to prepare the assignment.** Make sure that you understand it, and, if you have any doubt in your mind, reread the instructions first, then

mention it to the instructor. Generally speaking, it is better to ask the person who designed the assignment than to ask other students because they may be just as confused as you are. Asking during class also gives others the chance to benefit from a more thorough explanation. Figure 9.9 is an overview of the criteria faculty use most often to evaluate written work.

4. Go through your notes and cluster those ideas that go together. Some writers simply use the move-and-copy features of a word-processing program to sort out their ideas at this stage. Others find graphic organizers a helpful way to group their ideas about a paper. Still others find a rough outline helpful at this stage, but it is not essential. Experiment to discover what works best for you.

5. Develop a thesis statement. A *thesis* is the basic, overall idea of a piece of writing. A good thesis is developed as outlined in Figure 9.8.

6. Begin to think in terms of major sections for your paper. If there are any portions for which you have insufficient information, return to the library for additional background material. Do not forget to look in your textbook as well.

7. Keep chipping away at the assignment. If you really cannot write anything further at a work session, try rereading your notes, referring to your textbook or class notes, or begin typing the bibliography in the appropriate style, but continue to work on some aspect of the paper. Do not make the mistake of wasting time while staring at the wall and waiting for inspiration.

8. As you get closer to a finished draft, read your paper out loud. Reading aloud is a good idea for several reasons. First, writing has a rhythm to it, and reading aloud helps you discover that rhythm. If you doubt that this is true, read the following lines out loud:

> Altruism is an important human characteristic. Altruistic people are unselfish. They do good deeds without always expecting a reward. People in some professions are more altruistic than people in other professions. Nurses and teachers usually get high scores on measures of altruism.

Note that these sentences *sound* boring because the rhythm of the language is repetitive. The author did not vary the sentence length, so the words sound flat. Here is the same material, revised after it was read aloud:

> Altruism is an important human characteristic. People are altruistic if they are kind and unselfish but do not always expect to be compensated for their good works. Based on research, nurses and teachers are the two professional groups that consistently have the highest scores on measures of altruism.

Figure 9.9
Criteria for Evaluating Writing Assignments

Goals: Paper met the purposes outlined in the assignment.

Style: Paper is clear, well organized.

Content: Information is accurate and appropriately documented/cited.

Form: Paper is free of mechanical errors (spelling, punctuation, grammar) and is prepared in the correct format (number of pages, number of references, title page, style manual, etc.).

Quality: Paper shows evidence of careful thinking.

A second reason for reading aloud is that this simple procedure will sometimes help you *hear* where pauses and punctuation are necessary. Take, for example, the use of commas. Some students avoid this problem by not using commas or overusing them. Actually, the best guide for commas is to *listen* for places where a pause is needed. Reread the two sentences before this one quickly without the commas, and you will be able to tell the difference. The brief pauses indicated by the commas make the message clearer.

A third reason for reading papers aloud is that it enables you to identify sentences that do not make sense or words that do not form complete sentences. Read the following example from students' papers on the topic "Becoming Successful in College." See whether you can *hear* the errors.

> The use of the library will help me become a better student and the librarian will be able to give me some very helpful hints that will give me the inside track on some special information and these resources will help me with my assignments.

Notice that you had to take a deep breath to read this sentence. It just keeps adding more and more information, something that makes it sound disorganized. Run-on sentences waste words and the reader's time. Usually, they have been written in haste, and they show it. When a sentence is just a jumbled collection of ideas, it is called a *run-on sentence*. Here is that same sentence, revised after it was read aloud:

> Using the library will help me become a better student by providing me with specialized information that I can use in course assignments.

Another common problem in student papers that can be helped by reading aloud is the use of sentence fragments. Sentence fragments leave the reader with the feeling that something is missing, that the thought has not been completed. For example:

> And having good library skills.

Notice how this statement leaves us wondering who the author is talking about and why. It sounds incomplete when you read it out loud. But short sentences are not the only ones that are incomplete. A longer sentence can be a fragment as well. Read this one:

> Activities such as attending study groups and meetings, going to the writing center to seek help from the tutors, using the library to find information, and studying in a quiet environment.

Notice that, once again, we are left wondering, what about these activities? Who is doing them and why?

If you simply do not have an ear for language, ask someone else to read your paper and mark any places where they were confused, had to reread, or had a question that you did not answer. At this stage in your writing, feedback from a more experienced college writer (such as a writing center tutor) can be extremely helpful.

9. When you are nearly finished, examine each paragraph. As you have seen elsewhere in this chapter, each paragraph should be a neatly wrapped package. When you go back through your paper, make certain that each paragraph begins with a topic sentence and "hangs together." Everything that is discussed in that paragraph should clearly belong there and match the general idea stated in the first sentence of that paragraph.

10. Go back through your paper with better organization in mind. When your paper is completed, you should be able to write an outline that matches it or create a well-structured graphic organizer as a check on logical arrangement.

11. Use a word-processing program to make a final check on mechanics. Many word-processing programs and modern typewriters include programs for checking spelling or grammatical errors. Learn how to use these options to give your paper a polished look, but *do not assume that these features will eliminate the need for proofreading.* Even a built-in dictionary cannot identify whether you are using *to* when it should be *too* or *there* when you should have written *their.* It is also possible to push one wrong button and put the incorrect spelling for a word all through your paper. Be sure to proofread your paper two more times after you have said to yourself, "I'm finally finished!"

12. Analyze your habits as a writer. Experiment with different writing times and conditions. You may find that you write much more usable material early in the morning before your roommate or children wake up rather than in the afternoon or evening. If you need complete quiet and find it difficult to locate a quiet setting, try listening to a tape that does not distract you, such as jazz, classical music, or a relaxation tape on a set of headphones. By working to your strengths, you can make better use of your writing time.

13. Use the feedback your instructors give. If three different faculty members have read your papers and comment that you need to improve clarity in your writing, then you probably do. If you review the work that you have done and see the same comment more than once, such as "more detail needed in summary," then you need to make a change in your writing. Also note any particular errors that you have made, and make plans for avoiding them in the future. It seems to be human nature that after we have spelled a word incorrectly, we remain uncertain about the correct spelling. Some writers keep a personalized computer file on the errors they have made and refer to it whenever they need to be reminded about how to make the correction. You will find a reference book called an *English handbook* or *stylebook* to be a valuable reference tool for this purpose.

14. Learn to sound like an expert. Authority is an important feature of academic writing. When writing is authoritative, it means that it is backed up with evidence and reflects careful thinking. Usually, that careful thinking and documentation of facts are done by respected leaders in the field of study, or experts. Suppose that a professor gives you an

---

BOX 9.10 *Improvement in Action* ▐▐▐▶

When you are reading something, how do you decide whether the writer is an expert? What kinds of things provide evidence of credibility or lack of credibility? Make a list of some of these influences:

Tends to Enhance Credibility   **Tends to Diminish Credibility**

Why do we place any more faith in the information from a *New York Times* article than we do in an article on the same topic from the *National Enquirer?*

Figure 9.10
A General Process for Writing a Paper

1. Select a topic that meets the purpose and criteria identified by the instructor.
2. Complete your background reading and prepare notes.
3. Reread the information about how to prepare the assignment.
4. Go through your notes and cluster those ideas that go together.
5. Develop a thesis statement in an introductory paragraph.
6. Begin to think in terms of major sections for your paper. (Rearrange if necessary so that the information develops your thesis statement in a logical order.)
7. Keep working on the assignment.
8. As you get closer to a final draft, read the paper out loud.
9. When you are nearly finished, examine each paragraph.
10. Go back through your paper with better organization in mind.
11. Use a word processing program to make a final check on mechanics.
12. Write a concluding paragraph that brings the reader back to the thesis in reverse order (from your specific focus back to the general topic).

And don't forget to:

- analyze your habits as a writer,
- use the feedback your instructors give to improve, and
- learn to sound like an expert.

essay to read about oppression. Your job is to write a response to what you have read. Consider these opening lines for an essay. Which one sounds most like an expert?

> **Example 1:** "I think that there are three main ways of fighting people who are against you."

> **Example 2:** "Usually, people respond to oppression in three ways."

> **Example 3:** "Based on current theory and research, there are three basic responses to oppression."

Now, which one sounds most authoritative, most expert? Why? Clearly, the third example sounds most like an expert talking. Now think about *why*. In the first case, it sounds like pure opinion because the author uses *I* instead of referring to expert opinion. Also, the use of *I* and *you* makes oppression sound purely personal and individual when we all know that groups frequently oppress other groups. Second, the author uses language that is imprecise and contradictory. Peaceful protests and passive resistance could be one response to oppression, but the writer makes it sound as though open rebellion is the only type of response by using the word *fighting*. Therefore, it is incorrect to label all responses as "fighting" as the author does in example 1.

A general process for writing a paper is provided in Figure 9.10.

Conclusion

In their book on language, Temple and Gillet (1984) observe that many people have misconceptions about writing and believe:

BOX 9.11 *Improvement in Action*

Go back to the prereading questions at the beginning of the chapter. Can you answer them more completely now?

"good writing" emerges in final form, perhaps needing only to be copied over in ink, while "bad writing" has to be hacked at and refashioned, perhaps finally scrapped. We may even come to believe that writing well is a matter of talent and innate ability; or that writing is an art, in which few are lucky enough to be gifted, rather than a craft in which skills develop through practice and effort. In truth, writers are craftspersons; they are made not born. Good writing doesn't just occur. It is fashioned out of the raw material of words with patience and the skill born of practice. Few of us may become best selling authors, but almost everyone can become a more effective, articulate writer with instruction and practice. (p. 218)

As you think about writing in the future, try to remember that writing is

- a way to organize thinking,
- a way to communicate with various audiences for particular purposes,
- a strategic skill used to accomplish important goals,
- a craft that improves with practice,
- an authentic way of making meaning, and
- a means for encouraging responses from readers (Englert & Raphael, 1989).

It is said that shortly after the celebrated artist Michelangelo died, someone found a note in his studio he had written to his apprentice. It read, "Draw, Antonio, draw, Antonio, draw and do not waste time" (Dillard, 1989, p. 79). The same good advice that Michelangelo gave to his student about drawing is the advice we give to our college students about writing: "Write, write, write, and do not waste time."

66 99 *Voices of Successful Students*

"You have to make more than one draft and have more than one person proofread it. Go over and over it, and if you need help, go to the Writing Center."

"Use a variety of sources. Research the subject and know it."

"Don't procrastinate! Try to get things done ahead of time. Computers break (usually on the day things are due). You need time to review and revise toward perfection."

"Word processors are the way to go. Always use the spell check feature and then double-check by reading it again. Have other people proofread your paper. Some professors are willing to look over your assignment and give you advice before it is 'officially' turned in."

"Try reading your papers aloud to hear them. This helps you to notice where the writing is awkward or difficult to understand. You have to try out different things to find out what works best for you."

"Remember to do your writing when your mind is fresh and you feel alert. I found that I am a much better writer when I first wake up in the morning than I am late at night."

Extension Activities

Cooperative Learning Activity: Evaluating Essays

Here you will find five student responses to an essay question from Chapter 1. Work on one essay at a time using the following procedure:

1. Read the essay question in the next column, paying particular attention to what it asks you to do.
2. Then read the essays written by students one at a time. Use the following criteria to evaluate each on a scale from 1 to 10 (10 being the highest possible score):

Essay Evaluation Criteria

- Does the student answer the question?
- Is it clear that the writer understands the material?
- Does the writer use the key vocabulary?
- Are the features of learning experiences identified, explained, and illustrated with an example as specified in the instructions?
- Does the essay begin with a good introductory sentence?
- Is there sufficient detail?
- Does the writer follow instructions?
- Does the essay end with a concluding statement or a summary that "wraps things up"?

3. After you have finished rating the first essay, write a "prescription"—a statement that recommends changes the writer should make to improve on the next test.
4. Continue with the remaining essays following steps 1–4.

Essay Question

Use the five features of authentic learning experiences and apply them to a specific example of your learning. Take a moment to organize your thoughts before beginning, and sketch out your answer. Be sure to number and underline each feature of authentic learning experiences in your essay.

Essay 1

A specific time in my learning when I used all of these elements of authentic learning experiences is when I took my photo classes in high school. When I took this class, no one had to tell me to go out and take the pictures. This is the first step, which is **ownership.** I didn't know how to use the camera at first, but the class showed me how to use it. After a month, I excelled in the class so the teacher taught me some new ways to use the camera. This was the teacher using **appropriateness** to keep me at the right level of learning. Next was **structure**—getting organized and getting all of my ideas together for my final project and portfolio. By doing this, I have an effective way of finding subjects to take pictures of. To do this, I needed **collaboration,** interacting with other people. The way I did this was I talked to my teacher and some other teachers at the college and got some hints on how to make my project the best it could be. And finally, I have **internalized** because what I learned has become part of me. The way this happens now is that I look at things or people and visualize how I could make that into a photograph. So this is how I used the different features of authentic learning in photography.

Essay 2

Last summer I took a course for 6 weeks in which I had an ownership of my learning experience and it helped me do better on my SATs to get into college. I didn't have to take the course but I thought the appropriateness and structure were really there for me. It helped me collaborate with some other people in the same situations and it gave me a jump on everybody else in my senior class.

Essay 3

Ownership means to be responsible. I took ownership when I decided to come to college. College is a very big responsibility.

Appropriateness is to be at the right level of challenge. This means that you don't want to do something that doesn't challenge you to think. I considered appropriateness when I scheduled for the fall. I took a math class that I would be challenged in. It was between a simple and a harder class.

Structure has to do with organization. I became organized when I made up two schedules. I made a master schedule which has my classes on it and my work times. Then I make a weekly schedule to mark down my assignments and papers that are due that week.

Collaboration is human interaction. I collaborated when I started to come to classes. I talked with my classmates and found out who they are. I also collaborated when I went to the study groups at the Learning Center. You get to talk to a lot of people.

Internalization is to let what you study become part of you. This happened to me when I first started to study for the first class I had. We were to read a section on Amish culture. I understood what the author was saying and enjoyed reading it. So, after I read this section, it became part of me.

Essay 4

When I was in 11th grade my English class was mainly about reading books. I did not like to read books. My teacher told me you learn more just by reading books and if you don't know a word you will learn just by reading the story. I read the books and began liking what I was reading. Now most of my time I read books. I'm not good at it, but I try my best. My responsibility was to read those books I was given in class. I was wrong about not liking or getting along with reading. Now I learned more things than what I used to before reading. Reading is like a part of me now. It's like my hobby.

Essay 5

I'm going to use my experience of learning how to drive to explain the five features of authentic learning experiences. When I was ready to learn how to drive I had a sense of **ownership.** I took responsibility for gathering the information that I needed to study and get my license. My experience was **appropriate** because I had matured to the right level of challenge and was motivated to learn. There was **structure** to my learning because it happened gradually and was organized. I first got a job to save insurance money, then I was able to apply for my permit, and so forth. I **collaborated** with people such as my parents and friends. They helped me know the information for my driving test more thoroughly. Finally, my experience was **internalized.** Now, just like anyone else who has learned to drive, I can be off the road for long periods of time but when I have to drive, the information is recalled without effort.

Self-Improvement Strategy: Learning Logs

Read _____ and in your learning log write:

Any passage or item that puzzles you

Any items that intrigue you

Three things you agree or disagree with

How it makes you feel

What you think will happen next

Three new concepts and your definition of them

How this reading relates to your life

Two things this reading has in common with _____

What you think the author was like

Why you think _____ acted as he or she did

What you think it would be like to live in _____

A summary of this

Three things you would like the class to discuss

A cause-effect flowchart

How you can use this knowledge in your own life

Something the reading reminds you of

What you think it means, why you think that

What you would do if you were _____

Why _____ is important (Glaze, 1987, p. 151)*

Writing and Reflecting

Analyze the quality of the instruction you have received in writing. Note any deficiencies in your writing background, and describe strategies from this chapter that would help you overcome those obstacles.

---

* From "Learning Logs," by B. Glaze, in the Virginia Department of Education's *Plain Talk about Learning and Writing across the Curriculum* (p. 151), Richmond: Commonwealth of Virginia, Spring 1987. Copyright 1987 by Commonwealth of Virginia, Department of Education. Used by permission.

Reading Selections

Reading Selection 1: Writing as a Way to Improve Reading

Students who have a lengthy reading assignment, such as 30 pages in a college textbook, often "plow through" the assignment, then get to the end and realize that they didn't really understand it very well and cannot remember much of what they read. So, how do you solve this problem? One of the best things that you can do *as you read* is to pause periodically and put the ideas that you are reading about into your own words, or paraphrase them. This is something the most efficient and flexible readers seem to do "naturally," and it is something that you can begin to do to increase your understanding and memory of what you read.

One recommended way of monitoring comprehension is referred to as the *think-aloud*. In this approach, the reader actually goes through the reading material one short segment at a time, pauses, and then puts his or her interpretation of or thoughts about the passage into words. Researchers have used this approach to analyze what goes on inside learners' heads as they read and process information. You can profit from this strategy by adapting it to a "think on paper" approach in which you jot down your interpretation of text and ideas *as you are reading, one short piece at a time*. In other words, you can write as you read to monitor your own comprehension and analyze your own thinking—a very important metacognitive strategy (Wade, 1990). To illustrate, do the following exercise.

Think Aloud With a Poem by Maya Angelou

Maya Angelou is a leading author and prominent African-American woman. You may remember her from a poem that she read at the presidential inauguration for Bill Clinton. Perhaps you have read her powerful book, *I Know Why the Caged Bird Sings* (Angelou, 1983), which describes the abuse she suffered during childhood. Angelou has also produced some recordings of her writings read aloud that you may want to check out from the library. She has a beautiful, rich voice that she uses as an interpretive instrument to communicate the feelings behind her writings.

As you read her poem "Still I Rise" (Angelou, 1978) pause after each verse and try to interpret the meaning.* If there is anything you cannot understand, give it a try or simply write that you do not know. Then go back through your ideas after reading the entire poem and revise them as necessary. Notice what this approach to comprehension monitoring encourages you to do. First, you have to focus completely on what you are reading and what it means. Second, you have to transfer ideas from the author's writing to your writing. Third, you must stop periodically to check your understandings rather than just going forward without understanding and wasting your time. After you have completed your "Thinking on Paper" comprehension monitoring, look at the three student responses and compare them with your own.

---

* From *And Still I Rise* by Maya Angelou. Copyright 1978 by Maya Angelou. Reprinted by permission of Random House, Inc.

Still I Rise

You may write me down in history with your
    bitter, twisted lies.
You may trod me in the very dirt but still, like
    dust, I'll rise.
You may shoot me with your words, you may
    cut me with your eyes,
you may kill me with your hatefulness, but
    still, like air, I rise.
Out of the huts of history's shame, I rise.
Up from a past that's rooted in pain I rise.
I am a black ocean, leaping and wide
Welling and swelling, I bear in the tide
leaving behind nights of terror and fear I rise.
Into a daybreak that is wondrously clear I rise.
Bringing the gifts that my ancestors gave, I am
    the dream and the hope of the slave.
I rise, I rise, I rise.

Maya Angelou

Here are some students' thoughts as they read each line of the poem:

Think on Paper for "Still I Rise"

You could put me in history books as being bad or lies about things I do as bad, but she'll rise.

You may hurt me, but only if I let you. I shall rise because I won't let you hurt me.

You may call me names, physically abuse me, you may hate me because of my race, but I'll still rise.

Regardless of what history tells me I am or how bad I was, I'll prove you wrong.

I'll grow stronger and spread my thoughts to others.

Possibly meant that she'll rise and leave behind the nights when she was abused.

Future ahead of her is bright and she knows what she wants and how to achieve it.

She won't forget where she came from or her heritage or what her ancestors gave her, yet she'll take it with her and share it with others in hopes of preventing someone else's suffering.

Nicole Phillips

You may say your lies about me in the past.

Even though you drag me through the dirt, I'll come back.

No matter what you do to me, I'll be successful. (I'm not certain of what this part means.)

A black, beautiful person who keeps progressing and getting more powerful.

She's leaving behind all the negative things from her past.

She's reaching happiness and success.

She's using her intelligence, she's representing blacks.

Hubert Felton

She says she doesn't care what you say about her because she knows the truth.

You can't bring her down because she is determined to stay up.

You can say anything you want about me, but it won't hurt me.

She is saying just because her ethnic background has been done wrong, don't put it on her. She will stand up for the future.

She is open and has a lot of ideas. She will overcome all odds.

She has left behind all her troubles and worries and her abusive past and now she is rising to the top.

Leaving back her dark past and into a bright, sunny future.

Her ancestors gave her a gift of writing and now she is the dream of many slaves who couldn't become free.

She rose to the top!

Tamyra Terrell

Reading Selection 2: Procrastination

When a paper is assigned, do you find yourself saying, "Oh, I'll do that tomorrow" (or next week or next month)? Does putting off writing leave you scrambling at the last minute to get your paper finished? If this describes your behavior, you have a problem with procrastination. Monte (1990) offers advice on procrastination and writing.* Summarize his advice in a package paragraph.

Writing papers is the single college experience that yields to procrastination better than anything short of filing income taxes. Papers are frequently completed the night before they are due, and they show it. The student who does this also shows it—in wear and tear, bleary eyes, and an increased reluctance to do the next paper.

The reasons for procrastination are almost as varied as term paper topics, but they share a common underlying belief: putting off the task saves us from confronting the possibility of criticism, of not doing well, of

---

* From *Merlin: The Sorcerer's Guide to Survival in College* (pp. 123–124), by C. F. Monte, 1990, Belmont, CA: Wadsworth. Copyright 1990 by Wadsworth Publishing Co. Used by permission.

not being as adequate as we would like to believe. Here are some correctives:

- Believe that things don't happen until they do.
- Know that there is no more time than there is.
- Understand that intelligence is not related to perfection.
- Realize that personal limits don't excuse meeting realistic goals.
- Tell yourself the truth: Writing papers is hard. It's supposed to be. (pp. 123–124)

Reading Selection 3: Defining Plagiarism

What, exactly, is plagiarism? Try to write a definition. Then list some examples of student behavior that would be categorized as plagiarism.

Here is the *American Heritage Dictionary of the English Language* (Morris, 1980) definition for the word *plagiarize*: "to take and use as one's own the writings and ideas of another" (p. 1001). As you read the following selection on plagiarism, create a graphic organizer that shows the structure of the piece of writing.

Why Shouldn't You Plagiarize?

Don't. Ever.

Deliberate plagiarism is stealing and lying combined. Everyone knows it is wrong. It cheats the student of his or her education, it robs the person whose words or ideas are taken, and it deceives the teacher who assigned the work in good faith. (Monte, 1990, p. 124)

In college, two kinds of plagiarism should be avoided at all costs. One is to steal words and ideas from published sources such as books and journals. The other is to borrow or buy words from someone else, usually another student. Both of these practices are so unethical that they usually result in an automatic F for an assignment or even an entire course. In the case of blatant forms of plagiarism, students can be dismissed from college or lose their financial aid. Clearly, plagiarism is a serious matter.

How to Avoid Plagiarism

Most of the term papers you write in college are intended to help you survey what various experts have written, report on their words and ideas clearly, synthesize or weave together all of the material you have read, and, perhaps most importantly, document every source that you quoted or consulted.

In order to understand plagiarism, you must first understand the following terms:

References—any material that you refer to in preparing your papers

Citation—the act of giving credit to those whose words and ideas you are using and fully documenting the sources of that information

Paraphrase—to put an idea into your own words, to restate it yet remain faithful to the original

Monte (1990) offers the following guidelines:*

Never take the exact words of another, no matter how brief, and present them as your own. Indicate that these words originate from another source with quotation marks, the author's name, the publication date, the source of the material, and the page number on which it appears. (See the end of this chapter for specific referencing styles and check the stylebook required by your professor.)

Never use exact ideas of another person and expressed in your own words without indicating the source. You must give others credit for their ideas.

Whenever you are in doubt about whether to cite a reference, it is better to err on the side of giving too much credit.

Unless an idea has been so succinctly and beautifully stated that it would ruin it, paraphrase it and give credit to the original source. It is better evidence of your mastery of the subject matter to be able to express it in your own words than to collect quotation after quotation, even when they are appropriately cited. (pp. 125–126)

Reading Selection 4: Exercises on Purposes for Writing

Exercise for Summarizing

The following material appeared in a publication for college faculty (*On Campus*, 1992).* Summarize the main ideas in writing.

Students Tell What Works

When the academic going gets tough, the best watchwords for students to live by are "God helps those who help themselves."

To get the most value for their college time, says a Harvard researcher, students should be encouraged to work on their academic relationships with both their professors and their peers. The researcher, Richard Light, a professor in the Harvard Graduate School of Education, has been studying ways "to help students make the most of their few precious years at college."

As part of the Harvard Assessment Seminars, Light enlisted the participation of over 100 faculty at 24 institutions who interviewed close to 600 students. Their goal: to have students report on what has worked best for them to improve their learning.

The findings, reports Light, "carry several surprises." The clearest one is "that students who grow the most academically and who are happiest are those who organize their time to include interpersonal activities with faculty members or with fellow students built around substantive, academic work." Students who go to the trouble to seek out and meet regularly with peers in study groups learn more. Faculty should encourage such interactions.

Another finding Light found surprising was how deeply students care about their writing skills. The most successful students also used study groups to critique each other's work. The students also reported that being forced to write many short papers during the course of a semester, as opposed to one long one at the end, resulted in more time being spent absorbing the material.

Exercise for Comparing

Annie Dillard (1989) is one of the leading writers in America. In her best-selling book *The Writing Life*, she compares her struggle to control the writing of a book to lion taming.* As you read, *compare* by making a list of what these two tasks—lion taming and book writing—have in common.

I do not so much write a book as sit up with it, as with a dying friend. During visiting hours, I enter its room with dread and sympathy for its many disorders. I hold its hand and hope it will get better.

This tender relationship can change in a twinkling. If you skip a visit or two, a work in progress will turn on you.

A work in progress quickly becomes feral. It reverts to a wild state overnight. It is barely domesticated, a mustang on which you one day fastened a halter, but which now you cannot catch. It is a lion you cage in your study. As the work grows, it gets harder to control; it is a lion growing in strength. You must visit it every day and reassert your mastery over it. If you skip a day, you are, quite rightly, afraid to open the door to its room. You enter its room with bravura, holding a chair at the thing and shouting, "Simba!" (p. 52)

Exercise for Evaluating or Critiquing

To *evaluate* or *critique* means to determine the quality of the thinking behind a statement or a line of reasoning. Read "A Daughter's Inheritance" (Rath,

---

1995).* Rather than focusing on agreeing or disagreeing, make a list of the points that the author makes in her essay. Then list the specific examples she uses to support her ideas.

This essay was written by a 12th grader at El Cerrito (Calif.) High School in a composition class taught by Joan Cone. Cone encourages her students to explore issues of cultural diversity, stereotyping, and social responsibility by writing about their own lives. In this piece, Kate Rath reflects on her experience as the daughter of a gay man.

Explaining my father is impossible. I'm flooded with images of him: picking up objects with his toes, tickling me with his beard when he kisses me goodnight, writing me a note every morning, wishing me a good day or good luck on a test, attending Back-to-School Night and taking notes avidly, laughing when he is on the phone with my sister, calling for another garlicky dinner, dancing with me at our yearly Christmas get-together, swimming with me at the pool, giving me great bear hugs when I need them. This is my father. But for some people the fact that he is also gay overshadows this picture and keeps them from seeing him as a whole.

I have a weak spot, and it runs a straight course into the middle of my soul. I cannot take hearing another negative thing about gay people. When I do I become completely mute; I cannot speak. I just sit back and listen with agony.

First it was my grandparents (my father's parents) who told my sister and me that we should go to church so that we would not end up like my father. I knew they were not referring to his becoming a doctor and successfully raising two daughters. No, they were worried that we might also become gay. Their reaction reflected society's views. They were scared, and they reacted the only way they knew how. Shortly after the shock wore off, my grandparents were supportive of my father because he was their son and they loved him above all else.

Then it was other people who looked into our lives and made rash judgments. At a peace march during the Gulf War, a group of homosexual marchers were confronted by people with megaphones shouting that "all of the fags" were going to hell.

I often worry about my dad's safety because I know that many people out there judge him before they get to know him. Homophobia is accepted in our schools and in our community. Anyone can call another person a "fag" or a "dyke" with impunity.

Some people say they accept gays but still believe gays should not be allowed to raise their own children. My dad has been a better father to me than many of my friends' straight fathers who don't care about them. My father has been a surrogate parent for some of my friends who have grown up without one. My dad is the only one in my family who, while he is a doctor, still found the time to go to watercolor class and to sit down with me to review the SATs. I love that within my dad there is a warmth and an inner strength that makes me feel loved.

Above all, my father really believes in me. He supported me when I said I wanted to earn enough money to go to Europe. He ignored the hours I tied up the phone while I was the precinct captain for the Clinton/Gore campaign—in fact, he encouraged me in my activism. In the 9th grade when I asked my father how we could become more active in the community, he believed I was serious. I have been delivering meals to AIDS patients ever since.

One time I was having a pleasant conversation with a woman I met, and I mentioned that my dad was gay. She started telling me that my dad had a disease like drug dealers. She went on to tell me that the government should "take care" of people who are "that way." I was only 10.

I have heard my dad referred to as "that way" countless times. I guess that means the way of the gay person. I wish someone would tell me what being "that way" is all about because, in my opinion, it says more about the limits of their own vision than anything about gay people.

My dad is a doctor. He takes care of people in the emergency room regardless of color, religion, or sexual orientation. I have learned from him that it is important to see the whole picture. The people who refer to homosexuals as "that way" are keeping themselves from seeing the world around them. By categorizing gays and people who are not like them as "others," they ostracize a vital part of our community and our world.

I have learned in my life how important it is to educate ourselves so we can stop putting people into separate categories. College excites me for that very reason. I want to learn about different worlds, different cultures, and expand my knowledge so I can really help to improve this world for people who have been categorized as the "others."

Even though my father is comfortable with who he is, when he laughs I am aware of the pain that is in the background. I am aware of my hurt and my anger, and I remember my pride. I need to keep those memories so I will never have to hide from what I feel is right. (pp. 62–63)

Exercise for Taking a Position, Arguing, Defending, or Supporting

When an author takes a position, argues, defends, or supports, it means the writer approaches a writing task as if in a debate, adopts a particular point of view, and then moves beyond pure opinion by providing specific details and evidence to support that particular perspective. Read Shipman's (1994) "Fac-

---

* From "A Daughter's Inheritance," by K. Rath, 1995, *Teaching Tolerance, 4*, pp. 62–63. Copyright 1995 by *Teaching Tolerance*. Reprinted by permission.

ing Racial Differences Together."* Highlight every piece of evidence that she gives to support her thesis that we must begin to take a less emotional and more logical approach when considering the issue of race.

The horrors of racism are on the rise once again. Almost daily, the newspapers tell of new viciousness abroad or in the streets of our cities by people who have conceived and acted upon a deep distrust and dislike of those who are different from themselves. We did not defeat racism with the victory over Hitler and Nazism, nor have we banished it with equal-opportunity laws. Racism is a plague that continues to flourish, poisoning too many interactions and shredding too many communities to be ignored.

Because the study of racial differences is controversial and fraught with possibilities for misuse, scholars have for too long avoided—or been forced to abandon—research projects that might pinpoint racial distinctions. Yet identifying such distinctions could well have implications for better treatment of diseases, for more effective teaching practices, and above all, for the more peaceful integration of different peoples into productive societies.

On the face of it, *race* is a simple, benign-enough concept: a biological subspecies or a regional variant of our own species, *Homo sapiens*. Yet races are not separate genetic entities. While humans in Oslo, Lagos, and Beijing look different from one another, races continue to interbreed enthusiastically wherever they meet, thus insuring the genetic unity of our species. Most human populations today are the result of a delightful and thorough admixture of genes from many different groups.

Even those with strong ethnic identities are often a genetic mixture, including the erroneously labeled "race" of African Americans. According to research by the Stanford University geneticist Luigi Cavalli-Sforza, American blacks on average derive 30% of their genes from Caucasoid sources, the legacy of interbreeding that began in the days of slavery and has continued since. Does this mean that "African American" is not a valid group with which to identify? Not at all. But it does mean that African Americans are not a race, nor are Chinese, Serbians, or Hutus. Races are large, statistical entities whose composition varies with each new birth or death. Races are always fuzzy around the margins.

. . . From a biological perspective, the genetic variability among humans is trivial; after all, we share 99% of our genes with chimpanzees. And yet this mild genetic divergence is not wholly insignificant, for it arose in part as a means of adapting to different environments. Some of the genetic distinctiveness of different regional populations also arose by simple, random chance: the flukes of survival and reproduction that, in small populations, can change a rare gene into a common one in a few generations.

A combination of processes thus gave rise to the modern races, which must at the very least include Mongoloids, Caucasoids, Negroids, and Australoids: the native peoples of Asia, Europe, Africa, and Australia respectively.

To what extent is racism, too, a part of our heritage? The first populations of anatomically modern humans appeared between 100,000 and 200,000 years ago, about the same time that the first objects appeared that suggest an awareness of group identity. Some of these "identifiers" are portable art objects, such as bones engraved with complex geometric designs, which show regional variations in style and convention. Other identifiers include jewelry and similar items of personal adornment that symbolized the wearer's allegiance to a particular ethnic group or family.

Why did such objects appear suddenly in the archaeological record? Surely it must have been partly because of an equally abrupt rise in group consciousness, one that I would attribute to an increasing frequency of encounters with strangers. Some archaeological sites of this period, according to Margaret Conkey of the University of California at Berkeley, are of unprecedented size and contain objects made of raw materials gathered from a variety of surrounding regions.

Ms. Conkey calls these "aggregation sites" and argues that they are evidence of periodic gatherings of small, usually scattered, groups of people. For the first time, people apparently were meeting groups from beyond their local area with some regularity, probably to exchange information and find potential mates. Predictably, these encounters solidified people's identification with their own group, in the same way that colonials in foreign lands later would cling to the ways of their native countries.

This need to identify with a group is surely among the most basic and ancient human instincts. And it is in this instinct that racism is anchored, for racism is little more than a strong identification with one group, combined with fear and dislike of all others. Typically, the fear and dislike are fueled by unfavorable stereotypes, falsehoods, and half-truths, which serve to reinforce groups' boundaries. Is racism then an *inevitable* consequence of human variability? I think not. I believe that accepting racism is tantamount to condemning our species to misery and extinction. If we refuse to accept racism, what can we do to eliminate it?

The first step is to make a conscious attempt to broaden our group identity, uncoupling our need to belong from the dangerous temptation to hate others. Let our need for allegiance allow us to embrace a wider group than that narrow category "just like me." Whether we like it or not, we are irrevocably part of a broader community: a school, a state, a nation, a world.

The second step is to agree to investigate our differences and to do so honestly and rigorously. This is a task requiring great courage and broad participation by members of all groups in question. Ignorance and fear divide; the only potent weapon against them is knowledge.

---

* From "Facing Racial Differences Together," by P. Shipman, 1994, in *The Chronicle of Higher Education, 40,* pp. B1–B3. Copyright 1994 by P. Shipman. Reprinted by permission.

. . . My prescription is hard to swallow, but we must try. We might start by discussing our problems and differences openly, by damping down our fears so that we can listen to other points of view, and by including members of all groups in the planning and execution of investigations into racial differences.

Such investigations must be recorded with the utmost care and thoughtfulness. Above all, they must be carried out in an atmosphere in which we—the inclusive We—all agree that we will face the truth together. This means protecting and honoring the legal equality and moral worth of all races, *of all humans,* by every means possible. We have only one joint fate, and we must create it together.

Like a child growing to maturity, we must discover our gifts for this activity and handicaps in that. Knowledge and acceptance of self are integral, *essential,* parts of growing up. And the exploration of our differences will also reaffirm our vast similarities.

We must also recognize that although genetic and biological endowments surely vary, the fulfillment of individuals' potential is even more variable. A child with "tall" genes, if malnourished, will nonetheless be stunted; a child blessed with the eye of an artist will never blossom if the hand is not trained as well. A potential criminal, if such exists, will never terrorize or hurt if that potential is turned aside by altered circumstances and new opportunities for a productive life.

The responsibility for whether or not people live up to their potential is both collective and individual. We are collectively responsible for the appalling conditions under which so many people live, for the opportunities not offered, for the training never made available. We must acknowledge and redress these failures collectively. But we are also deeply and individually responsible for our own failures of potential: for the practice skipped, for the basic facts or skills not memorized and reinforced, for the opportunities that would have taken too much hard work to seize.

We must examine ourselves and accept responsibility for our behaviors, as does the growing child, or face the awful prospects of never reaching any sort of maturity.

As a species, it is time to grow up. (pp. B1–B3)

Exercise for Contrasting

Write the word *mistakes* in the middle of a piece of paper. Just think about the word for a moment and your ideas about it. Then cluster your thoughts into three categories: definitions or synonyms for the word *mistakes*, feelings that you associate with the word, and experiences you have had with mistakes.

Definitions:

Feelings:

Experiences:

Now read the following essay by W. A. Mathieu (1991), a famous musician, on how he looks at mistakes made by musicians.* As you read, highlight the key points in the passage.

We ordinarily use mistakes to fuel self-denial, as a proof of our incompetence. But since mistakes are inevitable, try turning them instead to your best advantage. Embrace your mistakes; accept the self who makes them. This is the creative response, one that allows music to find its true shape inside you.

Mistakes are your best friends. They bring a message. They tell you what to do next and light the way. They come about because you have not understood something, or have learned something incompletely. They tell you that you are moving too fast or looking in the wrong direction.

Mistakes might be detailed instructions on how to take apart and rewire physical motions, muscle by muscle. Or they might show you where you have not heard clearly, where you have to open up to the music and listen again in a new way. Examine a mistake as if you had found a rare stone. Run over the edges of it with your tongue. Peer inside the cracks of it. Hold it up to the sun, turning it a little this way and that. When you have learned what you can from it, toss it away casually, as if you didn't expect to see it again. If it shows up again later, be patient and polite and make a new accommodation. A mistake knows when it isn't needed and eventually will leave for good.

The goal is not to make music free of mistakes. The goal is to be complete in learning, and to grow well. (p. 92)

Exercise for Applying

Remember that the word *apply* means to use what you know or have read in one situation to interpret another. Students are often directed on an essay test, for example, to "use what you have been learning in this class" or "apply your readings" when responding to the question.

Now that you have read the passage on mistakes, try *applying* Mathieu's ideas to a different kind of mistake that has been troublesome for you. It could be a mistake in sports, school, or a social situation, for example. Remember that when you *apply,* you are taking his recommendations and *using* them in another situation. In other words, how could you use his advice in dealing with this other type of mistake?

* From *The Listening Book: Discovering Your Own Music* (p. 92) by W. A. Mathieu. Copyright © 1991. Reprinted by arrangement with Shambhala Publications, Inc., 300 Massachusetts Avenue, Boston, MA 02115.

Now add this section to your chart:

His perspective:

His advice:

His feelings:

References

Angelou, M. (1978). *And still I rise*. New York: Random House.

Angelou, M. (1983). *I know why the caged bird sings.* New York: Random House.

Ashton-Jones, E., & Thomas, D. K. (1990). Composition, collaboration, and women's ways of knowing: A conversation with Mary Belenky. *Journal of Advanced Composition, 10*(2), 275–292.

Banks, C., McCarthy, M., & Rasool, J. (1993). *Read and succeed*. Belmont, CA: Wadsworth.

Bloom, L. Z. (1991). Finding a family, finding a voice: A writing teacher teaches writing teachers. In M. Schwartz (Ed.), *Writer's craft, teacher's art: Teaching what we know* (pp. 55–67). Portsmouth, NH: Boynton/Cook.

Clark, W. I. (1975). How to completely individualize a writing program. *English Journal, 64*(4), 66–69.

Dillard, A. (1989). *The writing life*. New York: Harper-Collins.

Englert, C., & Raphael, T. (1989). Developing successful writers through cognitive strategy instruction. In J. Brophy (Ed.), *Advances in research on teaching* (pp. 105–151). Greenwich, CT: JAI.

Gardner, J. N., & Jewler, A. J. (1992). *Your college experience: Strategies for success*. Belmont, CA: Wadsworth.

Glaze, B. (1987). Learning logs. In Virginia Department of Education, *Plain talk about learning and writing across the curriculum* (pp. 149–154). Fairfax: Commonwealth of Virginia.

Kirszner, L. G., & Mandell, S. R. (1992). *The Holt handbook*. Orlando, FL: Holt, Rinehart & Winston.

Mathieu, W. A. (1991). *The listening book: Discovering your own music*. Boston: Shambhala.

Monte, C. F. (1990). *Merlin: The sorcerer's guide to survival in college*. Belmont, CA: Wadsworth.

Morris, W. (Ed.). (1980). *The American heritage dictionary of the English language*. Boston: Houghton Mifflin.

Murray, D. M. (1990). *Shoptalk: Learning to write with writers*. Portsmouth, NH: Boynton/Cook Heinemann.

On Campus. (March/April 1992). [Untitled], *11*(5).

Rico, G. (1991). Writer: Personal patterns in chaos. In M. Schwartz (Ed.), *Writer's craft, teacher's art: Teaching what we know* (pp. 3–20). Portsmouth, NH: Boynton/Cook.

Shipman, P. (1994, August 3). Facing racial differences together. *The Chronicle of Higher Education, 40*(48), B1–B3.

Temple, C., & Gillet, J. W. (1984). *Language arts: Learning processes and teaching practices*. Boston: Little, Brown.

Wade, S. E. (1990). Using think alouds to assess comprehension. *The Reading Teacher, 43*, 442–451.

Zinsser, W. (1990). *On writing well: An informal guide to writing nonfiction* (4th ed.). New York: Harper & Row.

CHAPTER APPENDIX

Reference Lists and In-Text Citations

REFERENCE LISTS

These examples show you how to type the bibliography or reference list that goes at the end of your paper.

Books

American Psychological Association (APA) Style
Used in most psychology and education publications.
Zinsser, W. K. (1990). *On writing well: An informal guide to writing nonfiction* (4th ed.). New York: Harper & Row.
Notice that this style is unique in that it does not use the author's first name, puts the date and edition information in parentheses, capitalizes only the first word in the title and after the colon, and indents each entry like a paragraph.

Modern Language Association (MLA) Style
Used in most English and composition publications.
Zinsser, William. *On Writing Well: An Informal Guide to Writing Nonfiction.* 4th ed. New York: Harper & Row, 1990.
Notice that this style puts the date last, uses full names, and indents the second line.

Chicago Manual of Style (CMS)
(also called University of Chicago Style or Turabian)
Used in general courses.
Zinsser, William K. *On Writing Well: An Informal Guide to Writing Nonfiction,* 4th ed. New York: Harper & Row, 1990.

Articles

Notice the differences in indentation, capitalization, use of quotation marks, ways of reporting page numbers. Only the *Chicago Manual of Style* requires the name of the month as well as the volume number.

APA Style
Wade, S. E. (1990). Using think alouds to assess comprehension. *The Reading Teacher, 43*(7), 442–451.

MLA Style
Wade, Suzanne E. "Using Think Alouds to Assess Comprehension." *The Reading Teacher 43* (1990): 442–51.

CMS
Wade, Suzanne. "Using Think Alouds to Assess Comprehension." *The Reading Teacher* 43 (March, 1990): 442–451.

IN-TEXT CITATIONS

When you refer to the source of the information that you consulted in the body of your paper, this is called in-text citation.

APA Style

Note that the date always follows the author's name and that the page number is required for direct quotations.

Examples of APA In-Text Citations

Paraphrasing: Anyone who can think clearly can write clearly (Zinsser, 1990).

Direct quotation: As Zinsser (1990) has pointed out, "Clear thinking becomes clear writing: one can't exist without the other" (p. 9).

MLA Style

Page numbers are used with paraphrasing *and* direct quotations.

Examples of MLA In-Text Citations

Paraphrasing: Anyone who can think clearly can write clearly (Zinsser p. 9).

Direct quotation: As Zinsser says, "Clear thinking becomes clear writing: one can't exist without the other" (9).

CMS

Note that this style uses footnotes or endnotes. References are numbered sequentially in the order in which they appear in the text of the paper. Any additional reference to a work already cited lists the author's last name and the page number rather than the entire reference.

Examples of CMS In-Text Citations

Paraphrasing: Anyone who can think clearly can write clearly.[1]

Direct quotation: In 1990, Zinsser said, "Clear thinking becomes clear writing: one can't exist without the other" (p. 9).

Footnote or Endnote: [1]William K. Zinsser, *On Writing Well: An Informal Guide to Writing Nonfiction* (New York: Harper & Row, 1990), 9.

5. If attending college had no effect on earnings, how many students would still attend college?
   a. half of all students
   b. one in three students
   c. four out of five students
   d. two-thirds of students
   e. three-quarters of students
   f. three out of five students

College Quiz Answers

1. b. Approximately 45% of American high schoolers begin college study.

2. d. Slightly over two-thirds of students find their classes engaging.

3. c. Four out of five college students are satisfied or very satisfied with their present college.

4. a. Half the students believe that the major contribution of a college education is the positive effect on their earning potential.

5. f. Three out of five would go to college even if it had little effect on their earning power.

Questions for Discussion

1. What might be some common characteristics of beginning college students?

2. What makes a class (high school or college) interesting for a student?

3. What, in your opinion, is the single biggest factor in selecting a college?

4. Fifty percent of the students surveyed believed that increased earning power was the major contribution of a college education. What other contributions does a college education provide?

5. What are your personal reasons for attending college?

Learning in High School

Think back to high school and describe several situations in which learning was really enjoyable. How did this experience challenge you? Why do you think you felt good about it? Be prepared to discuss your response in class. Make a chart like the one below.

Enjoyable Learning Experience	Reason

What do your learning experiences and reasons reveal about you as a learner?

Building Interest

Try to answer the questions about building interest in a subject.* Compare your answers with those produced by your small-group members.

1. It can be argued that some topics are so boring that there is just no way to become interested in them. Which subjects do you find most boring and why? How might you approach these subjects to make them at least tolerable for you?

2. Students tend to do well in courses that interest them. Students are generally interested in courses in which they do well. Which comes first, interest or success? What is the relationship between interest and doing well?

3. Choose a topic or course that you find or found very interesting. When you meet with your group, try to explain why it is interesting. Try to convince the other members of your group that there is something interesting about it even though others may disagree.

---

* From *The College Student: Reading and Study Skills* (4th ed.), by E. Spargo, 1994, Providence, RI: Jamestown. Copyright © 1994 by Jamestown Publishers, Providence, RI. Adapted by permission.

4. Some college faculty are well-known scholars and experts in the field but not very exciting to listen to in class. How can you benefit most from that type of professor?

5. Some professors conduct very interesting or amusing classes but convey very little information. Then, at exam time, you find yourself unprepared. How can you best cope with this situation and assure yourself of a good grade?

6. Some faculty contend that it is not their responsibility to make the subject interesting. They call this "spoon-feeding" students who are supposed to be adults and future professionals. What is your opinion of that attitude? Whose responsibility is it to make a class interesting? Is it possible that students and teachers might share in this responsibility?

7. What processes can you use to build interest even when the subject seems dull?

Technology on Campus

Visit your college bookstore or other store that carries electronic equipment. What products did you see for sale? How might these products assist you as a college student, or later, in your career?

Now visit the library, an office, or a laboratory, such as the writing lab or psychology lab on campus. Make a list of the hardware and software you see in use.

Compile your list with the lists created by other class members. What categories emerge? Design a graph to show your results. What are the major ways in which technology supports the operations of the institution where you are studying?

Internet Access to Professional Networks

Use the Internet to locate the following information about your major or a major that you are considering:

1. What are some of the major professional organizations in your field? Visit their Web sites and print out information about the purpose and goals of the group.

2. Choose a controversial topic that is being discussed in your field currently. Search for a bibliography on the topic and print out the abstracts of several articles. Select and read two articles, one that argues each side of the controversy. Present this information to the class.

Interview: Technology's Influence on Professional Practice

With the dawning of what is being called the "Information Age," technology is touching every profession. Through technology such as the personal computer, fax machines, modems, e-mail, and the Internet, professionals are more interconnected than ever before. To find out more about how technology has changed the way people work, interview a friend or relative who has been involved in the same type of work for at least 10 years. Ask him or her the following questions:

1. What technological changes have taken place in your profession? How has technology altered your job responsibilities?

2. In what ways has your job performance been aided by technology? What problems were encountered?

3. If technology continues to grow at the same rate, what do you predict for the future in your career?

Be prepared to share your responses with the class.

Corresponding via E-mail

Most people find it exciting to turn on the computer and find that there are messages waiting and people awaiting a response. With the advent of e-mail and the World Wide Web, you can transmit messages around the world in just a few seconds. Demonstrate your ability to use e-mail by performing one of the following tasks:

- Compose a letter to a friend or relative describing your college experiences thus far. Copy yourself on the message so that you can return to your letter in the future and reminisce about your earliest days of college life.

- Make contact with your academic adviser or an instructor for a class. Print out a copy of your exchange with your professor or adviser.

- Join a discussion group and participate in the discussion. Print out a copy of your contribution to the dialogue.

Exploring a School's or Employer's Web Site

As you begin to know the other students in your class, it is interesting to share information about your school or employer with others. Work in groups of 2 or 3 and search the Internet for these Web sites. A typical high school Web site includes pictures of some of the staff, sports scores, and information about various activities. You may want to investigate the Web page for the college, university, department, or major you are considering as well. Try to find out such things as the different programs that are offered, who teaches in the program, the types of jobs that graduates pursue, and what innovative projects are underway. An employer's Web site often describes the organization's purpose, achievements, and current projects. Compare/contrast the sites that you visited. Which were more effective? Why?

Assessing Personal Strengths

Think about the personal or professional skills, abilities, and interests that you have acquired over the years. What talents do you have? Do you have strong athletic tendencies? Are you very skilled in a particular craft? Do you know more than the average student about computers? Brainstorm a list of specific examples. For instance, sports may have taught you teamwork; crafts, persistence; computers, problem solving. In the chart here, describe some skills or interests you have developed. Explain how these skills will be useful during your college career. Then reflect on how these skills will enhance your professional or personal life after you graduate.

Skill, Ability or Interest

Usefulness During College

Usefulness After College

Managing Your Time

This activity will require you to work with a partner and to complete various tasks associated with a selected role. The roles include a time management expert and a noted reporter. The reporter's task will be to develop a list of questions that students frequently ask about time management, conduct an interview with the expert, take notes, and present a report to the class on the findings. The time management expert must have a thorough knowledge of the key points presented in Chapter 3 as evidenced by his or her ability to adequately answer the questions posed by the reporter. The expert must also be present when the findings are reported to the class. The expert must be prepared to answer any of the reporter's follow-up questions as well as any audience questions that may be asked.

Please note: Your instructor may choose to assign you and your partner to a specific area discussed in Chapter 3 such as time, study, stress, organizational systems, importance of goals, and so forth. You will have to prepare accordingly by focusing on that particular aspect of the chapter as well as your existing knowledge of the topic. Some sample questions are provided here to help you get started, but you are encouraged to develop more questions on your own, based on the material from the chapter.

Sample Questions

1. As a new college student, how do I determine how much time I need to spend studying each course?

2. How do people find time to study, work, take care of family responsibilities, and still enjoy life?

3. What, in your opinion, is the most effective time management technique currently being used?

4. What advice can you offer about making and keeping a schedule?

5. How can someone determine whether he or she is spending time wisely?

Know Your Instructor

Think about one of your favorite teachers for a minute. Can you remember any of his or her personality characteristics? For example, what kinds of verbal and nonverbal signals did he or she use when trying to make a point? Knowing your instructor's characteristics can be of great value to you because it helps you realize when an instructor is making an important point—a point worth writing down in your notebook. Provide an example for each category listed:

Movement

Change in voice tempo

Change in voice volume

Writing on the chalkboard

Repetition

Use of key words or phrases (verbal cues)

Pausing

Handouts

Types of tests

Can you think of other cues or signals teachers use that would enable you to identify important information more readily?

Activities and Support Services on Campus

Part of adapting to college life is understanding what there is to do on campus and where to go when you need help.

Review a copy of your college newspaper, and, with a partner, count the number of activities taking place on campus on a particular night or weekend. What did you find? Have you taken advantage of any of these types of activities? You and your partner may decide to attend one of these activities together and report your learning experiences to the class.

Now look at a copy of the telephone directory and undergraduate student handbook. What support services are available on campus? Figure out where you would go if:

you had a serious illness

you lost your class schedule

your student ID card was stolen

you were in danger of failing a course

you were depressed or anxious about a family crisis

you discovered an error on your tuition bill

you wanted to change your major

ACTIVITY
14

How to Develop Positive Relationships With Instructors

Brown and Holtzman (1987) offer these suggestions:

- Form your own opinion about your professors.
- Be in your seat when class starts.
- Be alert and ready to be attentive in class.
- Prepare your assignments as neatly and accurately as possible.
- Accept and learn from the constructive criticism offered by your professors.
- Work extra hard to compensate if you find you dislike one of your professors.
- Avoid excuses and flattery when asking your professors for help.

1. **Form your own opinions about instructors.** Do not let other students' opinions cause you to prejudge a teacher. The instructor in question may have demanded more effort than some students were willing to expend. Remember, as an active learner, *you* are responsible for finding value in all of your learning experiences.

2. **Be in your seat ready to begin when class starts.** Being late for class is not looked upon favorably, especially if it happens regularly. Most instructors feel that they have only a short span of time, one quarter or one semester, to convey their knowledge and understandings to you. Many would love to have extra time to expound on students' ideas and extend the learning activities. Since this is not possible, they feel each minute of class is valuable. Remember, you do not want it to look as though you do not feel the course is valuable.

3. **Be alert and ready to be attentive in class.** Instructors have little patience for helping students do well in their classes if the students are lethargic, look bored, talk to a friend all during class, or cannot manage to stay awake. These behaviors are distracting. Professors must concentrate fully on what they are communicating, both verbally and nonverbally. When one student is falling asleep, for example, the instructor cannot help taking it personally while wondering, "What am I doing wrong?" This

---

* From *A Guide to College Survival* by W. F. Brown and W. H. Holtzman, 1987, Iowa City: American College Testing Program. Adapted with permission.

distraction can force the instructor to lose his or her train of thought, making the learning experience less effective for the whole class. Get enough rest so that staying alert is not a problem.

4. **Prepare your written assignments as neatly and accurately as possible.** Do not let messy work give the impression that you do not care. Most instructors will either lower your grade or make you redo the assignment if it is not legible or complete. Use the writing and computing centers to help you if necessary. Remember, your work is a direct reflection on you.

5. **Accept and learn from constructive criticism offered by your instructors.** Do not take such criticisms personally. Rather, look at the suggestions as ways to improve your learning and mastery of the subject matter. If your work was perfect and there was not room for improvement, there would not be room for growth and learning. Constructive criticism is a part of every job, including your job as a college student.

6. **Work extra hard to compensate if you find you dislike one of your instructors.** Do not complain, act aloof, or show hostility, particularly in the classroom or a public place. Going to see that person during office hours may be a way to break down some of the barriers and get to know that person as an individual. You may find the professor to be a much different person when he or she is talking to an individual student who has made a special effort to get additional information outside of class. Remember to treat people respectfully, even if you do not agree with some of their behaviors. This courtesy is essential after you graduate, too.

7. **Avoid excuses and flattery when asking faculty for help.** Instructors are reluctant to devote extra time to students who try to manipulate them through flattery. Being straightforward with them and acknowledging your own weaknesses is a much better approach. Remember, a record of being a conscientious, hardworking student is the best way to assure that extra assistance will be offered when needed.

Now reflect on your behaviors. Which of these characteristics may be problematic for you?

Instructor Interview on Role Models and Mentors

Many college students find it helpful to choose a role model or a mentor. Someone with characteristics that we admire can serve as a role model. It is not necessary to know a role model personally, only to have the opportunity to observe that person. A mentor, on the other hand, is someone you know whom you respect and admire and is also in a position to help you achieve your goals. He or she can introduce you to useful networks where you can meet and get to know people who may be important when it is time to look for a job. Choosing someone you admire as a role model or mentor can be beneficial. Cypert (1993) believes "that role models provide shortcuts that allow us to avoid costly, time-consuming mistakes and focus our attention on proven techniques" (p. 136). A useful analogy is finding your way from one destination to another on a complex route. Most of us would rather follow someone else rather than try to make our way alone through a series of unpredictable twists and turns. A mentor is like that person whose path we follow.

Work in small groups to develop interview questions that can be posed to your instructor, adviser, or tutor. Some questions to get you started are:

1. Who was your role model or mentor as an undergraduate? as a graduate student? in your current job?

2. What characteristics do you look for in a role model or mentor?

3. What do you think the role model or mentor saw in you that made him or her willing to make an investment of time and energy into your career?

4. In what specific ways did these individuals contribute to your professional development?

Keeping Track of Extracurricular Activities

Participating in extracurricular activities, or activities on campus that are not directly related to your particular curriculum, does more than just expand your learning. It can provide you with valuable experience to prepare you for your future career.

Many times when college seniors are putting together their résumés and preparing for interviews, they have difficulty remembering the organizations and activities with which they have been involved. An employer may be looking for particular types of work experience, and keeping a record of what you have done gives you a valuable reference. Use the following form to keep track of the professional and service activities in which you participate.

Name _____
Academic Year _____

Type of Event	Date	Your Involvement	
Organization	**Position Held**	**Events**	**Dates of Events**

Sample Extracurricular Activity Record Sheet for a Sophomore Music Major

Name *Robin Kan*
Academic Year *1999–2000*

Type of Event	Date	Involvement
March of Dimes Walk-a-Thon	9/23	Participant—raised $100.00
"Musicfest"	10/19	Usher
Campus Holiday Celebration	12/18	Pianist
"Oklahoma"	5/27-5/29	Background singer

Organization	Position Held	Event	Date of Event
Student Senate M.U.S.I.C. Club M.U.S.I.C. Club Outing Society Member	Senator Co-chair Chairperson/Publicity	Annual dance	2/24

The Successful Reader

Do you consider yourself a successful reader? What are the characteristics of an efficient reader? What factors interfere with your ability to read and understand college material? In your small groups, complete the following activity. Begin by defining the word *reader*.

Reader:

List as many assets and barriers to reading that your group can think of for each of the categories identified here. Brainstorm possible solutions to the barriers. An example is provided in italics.

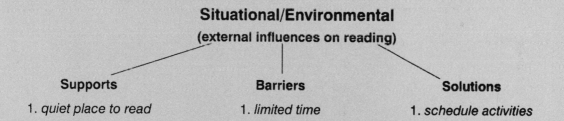

Situational/Environmental

(external influences on reading)

Supports	**Barriers**	**Solutions**
1. *quiet place to read*	1. *limited time*	1. *schedule activities*

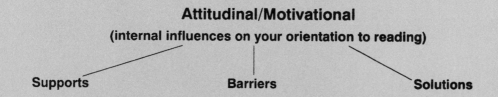

Attitudinal/Motivational

(internal influences on your orientation to reading)

Supports   **Barriers**   **Solutions**

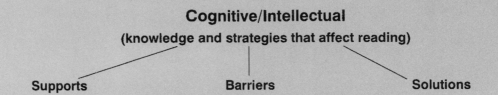

Cognitive/Intellectual

(knowledge and strategies that affect reading)

Supports   Barriers   Solutions

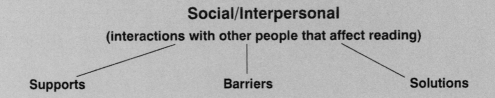

Social/Interpersonal

(interactions with other people that affect reading)

Supports   Barriers   Solutions

Recommending Reading

Have you ever been so excited about something you read that you could not wait to tell someone about it? Well, here is your chance to share that excitement with others as well as to learn about some great books and articles that you might enjoy reading.*

1. Select a book or article that you have read or that you are currently reading for pleasure. (Be sure that you will be comfortable recommending the selection to others and sharing the content.) If you are not currently reading a book for pleasure, try consulting the list of the top 10 books being read on college campuses in *The Chronicle of Higher Education* or at your campus bookstore.

2. Write a paragraph that describes the book or article and invites others to read it. Include the following information:
   a. Title
   b. Author's name (if you remember it)
   c. Short summary
   d. Personal reaction
   e. An invitation to read the selection

3. Share your paragraph with a partner or with members of a small group. Answer any questions they may have about the selection.

4. Revise your paragraph based on the questions raised and your classmates' feedback.

5. Use your paragraph as a guide for preparing a brief oral presentation on your selection.

6. As you are listening to the presentations, write down the titles and authors of those that you would like to read, and share, at a later date.

7. You may want to compile the class's five-star reading list, duplicate it, and distribute it in class.

Remember, the more you read, the better you will read!

---

* Adapted from *Reaching Adult Learners with Whole Language Strategies* (p. 99), by T. Kroeker and M. Henrichs, 1993, New York: Owen.

Reading Strategy Inventory

How do you handle reading difficulties? A skilled reader knows when comprehension breaks down and has a repertoire of "fix-up" strategies. This inventory will help you become more aware of what you do to build your understanding of what you read.* Circle *all* the responses that you think are effective.

1. What do you do if you encounter a word and do not know what it means?
   a. Use the words around it to figure it out.
   b. Use an outside source, such as a dictionary or expert.
   c. Temporarily ignore it and wait for clarification.
   d. Sound it out.

2. What do you do if you do not know what an entire sentence means?
   a. Read it again.
   b. Sound out all the difficult words.
   c. Think about the other sentences in the paragraph.
   d. Disregard it completely.

3. If you are reading technical material, what would you do to remember the important information you have read?
   a. Skip parts you do not understand.
   b. Ask yourself questions about the important ideas.
   c. Realize that you need to remember one point rather than another.
   d. Relate it to something you already know.

4. Before you start to read, what kind of plans do you make to help you read better?
   a. No specific plan is needed; just start reading toward completion of the assignment.
   b. Think about what you know about the subject.
   c. Think about why you are reading.
   d. Make sure the entire reading can be finished in as short a period of time as possible.

5. Why would you go back and read an entire passage over again?
   a. You did not understand it.
   b. You need to clarify a specific or supporting idea.
   c. It seemed important to remember.
   d. You tried to underline or summarize while studying.

---

* From "An Inventory to Pique Students' Metacognitive Awareness," by V. Miholic, *Journal of Reading*, 1994, *38*(2), 84–86. Copyright © 1994 by the International Reading Association. Adapted by permission.

6. Why did you not understand a particular sentence while reading?
   a. You may not have developed adequate links or associations for new words or concepts introduced in the sentence.
   b. The writer may not have conveyed the ideas clearly.
   c. Two sentences may purposely contradict each other.
   d. Finding meaning for the sentences needlessly slows down the reader.

7. As you read a textbook, what do you do?
   a. Adjust your pace to the difficulty of the material.
   b. Read at a constant, steady pace.
   c. Skip the parts you do not understand.
   d. Continually make predictions about what you are reading.

8. While you read, which of these are important?
   a. Recognizing when you know and do not know key ideas
   b. Realizing what it is that you know in relation to what is being read
   c. Accepting that confusing text is common and usually can be ignored
   d. Identifying different strategies that can be used to aid understanding

9. When you come across a confusing part of the text, what do you do?
   a. Keep on reading until the text is clarified.
   b. Read ahead and then look back if the text is still unclear.
   c. Skip those sections completely; they are usually not important.
   d. Check to see whether the ideas expressed are consistent with one another.

10. Which sentences are the most important in the chapter?
   a. Almost all of the sentences are important; otherwise they would not be there.
   b. The sentences that contain the important details or facts
   c. The sentences that are directly related to the main idea
   d. The ones that contain the most details

Reading Strategy Questionnaire

Answer the questions based on the techniques you currently use to improve your reading comprehension. You may have more than one answer to each question.*

1. What do you do when you encounter a word and do not know what it means?

2. What do you do if you do not know what an entire sentence means?

3. If you are reading technical material, what would you do to remember the important information you have read?

4. Before you start to read, what kind of plans do you make to help you read better?

5. Why would you go back and read an entire passage over again?

6. What are some reasons that might explain why you do not understand a particular sentence while reading?

7. What factors affect your pace or speed of reading?

8. How can knowing the main idea enable you to read more efficiently?

9. When you come across a part of the text that is confusing, what do you do?

10. Generally speaking, which sentences are the most important in the chapter?

Compare your answers with your group members'. Add any new strategies that you would like to try.

---

* From "An Inventory to Pique Students' Metacognitive Awareness," by V. Miholic, *Journal of Reading*, 1994, *38*(2), 84–86. Copyright © 1994 by the International Reading Association. Adapted by permission.

ACTIVITY

21

Interpreting the Great Quotations

Quotations are appreciated precisely because they say so much in so few words. As you read each quotation here, remember that your goal is to extract profound meaning from a sentence or two. This means that you have to go beyond literal meanings and consider the underlying message. Do not search for single-word answers or try to underline the correct answer. This strategy will not work. Instead, read the entire item and *think*. What is the message? What is the author's viewpoint, perspective, or purpose for making this statement?

Now, read each item and write down your own interpretation. If you cannot make much sense of it, at least write down a few thoughts/possibilities.

Next, meet with your group of four to six people to compare/contrast your answers and decide on the best interpretation. Write it on chart paper. It should be no more than a sentence or two at most. Then list the names of your group members on the chart paper and post it in the front of the room.

As a total group, we will compare your group's answers with the instructor's explanations.

Some Great Quotations

1. "That's what education means, to be able to do what you've never done before." —*Alice Freeman Palmer*

2. "The ultimate measure of a man is not where he stands in moments of comfort and convenience, but where he stands in times of challenge and controversy." —*Martin Luther King, Jr.*

3. "I do not believe that any peacock envies another peacock his tail because every peacock is persuaded that his own tail is the finest in the world. The consequence of this is that peacocks are peaceable birds." —*Bertrand Russell*

4. "As human beings our greatness lies not so much in being able to remake the world . . . as in being able to remake ourselves." —*Mohandas Gandhi*

5. "Illiteracy is *not* the *cause* of exclusion from the American Dream of the good life, but the *result.*" —*John Ogbu*

6. "Only those who dare to fail greatly can ever achieve greatly." —*Robert F. Kennedy*

7. "The longest absence is less perilous to love than the terrible trials of incessant proximity." —*Ouida*

8. "All cases are unique and very similar to others." —*T. S. Eliot*

9. "The philosophy of one century is the common sense of the next." —*Henry Ward Beecher*

10. "You have your brush, you have your colors, you paint paradise, then in you go." —*Nikos Karatzakis*

11. "The man who does not read good books has no advantage over the man who can't read them." — *Mark Twain*

12. "Self-development is a higher duty than self-sacrifice." —*Elizabeth Cady Stanton*

13. "If you treat an individual as he is, he will stay as he is, but if you treat him as if he were what he ought to be and could be, he will become what he ought to be and what he could be." —*Goethe*

14. "If the only tool you have is a hammer, you treat everything as if it were a nail." —*Abraham Maslow*

15. "When you cease to make a contribution you begin to die." —*Eleanor Roosevelt*

16. "Whoever gossips to you will gossip of you." —*Spanish proverb*

17. "Books give not wisdom where none was before. But where some is, there reading makes it more." —*Sir John Harrington*

18. "One doesn't discover new lands without consenting to lose sight of the shore for a very long time."—*Andre Gide*

19. "Settle one difficulty, and you keep a hundred others away." —*Chinese proverb*

20. "We need to restore the full meaning of that old word, duty. It is the other side of rights." —*Pearl S. Buck*

21. "We are our choices." —*Sartre*

Bring in some of your favorite quotations to share with the class.

Active Reading: The 3 × 3 Strategy

Reading is more than just deciphering words. It is a thinking process that can be conceptualized as three sequential stages: before reading, during reading, and after reading.

One recommended way for improving reading comprehension is called the 3 × 3 strategy.* To use this strategy you compose three key questions for each of the three reading stages:

Before reading—Focus on three things you already know about the topic or three things you want to know based on your preview of the selection.

During reading—Focus on three things that you are learning and put them in question form.

After reading—Ask three questions that are still unanswered.

Before reading, skim the article provided here called "Loneliness and the College Student: When Intimacy Is Lacking."† *Write three questions* in the space provided based on what you already know or what you would like to know about the topic.

Before-Reading Questions

1.

2.

3.

---

* Adapted from "3 × 3 Strategy," by T. Kroeker and M. Henrichs, in *Reaching Adult Learners with Whole Language Strategies* (p. 101), New York: Owen.

† From *Infancy, Childhood, and Adolescence: Development in Context* (pp. 480–481), by L. Steinberg and J. Belsky, 1991, New York: McGraw-Hill. Copyright © 1991. Reprinted by permission of McGraw-Hill, Inc.

Now read the article on loneliness. *During reading,* stop and *write three questions* that you can answer based on the information you have read. Use the space provided for your questions.

During-Reading Questions

1.

2.

3.

Loneliness and the College Student: When Intimacy Is Lacking

Late adolescence is one of the loneliest times of life. Adolescents need intimacy, but wanting independence too, many leave family and friends behind when they go to college. One study of UCLA students found than nearly half felt extremely lonely during their first months at a large, impersonal university where they knew virtually no one. Speaking with a researcher, two students expressed their feeling this way:

> *I do not feel my interests and ideals are the same as other people's. I get especially lonely when I realize that I am an isolated person, alone even in a group. It's depressing because I might always feel this way.*

> *This is a big impersonal school that treats people like numbers rather than people. . . . Here everybody cares about just one thing—grades. I like people. I like to be around them, and it was hard for me to realize that people don't really care for one another like high school, but for themselves and grades. (Cutrona, 1982, pp. 299, 303)*

All kinds of students were susceptible to these feelings of isolation, males as well as females, members of different ethnic groups, those living on campus as well as those living off.

For most UCLA students loneliness subsided by the end of the first year, but a sizeable number continued to feel lonely throughout their college years (Cutrona, 1982). Why couldn't they overcome their isolation and make some close friends? Part of the answer lies in the attitudes of these chronically lonely students. They did join clubs, strike up conversations, and go through the motions of meeting people, but they remained pessimistic about the chances of their social lives improving. Most became resigned to isolation, telling themselves that they didn't need friends or that their schoolwork was far more important. Ironically, these rationalizations probably increased their chances of staying lonely. To break out of a shell of isolation, a person apparently needs an optimistic outlook that things will get better, even in the bleakest of times.

In addition to a negative outlook, chronically lonely students may also be shyer than those who manage to make friends. Many adolescents suffer from shyness to some extent. In a study conducted at Stanford University, over 80 percent of 5,000 students surveyed admitted having a problem with shyness at some point in their lives, and 42 percent said that the problem still existed. For some of these young people the shyness is so acute that the security of a lonely room seems preferable to the pain of meeting new people.

Severe shyness is often related to a negative self-image, a feeling that you are not really a very attractive, interesting, or desirable companion. The problem is that with this negative self-image you are likely to behave in ways that promote the very social rejection you fear. "I'm so shy," said a 16-year-old girl named Tara, "that it's hard for me to look at another person, much less start up a conversation. Every time I try to talk with someone, especially if it's a guy, my hands start shaking, my mouth feels like it's full of cotton balls, and I blush like crazy" (Mackey, 1984). It is likely that Tara's awkwardness makes others feel uncomfortable around her, only adding to her negative self-image and isolation.

Psychologists offer several suggestions for overcoming shyness (Mackey, 1984):

- Learn and *use* friendly behaviors when meeting people. Instead of avoiding eye contact, defensively folding your arms, and mumbling a brief "Hello," practice looking the person in the face, extending your hand, and offering a very cheerful "Hi." At first, these behaviors may seem artificial, but keep working on them. The friendly responses you get in return should start to convince you that it's not *you,* but your normally reserved manner that puts people off.

- If when talking to a new person you temporarily run out of things to say, don't be embarrassed and assume that you must be boring the other person. All conversations have occasional lulls; lulls don't mean that the speakers are dull and uninteresting. Nor should you feel that filling a silence is solely your job. Your partner is probably just as eager as you are to find another topic.

- An easy way to keep a conversation going is to be genuinely interested in the people with whom you're speaking. Ask them questions about themselves, preferably ones that require more than a simple yes or no answer. Taking an active interest in others is also an excellent way to keep from being overly conscious of your own words and actions.

- Remember the statistics about how common a problem shyness is. If some 40 percent of Americans say they feel shy at least some of the time, the chances are good that the people with whom you strike up conversations are secretly feeling just as shy as you are.

After reading the article, use the space provided to write *three questions* that you have about the topic that are still unanswered.

After-Reading Questions

1.

2.

3.

For Further Discussion

1. How might shyness interfere with one's ability to be a successful student?

2. What suggestions can you offer a shy person for overcoming this problem in a classroom situation?

3. According to the article, attitude is an important element in overcoming shyness. It is also an important element in improving your reading and study skills. What advice can you give to others about the need for a positive attitude?

4. How was your mastery of the material improved by the 3 × 3 strategy?

5. How might your comprehension and retention of material differ if you simply read without using the 3 × 3 strategy?

Strategic Reading

What is an efficient reader? How does awareness of different study methods benefit an efficient reader? Wade and Reynolds (1989) define two broad categories of study methods used by efficient readers: observable study methods and in-the-head study methods.* The lists here identify various strategies that students use in each category. An efficient reader is not only aware of these strategies but knows how, when, and why they would be most effective. First, go through the lists and place a check mark in front of those strategies that you already use. Then, with your group members, complete the chart by answering the three questions presented for each strategy.

Observable Study Methods
(physical processes)

1. Highlight/underline

2. Copy

3. Write down in your own words

4. Outline

5. Draw a diagram

6. Others you know

---

* From "Developing Metacognitive Awareness," by S. E. Wade and R. E. Reynolds, *Journal of Reading*, 1989, *33*(1), 6–14. Copyright © 1989 by the International Reading Association. Adapted by permission.

	How do you use it?	When do you use it?	Why do you use it?
	1.	1.	1.
	2.	2.	2.
	3.	3.	3.
	4.	4.	4.
	5.	5.	5.
	6.	6.	6.

In-the-Head Study Methods (mental processes)

1. Look over before reading

2. Read at usual rate

3. Read slowly

4. Go back and read again

5. Special attention!

6. Review or memorize

7. Put together ideas in your head

8. Relate ideas to what you already know

9. Make a picture in your mind

10. Question or test yourself

11. Guess what comes next

12. Others you know (please describe)

How do you use it?	When do you use it?	Why do you use it?
1.	1.	1.
2.	2.	2.
3.	3.	3.
4.	4.	4.
5.	5.	5.
6.	6.	6.
7.	7.	7.
8.	8.	8.
9.	9.	9.
10.	10.	10.
11.	11.	11.
12.	12.	12.

Testing Your Memory

How would you rate your ability to remember information? What techniques and strategies do you already use to help you remember?

Try this memory game. The directions are simple. You have 2 minutes to memorize the 20 listed words. When the 2 minutes are up, you must cover the word list and use the space provided to rewrite as many of the words as you can remember.

1.	bookshelf	**11.**	identification card
2.	refrigerator	**12.**	textbooks
3.	notebooks	**13.**	laundry detergent
4.	computer	**14.**	bathrobe
5.	overdue notice	**15.**	desk lamp
6.	calculator	**16.**	car keys
7.	extension cord	**17.**	stamps
8.	videotape	**18.**	telephone
9.	radio	**19.**	checkbook
10.	highlighter	**20.**	snack food

Now cover the words—no peeking!

1.	11
2.	12.
3.	13.
4.	14.
5.	15.
6.	16.
7.	17.
8.	18.
9.	19.
10.	20.

How many words did you remember? What strategies did you use to help you remember the words? Share these strategies with the class and listen for new strategies used by others. In the space here, list some of the strategies identified. (Remember: Writing things down helps you remember!)

How might your memory strategy change if you were asked to memorize the list *in order?*

Evaluating Evidence

Why is one person's opinion on a topic any more valid than another's? What makes one piece of information more believable than information from another source? Questions like these have to do with evaluating evidence. Meet with your group and, in the space that follows, brainstorm a list of ways to assess evidence. Discuss your conclusions with the total group and compare them to the information presented in Chapter 4.

Work Area: Your Group's Ideas on Ways to Assess Evidence

Using the guidelines generated, read each statement and evaluate it. Here are possible responses:

A. This statement *is* backed up by *evidence* and appears to meet the standards for evaluating information described in Chapter 4.

B. This statement has *no* supporting evidence and fails to meet the standards for evaluating evidence.

C. This statement contains some evidence, but it is *improperly used.* In other words, the author has reached a conclusion that is not supported by the data.

_____ **1.** According to linguistic expert Frank Smith, when a reader stops comprehending what he or she reads, reading is no longer taking place.

_____ **2.** Anyone who experiences difficulty with reading can never succeed in college.

_____ **3.** Some of the people in my neighborhood say that nobody will give minorities a chance, so I guess there is no point in attending college.

_____ **4.** I read a letter to the editor of the newspaper complaining about a Philadelphia high school, so the whole school district must be inferior to any suburban high school in the country.

_____ **5.** Recent research by cognitive psychologists like Palinscar suggests that good readers set a purpose for reading and match their reading rate to that purpose.

_____ **6.** Statistics show that college courses in human sexuality and popular culture usually have high enrollments; therefore, this must mean that they are the most useful and well-taught courses on most college campuses.

_____ **7.** The National Institutes of Health reported that in 1987, only 13.5% of its budget was spent on women's health, so women should organize a protest immediately.

_____ **8.** According to statistics compiled by the Children's Defense Fund, over 40% of all children with a head of household under age 30 are poor.

_____ **9.** Most people today are pretty well informed about drugs.

_____ **10.** Now that all adolescents have the facts about AIDS, they will practice safe sex and, by doing so, halt the spread of the disease.

_____ **11.** Many college freshmen are undecided about their majors, so they should begin the decision process earlier while they are in 10th or 11th grade.

_____ **12.** National demographics experts project that by the year 2000, four out of five young mothers will not be married.

_____ **13.** The Centers for Disease Control reports that AIDS cannot be spread by casual contact; therefore, all people who test HIV-positive should be kept in isolation.

_____ **14.** I saw several rock stars on MTV who were involved in an organization called Greenpeace. If celebrities are endorsing something, it must be a worthwhile cause.

_____ **15.** Psychologists use the term _learned helplessness_ to describe the apathetic behavior and unwillingness to strive for a goal that results from repeated frustration and failure. A review of leading college textbooks found that explanations of learned helplessness are found in every leading textbook used in introductory-level psychology courses.

College Life:
A Mapping Activity

How confident are you in your ability to distinguish title, main topics, subtopics, and specific details? This activity will give you practice in this important skill. Begin by reading through the entire list. Write a title that could serve as a label for the entire list. Then go back through the list, this time placing a star next to the main topics. On a separate sheet of paper, create a web or map of your main topics. Then list subtopics under each main topic. Finally, match specific details to each topic and subtopics.

residence life
college newspaper
work-study programs
vehicle registration
medical file
room and board
student service agencies
résumé writing
honor societies
health center
college life
intercollegiate athletics
off-campus housing
parking information
interview opportunities
tutoring
student involvement opportunities
employer interviews
student housing
publications and media
wellness counseling
safety concerns
sororities
approved clubs and organizations
part-time employment
student government

financial aid office
lost and found items
commuter passes
job search training
learning resource center
mock interviews
Greek life
student loans
dormitories
parking ticket fines
health insurance information
student counseling
writing center
intramurals
career planning and placement office
parking permits
campus security
residence assistants
career advising
fraternities
time management advice
radio station
study skill help
internship opportunities
sports
scholarships

Draw your map here:

As you can see (even from this incomplete list), college life offers a wealth of opportunities to grow both personally and academically. Make the most of your college years by learning about the services that your college provides. Share any helpful experiences you have had using these and other college services.

Stating the Main Idea

Remember that the main idea is the essence, the basic point of whatever you have read, the major message of the piece of writing. Do not search for single-word answers. Read the entire item and *think*. What is the topic? What is the author's viewpoint, perspective, or purpose in writing about the topic?

Now, read each numbered item here individually, and state the main idea in the space provided. Then meet with your group to compare/contrast your answers. Decide on the best answer, and write it on chart paper or the chalkboard. Check (and correct!) your original answers against those presented in class. Write them directly on this sheet.

1. Those who have not visited a campus bookstore for many years are in for some surprises. Today's campus bookstore provides a much wider range of services than ever before. Visitors to most campus bookstores will now find not only textbooks and class materials but also gifts, food, clothing, computers and computer supplies, drug store items, and banking services. Increasingly, campus bookstores are a type of "one-stop shopping" for their students.

What is the main idea?

2. Credit card companies are constantly tempting people to spend money they don't have. After a person has established a good credit rating, it is not unusual to get unsolicited credit cards through the mail. Credit card companies are so anxious to get people started using these cards that they are often accompanied by blank checks that can be written for any amount up to the total credit limit. What these companies do not clarify is the fact that these cash advances are charged a much higher interest rate than regular credit card purchases—sometimes two or three times as high. So, before you even consider using one of the checks conveniently enclosed with a credit card or make a cash advance on your card at the automatic teller, read the fine print in your credit card agreement. If you need a loan, chances are you could get a conventional bank loan with a much lower interest rate and save yourself some money.

What is the main idea?

3. Cognitive style refers to the preferred, characteristic way that a person processes information. One dimension of cognitive style that has been researched extensively is reflectivity/impulsivity. Individuals

What is the main idea?

10. "Some 107 colleges and universities no longer require students to submit scores from the Scholastic Aptitude Test (SAT) or the American College Testing (ACT) Program for admission. But Bates College in Lewiston, Maine, made these college aptitude tests optional back in 1984 and recently reported on what has happened.

Basically, nothing has happened. That is, students who entered without SAT or ACT scores have done as well academically as anyone else. So how useful is the SAT? Ask Bates College (Hayes, 1992, p. 489).

What is the main idea?

11. "For better or worse, a revolution is at hand. Advances in hardware and software have made it possible for anyone with a computer and modem to attend college if he or she is otherwise qualified. But like all revolutions, this one will undoubtedly bring mixed blessings. As Chodorow, provost at the University of Pennsylvania, explains it in *The Chronicle of Higher Education,* 'We humans cannot thrive in a bodiless, frownless, smileless ecology, and our intellectual society cannot be complete without physical interaction.' In other words, distance learning can never replace the wisdom of one lone professor, fumbling for words, struggling to convey meaning, face-to-face in a classroom" (Bowers, 1995, p. 44).

What is the main idea?

12. In the following excerpt, Mike Rose (who is now a well-known college professor) explains how he and his former classmates in a vocational education program decided to learn as little as possible while in school. He also discusses the consequences of that decision. You may want to begin by looking over the synonyms for the vocabulary, then read each paragraph. Refer back to the word meaning as necessary while you read. The vocabulary is arranged in the order it appears in the reading selection.

Vocabulary	Synonym
groomed	carefully prepared
mediocre	ordinary, of average quality
somnambulant	sleepwalker
wherewithal	resources, both internal and external
stimuli	(plural of *stimulus*) external influences
diffuse	dissipate
cultivate	develop
malady	illness or affliction
gray matter	reference to the brain
flaunt	to show off in an extravagant way
materialize	to become tangible, real
neutralize	to counteract negative effects
exacts	requires, demands

None of us was groomed for the classroom. It wasn't just that I didn't know things—didn't know how to simplify algebraic equations, couldn't identify different kinds of clauses, bungled Spanish translations—but that I had developed various faulty and inadequate ways of doing algebra and making sense of Spanish. Worse yet, the years of defensive tuning out in elementary school had given me a way to escape quickly while seeming at least half alert. During my time in Voc. Ed., I developed further into a mediocre student and a somnambulant problem solver, and that affected the subjects I did have the wherewithal to handle: I detested Shakespeare; I got bored with history. My attention flitted here and there. I fooled around in class and read my books indifferently—the intellectual equivalent of playing with your food. I did what I had to get by, and I did it with half a mind. . . . The tragedy is that you have to twist the knife in your own gray matter to make this defense work. You'll have to shut down, have to reject intellectual stimuli or diffuse them with sarcasm, have to cultivate stupidity, have to convert boredom from a malady into a way of confronting the world. Keep your vocabulary simple, act stoned when you're not or more stoned than you are, flaunt ignorance, materialize your dreams. It is a powerful and effective defense, it neutralizes the insult and the frustration of being a vocational kid, and when perfected, it drives teachers up the wall, a delightful secondary effect. But like all strong magic, it exacts a price (Rose, 1989, pp. 27, 29).

What is the main idea?

References

Baumgardner, J. M. (1993) *60 art projects for children*. New York: Clarkson/Potter.

Bowers, J. (1995). A course of a different color. *Netguide, 2*(8), 40–44.

Hayes, L. (1992). News and views: Taking up the challenge. *Phi Delta Kappa, 73*(6), 489.

Nuland, S. B. (1993).*How we die. Reflections on life's final chapter*. New York: Vintage/Random House.

Rose, M. (1989). *Lives on the boundary: A moving account of the struggles and achievement of America's educational underclass*. New York: Penguin.

Main Ideas and Major Points

For each of the following passages, do three things. First, write a brief statement of the main idea, the major message of the piece of writing. After you have written the main idea, make a list of the major points included in the passage. State these major points succinctly as phrases rather than as complete sentences. Do not try to copy directly from the passage. Rather, try to paraphrase (put the main idea into your own words).

Second, meet with members of a small group to compare answers. Arrive at a statement of the main idea and list of major points that you can all agree on.

Third, compile your group's work onto paper or write it on the chalkboard. Be prepared to discuss your work and provide a rationale for your decisions about the main idea and major points in each passage.

1. When families do not fulfill their role or function, they are called *dysfunctional*. How do families that are dysfunctional and functional differ? Sipe and Sipe (1994) have identified characteristics that differentiate between functional and dysfunctional families. Functional families are successful in fulfilling seven significant roles:
   a. **Communication**—clear, open, frequent discussions
   b. **Cohesiveness**—feelings of closeness and connectedness; appreciation for the uniqueness of each family member while advocating a commitment to the family as a unit
   c. **Adaptability**—an ability to adjust to predictable changes as well as to overcome situational stress; seeking outside help when needed
   d. **Clear roles**—definite, yet flexible roles and responsibilities; equality for family members and a balance of power
   e. **Shared time**—quantity and quality of time together in which rituals and traditions abound
   f. **Shared values**—common core of beliefs, service to others, a sense of spirituality
   g. **Social support**—connectedness to extended family members, friends and neighbors, and the larger community; effective use of available services and resources (pp. 16, 40)

   These seven roles can be conceptualized as a set of standards for a family that is functioning well.

State the main idea:

List the major points:

2. The four basic food groups have been replaced by the food choice pyramid. The transition to the pyramid offers several advantages. First, the most healthful foods are located at the base of the pyramid, so it offers a hierarchical arrangement of foods and implicitly states how to achieve a balanced diet. Second, because the foods with the most recommended number of servings are located at the base of the pyramid, it offers direction in the relative amounts that should be consumed in each category. Finally, because the pyramid is a type of graphic organizer, it is easier to refer to, remember, and use. For all of these reasons, dieticians and nutritionists have given the food choice pyramid their enthusiastic endorsement.

State the main idea:

List the major points:

3. In the magazine called *It's New! Everything New under the Sun,* the editors have this to say about automotive collision warning systems:

> Over the last decade efforts have been aimed at automotive crash survival. Seat belts, crash absorbing frames, airbags, road improvement and education have all contributed to a dramatic decline in fatalities and injuries from traffic accidents. Airbags alone led to a 24 percent reduction in driver fatalities from frontal crashes.
> But today, technology exists that is capable of reducing the death and injury toll even more. The objective is to avoid crashes altogether by detecting unsafe driving conditions and potential conditions, then warning the driver, improving his or her ability to control the vehicle and ultimately interceding to prevent the accident (Editorial Staff, 1995, p. 43).

State the main idea:

List the major points:

4. Am I smart? This is a question that many people ask, particularly if they have performed poorly on some test. The first thing to remember is that a test is simply a sample of behavior taken under rather restrictive conditions. Psychometricians, psychologists who attempt to create tools that measure human abilities, recognize that psychometric tools (tests) have their limitations. Take for example, intelligence tests. Technically, intelligence refers to a person's overall capacity to store, retrieve, and process information. There is no test that can accurately determine all of that! Instead, intelligence tests give some indication of how much specific information a person has accumulated at a particular time and can recall on command. This is one reason why experts on learning have argued that intelligence tests in America are better at predicting who has a talent for schoolwork than at assessing overall intelligence.

Furthermore, as everyone knows, there are different kinds of smart—book smart, street smart, common sense, and so forth. Clearly, intelligence is not defined in the same way in different contexts and cultures. If you were volunteering to work on remodeling a house, for example, you might hold three Ph.D.s yet not possess the right kind of smart needed for the situation. Likewise, in an agricultural society, those with academic skills might be viewed as unproductive citizens. Typically, the most powerful members of a social group define what "counts" as smart for that group. If warriors are in power, those who "fight smart" are regarded as the geniuses; if technology is valued, those who "invent smart" and create new technologies are heralded as the brilliant ones. Therefore, instead of asking, "Am I smart?" it might be better to rephrase the question and ask, "*In what ways* am I smart?"

State the main idea:

List the major points:

5. "The relationships that we have with our brothers and sisters are, for most people, the longest-lasting ones we will have with anyone. They begin in infancy long before we meet our future spouses, and usually end in old age, generally long after our parents have died. Furthermore, there is an intensity and specialness to these relationships that is rarely duplicated. These are the people who share our roots, who merge from the same font of values, who deal with us more objectively than parents and more candidly than virtually anyone else we will ever know. Not surprisingly, siblings are a major influence on our lives" (Papalia & Olds, 1993, p. 203).

State the main idea:

List the major points:

References

Editorial Staff. (1995). *It's new! Everything new under the sun, 1*(3), 43–45.

Papalia, D., & Olds, S. W. (1993). *A child's world: Infancy through adolescence.* New York: Mc-Graw-Hill.

Sipe, J. W., & Sipe, D. S. (1994). Enough analysis and blame: Let's strengthen ALL families. *Student Assistance Journal, 6*(5), 16, 35, 40.

Reading an Autobiography or Biography

Most people are interested in the lives of other people. Every year there are movies, television programs, and books that attempt to capture the essence of a particular person's life. What autobiographies or biographies have you read? Perhaps you have read Maya Angelou's *I Know Why the Caged Bird Sings,* or Alice Walker's *The Color Purple.* Maybe you have read the life story of an athlete, rock star, politician, or religious leader. Usually, biographies are written by or about famous people or people who have had extraordinary lives in some way. Go to the library and find an article or book that is a biography or autobiography of a historical or contemporary leader in your major field of study. If you are a psychology major, for example, you might locate a book about Sigmund Freud. If you are an education major, you might find an article about John Dewey. Bring the complete bibliographic information about the book or article to class so that a reading list can be compiled.

Expanding Your Vocabulary

Educated people are able to communicate effectively because they can recall a word that expresses exactly how they are feeling or conveys precise information. Building a strong vocabulary is worth the effort. It is also an important part of the process of becoming a professional in virtually any field.

Make a plan to enrich your vocabulary. Find one unfamiliar word, write a definition in your own words, and give an example of a sentence using that word. Then, during that day, work that word into your conversation. Do this for one week and maintain a record that includes:

word   definition   example   results of my attempt to
                                              use the word

Words About People

What words would you use to describe yourself? Your best friend? Your worst enemy? Look at the words here and work with your group to write a synonym or a brief definition. Use a dictionary, thesaurus, or ask the instructor after you have tried to generate a definition in the group. On the next page chunk the words into one of three categories: words with positive connotations, words with negative connotations, and words with neutral connotations.

claustrophobic	misanthrope
skeptical	articulate
magnanimous	defiant
efficient	tenacious
prejudicial	duplicitous
indignant	evasive
atavistic	ingenious
anarchist	indulgent
amoral	vociferous
congenial	loquacious
dejected	dictatorial
conscientious	gregarious
dismissive	entrepreneur
diplomatic	confrontational
perverse	monotheistic
malevolent	disreputable
tactless	boisterous
altruistic	destitute
xenophobic	belligerent
indigent	enigmatic
nonchalant	transient
introvert	pessimist

Add your own "Words About People" in the space provided.

Positive

Neutral

Negative

Shades of Meaning

Would you rather be described as a conversationalist or a gossip? Both words have similar denotations or dictionary meanings, but their connotations or emotional meanings are quite different. Writers and speakers know that their choice of words can have a great impact on the reactions of their audience.

Draw a series of 19 horizontal lines across piece of paper. Leave space below each line. Create a continuum to describe the words' connotations by labeling the lines as follows: high intensity (on the left), moderate intensity (in the center), and low intensity (on the right). For each cluster of words given here, place them along the continuum according to their shade of meaning—high, moderate, or low. The first one, in italics, has been done for you.

Example: **Degrees of slender**
slender, emaciated, thin, lean, willowy, gaunt, haggard, slim

High Intensity	**Moderate Intensity**	**Low Intensity**
emaciated	*thin*	*slender*
gaunt	*lean*	*willowy*
haggard		*slim*

Degrees of Anger
angry, infuriated, irked, vexed, annoyed, irritated, aggravated, enraged, riled, bothered, provoked, peeved

Shades of Disagreement
disagreement, conflict, confrontation, controversy, diatribe, heated debate, a breakdown in communication

Levels of Difficulty
hard, difficult, complicated, complex, impossible, challenging, unattainable, incomprehensible

Types of Assertion
assertive, opinionated, dogmatic, frank, intractable, inflexible, aggressive, outspoken, candid

Degrees of Happiness
happy, pleased, elated, ecstatic, thrilled, delighted, euphoric, deliriously happy

Shades of Sad
sad, dejected, depressed, suicidal, miserable, unhappy, discouraged, despondent, inconsolable, sorrowful

Shades of Bad
bad, deplorable, appalling, terrible, awful, disastrous, catastrophic, poor, inferior, inadequate, mediocre

Levels of Disorganization
disorganized, cluttered, chaotic, in a state of disarray, sloppy, messy

Strength of Suggestions
suggest, mandate, recommend, require, insist, demand, decree, advise, counsel, command

Levels of Trustworthiness
trustworthy, unscrupulous, reliable, ethical, principled, dependable, above reproach

Levels of Confidence
confident, egotistical, poised, self-important, conceited, proud, self-assured

Types of Information
information, fact, opinion, proof, evidence, research, documented proof, conclusive evidence

Degrees of Strangeness
unusual, weird, bizarre, strange, incredible, ridiculous, outrageous, puzzling, mystifying

Levels of Interest
interested, fascinated, disinterested, captivated, intrigued, disaffected, bored

Types of Intelligence
intelligent, smart, sharp, astute, brilliant, insightful, perceptive, genius

Shades of Meaning for Old
old, vintage, antiquated, classic, ancient, dated

Levels of Foolishness
foolish, gullible, easily duped, ignorant, uninformed, naive, unenlightened

Degrees of Embarrassment
embarrassed, humiliated, mortified, chagrined, ashamed, an object of ridicule

Degrees of Fear
fear, terror, anxiety, panic, worry, concern, hysteria, dread, alarm, consternation, trepidation, dismay, stress

Headlines:
Interpreting Information

Read each headline and work with your group to arrive at an answer. If there are any unfamiliar words in the item, use a dictionary or thesaurus, or ask your instructor.

Entrepreneurial Spirit Alive and Well in Today's Freshmen

1. Are the freshmen being portrayed as ambitious and ingenious?

2. Is it likely that a few newspaper interviews accurately describe all or most freshmen?

3. What kind of research would be necessary to support the claim made in the headline?

Students Call Internet Registration
System a Technological Nightmare

1. Is the registration system working well?

2. What are some inferences you can make about the reasons for the problem?

3. Could the students have other reasons for disliking telephone registration?

Third World Country Subjugated by Rebel Forces

1. Is the country economically developed?

2. Is there political unrest?

3. What kind of evidence would be necessary to support such a claim?

Today's Parents Too Indulgent, Study Reports

1. Are the parents laissez-faire?

2. Is the information pure conjecture, or is it more authoritative?

3. What inferences can you make about how parents might spoil their children?

Employers Exploit Transients

1. Do the workers have permanent residences?

2. Are transient workers being treated fairly?

3. Who might issue such a statement?

Doctors Call for "Continuum of Care" for Elderly

1. Are the doctors functioning as advocates for seniors?

2. What type of health care are they proposing?

3. Could the views of medical professionals be slanted in any particular way?

Alumni Volunteer to Mentor At-Risk Students

1. Do the graduates of the institution sound altruistic?

2. How might students benefit from a mentor?

3. Why would the university want to publicize this information?

Disparity in Wealth Distribution Responsible for Insurrection

1. Are resources distributed equally?

2. How are people responding?

3. What kinds of evidence would be necessary to make such a pronouncement?

Pharmacological Breakthrough Makes Preemies Viable

1. What is being used to help the premature newborns?

2. What effect will this discovery have on infant mortality rates?

3. What sources of information are necessary to support such a claim?

Psychologists Concur That New Therapies for Depression Show Promise

1. Are the psychologists in agreement?

2. Have the treatments been thoroughly researched?

Publishing Empire Falls Under Charges of Widespread Malfeasance

1. What inferences can you make from the use of the word *empire?*

2. Are there suspicions of wrongdoing?

3. What evidence would be necessary to make such accusations?

Collaboration Essential to Career Success in the 21st Century, Futurist Contends

1. Who is making this prediction?

2. What work habits are predicted to lead to success?

3. How reliable is evidence of this type?

Film Star Makes Impassioned Political Statement at Awards Ceremony

1. Why might a celebrity use an awards ceremony to express political views?

2. Is this behavior appropriate, in your opinion?

3. What credentials does a film star have to speak as an authority on international policies?

Conversion to Metric System a Perennial Debate in U.S.

1. Why might Americans object to changing to the metric system when other countries around the world use it?

2. Is this an ongoing problem?

3. Who would be qualified to comment authoritatively on this topic?

Visual Aid Vocabulary

The purpose of this activity is to expand your active vocabulary and help you remember a variety of new words using your visual memory.

Things to Do Before Class

First, select a word with which you are unfamiliar. Choose a word that you are curious about and would probably use in your professional conversations. It might be a word that you come across in your reading.

Second, learn the meaning of the word. Do not rely exclusively on the dictionary definition. Look up synonyms in a thesaurus and/or ask someone to explain the word to you by giving examples.

Third, write the word on a large index card in colorful letters. Write the definition and an example on the back. For instance:

Front of Card	**Back of Card**
procrastinate	Definition: to delay or postpone. The old saying "Never put off until tomorrow what you can do today" is good advice for those who tend to procrastinate.

Fourth, create a visual aid that will enable class members to remember the word. The student who selected the word *procrastinate,* for example, brought two cassette tapes to class and said, "About 3 weeks ago, my friend gave me this blank tape and asked me to make a copy for her. Because I have a tendency to *procrastinate,* the tape still isn't made."

Suggestion for Sharing Vocabulary in Class

Assemble in groups of five and assign a number to each group. One student teaches his or her word to the group, then rotates to all of the other groups. When the first student returns to his or her original group, the second group member teaches and goes around to the remaining groups. This continues until all of the students are finished. Take a few minutes to make sure that those who were teaching have an opportunity to learn the words that they missed while they were teaching.

At the end of class, the instructor will gather all of the cards. Before each student is dismissed, the instructor reads one definition and the student has to identify the new word. Anyone who cannot remember the new vocabulary word goes to the end of the line and waits for another turn.

Good Listeners vs. Poor Listeners

Do you consider yourself to be a good listener? What role will listening skills play in your chosen career? What professions can you think of in which good listening skills are essential?

Look at the chart here.* Only the column labeled "Characteristics of Poor Listeners" has been completed. You and your group members must complete the second column by identifying the "Characteristics of Good Listeners." The first one in italicized type has been done as an example.

Characteristics of Poor Listeners	Characteristics of Good Listeners
1. allow their minds to wander	1. *focus attention on the message*
2. respond emotionally to "trigger words"	2.
3. let personal problems keep them from listening effectively	3.
4. succumb to distractions	4.
5. are unaware that their biases may distort messages	5.
6. react strongly to a speaker's style or reputation	6.
7. "tune out" dry topics	7.
8. hold the speaker responsible for effective communication	8.
9. listen passively	9.
10. mentally rehearse counterarguments during a speech	10.
11. feign attention, giving false feedback to the speaker	11.
12. avoid difficult material	12.
13. listen only for facts	13.
14. seek out entertaining messages	14.

Are there any additional characteristics that you can add to the list? What changes in your listening habits do you need to make in order to become a more proficient listener?

---

* From *Public Speaking* (3rd ed.), by R. Osborn and I. P. Osborn, 1994, Boston: Houghton Mifflin. Adapted by permission.

Mapping Your Interests

Have you ever experienced that feeling of panic when an instructor assigns a speech? One reason why you may feel uneasy is because you have not decided what you will talk about. Most experts in the field of public speaking suggest that you select a topic that interests you and will interest your listeners.*

This activity has several parts. The first part requires you to consider your own broad areas of interests. Then, use the topics you list to generate related but more specific topics for your speech. Remember to keep your audience in mind. What would interest them? Finally, generate some questions you could research about the topic by using one or more of the following question words: who, what, when, where, why, and how. An example follows.

Personal Interest/Activities	**Specific Topic**	**Audience Interests**
winter sports	downhill skiing	physical education class/interested in sports

Questions

Who can participate in downhill skiing?

What equipment is required?

When and *Where* is the best skiing?

Why is downhill skiing popular?

How is training completed?

---

* From *Public Speaking* (3rd ed.), by R. Osborn and I. P. Osborn, 1994, Boston: Houghton Mifflin. Adapted by permission.

Abbreviations and Speedwriting Techniques

Do you ever find it difficult to keep up with the pace of the class? Do you sometimes get frustrated because the instructor is already on the next point when you are still trying to write notes about the previous one? Did you ever envy the person who has learned to take shorthand and uses it for class notes? If you answered yes to any of these questions, then you need some help in abbreviations and speedwriting.

Quick: In the next 2 minutes write down as many abbreviations as you can think of:

Share your abbreviations with fellow class members. Can you chunk or group the abbreviations into categories (e.g., Measurements, Titles, States, Corporations, Athletic Teams, etc.)? You probably know more abbreviations than you realize. The trick is to practice using abbreviations and to know and use a few speedwriting techniques. Look at the speedwriting techniques listed here, and compare them to the abbreviations you have identified. Then try the examples in the right-hand column.

1. Eliminate vowels unless the word begins with a vowel. Try eliminating consonant letters in longer words, too (e.g., *mtn* for *mountain; amt* for *amount; rv* for *river*).

   a. around
   b. guilty
   c. anthropology
   d. development

2. Use simple synonyms for longer words (e.g., *job* instead of *occupation; same* instead of *uniform.*)

   a. consumed
   b. imitation
   c. demonstrates

3. Use the first syllable of a word (e.g., *char* for *characteristics; rep* for *representative*).

   a. dormitory
   b. socialism
   c. development
   d. demonstration

4. Use numbers and one or two letters (e.g., *2* can stand for to, too, two; B4 stands for *before; w/* for *with, w/o* for *without; G/L* for *Greenland*).

   a. understand
   b. eight o'clock in the morning
   c. the sixteenth of June
   d. manuscript

5. Use symbols (e.g., % for *percent;* & for *and;* $ for *expensive* or *money;* ~ for *approximately*)

a. therefore
b. the
c. question
d. positive, negative

6. Use apostrophes to eliminate letters (e.g., *accd'tal* for *accidental; b'ful* for *beautiful*).

a. homeless
b. additional
c. international
d. development

7. Use key words and phrases (e.g., "There will be a track meeting in the gymnasium on August 9 at nine in the morning" = "trck mtg 8/9 9 AM in gym").

a. Mapping helps a reader condense textbook material.
b. You are three times more likely to remember information you recite out loud.
c. Good notes are your insurance against forgetting.
d. See you at the library next Sunday afternoon.

8. Use or make up acronyms for frequently used phrases (e.g., *SAM* for *South America*).

a. Great Lakes
b. Supply and demand
c. North Atlantic Treaty Organization

9. Use a combination of these techniques.

Now revisit your own abbreviations. How many of the speedwriting techniques listed did you use? Can you revise any of your abbreviations using the techniques listed? Can you add any new techniques to the list?

Remember: Good notes always include the topic, date, and corresponding textbook chapter. In most cases you should be able to use the words and phrases surrounding your abbreviations as clues to their meanings. Rewrite any new abbreviations as soon as possible to avoid forgetting.

Are you ready to put all of your speedwriting techniques to use? Try using as many techniques as possible as you use speedwriting to rewrite the following sentences. *Hint:* Do not forget about using key words and phrases.

1. Visualization is a powerful tool for remembering.

2. Three signals of abbreviations are periods, capital letters, and apostrophes.

3. Spaced review is more effective than massed review or cramming.

4. Some characteristics of a good study location include proper lighting, a table or desk, and all necessary materials close at hand.

5. A summary is a brief statement written in your own words that includes main ideas and major details.

6. Efficient readers vary their reading speed to suit their purpose or reason for reading.

7. Prewriting is important in all writing situations, especially when you are writing under pressure.

8. Most students spend more than half of their day listening, so active listening is important.

9. Study groups are particularly effective when dealing with difficult material.

10. Speedwriting techniques will become more useful with practice.

Compare your speedwriting with those of your classmates. Yours may not look exactly like any of the others, which is okay, as long as you can read your notes, used several of the speedwriting strategies, and did not lose meaning in the process of translating from the original to the abbreviated version. *Remember:* These techniques get easier with practice. You can develop your own techniques, too. Just be certain that you can look at the abbreviations at a later date and figure out what they mean.

Understanding and Remembering Through Visual Images

Visual imagery is a technique that can help you understand and remember textbook and lecture material.* After reading a textbook section or listening to a lecture, it is helpful to design a visual image of the key concepts that were represented. Listen to the teacher read a short excerpt and then design a visual to help you remember the important information.

1. Listen to the teacher read an excerpt from Abraham Maslow's "Hierarchy of Needs." Take notes in the usual way, then complete the brief quiz. Write your quiz score here: _____.

2. Now listen to the excerpt a second time. On a sheet of paper, design a picture that represents the most important aspects of the selection. You may use single words and short phrases as part of your visual.

3. Share and explain your visual image with a partner.

4. Retake the quiz after studying with the visual image approach. How did the use of the visual images affect your score?

5. Discuss your ability to remember the concepts using this technique and how you might apply it in your course work.

Quiz

a. Who is Abraham Maslow?

b. List the steps of Maslow's needs hierarchy in order from lowest to highest.

c. Give an example for at least three of the items in the needs hierarchy.

---

* Adapted from *Reaching Adult Learners with Whole Language Strategies* (pp. 91–92), by T. Kroeker and M. Henrichs, 1993, New York: Owen.

The 2-Minute Synopsis

In your small groups, read and annotate (take notes on) an article from the magazine *Time* or *Newsweek*. Use the chalkboard or scrap paper to identify the main points of the article in the form of a map, list, drawing, or some other format. Then use the chalkboard or chart paper to create a visual of the main points of the reading. Formulate a plan for presenting this information to the rest of the class in 2 minutes. Make sure everyone has a part in the presentation. Make it interesting and fun. Do not forget to add your own advice to students based on your personal experiences. This is what will make each presentation distinctive and interesting.

Public Speaking Advice: Top 10 List

Think about the last time you were asked or required to make a speech. Think about the best (and worst) speeches you have ever heard. Read the list of factors here, and for each one, think about the best and worst advice you could give to a speaker.*

Factor	Best Advice	Worst Advice
1. Preparation	**1.**	**1.**
2. Selecting a topic	**2.**	**2.**
3. Eye contact and nonverbal communication	**3.**	**3.**
4. Analyzing the audience	**4.**	**4.**
5. Using visual aids or props	**5.**	**5.**
6. Method of presentation	**6.**	**6.**
7. Room set-up	**7.**	**7.**
8. Overcoming nervousness	**8.**	**8.**
9. Forgetfulness	**9.**	**9.**
10. Your choice	**10.**	**10.**

* From *The Public Speaking Book* (p. 6), by I. J. Rein, 1981, Glenview, IL: Scott, Foresman. Copyright © 1981 by Irving Rein. Adapted by permission of the author.

The Great Debate

In the next few minutes work with a group to brainstorm a list of controversial topics that are currently a concern in the community or area where you live. Look over the list and select one topic that your group would like to debate. Write that debate topic in the form of a question in the space provided:

Question: _____

     Who are the people most affected by this issue? What perspectives would these people bring to a debate on this topic? In your group make a list of the various roles that could be played during the debate. Then have each member select a role as well as a position (pro or con) that they will play during the debate. Brainstorm ideas and responses that you think are relevant to the role you are playing. Also, find at least one article in the library that supports your position. Be prepared to discuss your points for a maximum of 2 minutes during the debate.

     Complete the graphic given here to help you get a general overview of the issues.

The Debate Question: _____

_____

_____

Pro Position	**Roles**	**Con Position**
	Debate Moderator	
	Timekeeper (optional)	
	_____	
	_____	
	_____	
	_____	

Learning About
the College Library

Successful college students spend a great deal of time in the college library in order to complete their assignments. Knowing what resources are available for your use and where those resources are located will enable you to use the library effectively.

   Listed here are some basic sources of information found in most college libraries. Members of your small group are to spend today's class in the campus library. Your objective is to make a graphic organizer to share in class that shows the location of the places and materials listed below along with a brief description of their contents or purposes.*

   circulation desk

   interlibrary loan

   reserve desk

   card catalog

   on-line card catalog

   reference desk

   specialized encyclopedias

   general encyclopedias

   biographical indexes

   citation indexes

   atlas

   CD-ROMS

   InfoTrac

   ERIC database

   MLA bibliography

   PsycLIT

   religion indexes

---

* From "Scavenging for Better Library Instruction," by T. S. Cocking and S. A. Schafer, *Journal of Reading*, 1994, *38*(3), 164–170. Copyright © 1994 by the International Reading Association. Adapted by permission.

microforms

ERIC documents

bound periodicals

current periodicals/newspapers

journals/newspapers

general collection

video library/media resources

music library

special collection

children's collection

copying machines

group study rooms

others

Compare your completed graphic organizer with those of the other groups for accuracy. Then, through group consensus, select five sources that you feel the least confident using. Arrange one additional library time to review those specific sources.

Summarizing: What Employers Want

Many college students have part- or full-time work experience before and during college. Think for a moment about what employers are looking for in their employees. Then read the following article for some information on "Workplace Know-How."* Underline some points worth remembering as you are reading. When you are done, use your notes to write a summary of the article. As you begin your summary, write your name on the back of the paper. Later, you will be exchanging papers with another student who will rate your summary using the summary evaluation guidelines that are provided. (The reason for concealing your name is to get an impartial rating of your summary.)

What Employers Want: "Workplace Know-How"

The Secretary's Commission on Achieving Necessary Skills (SCANS) recently published its first report on the skills and knowledge that graduates will need to make the transition from school to work successfully.

What SCANS refers to as "workplace know-how" consists of two elements: a set of foundation skills and a set of five competencies that are at the core of job performance. According to SCANS, these will be needed of all graduates, both the college-bound and those directly entering the workforce.

There are three foundation skills: *Basic skills,* such as the ability to read, write, perform arithmetic and mathematical operations, and listen and speak effectively; *thinking skills,* such as the ability to think creatively, make decisions, solve problems, visualize, and know how to learn; and *personal qualities,* such as displaying responsibility, self-esteem, sociability, self-management, and integrity/honesty.

Five broad competencies complete the picture. SCANS says employees need to be competent in the areas of:

- **Resources.** Employees need to be able to identify, organize, plan, and allocate resources (such as time, money, materials and facilities, and human resources).

- **Interpersonal skills.** Employees should be able to work effectively with others. Examples are the abilities to participate as a member of a team, teach others new skills, serve clients or customers, exercise leadership, negotiate, and work with diverse people.

- **Information.** Employees need to be able to acquire, evaluate, interpret, and communicate information, as well as to use computers to process information.

- **Systems.** Employees must understand complex interrelationships. They must be able to understand systems, monitor and correct performance within the system, and improve or design new systems.

---

* From "What Employers Want: Workplace Know-How," by J. O'Neil, *ASCD Update,* 1991, *5*(33), 5. Alexandria, VA: Association for Supervision and Curriculum Development. Copyright © 1991 by ASCD. Used by permission.

■ **Technology.** Employees should be able to select appropriate technologies or tools for a task, apply technology to a task, and maintain and troubleshoot equipment.

To illustrate: a worker in the manufacturing sector might be expected to develop a plan to show how a production schedule can be maintained while staff members are being trained in a new procedure (resources); help brainstorm ways to involve two limited-English-proficient team members in quality control discussions (interpersonal); analyze statistical control charts to monitor error rates (information); analyze a painting system and suggest ways to minimize system downtime and improve paint finish (systems); and use appropriate resources to evaluate and make recommendations to management on three new paint spray guns, taking into account cost, health, and safety (technology).

SCANS will be working with pilot schools to integrate the competencies and foundation skills in school programs, says John Wart, SCANS deputy director. The commission, which is expected to complete its work early next year, will also issue reports on creating an assessment system that certifies student competencies and on how school curriculums and teacher training might address SCANS' findings.

Summary Evaluation Guidelines

As you are writing your summary, use the evaluation guidelines developed by Casazza (1992). Then use the criteria to assess one of your classmate's summaries after you exchange papers.

1 = **never**	**2** = **sometimes**	**3** = **frequently**	**4** = **always**

The student:

	1	2	3	4
deletes minor details	1	2	3	4
combines/chunks similar ideas	1	2	3	4
paraphrases accurately	1	2	3	4
reflects author's emphasis	1	2	3	4
recognizes author's purpose	1	2	3	4
identifies the topic	1	2	3	4
identifies the main idea	1	2	3	4
stays within the appropriate length (1/3 of text)	1	2	3	4
does not include own opinions	1	2	3	4

Total Possible Points = 36   Your Score = _____

Based on your evaluation, revise your summary to make it better.

Reference

Casazza, M. E. (1992). Teaching summary writing to enhance comprehension. *Reading Today,* 9(4), 26.

Introductory Sentences in Essays

Answering essay questions can be a little nerve-racking. Prewriting is one technique that can be very useful. The process can help you formulate the thoughts that you would like to include as part of your answer. Another good technique is to start your essay response with a main idea sentence. One of the easiest ways to do this is to take the essay question or part of the question and turn it into a sentence. This will help give some organization and focus to your writing.

Example: Compare the arachnid to a crustacean. Be sure to include at least five points about each.

Sample main idea sentence: There are many likenesses and differences between arachnids and crustaceans.

Try to convert the following essay questions into main idea sentences:

1. Discuss the benefits of the mapping technique.

2. Explain the procedure you would follow for organizing a study group.

3. Define the term *mnemonics* and describe three different mnemonic devices.

4. Identify the steps involved in the process of writing a summary.

5. List and explain at least three reasons why listening skills are so important during college study and later in professional life.

6. Describe a step-by-step procedure for how you would prepare a group presentation.

7. Why is it important to be a flexible reader? What factors could influence your reading rate? (Notice that this is really two essay questions.)

8. Define interest. Discuss barriers to interest and influences that build interest.

Now write three essay questions of your own based on your assigned reading for this week. Then *convert each one into a main idea sentence.*

1. Essay Question

   Main Idea Sentence

2. Essay Question

    Main Idea Sentence

3. Essay Question

    Main Idea Sentence

Thinking About Texts

Remember how you felt the first time you purchased a textbook in the college bookstore? You may have browsed through the book and wondered how you would ever understand all of the material. The first day of class finally arrives, and you walk in armed with notebook, pens, and your new textbook. Your instructor follows the usual routine—roll call, attendance policy, required texts, and course syllabus, but soon you find yourself faced with the prospect of your first essay test! The instructor says, "At our next class meeting, you will have 1 hour to complete your first essay answer. Please be sure to bring a blue book to class and your best essay writing strategies. The topic of the essay is simple—What is your textbook about?"

Select one of your textbooks, and use the space here to brainstorm some ideas that you might include in your essay. Consider making a map or an outline of what you intend to include in your essay answer.*

Share your ideas with your small-group members. Compose an essay answer that explains how your group would prepare for such an essay examination. Refer to the guidelines for essay writing presented in Chapter 8 (pp. 209–246) as you compose your answer.

Share your completed essays with the class. Offer some recommendations for each essay answer.

Essay Ideas/Prewriting Notes

---

* From *The College Student: Reading and Study Skills* (4th ed., p. 213), by E. Spargo, 1994, Providence, RI: Jamestown. Copyright © 1994 by Jamestown Publishers, Providence, RI. Adapted by permission.

Dealing With Exams and Exam Tensions

Most of us have experienced the feeling of panic that occurs when an instructor announces a midterm or final examination. Fortunately, several strategies can be used to help turn this uncomfortable feeling into positive action. This activity will help you focus on those strategies that lead to improved test preparation and performance. In your small group compose a response to the following scenarios.

Scenario 1

Dr. Zamboni has just announced that, due to unforeseen circumstances, the midterm will be 1 week earlier than had previously been stated in the syllabus. Dr. Zamboni reassures everyone by her words, "If you have read the assigned chapters, participated regularly in class, and taken notes, you should have no problems with the exam."

What kinds of questions will you ask Dr. Zamboni in order to help you prepare for the exam?

Scenario 2

You have studied all week to prepare for this math test and you think you are ready, but as soon as the instructor hands you the test you freeze. Your mind cannot think, and your heart starts to race.

What do you do?

Scenario 3

The teaching assistant for your microbiology course has just informed the class about the upcoming lab practicum. He has indicated that he will place a sign-up sheet outside the lab so that students can schedule the time for their practicum. This scheduling is done on a first-come, first-served basis. Individual students will have 15 minutes within a 4-hour block to complete activities at lab stations that will be set up throughout the room. These activities will range from identifying parts of laboratory equipment, identifying structures in slides, demonstrating knowledge of laboratory safety procedures, and demonstrating knowledge of the key concepts discussed during lab this semester. The teaching assistant will be available in the lab for 1-hour help sessions on the two evenings prior to the practicum. This practicum represents one-third of your lab grade.

How should you prepare for this practicum?

Scenario 4

Your philosophy instructor has indicated that the midterm examination will consist of six essay questions based on the six chapters that you have read in the textbook so far. The questions will focus on the major themes and ideas discussed in class. While you have to answer only four of the six essay questions, the instructor says that you will have to include pertinent information and key terminology from all of the chapters in order to answer each essay question completely.

How will you prepare for this examination?

Now prepare your own examination scenario based on an experience that you had. This scenario can focus on actions taken before, during, or after a testing situation. Write the scenario in the space provided. Share your scenario with your group and encourage them to respond. If you are willing, share your own response to the situation with the group and discuss any positive or negative outcomes based on the strategy you used.

Your Scenario

If faced with a similar situation, what would you do differently?

What actions would remain the same?

Words in Essay Exams and Assignments

Imagine that you are reading an essay exam question or instructions on writing an assignment for a class. What do each of the following terms mean? In other words, *what is the instructor expecting you to do?* Work with your group to arrive at a consensus on the meaning of each word.

compare/contrast

What strategy would you use to prepare for writing a compare/contrast question?

define

What strategy could you use to make it clear to the instructor that your definition comes from an authoritative source?

describe/discuss

What strategy could you use to make it clear that your description and discussion are based on your readings?

synthesize

How could you demonstrate that you are synthesizing information?

summarize

What are some ways to prepare *before* you begin writing a summary?

analyze

How will you impress upon your instructor that you have conducted a careful analysis? What evidence could you provide?

critique/evaluate

How is a critique or evaluation different from summarizing?

explain

How is explaining distinct from discussing?

agree/disagree

Will an instructor be satisfied with your unsubstantiated opinion? How can you use evidence to back up your opinions?

apply (as in "Apply the principles of active learning to your situation in this class")

How can you show your instructor that you know how to use information you have studied?

Class Skills and Job Skills

Take some time to think about how the skills you have learned in this book will help you get and keep a job. Consider the job skills sought by today's employers listed in Activity 43, p. 383–384 that you will use beyond your graduation. For example, the presentation skills that you read about in Chapter 7 could assist you in a job interview and the active learning strategies that you read about in Chapter 1 could help you to stay current in your field. Think more specifically about your chosen profession in relationship to the content of each chapter and complete the following chart.

Strategy	Usefulness in Career
active learning	
critical thinking	
managing time	
coping with stress	
reading and study	
listening and note taking	
making presentations	
developing skill in self-evaluation	
writing effectively	

Life Lessons From Thomas Alva Edison

Can you imagine life without light, music, or movies? Thankfully, you do not have to largely because of the time and talents of Thomas Alva Edison, quite possibly the world's greatest inventor. The lessons of his life offer some valuable ideas on how you too can make the most effective use of your time and talents.

Paul Israel, Ph.D., associate editor of the Thomas A. Edison papers at Rutgers University, uses Edison's experiences as an aid in teaching others valuable life lessons. After reading each excerpt here, identify the lesson learned from Edison's experiences.* Use your skill in making inferences to help you with this activity.

Self-Education

Edison had an incredible amount of curiosity and eagerness to learn. He only had a few months of elementary school before his formal education ended, but his mother, a former teacher, continued his schooling at home. The love of reading and knowledge that Edison learned from her continued throughout his life.

Edison recalled, "My mother taught me how to read good books quickly and correctly, and as this opened up a great world in literature, I have always been very thankful for this early training."

What lesson can be learned about education from Edison?

Using Time Wisely

Edison's education did not stop when he went to work at age 12 selling candy and newspapers on the railroad. When the train was laid over in Detroit, he raced to the public library to read for a few hours.

While working on the train, Edison also took the opportunity to study business practices. He soon discovered that by wiring ahead to the next train station that there was news about a Civil War battle, he could increase the sales—and price—of his papers when he arrived. He started his own newspaper that featured news and gossip about the railroad and the towns along the line.

Edison printed his newspaper in the baggage car. He also set up a small chemistry laboratory in the car and spent his remaining free time conducting experiments described in a chemistry textbook.

What lesson can be learned about using time and space from Edison?

---

* From "Life Lessons from Thomas Alva Edison," by P. Israel, *Bottom Line Personal*, 1994, *15*(4), 13–14. Reprinted with permission of Boardroom Reports, 55 Railroad Avenue, Greenwich, CT 06830.

Persistence

When Edison made his famous statement that genius is 1% inspiration and 99% perspiration, he wasn't joking. When he set out to develop a new device, he never gave up. If one approach failed, he would try another . . . and another . . . and another . . . until he succeeded. In the early 1900s Edison set his lab staff to work to develop a new storage battery. After testing a huge number of possible compounds—50,000, by one account—one of his workers asked the great inventor if he was discouraged by so many failures and the lack of results.

Edison's response: "Why, man, I have gotten a lot of results. I know several thousand things that won't work."

What lesson can be learned about failure from Edison?

Taking the Broad View

Edison had to focus on the finest details as he perfected his many inventions. But despite his focus on detail, he never lost sight of the big picture. Some examples of his broad vision:

Commercial vision: After 4 years as a roving telegraph operator, Edison applied for and received his first patent in 1869, when he was only 22. It was for an electric vote recorder. When nobody wanted to buy one, he resolved that he would never try to invent anything unless he could identify a commercial demand for it.

Industrial lab: Within a few years, Edison had earned enough money to build a machine shop where he could manufacture the various improved telegraphs and other machines he constructed. He soon realized that he would not be satisfied with his life just as a successful manufacturer—he had too many ideas and knew he could not develop them all by himself.

That problem led him to conceive of one of his greatest inventions—a major laboratory with state-of-the-art chemical and electrical equipment and a skilled staff of expert technicians and scientists, all dedicated to developing new profit-making devices. In short, Edison invented an "invention factory."

Competition: Edison realized that in a competitive world, it was not enough just to make a good product. He kept making minor improvements to everything he invented. And even after mastering one way to do something, he continued to search for other better ways.

Electric light: Edison was not the only inventor who was trying to develop the electric light at the time. But he was the only one with the vision and financial backing to solve the practical problems of creating a world lit by electricity. This vision involved developing not just a superior light bulb but a whole system that included improved generating and distribution equipment.

Example: Edison first made an intensive study of the well-established gas-lighting industry. He decided that his system would be more acceptable to the public if he developed an underground transmission system—parallel to that used for piping gas—to avoid adding to the tangle of overhead wires from telegraph and telephone poles that were beginning to disturb the public. (pp. 13–14)

What lessons can be learned about being a winner from Edison?

Questions for Discussion

1. How do these life lessons apply to learning and study in college?

2. What memorable life experiences have enhanced your own ideas concerning the productive use of time and talent?

3. How can "seeing the big picture" be advantageous to college study?

Establishing Goals

How do you make goal setting a part of your life? What do you envision yourself doing in the next 5 years? Read the article here and learn how one student's commitment to a personal goal altered the course of his life.* As you read, underline the main ideas (most important points) with a double underline. Underline any details that help explain, prove, or support the main idea with a single line. Compare your notes with the notes taken by another student.

The Role of Personal Goals

The work in motivation by researchers and theorists like Schunk (1985, 1990) indicates that people are most motivated when they are pursuing personal goals, and it is when they are motivated that they are most likely to use productive habits of mind. In other words, it is when we are trying to accomplish a personal goal that we are most likely to have a need to plan, manage resources, seek accuracy, work at the edge rather than the center of our competence, and so on.

One of my favorite ways of illustrating this point is to relate a story about my son, Todd. Although not a terribly poor student in high school, Todd was certainly not at the top of his class. He took as few academic courses as possible, and his 3.00 GPA was essentially the result of A's in metal shop and phys ed and C's in mathematics and science. In the middle of his junior year, he announced that he was not going to go college. His logic was that he was not academically oriented (which was true), did not like school (also true), and was talented in auto mechanics (true again). Being the second son of Italian immigrants who stressed education as the way to a better life, I was extremely upset. Of course, I gave many unsolicited speeches about the importance of going to college and the probable effect that not going would have on his life.

At some point during this traumatic period, Todd went to see *Top Gun,* a movie about a modern-day navy aviator. Immediately after seeing the movie, he announced that he wanted to be a fighter pilot. This discouraged me because I believed my son was setting unrealistic goals. A happy turn of events (from my perspective) occurred when my son announced that he was going to college, because "you have to have a college degree to be a fighter pilot." I thought that if I could get him into college under any pretense he would soon abandon the foolishness of trying to be a fighter pilot, given the academic rigors involved. Since Todd had not distinguished himself in science and mathematics in high school, how could he possibly master the advanced mathematics and science he'd need to be a fighter pilot?

To my utter amazement, Todd attacked the science and mathematics courses in college with a fervor I had previously not witnessed in him. He made detailed plans about how to transfer from an open-enrollment community college (the only one he could get into) to one of the best engineering schools in the country. He managed his time and money at a level of detail that bordered on obsession. He strove for accuracy in all his academic classes and surely worked at the edge rather than the center of his competence every day. As I write this book, I can proudly report that Todd is about to graduate *magna cum laude* with a degree in aerospace engineering from the third best engineering school in the country. Recently, he was inducted into a prestigious engineering fraternity. And along the way he obtained his private pilot's license, receiving a score of 100 on the examination given by the Federal Aviation Administration (the

---

* From *A Different Kind of Classroom* (pp. 140–141), by R. Marzano, 1992, Alexandria, VA: Association for Supervision and Curriculum Development. Copyright © by ASCD. Used with permission.

first time in fifteen years anyone from our region received such a high score). Finally (and most important to Todd), he was one of only two candidates from the state accepted into the Aviator's Officer Candidate School of the United States Navy, which is the navy's first and biggest step to becoming a fighter pilot. In short, when Todd identified and began actively pursuing a goal that truly excited him, he cultivated mental habits he had previously ignored. In retrospect, this makes perfect sense to me. . . . The vast majority of people commonly do not like to plan, manage resources, or attend to feedback because of the time and energy involved. We usually do not avoid impulsivity or seek accuracy and clarity because not doing so is easy. For similar reasons, we usually do not work at the edge rather than the center of our competence, persevere even when answers or solutions are not readily available, and so on. But we *do* use these mental habits (which I tend to think of as being at the apex of human thought) when we are striving for something we truly desire.

The implication of this principle is that students should be encouraged to set personal goals—goals that really "turn them on," as aviation did Todd—and then supported in their efforts to accomplish those goals. (pp. 140–141)

Additional Questions for Discussion

1. What thoughts or reactions did you have as you were reading this selection?

2. What, in your opinion, are some examples of "productive habits of mind"?

3. How do you learn these "habits"?

4. What are the motivating forces in your life?

5. How effective was selective underlining as a note-taking technique?

Personal Stairway to Success

Todd, whose story was described in the previous activity, certainly found his way to success in life by clarifying his goals and the steps needed to attain them. You can create your own stairway to success by completing the following activity.*

Draw one set of stairs consisting of 8 to 10 steps (you can use more or less steps). At the top of the stairs, write down what you hope to achieve from your college education. This is your long-range goal—what you are working to accomplish. In the middle of the stairs, identify and list any mid-range goals that are necessary to achieve your ultimate goal. List any short-range goals that are necessary first steps in the process. Share your stairway to success with members of your small group. Here is an example of Todd's stairway to success:

Long-range goal: become fighter pilot

Mid-range goals: acceptance into the Aviator's Officer Candidacy School of the United States Navy; pass test administered by FAA; graduation from a prestigious engineering school; induction into engineering fraternity; obtain private pilot's license

Short-range goals: get accepted into good engineering school, learn to budget money and time efficiently; work hard in science and mathematics classes; attend community college

---

* From *How to Study*, by R. Fry, 1991, Hawthorne, NJ: Career Press.

Exploring the Professional Journals in Your Field

Whether you want to know more about becoming a physical therapist, school coun-selor, or news anchor, you will need to consult the publications in your area of spe-cialization. Unlike the popular magazines on sale at newsstands everywhere that are written for general audiences, professional journals are written by experts in a chosen field for other experts in that field. To become more knowledgeable about the field you are interested in, do the following:

1. Go to your library and print out a list of journals that you will be reading as part of your education in the profession.

2. Show your list to someone who is knowledgeable in the field and ask if they have any additional suggestions of reading material.

3. Select one article to read. Include the following information:

■ All the bibliographic information, including the author's complete name, the year and the month the journal was published, the complete title of the article, the name of the journal, the volume and number of the issue of the journal, and the inclusive page numbers on which the article appeared.

■ Briefly explain the topic of the article. Then make a graphic organizer of the main points the author was trying to make and the evidence used to support each point.

■ Tell why you selected this article. How will this information help you in your chosen field?

Are You Ready for College?

Use the following questions to conduct a candid self assessment. If you can point to evidence of being self-sufficient, a good thinker, self-directed, focused, and capable of handling both stress and success, your chances of succeeding in college are greatly enhanced.

1. **How self-sufficient are you?** Have you been responsible for attending to your basic needs for food, clothing, and transportation? Can you live on a budget? Can you manage your time and maintain a schedule?

2. **What kind of thinker are you?** How flexible is your thinking? How do you respond when your assumptions are challenged? Do you expect one right answer all of the time or can you accept that the answer to a worthwhile question is often complex and uncertain?

3. **How self-directed are you?** Are you easily influenced by peers or do you think for yourself? Can you begin and complete work, even work that you don't particularly like, without constant supervision? Can you persist at a task, even when it is difficult or unrewarding? When you had a major project due in the past, were you able to do a good job and turn it in by the deadline?

4. **How focused are you?** How involved were you in making the decision to go to college and selecting a particular college and program? Do you have clear academic goals? Career aspirations?

5. **How well do you handle stress?** Are you proficient at coordinating many different tasks simultaneously? What ways do you use to cope with conflict? Do you blame others when things don't go well or are you able to admit mistakes and learn from them? How do you respond to criticism from supervisors?

6. **How do you respond to success?** When you perform well, do you "slack off"? When you excel as the result of hard work, do you attribute your success to good luck? After you have succeeded, do you worry excessively about whether you will be able to "live up to" the same level of performance?

Letter to Next Year's Class

The purpose of this activity is to culminate our class together and share the wisdom you have acquired with others. During this class, you have learned many things about college reading, study skills, and college life. Imagine for a moment that you are returning to this room at the same time next year to speak with students who are beginning the college course that you are now completing. What advice would you want to give to these newcomers?

Within your group, consider what you could say that would be helpful to beginners. You may write your advice in the form of a friendly letter. If you want to get more creative with the assignment, you might choose a slightly different format—a list of guidelines, words of advice written artistically (like a graffiti board), a brochure that advertises this class, the script of a 60-second commercial, a magazine-type advertisement for the class, and so forth. Whatever format you choose, keep in mind that *you want to offer sound advice to those who are beginning the class just as you did several weeks ago.* The products of your work will be shared with next year's class by your instructor.

Index